Big Boss Man

The Life and Music of
Jimmy Reed

by Will Romano

Backbeat Books

San Francisco

Published by Backbeat Books
600 Harrison Street, San Francisco, CA 94107
www.backbeatbooks.com
email: books@musicplayer.com

An imprint of CMP Information
Publishers of *Guitar Player, Bass Player, Keyboard, EQ* ,and other magazines
A CMP Information company

CMP
United Business Media

Distributed to the book trade in the US and Canada by
Publishers Group West, 1700 Fourth Street, Berkeley, CA 94710

Distributed to the music trade in the US and Canada by
Hal Leonard Publishing, P.O. Box 13819, Milwaukee, WI 53213

Text Design and Composition by: Maureen Forys, Happenstance Type-O-Rama
Cover design by Richard Leeds — bigwigdesign.com
Front cover photo © Michael Ochs Archives / Ray Flerlage

Library of Congress Cataloging-in-Publication Data

Romano, Will, 1970–
  Big boss man : the life and music of Jimmy Reed / By Will Romano.
      p. cm.
  Includes bibliographical references (p.   ), discography (p.   ), and index.
  ISBN-13: 978-0-87930-878-0 (alk. paper)
  ISBN-10: 0-87930-878-8 (alk. paper)
  1. Reed, Jimmy, 1925-1976. 2. Blues musicians—United States—Biography. I.
Title.

  ML420.R2985R66 2006
  781.643092--dc22
  [B]

                              2006016363

Printed in the United States of America

06 07 08 09 10   5 4 3 2 1

Contents

Preface

Brayton Fogerty meets me at the front of his low ranch in rural New England. The house and the front lawn are covered in snow—fallout from one of the worst snowstorms of the last few years in the East. When I get out of my car, Fogerty asks if I made it here all right, and I did, besides taking a wrong turn down one of the winding, hilly, woodsy roads.

Fogerty is the executor of Vee-Jay Records, a limited partnership—a mere shadow of what it once was in the 1950s and 1960s, though it still licenses the catalogs of Jimmy Reed, Dee Clark, and others. I had spoken with Fogerty a few times before coming over to his home office to discuss Reed.

One of the first things he does is show me a few written accounts of Reed's life and even some official documents. He shows me one LP review and says, "Look at this. Look how this writer spelled Reed's name: Matcher Reed. O.K.?"

Fogerty throws down the article, and thumbs through some more material. He finds what he is looking for and shoves it in front of my face: "Now, look at this," he says. "M-a-t-h-i-s Reed. Two different spellings."

And there are more—each reference slightly different from the last. This is indicative of the kinds of conundrums that I, and apparently he, got caught up in while trying to unravel Reed.

On tap next is a trip to a nearby storage facility where Fogerty had tucked away the Jimmy Reed Vee-Jay master tapes. This could be a potential goldmine, I think to myself, especially since the tapes include production notes. But good luck finding out just what was written in those notes, or by whom. It's all chicken scratch on yellowed papers and stickers, barely legible, and there's not a lot of it.

It's a wonder that anything at all is known about Reed and his music. And it was Reed's music that drew me to his life story. Defining Jimmy Reed in his musical milieu was simple: the pained, high-squeal harmonica style and mush-mouthed vocal delivery—the trademarks of his sound—plus the hypnotic, laidback shuffle courtesy of Eddie Taylor, one of the greatest blues guitarists ever to grace the streets and clubs of Chicago. But Reed's life was not as readily deciphered. It came in bits and pieces, with an ounce of doubt and a pound of skepticism every step of the way.

I had wanted to speak with Mary Lee Reed—Mama Reed, Jimmy's widow—but just before I started this project she died, in the fall of 2003. I never got a chance to sit down with her and tell her how much her husband's music had changed the world for the better. Something tells me she knew.

My hope is that you will join me as I track Reed's extraordinary life and explore what it was like to grow up in the Dunleith, Mississippi, area in the 1920s, work in South Chicago in the boiling heat of steel/iron mills and on the "killing floors" of meatpacking plants, and become the Windy City's foremost blues talent by the 1960s.

I still wonder why Reed sold more records than Wolf, Muddy, Sonny Boy, and Little Walter in their heydays yet is somewhat forgotten today. Is it perhaps that his influence has been so pervasive, so fused with the fabric of popular American rock/R&B, that it has simply been taken for granted?

Indeed. We in the twenty-first century can still relate to songs (some now over 50 years old) that Reed wrote and/or recorded, like "Honest I Do," "Big Boss Man," "Bright Lights, Big City," "Take Out Some Insurance," "Ain't That Lovin' You Baby," and many, many others. With all due respect to today's artists (particularly pop), I ask, Will we be listening to their songs and discovering—and rediscovering—them some 50-plus years from now?

Paradoxically, the faster and faster we speed into the future, the more and more we owe to the blues. In fact, those same "simple" blues tunes are so definitive of human nature that they cannot be outdone, or reproduced.

In an odd and creepy coincidence during my research for this book, I was just blocks from the Burr Oak Cemetery in Alsip, Illinois, when the body of Emmett Till was being exhumed by police and FBI agents in early June 2005. (Till was an African-American teen who lived in Chicago and was reportedly abducted from his uncle's home in Mississippi and killed for allegedly whistling at a white woman in 1955. Till's death, like that of Medgar Evers, helped spark the civil rights movement.) I was at the nearby Lincoln Cemetery (South), looking for Jimmy Reed's headstone.

It was hard to find. I painstakingly examined each gravesite within three separate areas of the cemetery. Parched and exhausted from baking in the hot afternoon sun, I finally came upon it. While there was a modest tribute to the man engraved upon the stone, there was no marker—nothing to draw your eye to it. In fact, if you blinked while passing, you'd miss it.

In the language of the land, "That's a shame, shame, shame."

Chapter 1
From Deep Inside the Hellhole

Jimmy Reed is playing at the Savoy Tivoli in San Francisco's North Beach on Saturday night, August 28, 1976, talking through his smiles to an audience—a predominantly white audience—that howls and shouts requests for some of his greatest material.

It's late, but the crowd at the Savoy won't let Jimmy go. They show no signs of fatigue or boredom, and give him a standing "O"—some people bold and carefree enough to stand on their chairs, egging Reed on. Sitting on a wooden chair directly in front of the raised stage platform, Jimmy diddles his guitar strings with his fingerpicks and chuckles, getting a kick out of the audience response. Every time his chest heaves, the harmonica rack resting on his neck bounces up and down.

It is a worn and weathered Reed—but a live one. Those squinting eyes, that salt-and-pepper hair, those deep lines on his brow like fissures carved by water on rock appearing each time he parts his full lips and flashes his broad smile. Despite being only middle-aged, Reed has the appearance and countenance of a seasoned seer, spreading truth through his bluesy romanticism.

"It was always with these little anecdotes—on and off the stage," remembers Mike Henderson, a musician who played with and opened for Reed during his stand at the Savoy. "He was like a...well, he wasn't like a grandfather, he was like being around a sage or somebody like that. Maybe not like a priest, but a wise man, you know? He was loving life and he was loving his life. And everything he said to me or the audience or about himself, was about how he enjoyed life so much."

Reed attempts to speak over the crowd and tell them "good night," but to no avail. With every word he speaks, the buzz from the audience grows louder. They want more, and Jimmy soon finds himself in the middle of an encore longer than the original scheduled set. "He might play 'Big Boss Man' three times a set, and every time he played it, the crowd cheered louder," says Stephen Gordon, who ran the Savoy back then.

Late August 1976 was a crucial period in Jimmy Reed's career—a moment when it seemed this Sisyphus would finally roll the stone up and over the hill, defying logic and rewriting myth. It's almost inconceivable to think that in the previous months and years Reed had been presumed dead. And when he was not presumed dead he was thought a ghost—a vanishing ghost that made for a risky business proposition. If Jimmy decided to get sauced instead of staying at arm's length from the bottle as he should, he'd be hard to drag to the venue. Or if he was incapacitated by his epilepsy, the venue was out of luck. Thousands of dollars would have to be refunded, not to mention the irreparable, incalculable damages a venue's reputation would suffer because of a "no-show."

But that's all behind Jimmy now. He's onstage at the Savoy Tivoli because he wants to be—no one is pushing him to play the gig; no manager is hounding him; no monkeys are on his back. Reed has battled alcoholism, epilepsy, and bad business decisions. His nearly miraculous turnaround and perseverance is surely a sign that he has more to give the world, as if some divine force has deemed his career no longer needs life support. By all rights, with all the miles he has tracked, all the abuse his body has suffered (much of it self-inflicted), Reed shouldn't have lived to see the age of 50. Yet, here he is.

Reed has scratched his way back to become a beloved—and visible—artist once again, after an extended period of hibernation, followed by a string of less-than-stellar live performances and a litany of expletive-spewing booking agents. On Saturday, August 28, 1976, the audience at the Savoy Tivoli is not seeing an apparition; they are seeing the real Jimmy Reed, in the flesh.

Yet, ironically, it is almost like a dream. Although his family relationships had been disjointed and strained for some time, Reed is now joined onstage by his kinfolk—his people—for a performance peppered with equal doses of poignancy and crowd-pleasing tunes. Maybe that's why Jimmy is so relaxed. Maybe that's why he is full of so much renewed vigor.

Maybe the warmth of the West Coast has enveloped him and for one shining moment it seems that all is right with the world.

The face bathed in sweat, the glistening, pencil-thin moustache, the quivering, thin body frame, and the gap-toothed smile all speak of a man in jubilant exhaustion. How could he have arrived at this Savoy splendor? How far had he fallen in order to claim this comeback? And how long could he sustain this personal victory without backsliding, or worse?

The answers lie in the story of the Big Boss Man, one that is rife with God-fearing humility, virtue, vice, unspeakable humiliation, and unexpected and unparalleled successes.

On weekends in the early 1900s, Leland, Mississippi, was the height of debauchery, criminal activity, and laborers exorcising their demons. Once called the "Hellhole of the Delta," Leland was a bawdy beacon for otherwise righteous and God-fearing people who flooded the city streets on weekends (particularly on Saturdays), leaving behind their day jobs—and sometimes their dignity—on the plantations to the north, west, east, and south. Current residents choose to ignore Leland's rough-and-tumble past and scarcely think violence was a hallmark of the city—let alone that it existed smack-dab in the middle of Broad Street.

At the time of this writing, the town boasts a more pleasant, family-oriented image through its annual festivals and disarming unofficial mascot, Kermit the Frog (the amiable toad hatched from the imagination of Leland native Jim Henson, creator of the Muppets). It's been a hard road back for the town, overcoming its social ills and even over-the-top bad publicity. It was once said that in Leland's business district every third or fourth door was the opening to a saloon. Weekly the local papers reported on the random murders by stabbing or shooting, regular crap games, secret basement saloons (aka "blind tigers," which referred to the types of animal-oriented advertisements appearing on the window blinds of saloons to conceal their true purpose), and other such lawless activities. Not to mention the racism, which was rampant on both sides of the aisle.

On the weekends back then, mostly black laborers and sharecroppers from places like Dunleith, Holly Ridge, and other farming communities throughout the northwestern Mississippi cotton belt descended upon the big town to shop at all-hours stores and complete their weekly errands. By default and mere proximity, their nearby hamlets became guilty of the same harsh categorization Leland received. This was all much to the white population's dismay. *Collier's Weekly* magazine in 1908 coined the phrase "Hellhole of the Delta" in reference to Leland, and the ignoble title was propagated by nearby Greenville, a competing town that resented the attention and commerce Leland was gaining through its criminal elements. "On the door of one saloon, there was a sign that read 'No white folks allowed at the crap games'," says Dorothy Turk, author of *Leland Mississippi: From Hellhole to Beauty Spot.* "We had a cocaine problem as early as 1906 and 1908, and there was a lynching right in the middle of downtown Leland. Just about anything could happen in Leland."

Like many sharecroppers of the area, Jimmy Reed's family would arrive at the plantation commissary to buy their groceries for the coming week or head into Leland for special goods.

Jimmy Reed's birth certificate.

The Reeds were hard workers and squeezed every ounce of potential from their family members that they could. Life on the farm meant relentless, backbreaking work: rising at dawn and picking cotton in the first rays of morning light and not ceasing until sundown. It was common for Southern blacks to have a big family. In a way, it meant more hands to work the fields to generate a larger number of cotton bales, which in turn meant more money for the sharecropper parents to provide a stable home environment.

Mathis James Reed was born in the Hellhole of the Delta on September 6, 1925. (Though Leland is listed on Reed's birth certificate, Reed may have instead been born "in the country" with the aid of a midwife near Long Switch, Mississippi, and the Collier plantation.) The youngest of a family of ten children born to Joseph Reed and Virginia Ross, Jimmy was a fast learner and had a great sense of self. Those who remembered him as a child told of his being a decent human being, but one who could stand his ground. Virginia and Joseph were God-fearing, hardworking African-American parents, and they instilled in Jimmy a humility he would take with him beyond the Delta and into his stomping ground of Chicago.

It was in his early years that Jimmy—or Mathis, or the derivative "Mack," as his dad and others called him on occasion—developed an interesting mixture of pride and self-deprecation. Reed never forgot his humble beginnings. Indeed, he used them to his advantage (his country-boy personality and thick Southern drawl helped him became an international "pop" star), yet he demanded more of himself and his life than others perhaps had planned for or expected. Reed also tested the limits of his life and his very existence, time and time again: down on the farm, in the studio, on the road, and in his personal life.

Reed also had the opportunities—whether by luck or perseverance—that countless others who would fade in and out of the historic record didn't, or couldn't. Reed's life was very similar to other African-Americans who grew up in the area and acquired some musical skill to entertain, to touch a universal nerve with often personal and veiled or overt social commentary and while away the hours.

On the Stoneville farm, owned by the Weilenman family, sharecroppers who lived on the land and frequented the plantation store played music every Saturday night to entertain themselves and others. "Our grandfather bought a country store mainly with his plantation in 1900," says Bill Weilenman, descendant of the original owners. "On Saturday night there would be different musicians who would play the guitar and would play with feeling and skill. So did my father, who played guitar by ear. On Saturday night there could be 150 or more people outside the porch or inside the building and occasionally they would stop the nickelodeon and whoever wanted to play would do so. Really everybody would pack in there as close as they can get so they could hear whoever it was. It was all blues."

It was in this milieu that Reed spent the better part of his early years. It all started on a farm not far from where Charley Patton—one of the most revered Delta musicians, who would influence generations of country and urban bluesmen alike after him—had laid claim later in his life, playing the fields and juke joints of northern Mississippi. "[The Reed family] lived on our farm, the Collier plantation," explains Hampton "Hamp" Collier (no relation to *Collier's Weekly* magazine), son of John Collier, who owned the Collier plantation. "The Reeds had a house—great big ole four-room house with a tin-top roof. Their house was north and west of where I lived, just a little ways away. Jimmy came from a good family and they were all good workers."

Life was tough, but simple. "We used the mules to plow the land with," Hamp says. "When I was young we didn't have any tractors. It was all mule farming, you know? We kept all the mules and hogs in front of where we lived in a large barn, where my daddy's house was. There wasn't much vehicles around there, it was just like you'd see on that TV show *Gunsmoke*."

Many of the communities in Mississippi at that time (much like today) were made up of farming lands that were not incorporated towns. The nearest "towns" were farming hamlets such as Long Switch and Dunleith, but as Hamp notes, "Dunleith wasn't really a town. It was more like just a country store, post office, some land, and a few farms. The train would come through there, sure, but I can tell you that *our* plantation was in the middle of nothing. We were not really a town. It was what they called 'being out in the country.'"

It was an auspicious early childhood for Jimmy Reed. Ironically, a local landowner in virtually the same spot shared his name. (Not to suggest this is reason to link "Reed" with the regal everyman of the blues so many would know and love—but his name, at least in the vicinity of his birth, was synonymous with success.) Hamp Collier explained that a source of much confusion has arisen over the years due to the two Jimmy Reeds. The difference is, of course, the landowner was a Caucasian unrelated to the bluesman. When I asked about Jimmy Reed, Hamp spoke about his neighbor who ran the Dunleith plantation. "*That* Jimmy Reed was a white man on the next plantation—the Dunleith plantation," Hamp says. "Dunleith was the closest place to our farm, which was about a mile's walk. There really were no division lines between the two. I knew Jimmy Reed *the musician*. I used to call him 'Mack.' I was raised with him and he was about my age."

As a child, Hamp knew Jimmy "Mack" Reed to be an active kid. "In those years, Jimmy Reed didn't even fool with a guitar until a little later," Collier says. "I was very familiar with Jimmy, because we grew up as kids, and we both lived on the same plantation. He had a big family—lots of boys and girls. We would go on Saturdays, I remember, picking up pecans together. We had a lot of wild pecan trees on the farm. Saturday we'd get all the little kids together and go pick up pecans. We'd get half of what we'd pick up and that would be something, you know. Mostly we ate 'em. We played and we went rabbit huntin'. Rabbit huntin' consisted of putting a bolt at the end of a stick, and you'd be surprised what good a weapon that was. You threw it like a boomerang and I learned how to do that, too. We run down rabbits and there would be maybe ten or 15 kids out there doing it."

Reed was a strong individual as a child. This quality would stay with him throughout his life. "He had a very definite personality," Hamp says. "He was a go-getter type. He did not let people run over him. So, he was not a tough guy, but he was not afraid of people, either."

Collier says it was Reed's brother who was the real musical talent early on. "Jimmy's older brother—used to call him 'Buddy'—played the guitar real good," Collier says. "He was just a wonderful guitar player. We called him 'Buddy' but his name was Joseph, after his father."

John Allen Collier, Hamp's older brother, now deceased, remembered the Reeds. "I was the same age as Jimmy Reed's older brother, Buddy," John Allen told local historian Billy Johnson in 2001. "My younger brother, Hamp, and [Buddy's] younger brother, Jimmy, were both born in 1925 and came up playing together. I remember that guy [Charley Patton] from the Holly Ridge store that made records would come and play. A younger fellow named Bull Cow [Howlin' Wolf], who was a great big guy, would get excited and cross his eyes when he played."

Musicians from far and wide would travel the rails and get off at the local stops throughout these tiny Delta hamlets. Every plantation in the area had a country store, and nearly every plantation had a musician who would play in the fields or at that store. Traveling musicians, wayward and adventure-seeking alike, would hitch a ride on the train that wound through plantation towns. They'd jump off and walk with their guitars over their backs to a nearby store, which would host music nights, usually Saturday. "Dunleith, Long Switch, and Holly Ridge were just train stops back when people used trains as a means for transportation," says Johnson.

Jimmy had traveled to these local stores and seen these musicians and he, too, would start plucking an acoustic guitar around the age of nine. At first he was a bit frightened of his taste for music. He wanted to play his brother's guitar, but if he laid his hands on it, his brother would be fuming. He eventually received his own guitar from a family

Musicians such as Charley Patton, Howlin' Wolf, and Jimmy Reed reportedly played at the Holly Ridge Store.

member. "I had a regular guitar…but I just had a regular box—we called [the guitar] a box," Reed told radio interviewer Bill Scott.

Despite the music ringing in his ears, Reed successfully managed to work in the field and go to school when he could. That wouldn't last for long. He never made it to the fourth grade. By then, he was too valuable as a field hand, and was yanked out of public school to work in the fields full-time. Despite—or perhaps because of—his third-grade education, Reed followed his muse. It was in these days, out of school and in his preteens, that Reed was formulating song ideas, musical lines, and even copying spirituals. Reed knew he had natural talent, he said, because he didn't have any "learning" of music or music theory. "Well, I just have to tell the truth…. I think it just [came to me] out the clear blue sky because I didn't get to go to school, and therefore I know I can't read—didn't nobody teach it to me," Reed told *Living Blues*. "I used to play M. Hohner [harmonicas] then, and that was just when I was tryin' to try to blow the harmonica."

The Collier plantation no longer exists, but this street sign reminds locals of the area's past.

Hohners were cheap then. Reed would pay a mere twenty cents for a harmonica (he bought them with more regularity as he got older and better on the harp). Years later, Reed was introduced to Hohner's diatonic Marine Band harmonicas when he went to Chicago, and he never returned to the old Hohners again. Reed had complained of not being able to choke the harp the way he wanted, but something about the keyholes of the Marine Bands allowed him to capture the sound he wanted.

Music and musicians abounded on the Collier plantation. Willie Foster, the late harp player, was born in 1921 (while his mother was working in the cotton fields) and, like Reed, grew up on the Collier farm, his family having moved to the area when he was six years old.

It is no surprise that both Reed and Foster took up the harmonica. "Willie had told me stories of he and Jimmy playing together as kids even before music was in the the picture," says Brad Webb, Memphis guitarist and producer who recorded Foster before he died in 2001. "I can't think of any young person at that time who didn't fool with the harmonica," Hamp Collier says. "I think a lot of people knew the harmonica was cheap to come by and you could get them. Willie Foster got famous from his. He and Mack and I lived at the same place. I didn't have enough to get famous with the stuff, but they did."

Hamp respected Reed's apparent talent, but didn't realize Reed became a famous musician until much later. "After years we found out that he ended up being famous," Collier says. "We thought it was some other Reed. We did not know for the longest time that this was the same Reed—Jimmy. Not even the folks on the farm knew it was the same Reed. When I heard about Jimmy Reed being famous, I always thought they were talking about his brother Buddy Reed, for some reason. But it wasn't. That made me feel like a fool for 20 years. I guess Mack adopted that *Jimmy* Reed after he left our farm and started playing—he had to pick him up a trade name, I guess you'd call it. So, he picked up 'Jimmy' Reed."

The Reed family left the Collier plantation in the late '30s and went to Shaw, Mississippi, some 17 miles outside of Leland, to pursue other farming opportunities. Shaw was a small town with many black-owned businesses (most of which have long disappeared as of this writing), stores, gin houses, and movie theaters where patrons could see picture shows for only a handful of pennies. Education took place in the local churches (tales have been told of teachers walking from Shaw to Meltonia just to teach classes in large church houses).

Though class was being held in church, Reed would have none of it. Ironically and suddenly, the most important aspect of his life became his spiritualism. Jimmy was showing signs of being quite a good singer, and he was urged by his family to sing praises to God. An opportunity opened when his parents joined the Pilgrim Rest Missionary Baptist Church, a church founded in the years following The Reconstruction and located just west of the Shaw limits on Highway 448.

Reed fell into a vocal singing group with distant relatives James Cleveland Phillips and his brother Erman, and their friend B. Shaw. Herstine Franklin, another distant relative to Jimmy, remembers seeing a young Reed in a gospel quartet in Shaw. "The group was good, and a fellow by the name of Sam Turner used to manage them," Franklin says. "Jimmy Reed was none of but ten years old or maybe a little bit older when he was singing. He was singing with this quartet, and they would sing all over Bolivar County in different churches. They would sometimes be eight of them in a choir, but usually it was just the four. Then Jimmy stopped singing spirituals and started singing those blues."

In the church, they grabbed you early. Perhaps the church elders and churchgoers knew that if the young and impressionable were to be exposed to music from the dark side, there would be no return to the light. There's no evidence to suggest that Reed lost his way, even as he became the biggest blues name in the country, but his is a familiar story.

Luckily for Reed, he had a great support system in his relatives. "Everybody seems like family," Franklin says. "Everybody knows each other. They always say to each other and me, 'Hey, cous.'"

Years later, when Reed triumphantly returned to his native digs after he had made a name as a crossover blues artist, he performed for the residents of the Delta town and the surrounding areas. "Jimmy left here and then went up North after a while," Franklin says. "Jimmy would come through this area and perform for Negro towns. We all liked that. He never did forget where he came from."

There's a good deal of guesswork involved in reconstructing the life of Jimmy Reed, mainly because many of the markers meaningful to his life are all but gone. The Collier plantation and the surrounding areas, such as Dunleith, just don't look like they did when Reed grew up there. You might find the occasional shack or abandoned farmhouse, similar to the Reed family house, I suspect. You will also find large tracts of farmland and shotgun housing that did not exist when Reed was in the area. In the years after Reed left, the land was carved up by newer owners and now numerous farms with a fairly long history in the area have laid claim to the land. The old Dunleith plantation no longer exists, and neither does Collier's farm.

The landscape has changed and the very byways that were once populated are all but forgotten. Highway 10 once snaked through northern Mississippi hamlets such as Magenta, Stoneville, Dunleith, Long Switch, Holly Ridge, Indianola, Itta Bena, and Greenwood, intersecting Highway 82 at different points. As I drove through the area, I followed a railroad track that ran along the automobile path. (There is one scary stretch in which drivers virtually face head-on train traffic before they are routed to a bend in the road.)

Apparently, Highway 10 is just as mysterious to natives as it is to anyone else. "That is the first time it has come to me," says Little Arthur Duncan, who migrated to Chicago in the 1950s. "I know about 82 going through Indianola, and 49. Then the next one is 61 and then Highway 3. I know Highway 8 runs out through Leland. I used to go up through Slaughter and Itta Bena. It might have been a gravel road that they just blacktopped."

Don Otha Baker, longtime area resident, remembers Highway 10. "It had gravel on each side and it ran from Greenville to the Washington County line," says Baker. "This was when I was a little boy, which was, I guess, about 70 years ago. It came from Greenville to Leland and then it went south and came back around and went up to Dunleith. Then it turned down the railroad."

"Once Highway 10 was straightened and became part of US 82, locals quit using it as the east-west highway and started using US 82 in the mid-'30s," Billy Johnson says. "It took about 30 years, but all of those little stores dried up and all of those little towns dried up once the highway traffic quit going through there."

It seemed once Highway 10 dried up, the plantation—and its home-grown musical talent—were out of sight, out of mind. But Reed had played, worked, and gallivanted along it. "A lot of historians missed this highway when they came through here," Johnson says. "The old Highway 10 runs through the Dunleith area, where Jimmy Reed was born. It goes down about three or four miles through Holly Ridge where Charley Patton lived and where he is buried. That old road wound out across the Delta. I mean Jimmy Reed and B.B. [King] were born 20 miles and ten days apart, basically along this highway. It really is the forgotten blues highway."

Perhaps one of the last true vestiges of the Reed era is the Holly Ridge store along the dirt road that used to be Highway 10. Beverly Reginelli, store manager, explained that a number of local bluesmen played at the commissary on Saturday nights. She claimed people like Jimmy Reed, Howlin' Wolf, and Charley Patton played there, and that Patton lived in the back of the store, playing with local musicians including the store owner, before he died in 1934. (Patton's grave also happens to be along the same dirt road, the old Highway 10, about a mile away from the Holly Ridge store, in a deserted field marked by decades-old gravestones and dead grass.) While there is no hard evidence to support Reginelli's assertions, we do know that the tradition of musicians performing at the store was upheld through the 1990s.

Charley Patton's final resting place along what was Highway 10.

After a brief stay in Meltonia (another small town in the northern Mississippi county of Bolivar), Reed pulled up stakes as a young teenager and headed out on the road to Duncan, Mississippi. "I don't know what give me the idea to get up and want to leave from down there and go somewhere," Reed told *Living Blues*. "I went and spent a while with my brother [Joe] in Duncan, Mississippi."

Like so many other communities in Bolivar County, Duncan was a small town located on Highway 61 (20-plus miles north of Clarksdale), with two pharmacies, one dry cleaner, one bank, one doctor's office, and three gasoline filling stations. The town's main source of income for both white and black residents was cotton farming. It was only a few years prior to Reed's arrival that Duncan had its roads blacktopped for vehicle and horse travel. It was virtually a nineteenth-century town, one that had been beat up and battered around. Duncan was learning to rebuild itself in the wake of a tornado in the late '20s that had left deep emotional, physical, and, in all cases, financial scars.

A brick school for "coloreds" was built just a few years before Reed came—the very school Reed would have attended had he continued on the educational track. Blowing off school (he was getting closer and closer to graduation age anyway), and largely unsupervised, Reed was making his way in the world as an adult. Which meant he was susceptible to adult vices, like participating in the still-booming moonshine industry. It was around Reed's 13th or 14th birthday that he would get his first taste—literally—for alcohol.

"[I was] just a little kid, you know what I mean?" Reed told radio interviewer Norman Davis. "An old guy, he, his name was John Henry Johnson, but he always call me 'Maxim House.' That was about the time this guy come out with this Maxwell House coffee.[i] He called me Maxim House. So, mostly he called me 'good coffee.'…But he had a whiskey still, you know? And he had to work daily, so he used to give me somethin' like a couple dollars a day to go out there and sit around his still and check it out for him, and all that. Well, I didn't mind a couple of dollars, you know? I had a teacup out there and… I could sample his stuff. I'd taste it, and if I wanted to see how it could taste, like it was pretty strong, or something, and all that kind of stuff, I'd be running off and set up some mo' for him. That is the way I got started to drinking."

During Prohibition, farmers and locals would sell their homemade hooch to small area shop owners, who would in turn market these products to customers and the musicians who played their stores. "When I got something like about 14 or 15—well, I should say about 15 or 16, something like that—[I went] out to the liquor store [to] buy me some of that stuff," Reed continued. "See, they would sell it to ya then in Mississippi. They had whiskey stores where you just go and buy you some liquor. They wasn't worried about how old you was. If you had the money you just, you just got it."

At the same time, Reed's musical counterpart, some 20 miles away in Benoit, Mississippi, was formulating his own musical style.

Eddie Taylor, born in 1923 and nursed by the musical Memphis Minnie (Lizzie Douglas), was not yet three years old when his parents split. "Memphis Minnie and my mother went to school together," Eddie told writer Mike Rowe. "She used to nurse me when I was a baby…and I used to listen to her play the guitar…."

Being the oldest male of three children, Taylor went to work early in the fields. He once said he'd pick 200 to 300 pounds of cotton a day at his best, as well as milk cows, do his homework, and chop wood. Despite being the man of the house—and knowing that he needed to support the family—Taylor found himself inextricably drawn to the sound of the guitar. He was fascinated by the music Minnie made, and it was through her that Eddie was exposed to the kings of Delta blues: Robert Johnson, Charley Patton, and Son House. "I was about seven or eight years old at the time and I'd see them play at house parties," Taylor explained in the early '70s. "See, at those old house parties they'd play cards, shoot dice, and somewhere up the front of the house, they'd have guitar playing, and dancing."

Taylor would follow these and other local Delta musicians from plantation hamlet to plantation hamlet, through towns like Leland and north through Stringtown. A self-described "sneaky little guy," Eddie crawled under houses (those lifted above the ground by cinder blocks or stilts of some kind) to listen to musicians play devil blues in the jukes—jukes he knew he had no business even being near. Comforted and caressed by the rhythm of music, ringing of the guitar strings, and pulse of pounding feet on the floor above him, Taylor would be lulled asleep by the dynamics of the musical notes floating above. With the music swirling in his head, Taylor would then rush home and attempt to play his guitar—one his mother bought him from a Sears & Roebuck catalog for $12. Though Taylor cited Tommy McClennan and Peetie Wheatstraw as two early influences, it was Robert Johnson who had the most lasting impact on Taylor's eventual style, one that would also inform the "Jimmy Reed sound," as it is often called. Johnson's bouncy bassline underpinnings (an important component of his polyrhythmic approach) are in direct correlation to the bedrock, the foundation, of the classic Reed shuffle.

Having gotten up the gumption and facility to do so, Taylor tagged along with Patton to Stringtown when he was just a young adult and began playing on the streets for money. He also picked up cues from other musicians, such local legends as Popcorn Jesse (whose last name has been lost to the mists of time), Little Quick, and Boots. Eddie's family would later move to Stringtown, giving him the opportunity to play in his hometown and nearby Leland with Big Joe Williams, Son House, Howlin' Wolf, Floyd Jones, and Jimmy Reed.

Taylor got so good he became competition for the then more sophisticated players, such as David "Honeyboy" Edwards. While Edwards could play those blues, Taylor was adept at a cross section of music—from hillbilly to popular standards—the kind white folks would stop and listen to and, more importantly, tip him for playing. "That's how I got more money than he got," explained Taylor to Mike Rowe for his book *Chicago Blues* (originally *Chicago Breakdown*). "He never did get but over maybe six or seven dollars [in his can]. Mine be twenty-five to thirty dollars...."

It was in Eddie's travels through the tiny plantation hamlets of western Mississippi that he met Jimmy Reed. Striking up a friendship was easy. Reed was affable and talkative, and Taylor was a good listener. And as musicians they complemented each other. Taylor would play the more groove-oriented elements he had heard in Patton's and Johnson's style, and Reed would fool around trying something new.

After a day of work in the fields, Taylor, Reed, and others would play music on their boxes and dream of getting out of the steamy Hellhole towns where they worked and played, and one day bust into the busy streets of Memphis and Chicago. "In Mississippi we come up just two little ole boys together," Reed told Norman Davis. "When sundown come and they get us ole guitars, little ole soapbox—the one with the hole in the middle—we'd go out and sit out under the tree, I should say, until twelve or one o'clock in the morning or something like that. Just foolin' around with the box—just seeing what we could do. [Taylor] was way better than I was. That's a whole lotta different things he did on his box, which he didn't show me how to do it. But I heard the way it sounds and then…even if I wasn't with him, to get this box and still be thinking about the way that sound was sounding that time, and just keep on working on mine till I could get mine to sound just like that sound when he had it on his, going like that night, or so. And I get mine to sound like that."

Years later, the Jimmy Reed "lump," boogie beat, or the "Jimmy Reed sound" would become an international success. The simplicity— even elegance—of the rhythmic groove (pumping life into the essence of the tune like the warm pulse of a strong heartbeat) became synonymous with the very name Jimmy Reed.

Some critics debate the accepted version of reality: that it was Eddie Taylor who taught Jimmy Reed how to play guitar. Some in Jimmy's native land don't accept it either. "Jimmy Reed had an older brother named Buddy who ended up being a preacher," historian Johnson says. "Buddy was the one who taught Jimmy Reed to play. All this shit about Eddie Taylor taught him how to play is bullshit." Hamp Collier adds: "Buddy was the one who taught Jimmy how to play the guitar."

"The only thing about it is that Eddie and Daddy were together quite a bit," explains Reed's daughter Loretta Reed. "When [Jimmy Reed] went to Gary, Indiana, Eddie basically went with him. So, all we can say is that together they made what is known as 'the Jimmy Reed sound.' From our perspective, it was Daddy, but I can see Eddie's kids saying the same thing."

Eddie Taylor had always maintained that it was he, and *he alone,* who came up with the classic Jimmy Reed sound that made Reed an international star. "I taught Jimmy how to play guitar," Taylor told *Living Blues*. "Jimmy wasn't doin' nothin', just playin' a little. He mostly learned from me. The Jimmy Reed style is my style. [Jimmy] don't have no style. And I got the style from Charley Patton and Robert Johnson."

Reed himself acknowledged that it was Eddie who had the greatest influence on his sound, but stopped short of saying Taylor actually taught him to play. As he explained to radio interviewer Davis, "I just listen to him and that sound just stay in my head whether I sleep or woke.... I never would ask him to show me how he did that sound or nothing.... Just like I am sitting up here talking to you now, that sound would still be in my head. When I get out of here, I would go get that box...."

It is easy to see why the point is and was hotly debated. A whole generation of blues and rock 'n' roll musicians was influenced by Jimmy Reed—they took his cue and ran with it. Some were out-and-out copycats; others took elements of his 12-bar blues shuffle and added to it, perfected it. Some musicians picked up harmonicas for the first time, and others merely covered his material as homage. Artists like the Rolling Stones, the Animals, Neil Young and Crazy Horse, Bob Dylan, Lou Rawls, the King Elvis Presley, the Yardbirds, Them with Van Morrison, and countless others owe more than just a debt to Jimmy Reed. They used his music as a virtual blueprint for some of their own recorded output. These second-generation musicians (separated by more than age—an ocean, in some cases) internalized the loping movements of Jimmy Reed's shuffle and spat it out for a whole generation of hi-fi-hungry listeners. In fact, Jimmy Reed is so embedded in the vernacular of a musician's universe, when a bandleader asks a musician to do "a Jimmy Reed beat," the player knows exactly what's being asked—and what to do. It winds up coming out similar to Reed's song "Close Together"—a variant of the 12-bar, I-IV-V blues in *E*.

There is still a good amount of wonder and mystery about the Jimmy Reed sound and how it is achieved. Producer Jim Dickinson told writer Joe Nick Patoski: "The thing about the lick...it's obviously 'Honky Tonk,' until you get to the V chord, which would be *B7* [in *E* major scale] if you are playing the lead, the turnaround, the blues pattern. Then Jimmy Reed does something. He plays this thing, this riff, *instead* of the V chord—that eluded me for 20 years, I guess, until Keith Richards showed me backstage at the Astrodome. 'This is the way you do it.' And it is."

In all probability, it was Eddie who provided the backbone of the sound, but we may never know. For some, that is enough of an answer. "I'll answer that question for ya, and Billy Gibbons [of ZZ Top] agrees," says blues-rock guitarist George Thorogood. "Some things you are not supposed to know. There is no mystery.... We are looking for the answers…but it is like baseball. No one can tell who invented it. It drives Americans mad."

"I think Eddie was responsible in large part for that groove," says blues vocalist Angela Strehli, who had a front-row seat to Jimmy Reed's performances when she was in Austin in the 1970s for the Antone's club scene. "When I was first learning in the '70s, because Jimmy was popular and his songs were so simple, people would say, 'Oh, yeah, we can cover that.' They would insinuate that anybody could cover a Jimmy Reed song. The truth of it was that almost nobody ever covered Jimmy Reed and pulled it off. I used to just laugh at people."

It was in the fields that Reed first heard B.B. King, Sonny Boy Williamson I, and Sonny Boy Williamson II on the radio. Sonny Boy I's "Good Morning, Little School Girl" would be one of the first songs that Reed had gotten proficient at playing on his harmonica.

Tracing an artist's influences and their effects on playing style is sticky work, with dead ends and winding avenues that sometimes lead to nowhere. However, it is impossible to believe that Reed didn't hear an element he'd exploit in Sonny Boy Williamson I's first- and second-position harp blowing, or over-the-meter harmonica playing in "I'm Tired of Trucking My Blues Away," or his trembling, mush-mouthed vocal delivery in "Jackson Blues." Sonny Boy Williamson I (John Lee Williamson) was an important link between the pre-war Delta blues style and what would become the electrified Chicago blues, though he has been eclipsed by his successor, Sonny Boy Williamson II (Aleck Ford, aka Rice Miller), in the eyes of the mainstream public.

By the early '40s, Sonny Boy II and guitarist Robert Jr. Lockwood were playing for ten minutes each day on Helena, Arkansas' KFFA on "King Biscuit Time"—generally seen as one of the first national live blues shows, if not *the* first. ("King Biscuit Time" is the longest-running daily radio broadcast in history.) Since Sonny Boy I did not make many, if any, personal appearances in Arkansas, and since Rice Miller was not yet recording under the name Sonny Boy Williamson II, KFFA apparently felt it was practicing safe business when the station coveted the name to boost their advertising sales.[ii]

Sonny Boy II's show took off among the radio-listening public throughout the Deep South, with Jimmy Reed an eager listener. Whenever Reed had a break from the fields, usually around midday, he would sit and listen to the radio, and liked what he heard. "See, Sonny Boy was advertising King Biscuit Flour," Reed recounted to Davis. "I go up there and get a chance to turn on the radio and listen to him do his thing on the radio…. He was blowin' his harmonica, and boy, he was stone pushin' it."

"[Sonny Boy II] was my biggest favorite because he was about the onliest one who could play the blues," Reed told interviewer Bill Scott. "He made me listen…. I skip out to the cotton field, you know, and go up there to get a drink of water and turn up the radio and listen to him for some 15 minutes [to]…King Biscuit Flour, and all that kind of stuff."

Reed was then employed on the McMurchy farm—what he had once referred to as the McMulty farm, run by a Lynn McMulty. My research revealed that there was, and still is, a McMurchy plantation in Duncan. "There is no such thing as a McMulty and there hasn't ever been a farm here by that name, as far as I know," said Betty McMurchy, who kept the plantation records and was nearly 80 at the time of our talks. (Oddly, Lynn is the name of Betty's 56-year-old son, and her deceased husband's name was Ernest Lynn.) Betty did keep meticulous records, though it appears she didn't do so until Reed had left the area. She could remember no Mathis, Matcher, or James Reed, and has no record of any other Reed.

It is reasonable to assume, then, that Reed was most probably a fieldhand who drifted for a year or so in and out of the Duncan area (he was living with relatives at the time). Reed most probably did work on McMurchy's farm, but no records have come to light to prove it. It's doubtful he would lie about this. After all, why would an African-American state he was a fieldworker if he really wasn't? What's to be gained?

Nothing. In fact, Reed was beginning to realize this himself. His days as a farmhand for old man Ernest Lynn McMurchy were numbered, and the reason can be traced to one specific event, a story that Reed told many times throughout his life:

Reed apparently had some special powers over the mules he was leading in the fields, like a Delta-style Dr. Doolittle. They would allegedly only listen to him—no one else. "I could just go ahead and work the mules," Reed explained in a Q&A with Scott. "So this guy come by and told me, he said, I don't know what was on his mind this morning, or what had him shook up, but he said, 'Look, don't you stop them [mules]. I don't want you to stop them for nothin'.'"

"This guy" was a field supervisor, and he had it in for Reed this day. Reed was beside himself. What had crawled up *his* ass? Maybe it was the fact that Reed played harp, or that mush-mouthed drawl, or Reed's clownish exterior, or that he was black. Or maybe it was simply the fact that Reed's general good nature made him an easy target.

Reed didn't want any trouble and tried to carry on without giving the man another thought. Reed said the supervisor was going to get a trailer behind his truck "and he was going to get a load of hay to take up to the barn to stash for the mules to eat…." When the plantation overseer, instead, came back from the barn, he found Reed getting a drink of water. He barked at Reed for having stopped the mules: if Reed stopped them, no one could get them to start. "Man, whatcha mean don't stop them mules?" Reed asked. "I want some *whadda*."

The plantation overseer was persistent and losing his patience with this fieldhand. "Don't you think I can get me some water?" Reed asked. Disgusted, the plantation man cursed Reed, but Jimmy shook it off. "I didn't do no arguing with him," Reed admitted. "I just start walkin' on off on him, you know?…There was a little ditch between me and the mule. I just went to step 'cross the ditch and just as [I] reached up one feet and went to step 'cross the ditch…he taken [his foot] and pushed me 'cross the ditch."

The overseer kicked Reed over to the other side of the field and forced him to get back to work. This overseer was never a favorite, but he had never done anything like this before.

We all, at some point in our lives, have had to suffer an indignity from a superior. Most of us look at the overall picture and generally let things slide down our backs, keep our mouths shut, and deal with it.

Reed did keep his mouth shut, but his anger swelled. "I got the mules and plowed them on down to the other end of the field and turned them 'round…like everybody else was doin'," Reed said. When the mules stopped, "I just started walkin'. I ain't seen him no more…and the mules, either."

That was it. Reed walked out on the job, literally. He didn't stop until he left Duncan and found himself moving from one stinkhole to the other. He looked up and there was the city limits sign for Leland.

Reed stayed briefly with his brother Joe there, but he had rambling on his mind again. He wanted to get out of Mississippi and be done with it. He knew his second-oldest brother, Tommy, lived in Chicago. Now 18 years old, Jimmy was beginning to formulate his escape plan, as so many others of his generation had done. Going up north meant a new life, one where he could work without the same kind of backbreaking indignity. With what little money he had, and some he borrowed from his brother Joe, he bought a one-way train ticket (he wasn't planning on coming back) for $10 on the Illinois Central Railroad line from Leland station and was off to the new Promised Land: Chicago, Illinois.

When the train pulled into Chicago a few hours later, Reed's anticipation was running high. His mind was racing: Where would he live? Where would he work? When he surfaced and found his way to his brother Tommy, his brother assured him that he could find an apartment for him immediately. Much to Jimmy's surprise and delight, he would live in the same building as his brother. " [He] was living over there at 4735 Langley, and therefore I had done come up…and I started stayin' with this old man," Reed told *Living Blues*. "[He] gave me a place to stay there and he let me have this place for, I think it was, $70 a month."

Reed, barely able to write his own name, was ready for work—work that didn't involve mules. For the first few weeks and months of his stay in Chicago, Reed relied heavily on his brother. Tommy did everything for Jimmy, including getting his brother a Social Security card application and filling it out for him.[iii] Said Tommy, having a Social Security card meant better opportunities for the black man. It showed a prospective employer that you meant business, that you were serious about employment, and that you were "official."

While Reed was waiting for his card in the mail, he quickly took a job as a janitor at the YMCA at 826 South Wabash between South Champlain and South Evans (today it is a movie theater). His job description? "Mopping the floors, cleaning various rooms, and doing odd jobs from the 11th through the 20th floors." Not exactly glamorous work, by any means, but it was a living. And it beat picking cotton and getting a kick in the ass for it. Within two weeks, the postman delivered his Social Security card and he gave his notice at the YMCA, hopeful for better employment. That was, after all, the idea of being legitimate and having a card in the first place. Reed opened the letter, unveiled the card, saw his number, looked below it, and *what?* Thanks to Tommy, Reed's name was misspelled on his card. Instead of the card reading Mathis James Reed, or simply James Reed, it was printed with "Matcher" Reed.

A period postcard from the YMCA on South Wabash, mid-1930s.

But Reed could hardly complain. He was asking for help—help he needed, and Tommy had known that Jimmy's nickname had always been Mack. What was that short for, Mathis? No, it was Matcher. Or so he thought. It would cause some confusion later on.

Misspelling aside, Reed did find work more easily. His brother was right. Reed was hired at the South Chicago firm Hefter Coal Company as a "coal hiker," punching in and out on the time clock and being paid by the volume of coal he shucked. (Very similar to the way a sharecropper might be paid at the end of a harvest.) Reed would later say he enjoyed the job, but this seems doubtful. It was manual labor that was not very challenging or fulfilling. And its similarity to the backbreaking work of a fieldhand in the South must have proved too close for comfort for Reed.

Burning in him was an angst, a sadness and expectation of a better life that didn't seem to be coming anytime soon. No one is promised anything in this life, least of all an illiterate laborer in the early '40s. The only way he could soothe his soul was through music. Having stopped playing for a few months, Reed picked up the guitar again and fooled around a little bit. It was nothing serious, but he was keeping his hand in the part of life he enjoyed the most. His landlord, John Ford, offered him an acoustic guitar for seven bucks. Reed forked over the dough, along with his monthly rent, and plucked and strummed the hell out of it.

Jimmy was reclaiming his dexterity on the instrument and hitting upon some ideas. Having heard the Memphis, New Orleans, and Chicago blues and jazz piano players on the radio, he was attempting to transfer some of their piano lines to his guitar. Reed knew he would never be a guitar legend like Lonnie Johnson, but he had transmogrified bits and pieces.

Reed might have gone on to be a professional musician within six months—if he had stayed in Chicago at the Hefter Coal Company. But that was not to be. By 1943, Reed was drafted into the United States Navy and required to report to boot camp with Company X190 in Bainbridge, Maryland, which was one of the three training bases equipped to handle 20,000 recruits during the height of World War II.[iv]

Reed finished his basic training, but two days before deployment he came down with the measles and a 103-degree fever. Suddenly Uncle Sam would have to wait for this sailor. The only place he was being shipped was sick bay. Standard procedure for any serviceman with an illness was to quarantine him. Reed was exiled for two weeks. Within those two weeks, Company X190 shipped out.

No one could accuse Reed of being a coward—and he certainly didn't plan it this way—but he was happy that ship had sailed without him. Reed thanked his "Good Lord Jesus," he said, for not being shipped out with X190 on the open waters of the Atlantic. When a second company came through Bainbridge, Second Company X233, Reed was required to join this one and stayed with it through his military service.

There was no getting around this company's deployment. Reed was about to be shipped out with Second Company X233 to Riverside, California. There he was given a job in the galley, where he wiped the tables, set up the utensils, plates, and cups, and cleared and cleaned the tables of garbage when the men were finished. All in all, not the worst job a person could have. At least there were no bombs being chucked at him. And Reed was free to leave the premises via a bus and find the world outside. Reed did leave on occasion, but more often than not he stayed on the base and within its gates.

After some months of monotonous cleaning, sharing cigarettes with the galley crew, Mack Reed, also known as Cousin Peaches, was steadily becoming friends with some of the men in his company. The men knew Reed as the guy with the Southern drawl who also happened to be a very good swimmer, showing a genuine affinity for the water. Reed was not an outgoing man, as the men would find out, but there was an endearing quality to his personality that instantly made people like him. He was to get real chummy with one seaman, and he'd regret this unfortunate, though ultimately comedic, episode.

After about a year with the company, Reed ran into a dishwasher in the galley who shared the same taste for alcohol. He told the story to Scott:

"We all called him 'Pappy.' So, for quite a little while, I should say about three weeks or somethin' like, about, a good month or month and a half, I see him staying pretty late and all that kinda stuff. And I was wondering what was happening, 'cause they kept buses down at the main gate where we could get a free ride to Riverside, California, when we want to…just as long as we get back to the base before nine o'clock. But they never did see me go out…. And [Pappy] never did go out either. I was watching him."

Reed became suspicious because ole Pappy would never go out, yet he seemed to be getting lit just the same. So, where was the saloon? "I told him, I said, 'Pappy, look…now I know you don't leave away from this chair here, this dishwasher, here this sink, and all that. And I say, 'But you seem like you be feelin' pretty good every time I see you…. Won't you let me in on that? Now, you know I ain't got nothin' to do with it, but I-I-I know good and well you don't go out that gate.' He said, 'Yeah, Reed, you right about that. It ain't nobody's business but mine and yours….' "

Pappy reached under the sink and forked it over—nearly a gallon of pure-grain alcohol—and Reed's eyes lit up. "That was what he was getting lit off of and he would get him a little teenie-weenie bit of. That was lighting him up. I take mine, it looked so much like gin, I thought it was gin, and I take mine and drink it down. You know, with no water. No nothing. I said, 'Anyway, what was that?' He said, 'Maaaaaan! That was alcohol. Pure-grain alcohol. That stuff'll burn you up!' "

Pappy was shocked at Reed's overenthusiastic approach to drinking: "You ain't supposed to drink that stuff straight!"

John Henry Johnson's 'shine back in Duncan, Mississippi, was nothing like this. So, Pappy gave Reed a big glass, filled it up, and mixed the pure grain with water. Pappy handed it to Reed and told him to drink it. Reed did, and it went down a little smoother this time. As Reed drank up, Pappy put a little more in his glass. When Reed was finished—each time—Pappy was right there as his impromptu bartender, filling his empty glass. "I must have stayed high for something like about two or three days off that," Reed said.

Reed admitted that the pure-grain alcohol—which he estimated to be 190 proof—tore up his stomach something fierce and landed him in sick bay, his one-time sanctuary from deployment. Ironically enough, while in sick bay, he heard that Company X190 had been hit pretty rough. Reed's luck appeared to be as strong as ever.

Reed had evaded being a casualty thus far, and he wanted to keep it that way. But after he was patched up, he was finally put on the spot: his name was chosen for survey duty—to God knows where.

His luck was intact, though. Instead of being shipped overseas or going into battle, Reed was given his walking papers.[v] He was free to go back to Chicago or Mississippi.

Just a few months earlier, while on leave, Reed had married Mary Lee Davis on May 26, 1945. A girl who hailed from Lambert, Mississippi, and was the sweetheart of his teen years, Mary Lee grew up on a plantation that joined Collier's. She and Jimmy made quite a pair. A husky woman even at a young age, Mary Lee received very little in the way of education. She attended a black public school until her parents needed her help on the farm. After initially leaving school, she returned at age 11 (to the sixth grade), only to be called back to work in the fields. She never returned to school.

Mary Lee would be the love of Reed's life, his rock, and they would have eight children together. They met in 1943, before Reed was shipped off into the Navy. While the relationship was rocky at times, Mary Lee, or "Mama," as Jimmy would call her, never abandoned Jimmy—even in his most selfish, self-destructive, and insensitive moments.

When Jimmy returned to Chicago, he and Mary Lee decided to head back south and stay with family. In a kind of reverse migration, Reed had seen enough of the big city. Though he would never admit it, he felt defeated. He didn't have any real aspirations of being a professional musician, and since he still couldn't read and write (though he had improved under the tutelage of Uncle Sam), he figured Chicago's job market wasn't much better for him than when he left it.

As a final act of kindness, brother Tommy gave Reed a guitar as a parting gift. Truth be told, Reed didn't know what to do with it—or if he should do anything with it. It was time to roll.

Back in Mississippi, Reed, though disillusioned, decided to try his hand again at the farming lifestyle. Maybe in some bizarre way, this was truly what was meant for him. It was all he really knew. Plus, he knew he didn't have much choice. Being black, married, and poor, farming was more of a necessity.

Jimmy and Mary Lee had become accustomed to living in tight quarters. They lived with Reed's parents for a time, until they found their own place in the Leland area. Cousin Peaches and Mama Reed had a year of marriage under their belts, and like many young couples they argued, loved, and argued. The substance of their verbal bouts dissipated, but after a particularly nasty one Mary Lee walked out on Jimmy.

It was then that Reed's mind started wandering again toward Chicago. What was in Mississippi? Dead-end farming jobs and nasty boss men who mistreated and even attacked their fieldhands. With Mama out of the house, Reed had a tough choice to make: Should he go back after her—with little to no money in his pocket for a train ride? Or should he try to drum up enough cash to get to Chicago by train— and stay there? Jimmy would later say that he begged his parents and sister for the money he needed for a train ticket to Chicago.

He placed his money on the counter of the Illinois Central Railroad station and hopped the next train to the Windy City, where three of his siblings had recently migrated. They'd be more than happy to help him—again. But would he have the gumption to stay this time?

Chapter 2
Slag Valley and the Gary Stomp

The hustle and bustle of Chicago's "Jew Town"—the open-air market-place of Maxwell Street—in the late '40s and early '50s was a beacon for musicians. Its crowded streets were a playground rife with musical exploration and education.

Jimmy Reed was drawn to Chicago and the spectacle of Maxwell Street. After all, so many of his fellow Southerners had come up to Chicago from places like Mississippi, Louisiana, Arkansas, Georgia, and Alabama—people like Muddy Waters and Little Walter—dipping their beaks into the rich Chicago blues gigging circuit and recording indus-try. Versatile guitar virtuoso Lonnie Johnson had done his first show in Chicago some years earlier, and people like Sunnyland Slim, Sonny Boy Williamson I, Eddie Boyd, Big Bill Broonzy, Kokomo Arnold, Big Maceo Merriweather, Floyd Jones, James "Snooky" Pryor, Memphis Slim, Johnny Shines, Homesick James, Daddy Stovepipe, Tampa Red, and Jimmie Lee Robinson (among many others) were playing there regu-larly—fashioning a new musical sensibility, laying the groundwork for both the electric Chicago blues and, later, rock 'n' roll.

Though being a musician didn't occupy Reed's every thought, he did have a mind to get back to playing again. He frequented the local clubs and dug the vibe of jazz and blues that seemed to be emanating from the very street corners of this urban environment. Reed had learned a few things on the harp, which sounded like both Sonny Boys (things he had heard on the radio), but a gnawing and burning sensation inside him forced him to retreat from being a generic copycat. Jimmy knew his musical style and voice were still raw, still developing, still largely for his own personal entertainment, but he wanted to be plugged in to the Chicago blues vibe somehow. He knew he had to do it his own way—there really was no other option. Either out of stubbornness or lack of facility, Reed *couldn't* do it any other way.

In an unfortunate turn of events, one of the genre's true pioneers would soon be making room for Reed. Early in the morning on June 1, 1948, Sonny Boy Williamson I, drunk and staggering out of the Plantation Club on East 31st Street in Chicago, was finding his way home. He was nearly at the door of his home at 3226 South Giles when he became a victim of a violent mugging. He was robbed and left for dead. Bloody and half dazed, Sonny Boy crawled to his door where his wife, Lacey Belle, who Sonny Boy referenced in his music many times, found him incoherent and half dead. A few days later, Sonny Boy fell into an irreversible coma and died. Just two months prior, he had turned 34.

With his passing, Chicago—and the world—lost one of the greatest blues harp players ever to record. But Chicago would soon gain another, one who would take the concept of blues artist to a height not achieved by many before him.

While Sonny Boy I would soon be eclipsed by the likes of Walter Jacobs (aka Little Walter), there was a feeling of tremendous freedom, of the playing field being wide open for newcomers. For Reed, the welcome wagon would have to wait. With his small family, Reed had to spend most of his time thinking about bringing home the bacon.

Being a veteran of World War II and a hard worker, Reed found it easy to get work without too much fuss from employers. Besides, employers, particularly in the booming industry of steel, were hiring in record numbers. As long as a worker kept his nose clean and was not blacklisted (and Reed wasn't), he could pretty much experience smooth sailing.

It seemed the worst jobs, however, in the mills and the like were reserved for blacks—jobs that had been done by ethnic whites just a few years prior to the half-century mark. It was work, nasty, unforgiving, and unappreciated work at times, but if you played your cards straight, you could have a job for life—and have a career. And that was what many of the poor Southern blacks who had come north to Chicago and east into Gary, Indiana, had hoped for. They just wanted a better life, and the chance at long-term employment. They wanted a respectable position, and then someday, who knows? Maybe they could be foreman.

Jimmy found a job immediately in the union-friendly Wisconsin Steel Works mill located in the Irondale district, where many steel workers lived. With the coming of the Korean, Cold, and Vietnam wars, America was experiencing a steel boom. At Wisconsin Steel alone, two open-hearth furnaces were installed just before the attack on Pearl Harbor. At the same time, social projects were being devised, such as FDR's great vision for a nationwide superhighway system, later to be developed and elevated (literally) by Eisenhower. As more and more people wanted and could afford cars, the need grew for an expansive highway system. Production stepped up. Wisconsin Steel Works alone had been averaging 88,000 tons of open-hearth steel a month.

Reed was one of the many blacks who had flocked to Chicago's South Side to be close to their place of employment. He was living a few doors off the corner of 90th and Mackinaw, not far from the mills (and, incidentally, not far from the bars). According to data put forth in William Kornblum's book *Blue Collar Community* (a study of Wisconsin Steel Works and the urban environment surrounding it), 70 percent of the workers in Wisconsin's Number 3 mill, from 1950–1954, were African-American.

"The story of Wisconsin Steel Works is not just the story of a company," wrote R.A. Lindgren, general superintendent of Wisconsin Steel Works circa 1951. "It is the story of people; the story of employees and management alike who have pulled together to establish and maintain an enviable reputation in the community and the trade."

This all looks clinical and sanitized on paper. Living it was another story. Iron is typically poured at 2,700 degrees Fahrenheit and steel at hundreds of degrees higher than that. Reed and his coworkers in Wisconsin Steel loaded furnaces and combated stifling heat and silent-but-deadly carpets of dust particles every day. "Steel work is dangerous," remembers Al Cabaj, who worked at Wisconsin in the early '50s. "My pa was a scarfer and I mean he ate a lot of junk in his time." (Scarfers removed imperfections with torches that cut through steel.) "When you are at the open-heart furnaces you could be pouring liquid metal on a very large scale—maybe 300 tons of liquid into various molds."

An aerial view of the Wisconsin Steel Works, circa 1950.

Horror stories frightened the locals, stories of men losing their neighbors, best friends, and even their own body parts in vats of molten metal. The ventilation problems, let alone the heat, made for long-term health problems. At Wisconsin Steel, in the unbearable heat, workers loaded the blast furnaces with limestone, coke, and iron ore—making a kind of industrial sandwich, which would turn to liquid in the oppressive hellfire. Limestone, being lighter than iron, was used to help float impurities. Those impurities are skimmed, or slagged, off the top and thrown away. The purified iron ore then gets shoved into the open furnace to make steel. "It was a dirty son-of-a fuckin' place to work," says Cabaj. "The stuff that was slagged off, that scum, that would be dumped—when it was cherry red still—right on to 100th Street. After it cooled it would be picked up and put in buckets. It was shipped away, processed and broken down."

At the nearby US Steel factory in Gary, Indiana, the workers would pour the impure runoff into water and it would break up. The workers called it "popcorn slag" because of its shape. As with Wisconsin, nothing went to waste. The dumped slag would be recycled and used, for instance, to make new streets. But the very idea of runoff made most people uneasy and, frankly, nauseated. The entire steel mill quadrant became synonymous with this most unpleasant runoff. Locals and even the workers at the mills identified and labeled the area "Slag Valley."

The term is rich in double meaning, of course. Millwork was gut-wrenching under the worst conditions imaginable; it wasn't for people who didn't like to get their hands and entire body dirty. Reed stuck it out for a while, though deep down he knew he wouldn't get far at Wisconsin Steel. Talk of racial inequality in the mill as well the company's advancement policies made it nearly impossible for Wisconsin to consider a borderline illiterate country boy as a leader of workers and as a problem solver of daily crisis situations.

Somehow, Reed knew the gray drabness and the dirty darkness of the mill were only temporary, as music—specific musical figures—began to take shape inside his head. "I must have stayed out there for somethin' like a year or maybe a little better," Reed said in *Living Blues*. "Or could've been two years or more. And that's the time I started foolin' around with that box all over again."

One morning after a typical 11:00 P.M.–7:00 A.M. shift (the grave-yard shift), Reed went to the alley behind his apartment in South Chicago to blow his harp and maybe pluck the strings of his acoustic guitar for a while. Then, an idea came to him. Why was he playing these two instruments separately? *Jimmy*, he said to himself, *why not try to get both of these things together?*

Jimmy left the alley, reached into the back of his truck, pulled out a pair of pliers, and headed straight for his bedroom. He riffled through his closet, found a wire hanger, and went to work. After stretching the hanger, he fitted it over his head and rigged the harp with wires to keep it attached to this makeshift holster. The device seemed to work for the time being: it allowed him to strum a guitar and blow harp simultaneously. But it would never do on the streets or on the stage; it was just too unstable. He needed a professional rig, but where to get one?

Reed checked out the local Brown's Music Shop on 92nd and Commercial Avenue and bought himself an amp and an electric guitar. He eventually bought a professional harp rack from a music store on Halsted, and the first time he placed his neck through it and rested it on his shoulders, it was as if he had truly found himself.

"Guitar you can be taught," Jimmy told *Melody Maker* in 1964, "but harmonica is something you can't teach a person. So, I tried and tried and tried and finally got to play some things on harmonica that I had going on guitar. When I found I could, I decided to play both at once."

Reed would later say that he had never seen anyone play two instruments at once, same as he did, but it wasn't a new concept, of course. The European folk tradition, for instance, saw musicians play a pipe (much like a recorder with only three air holes) in one hand and tabor (usually a long barrel with two rope-tied heads on either end) in the other. Musicians like Jesse Fuller, Doctor Ross (Isaiah Ross), Joe Hill Louis, and Daddy Stovepipe blew harp, played guitar, and sang, and in some cases were virtual one-man bands, adding drums to their acts. Reed undoubtedly saw the two being played together in the plantation towns in Mississippi, as it was indigenous to many Southern states.

By 1952, Jimmy bounced over to nearby Valley Mould Iron Foundry, on 106th Street across the Calumet River, and took a job as a "shakeout" man. Valley Mould was a service mill, casting iron for other mills—barely a blip on the industrial map. It employed only 330 workers or so, while neighboring mills like Republic and US Steel had thousands on the payroll. To say that Valley Mould was a less-than-desirable place to work was putting it mildly. In the summer when the outside weather was 90 to 100 degrees right on the river (taking into account the humidity), it would be at least 20 to 30 degrees hotter inside the factory. Amid this intense heat, Jimmy, as a shakeout man, would pour hot iron, wait till it cooled, and then, once the iron was solid, shake out the sand with an eight-pound hammer. "It was the dirtiest fucking place in the world," says Ed Sadlowski, a former Valley Mould employee and resident of "Slag" or "Death" Valley. "Because of all the silicon, sand, dust, and dirt flying around—the foundries were inherently dirty—some people called it 'Death Valley.'"

"Once the sand was shaken off, the air was full of black dust," explains Raymond Monroe of the Steel Founders Society of America. "It is arguably one of the worst jobs, next to tunnel men who worked below the foundry, in the factory because you had to pick up the heavy casting in an awkward position in an area that was most hot and dusty."

A fine-layered soot, the blackest color, would manifest from nearly every crevice and orifice of Jimmy's body. This was before the time when environmental and union groups made a concerted effort to clean these mills to make a safer work environment. The only way to fight the dust was to wear something over your face. Looking something like a Wild West bandit, Reed would drape a handkerchief over his face while he was at work. Prolonged exposure to the atmosphere in the mills led to silicosis (silica poisoning; silica is the main component of sand). The men wouldn't even realize it until it was too late.

"The horseshit jobs were reserved for the black guys," Sadlowski says. "Ninety-something percent of the horseshit jobs then were filled by black guys."

Still, there were plenty of watering holes where people could forget their troubles. Nearby taverns were kept in business by laborers who needed a good stiff belt at the end of a long day's work. Many longtime Chicagoans I spoke with all said the same thing: "There were more taverns than churches."

Ironically enough, it was just such a watering hole where Reed found sudden inspiration. Club Jamboree was only a few doors down from Reed's house, and he would stop in there for a drink after work. He had already been playing for fun with neighborhood musicians in the alley outside his house. They'd sit in the alley as Reed would plug in his new amp from Brown's Music and local musicians, young and old—all amateur—would play and drink and bullshit. But after seeing these professional musicians at the Jamboree, a little light went off in Reed's head. "There was a tavern—it wasn't no club—across the street from my house when I was living in South Chicago," Reed told *Guitar Player*. "I said to myself, 'Well, if these guys can play in here—I don't see too much that they're doing—I think I could do some of the same thing.'"

As if inspired by his new musical vision, Reed left Valley Mould to do odd jobs for a mobile home manufacturer on Stony Island Avenue. There was also a practical reason for leaving: Jimmy's health was being affected by the work environment at Valley Mould. "[Daddy] wasn't able to work certain places," explains daughter Loretta Reed. "He couldn't work in the steel mill. It would make him sick."

At his new job, Jimmy met fellow musician Willie Joe Duncan, nick-named "Jody" or "Joe D." Reed quickly became friends with Duncan; they'd share beers, laughs, more beers at local taverns, and exchange musical ideas while playing on their breaks. Duncan would go on to record his signature "Unitar Rock" for the Specialty label. The monotonous yet strangely unforgettable song was created on Duncan's one-string instrument dubbed the Unitar (a broom wire tuned to A).

Reed and Duncan polished their act at Jimmy's house, but soon they took it to the streets, to places like Robbins, Illinois, taking requests from small crowds on corners and in front of grocery stores. As Reed told *Living Blues,* "We'd just run here and there, just stop some of anywhere. And [Duncan] was doin' this old crazy thing, with this one strand of wire, he wasn't lettin' me lose him nowhere.... We got pretty good together."

Reed's love for music soon escalated. He and Jody floated on up to 92nd Street to Brown's Music Store and cut some dubs. Though some of the names have been lost to time, Reed remembered one of the demos as "Found My Baby Gone." There was nothing fancy about it; Reed just wanted to "hear himself back" and perhaps even get a read on whether he had what it took to sell his music. Reed thought it half a gag, half a step in the right direction to entice a distributor who could put it in local jukeboxes.

"That old thing, you could play something and you could cut it yourself," Reed told Bill Scott in a radio Q&A. "Then you could flip it and it would play it back for ya. So, I had taken that thing out, a 78 side."

Emboldened by what he had heard, Reed's confidence grew. He began playing with street musicians less and less and started falling in with such established professionals as drummer Kansas City Red and his piano player, Blind John Davis, in Chicago Heights at the Black and Tan Club. Kansas City Red had played with Robert Nighthawk and Earl Hooker, Big Bill Broonzy, Tampa Red, and Sonny Boy Williamson I (one of Reed's idols), among others. "I met Jimmy Reed in South Chicago," Red recalled. "He was messin' around with a guy with a tub—just goin' out and playin' with me out in South Chicago."

Reed won a spot at the Club Jamboree near his house and he'd often show up and hope for the best. He'd always bum a guitar off of whoever might be making an appearance that night with him; sometimes it was Homesick James, other nights it was Baby Face Leroy. As luck would have it, Eddie Taylor, Jimmy's old friend from Mississippi, was playing there regularly. The two rekindled their friendship and each was curious as to what the other had been doing.

A lot had happened since Taylor had seen Reed. For one thing, Jimmy had become increasingly more capable of playing guitar, singing, and blowing harp. Taylor, meanwhile, had sat in with Homesick James, Elmore James, Walter Horton, Johnnie Shines, and B.B. King in both Chicago and Memphis. While Reed had been bouncing around Mississippi, Taylor had been playing with Floyd Jones and Big Joe Williams.[i] Taylor had recently moved to Chicago from Memphis and immediately gone to work in the packing department of a TV and radio station in Chicago. He'd often mosey down to Maxwell Street on his days off, and later began playing there as well as other places in the city, most notably with Jimmie Lee Robinson at Jake's Tavern on Kedzie.

With Robinson the pay was minimal and the boys didn't have much, but they hustled from that gig to others around the city, carrying their equipment wherever they went to make an extra five dollars or even ten. As he told Mike Rowe for his *Chicago Blues: The City & the Music:* "We played there for three dollars a night," Robinson said, "from 7:00 P.M. till four or five in the morning. I had only one suit; Eddie had no soles in his shoes. We walked everywhere to these jobs, carrying the amplifiers, and play for five, eight, ten dollars a night. Yeah, we did that for a few years."

Taylor and Robinson gigged at Club Alibi until Eddie began going out himself, finally hooking up with James Scott, Jr., at the Congo Lounge. Eventually, Taylor gravitated toward Memphis, Tennessee, where he was working on a pitch to snag harp player Walter Horton for a gig Taylor had at Chicago's Club Jamboree.

Horton, born in 1916 in Horn Lake, Mississippi, was a child prodigy at five. His harp playing would entertain neighbors at house parties and communal dances. The Memphis Jug Band took Horton under its wing when Horton's family moved to Memphis in the mid-'20s. Horton learned—and learned well—from Willie Shade (of the Memphis Jug Band) and took pointers from Memphis harp legend Hammie Nixon. Synthesizing what he was shown, Horton took to the streets and jammed with such accompanied luminaries as Robert Johnson and Honeyboy Edwards. By 1940, Horton had staked a claim to bustling

Maxwell Street and met Eddie Taylor. Despite having met Taylor, Horton returned to Memphis to record with Sam Phillips. He had made a few recordings for Chess, Modern, Sun, and RPM when he and Taylor crossed paths again. Taylor finally coaxed Horton into coming to the Windy City one more time, and Horton was convinced.

Taylor and Horton resurfaced in Chicago, but it would be a short-lived reunion. Not surprisingly, given Horton's track record, after just a couple of weeks the harp player told Taylor he had to split so he could rendezvous with Muddy Waters as a replacement for Junior Wells.[ii]

With the loss of Horton, Taylor needed a harp player. As luck would have it, Reed happened to be playing the Club Jamboree himself. "I was playing a little way from where Jimmy [Reed] was living," Eddie Taylor told writer Mike Rowe. "He came over there one night and saw me—that's why we teamed back up together. At that time he wasn't going nowhere. Wasn't hitting no nothing. Just rapping on the guitar and blowing on harmonica. So I just told him, lighten up off his guitar and blow his harmonica and I put the beat to it."

Reed and Taylor renewed their musical partnership at the Jamboree—jamming with the likes of Floyd Jones, Snooky Pryor, and Junior Anderson—and sometimes joining Kansas City Red and Blind John Davis at the Black and Tan.

One more piece of the musical puzzle appeared to be clicked into place. Despite this, Jimmy maintained a day job. He had moved on from his odd jobs and was working in the packing industry as a "shoulder man" for Armour Packing Company. Being a shoulder man meant he cleaned and removed the hide from the shoulder of the butchered animal.

The stockyards have been romanticized and even immortalized: Howlin' Wolf entitled one of his most famous songs "Killing Floor"—a reference to the stockyards (although the song itself is not about the stockyards). Frank Sinatra's original "My Kind of Town" mentioned the union stockyards, and Upton Sinclair's sobering novel/social commentary *The Jungle* concerned turn-of-the-century immigrant workers who eked out an existence in the Chicago stockyards, lived in squalor, and battled disease and tragedy despite their pursuit of the American Dream—or perhaps because of it.

Armour, like so many other packing companies down at the Chicago stockyards, hired many uneducated workers who needed employment. Some historians estimate there were as many as 6,300 people working at Armour circa 1952. The strongest, of course, got the most work. And Reed was no slouch. He was thin, solid, and wiry, but he had a vise grip. The man's hands were rocks. He was nearly born to be a shoulder man. But no one is born to do such work; it is an acquired skill applied in ungodly surroundings.

"I used to want to vomit when I first worked at Armour," says Jim Stevens, president of Lincoln Provisional packing company, who worked for Armour Packing from 1952 through 1959 and lied about his age to get the job.

"They even used to stop Chicago White Sox games when the wind was blowing in a certain direction," says Franco Chiappetti, marketing director for Chiappetti Lamb and Veal, one of the last standing meat-packing companies of the Chicago stockyards. "The smell was just appalling."

The sights, the sounds, the smells—it was grotesque. After a while, workers got used to the animal shrieks and the odor of blood and death. There was even a kind of gallows humor in seeing angry cattle stampeding and chasing workers around the floor until being shot with a rifle by someone from above. Workers would laugh off such incidents, and it was all they could do to stop thinking about what had just happened.

Yet, for all the grotesqueries and harsh realities, the stockyards were a hub of activity. What with the rails transporting millions of livestock; wide-eyed tourists clamoring for a look at how meat is processed (many becoming ill at their new knowledge); the neighborhood stores, street vendors, and restaurants attracting customers; the confluence of ethnic backgrounds creating a kind of linguistic and aromatic tapestry; and the booming by-product plants (everything from violin strings to soap), Monday morning in the stockyards looked like a carnival on Saturday night.[iii]

Although he knew he was being exploited by a system that was unfair to people of color—and that he would escape it someday—Reed found a new kind of challenge and graduated skill level in working for Armour. "I had done got pretty good, man, bonin' them shoulders as they come down the line," Reed explained to *Living Blues*. "And them couple of knives I had was so sharp till I could cut the skin offa them shoulders so quick till it just didn't really look like it was happening."

To top it off, Jimmy never complained about the penetrating stench that would linger with him even long after he had left the slaughter-house, or the renegade cattle, or the blood-curdling animal shrieks. He became less sensitive to them over time.

Stamped August 12, 1952, an issued Chicago musicians union card read: "Reed Matcher James." While this commenced Reed's long—and quite bizarre—relationship with Chicago's local musicians union (Reed would be deleted from membership rosters, then reinstated, then deleted and reinstated again), the union card, like his Social Security card, meant Reed was "official." It gave him free rein to go where he wanted in Chicago and places like nearby Gary, Indiana, without fear of being dragged off the stage or having local authorities side with club owners and block him from performing without a union card.

MEMBERSHIP RECORD CARD   C32

FULL NAME REED MATCHER JAMES
           Last Name   First Name   Middle Name

SOCIAL SECURITY NUMBER 355-20-▉

BIRTHPLACE Leland, Miss, DATE OF BIRTH Sept.6th.1925

DATE JOINED LOCAL 8-12-52 INSTRUMENT Guitar Harmonica

BENEFICIARY Mrs.Mary Lee Reed RELATIONSHIP Wife
    same add.

SIGNATURE OF MEMBER ✔ *Matcher J Reed*

DATE FILED WITH SECRETARY AUG 12 1952

◀● 385

ENTITLED TO GRADUATING DEATH DONATION
(SEE REVERSE SIDE)

The 1952 union card issued to James "Matcher" Reed.

Gary was the steel capitol of the world. Seduced by the promise of a good life and good jobs, lured by US Steel ads in local papers like the *Chicago Defender,* people of all colors came to Gary and the population exploded from just 300 to nearly 17,000 in four years. Shacks and tents that once dotted the landscape were replaced by homes, churches, schools, and parks. Even the terrain was changed to accommodate the construction of the US Steel mills—swamps drained, the mighty Calumet River diverted, and railroad tracks ripped up and relocated. Gary became a boomtown: employees of US Steel numbered more than 20,000 by the mid-'50s.

This statue in downtown Gary, Indiana, is dedicated to Steel Town's founder.

Bill Hill, jazzman and Gary music historian, remembers Jimmy Reed spending a lot of time in Gary, playing places like Pulaski Bar. "It was a magical time, as I look back," Hill says. "The sidewalks of Gary then used to be four and five deep, both sides of the street. There were so many people going from joint to joint. All the joints had crowds because there was always different types of music going on. I sat in with Jimmy Reed, and he would sometimes come in and sit in with us in our intermission. After hours—that was when music was really played. In fact, at 19th and Broadway, it was The Hurricane upstairs and in the basement it was Club Dreamland. So, we started playing upstairs and then we would continue downstairs until four, five, six in the morning."

Jimmy was still working at Armour and needed to bring home money for his family while moonlighting at clubs in Illinois and Indiana. He began accompanying guitarist and songwriter John Brim and his wife, Grace (a drummer, singer, and harp player), around Steel Town. The three became very close. It was John and Grace who would take Jimmy in overnight sometimes, after late-night gigs across the river.

Brim completed "Rattlesnake" (which bore an uncanny resemblance to "Hound Dog") and "It Was a Dream" for the Checker label (a subsidiary of Chess) with what was essentially the Aces—Little Walter on harp, Fred Below on drums, and the Myers brothers (Dave on bass, Louis on guitar) in March of 1953. (Little Walter's smash hit "Juke" was still on the air and became the standard for harp players everywhere. It's easy to hear why: his jazzy side and sax-like phrasings were miles ahead of what any other blues harp player was recording then.) Brim followed that session with one in May that included Walter, Eddie Taylor, and Elgin Edmonds on drums and yielded "Lifetime Baby" and "Ice Cream Man." (This outrageous double entendre extraordinaire was covered by a little hard-rock band called Van Halen in 1978.)

Originally from Hopkinsville, Kentucky, John taught himself to play harmonica (much like Reed) and from an early age was inspired by Tampa Red and Peetie Wheatstraw, among others. He later played with the man known as "Peetie Wheatstraw's buddy," Harmon Ray. After letting his creativity incubate in Indianapolis, Indiana, Brim charged Chicago, coupling with old music partner Homer Wilson, a fellow guitarist. A dry cleaner by day and musician by night, John fell in with people like Muddy Waters, Sonny Boy Williamson I, and groundbreaking piano player Maceo Merriweather, who had played with Big Bill Broonzy and Tampa Red.

Merriweather ultimately paved the way for many Chicago piano players, from Johnny Jones and Henry Gray to Otis Spann, who would define and frame the very essence of Chicago blues piano cool. But his drinking got the best of him and he suffered a stroke in 1946. He continued to play left-handed piano—his right-hand dexterity was severely hampered by the stroke—and John and Grace performed with him right up to his death in February 1953.[iv]

1640 Broadway in Gary, Indiana, the one-time home of Vee-Jay Records.

Though far from being in such poor physical condition, Reed presented a kind of vulnerability that Brim recognized from working with Maceo. It was obvious that Reed was a natural, but the record and music industry's choppy waters could be fatal for the uninitiated and undereducated. Reed did fine in the clubs, but could he survive? For Brim, watching Maceo deteriorate—as noble as it was for him to continue performing after his stroke—was a cautionary tale.

Things were moving fast. Jimmy was being noticed, and he and an independent, black-owned record company called Vee-Jay were about to put Gary, Indiana, on the musical map.

Vivian Carter, a local DJ, hosted the radio shows "Vivian Carter Show" daily from 9:30–11:30 A.M. and "Vivian's Spiritual Hour" from 9:00–10:00 A.M. every Sunday on WGRY. Vivian got her start in radio on WWCA with the "Living with Vivian Show"—one of the few national R&B radio broadcasts—and went on the air Thursday evenings with "Upshaw's Famous Door" and the "Roger Turf Lounge" on Saturday afternoons.

Vivian had opened Vivian's Record Shop at 1640 Broadway in Gary, and it was her husband, Jimmy Bracken, who urged Carter to establish a record label. Stories conflict, however, on just how Carter and Bracken raised the start-up capital and just how much. "Vivian and Jimmy borrowed $500 to produce the first record, borrowed it from a pawnshop," explained Vivian's brother Calvin Carter, who would become the label's main producer. "The pawnbroker's name was Maurice Tepper." Another source says it was $300 Jimmy earned by selling his car.

Regardless, the Vee-Jay label (a name created with the initials of their first names) went live. The first band they recorded was the Spaniels, with lead singer James "Pookie" Hudson. "The Spaniels graduated from the same high school my sister and I went to—Roosevelt High School in Gary," Calvin said.

Accounts differ on how Jimmy Reed met Bracken and Carter. Most think Reed was urged by Albert King, who was playing in Gary as a drummer for Jimmy Reed, to send his material over to Vee-Jay right away when word of the new label got out. Reed was encouraged by the demos he had made at Brown's, but instead took them to the reigning king of recorded Chicago blues music: Chess Records. Chess and its Checker division were having success with Little Walter, Muddy Waters, and Willie Mabon, and Reed would have liked nothing better than to have been mentioned in their company.

Reed was hopeful, until Leonard Chess heard the records. "They were too great for me," Reed said of Chess Records to *Living Blues*. "I took three of those [demos] to Leonard Chess and he said I had to come catch him later, because…he had just a little bit too [much] tied up right then. They had him strung out as such, Muddy Water[s]…and Little Walter and they said they had him tied down. He said he was very busy so I had to catch him one day later."

Vivian Carter, Vee-Jay co-founder.

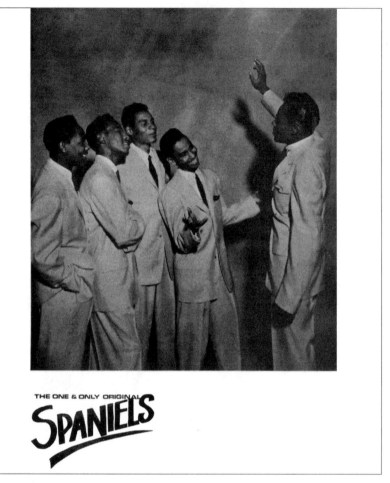

THE ONE & ONLY ORIGINAL **SPANIELS**

A publicity photo of Vee-Jay's first recording artists, a vocal group called the Spaniels.

"My dad went to Chess and he said that Chess was telling him that they wanted Little Walter to play harmonica for him and [they] wanted Muddy Waters to play guitar," Jimmy Reed, Jr., says. "Dad said, 'Why should Little Walter play harmonica for me when I can do it myself? And I can play my own guitar.' Apparently, that was the only way that Chess would have received him, was under those terms. He didn't buy it."

Calvin Carter told a tale of how Reed wound up on the Vee-Jay label. "When we first met Jimmy Reed in 1953, he was actually working in Chicago in the stockyards, where he was cutting up cattle,"

Calvin told interviewer Mike Callahan. "He was playing harmonica for a guy called King David that we were interested in. So we were having a rehearsal with them one day and we heard Jimmy play. We asked him, 'Do you have any songs that you've written?' And he said, 'No, but I've got some I made up.'"

Reed remembered: "Vivian said, 'I'll tell you what…let's go out to my mother's house, 'cause fact of business, I want to hear them records what you taken let Chess heard.' She played that and she said, 'Get your box and your harmonica, I wanna hear you play this thing.' So, I got my box and everything and I start playing for her. She just said, 'I think that is very nice. Will you record some records for me if I can get this started?' I said, 'When are you planning on doing it?' I was strictly just interested in hearing myself either over the radio or over the jukebox. I didn't know what it meant or what it might be. I just wanted to hear myself back."

As 1953 was spiraling, Jimmy Reed was invited to two recording sessions. The first one was John Brim's. Brim had asked Jimmy and Eddie Taylor to accompany him and Grace on two sides (of the same single) for Al Benson's Parrot label. The four musicians were billed as John Brim and His Stompers and recorded "Gary Stomp," an instrumental, and "Tough Times," a Muddy Waters–style stopgap stomp. If Reed had ever sounded like Little Walter, it was in late 1953.

Brim's career at Chess/Checker wasn't taking off, but his songwriting talents were still intact. His ability to speak truth and cut to the bone with a healthy dose of wit, humor, and candor were evident on the session he did with Reed and Taylor. "Tough Times" is a kind of rarity. While some bluesmen were certainly speaking about conditions in America, and how African-Americans were being locked out of the American Dream, the examples were few and far between. Brim wasn't naming names, or placing blame, but he certainly was weary of the economic situation he and—by default—others were forced to face.

The irony of the song is that while it doesn't exactly mock the trials and travails of the working man, there are equal parts sarcasm and melodrama as the lyrics showcase the sharp divide between African-Americans and the larger white majority: "I had a good job/working many hours a week. They had a layoff and they got poor me…can't find a part-time job…nuthin' in my house to eat."

Perhaps most notable about "Tough Times" is Reed's squeaking and trembling harp. He plays an amplified harp, a technique that the Chicago harp player Little Walter had pioneered. Reed's sharp, metallic bite, his masculine, sax-like blowing on the Brim tracks is in stark contrast to the toy-ish, acoustic high squeals (a feminine tone) the world would soon come to know. Far more significantly, Reed had his first solo recording date with the newly formed Vee-Jay Records. Carter and Bracken had big hopes for Jimmy Reed. They thought they had put something over on Leonard Chess; his lack of interest was their gain. Reed, with pre-guitar hero Albert King on drums, Brim on guitar, and an unknown bass player (his name has been lost to time), banged out four tunes that one afternoon: "High and Lonesome," "Jimmie's Boogie," "Roll and Rhumba," and "I Found My Baby."

"Roll and Rhumba," as the title suggests, is caught somewhere between a rock 'n' roll number and a Latin dance feel—a variation of the Afro-Cuban musical style called the Cuban Son. (A similar combination by Chess recording artist Chuck Berry would be exploited for the 1957 hit "Rock & Roll Music.") In Reed's song, the guitars are barking dogs, Reed's harp is akin to a high-pitched whistle, and Albert King's syncopated rata-ma-tat clicking on the rims of his drums sidestep a "two and four" backbeat pattern. The drums sound *so* primitive, in fact, that they bear some resemblance to the timbre closely associated with an overanxious youngster banging on pots and pans while stomping his feet to keep time.

"I Found My Baby" is perhaps one of the most straightforward blues in the Reed catalog. Reed sings: "When I found my baby/she set right down in the road/I know she was so sorry/to know what she done to me." It is a rare occurrence to see Jimmy as a victim who has no restitution. It seemed his lyrics, more often than not, portrayed him as someone with something up his sleeve.

It was "High and Lonesome," however, that would most closely resemble the template known as the "Jimmy Reed sound." Reed's second-position harp playing echoes to the country fields he worked and lived on as a child. Reed's harp is tuned to *A* and he is playing in the key of *E*. (Second-position playing is in the 5th of the key of the tuned harp.) John Brim plays a variation on a I-IV-V blues in *F* that is quite nearly the blueprint for the rockin' shuffle that would become Jimmy's trademark.

This country feel seems to belie the urbane wittiness of Reed's lyrics. This is not your typical "my lady done me wrong" song ("Well, now you're packed up, wanna leave me/and I'm not gonna let you stay…"). Jimmy Bracken took credit for co-writing this song, but this seems unlikely. Nonetheless, the raw, grooving, and raucous number is a wonderful slice of Americana. Reed's song was truly without boundaries.

Critics and writers would apply terms to these four songs for years to come, but they were (especially "High and Lonesome") "folk" music in its purest sense—a point that seemed to be underscored by the fact that Reed was evoking, though not in the academic musical sense, the Appalachian/bluegrass "high lonesome" motif.[v] Reed was as much a "folk" artist as anything—his music being "of, by, and for" the people.

Of course, Reed's style and his substance was *not* bluegrass and, despite his somewhat nasal vocals, he was not hitting notes in the high registers. However, he did share a sort of kindred spirit with the father of bluegrass, Bill Monroe, who tagged his own music and singing voice "high lonesome" and sang of life with all its hurt, need, and longing.[vi]

Reed's electrified vision of down-home blues certainly fit into the history of African-American folk music as well. The "blues" worked its way through nineteenth-century minstrel music (combined with the popular "juba" dance forms), post–Civil War Euro-American standards, spirituals, field hollers, and into twentieth-century popular culture as the musical format *A-A-B*. This folk tradition eventually arrived at (for example) something that resembles Mississippi John Hurt's "Stack O' Lee Blues"—arranged by storyteller Hurt and recorded at the end of 1928, or Blind Willie McTell's "Travelin' Blues" recorded in 1929—and is carried on by Reed.

Even from these early sides, Reed did, and did so well, distill the rawness of the blues: he took the edge off a darker and more fearsome brand put forth by the likes of contemporaries Howlin' Wolf and Muddy Waters, scaled it to a sugar-packed 12-bar (or sometimes more) blues, added accents to the eighth-note feel of the rhythm, and sprinkled in the occasional variation from the theme.

Vee-Jay Records thought they had a hit. They had bridged the country and urban blues planes in Reed. But that was not how the general public heard it. "High and Lonesome" was far from being a big seller, falling short of the Spaniels' side "Baby, It's You." "High and Lonesome" with B-side "Roll and& Rhumba" was released on Vee-Jay and then leased to Art Sheridan's Chance Records for wider distribution. Despite a good review in *Billboard* proclaiming that "Roll and Rhumba" could "catch juke loot in the Down South Market," sales showed little improvement. ("I Found My Baby" and the instrumental "Jimmie's Boogie" went unreleased at the time.) Vee-Jay was wondering if they had made a mistake by putting money, time, and effort behind their adorable country-blues man with the high-pitched drawl.

Jimmy Reed's first sides were issued on Vee-Jay and Chance.

Jimmy Reed needed a hit. The sales of "High and Lonesome" were disappointing, and Vee-Jay was itching to drop him if the public failed to connect with his next recordings. Despite Vivian's and Jimmy Bracken's lack of record industry acumen and experience, they knew a monetary dud when they saw one. Maybe it was time to wrap up this failed experiment. *Maybe*, they thought, *Leonard Chess was right in having passed on Reed!*

But the company decided to give it one more shot, hoping to at least get back some of its investment. The two-day recording session, probably at the tail end of December 1953 (studio records are unclear; it appears there were dates on December 29 and 31, and/or in early January 1954), was remarkable—if only because Reed invited Eddie Taylor to attend.[vii]

Jimmy Reed's first hit, "You Don't Have to Go" (bottom left, sent him on the road.

Jimmy also called back Albert King as a drummer.[viii] Along with guitarist Johnny Littlejohn, Reed, Taylor, and King cut 4 tracks: "You Don't Have to Go," the instrumental "Boogie in the Dark" (with honky tonk overtures, a walking bassline supplied by Littlejohn and Taylor, and Reed on slide playing in sympathy with his harp), "Shoot My Baby," and another instrumental (and more slide from Jimmy), "Rockin' with Reed."

You Don't Have to Go" plays havoc with the traditional 12-bar blues standard. For one, Reed's cracking and crackling vocals enter the song at a weird angle (mysteriously, Reed's voice is as "stable" as the shifting sand: at points it is strained and at others it is clear as a bell). The harp solo also plays tricks—Reed quickly rises up the sonic ladder (he's using a combination of draw-bent, drawn, and blown notes). Reed's droning and mournful harp burps are played in *F*. (Reed is using a harp tuned in *B flat* here, which means he is playing in second position.) To get in sync, Reed, Taylor, and Littlejohn capoed their guitars at the first fret (or tuned up a half-step from standard tuning).

What's so great about Reed's art (though he would not have referred to what he did as "art") is the strange little subtle things that happen inside the music. A close listening to "You Don't Have to Go" reveals a kind of sonic weirdness, a dissonant riff (about 2:19 into the song), which nearly threatens to tear the song apart. The slight dissonance is caused by the rhythm guitarist—probably Taylor—playing a C7, which is the V chord of the song's choral progression, on the 4th fret with the fifth string open, mingling with scale tones C7 to E on top of a *Bmaj7*. The song is a variant of the 12-bar form, beginning on the IV, or *Bmaj7*, chord. Somehow, the song holds together by a slender thread.

Eddie Taylor's impact was felt immediately. It was *the sound*: the sound that had been alluded to on "High and Lonesome"; the sound that was now solidified. Jimmy was leading with his harp and flash chords while Taylor (with Littlejohn, of course) played a rock-solid "lump" shuffle.

The point has been belabored, but this session, and "You Don't Have to Go," would not be the same without Eddie Taylor's skill and instinct. Eddie had a very efficient way of holding down the syncopated bass beat. He'd mute the strings with the edge of his right hand to clamp down the sound. Eddie was also a hard picker: he'd use fingerpicks—which made for a bassy and punchy string resonance that was streamlined enough not to overwhelm Reed's musical persona, yet full enough to create a sonic bed.

Taylor was the perfect complement to Reed. When the band played in *F,* Eddie had the plucky and deep tones covered, while Reed, using fingerpicks himself, would let his capoed strings ring out for a chimey sound.

There was some controversy for a time concerning "You Don't Have to Go." Big Joe Williams had said that Reed borrowed a thing or two from his "Baby, Don't You Want to Go" for "You Don't Have to Go." There are two things wrong with this argument, however. Firstly, Williams' song is in C (at least to this writer's ears); Reed's is in *F.* Secondly, the Williams song is basically a derivative of the Robert Johnson classic "Sweet Home Chicago." Reed would later dismiss Williams' charge, saying that there have always been people who tried to horn in on his writing credits—from both inside and outside his ranks.

It's hard to imagine anyone else coming up with the lyrics of "You Don't Have to Go," which are a kind of send-up to every heartbroken schlub in the world who wanted to tell off their mistreatin' woman: "You don't have to go…because I will." In a kind of complement to "High and Lonesome," Reed sings: "Oh, baby/you don't have to go/I'm gonna pack up darlin'/down the road I go." With "Shoot My Baby" about as violent and misogynistic—and rockabilly—as Reed would become, "You Don't Have to Go" politely disses and dismisses the object of the singer's derision.

JIMMY REED

Exclusive
VEE JAY RECORDS, INC.
2129 SO. MICHIGAN AVENUE
CHICAGO 16, ILLINOIS

A PR photo of Reed, probably from the mid-to-late '50s. The signature may have been fudged by Calvin Carter or Ewart Abner.

Billboard pegged it right when they called the single a "sleeper." The song was not a hit, though Reed's performances were part of a musical mushroom billowing in all directions, mixing "race" (R&B) and hillbilly music into a new feral beast called rock 'n' roll. Of course, Reed's lackadaisical style was not exactly the same as that of rockabilly cats like the sharp-dressed, slick-pompadoured guitarist Eddie Cochran (who began recording in 1955), but his raw, dancey bop, heard in songs like "Boogie in the Dark," landed him right in the thick, if not at the very beginning, of the entire rock 'n' roll revolution.

Cases in point: Chuck Berry began recording for Chess Records in mid-1955 (though he had been playing "hillbilly" music as an African-American before that). Fats Domino crossed over with "Ain't That A Shame" in 1955. Elvis was making history at Sun Studios in 1954. Inspired by New Orleans gospel music, Little Richard brought forth a more electrifying brand of R&B—called rock 'n' roll—when he kicked out "Tutti Frutti" in 1955. Carl Perkins' 1956 rockabilly "Blue Suede Shoes" was a hit and put the Hank Williams–inspired guitarist on the map. And in 1951, Bill Haley, whose importance is sometimes overlooked, had recorded a cover of "Rocket 88," releasing what is viewed by many music historians as the first "white" rock 'n' roll record. Haley's "(We're Gonna) Rock Around the Clock" would follow in 1954 and Bill Haley and His Comets would become national stars. Jerry Lee Lewis' breakthrough wouldn't come until 1957 with "Whole Lotta Shakin' Going On" and "Great Balls of Fire". Buddy Holly's breakthrough wouldn't come until 1957 with "That'll Be the Day."

Strangely enough, Vee-Jay held back Reed's second session and didn't release any of the material straight off. As it was explained to Jimmy, the company still wanted to see what the first single would do. More likely, Vee-Jay was waiting for the right time to release this material in order to ensure it did well. They thought Reed needed all the help he could get. It wouldn't be until the fall of 1954 that "You Don't Have to Go" (with B-side "Boogie in the Dark") saw the light of day.

The long wait was over. It was released, and…nothing. Vee-Jay's worst fears had come true. The record *was* a dud. Reed's mind flashed back to when he had asked Vee-Jay why they had sat on his material: he wished he could take it all back. But perhaps there were worse things,

Reed kept telling himself. Besides, he had other things to think about. He still had Mary Lee and a family (a growing family that would soon see the addition of twins) and a job he liked, for a change.

Months passed. Then something startling happened. On his way home from Armour, Reed heard a song on the radio. It was "You Don't Have to Go." "The announcer said, 'That's Jimmy Reed,'" Reed recounted to *Guitar Player*. "He's going to be out in Atlanta, Georgia, this Friday and Saturday night." Reed panicked: no one had told him…and this was Thursday evening! "I didn't know I was booked in Atlanta," Reed said. After Jimmy spoke with Eddie Taylor and convinced him that he needed him on the road, the two set out for their first tour together for Vee-Jay Records.

All of a sudden, people started to take notice of the song. "You Don't Have to Go" was scoring high marks with DJs in key markets. Fans in Los Angeles, Chicago, Baltimore, the nation's capital, Nashville, Cleveland, Detroit, Pittsburgh, Buffalo, St. Louis, Durham, and the Big Easy were buying "You Don't Have to Go" like nobody's business. Reed would later say that it was "You Don't Have to Go" that sent him on the road—the song was his launch pad. In November 1954 *Cashbox* declared "You Don't Have to Go" an "effective wax" and observed: "Jimmy is really in there pitching as he handles the slow, bouncy blues with feeling and gusto."

Reed's music was reaching straight across the country, and to some unexpected places. Tommy Dukes, who patterned himself after Jimmy Reed and had learned to play guitar and harmonica before his teens, moved to Arizona when he was just ten years old from his native Hattiesburg, Mississippi. Dukes remembers hearing Reed's music on his dad's transistor radio in both Winslow, Arizona, and Hattiesburg. He claims Reed had played in southern Mississippi in many of the white-oriented clubs—unlike many of the blues artists of the day. "And everybody liked Jimmy Reed—white and black," Dukes says. "I remember a lot of black folks listening to him as well. A lot of black teens were listening to him, and my dad, back in Hattiesburg, would get up and dance, hit that floor, and just yell, 'Yeah,' every time Jimmy Reed come on the radio."

The irony was so thick you'd have to cut it with a knife. "You Don't Have to Go"—given its title, especially—had made Reed a not-so-instant rising star but a rising star nonetheless, and this was after Vee-Jay guarded against the possibility of signing the Southern gentleman to a multi-song deal.

Jimmy quit his job at Armour and was soon seeing the world from the window of a tour bus. (Reed would soon be able to travel the way he wanted: in his own big white Cadillac.) It was a different lifestyle, one that Reed was not used to, but one that he enjoyed. It would also be a life he would learn to manage, or mismanage, depending on his state of health and mind. The road was unforgiving, but it was truly the only home for Reed for the next several years. With success came a price. He had to share some of the greatest and worst moments of his life with fans.

After not recording for the entire year of 1954, Reed returned, unceremoniously, to Universal Recording Studio on January 18, 1955, to cut one track, "You Upset My Mind," with Eddie Taylor and drummer Ray Scott in tow. Reed's instinctual sense of the complex led to a strange duck in "You Upset My Mind." The song was recorded in third-position harp, meaning he was playing an *A* harp in *B*. But Reed knew exactly what he was doing. He was hitting note bends and hitting them in harmony with the band. When Reed hits a bend, he is bending from *D to C#* so that it's sympathetic to the *V chord* being played. Above all, Reed had great ears, and didn't play any major thirds over the IV chord.

The industry was learning to respect Reed. *Billboard* spent plenty of ink in covering Reed's "You Don't Have to Go." In the "Rhythm & Blues Notes," Paul Ackerman wrote: "Another point of interest this week is the appearance in the national bestseller charts of Jimmy Reed's 'You Don't Have to Go' on the Vee-Jay label. This is the second Southern blues type of R&B wax which has proven strong enough—in recent wax—to break out as a good seller on more than one regional basis."

By March 1955, *Billboard* had ranked "You Don't Have to Go" in the Top 20 bestselling records among dealers surveyed throughout the country, with the flip side, "Boogie in the Dark," being a particular favorite of fans in Atlanta. *Cash Box* proclaimed "Boogie" was "infectious music that is good for jukebox." They were right, of course. Jimmy Reed's music was tailor-made for jukeboxes. The lows of a 78- or 45-rpm record were pumped through the machine's speaker and got the nightclub crowd up and dancing. There was something about the depth of the bottom end that hit listeners in their soul and forced them to get up and leave their tables. None of the sonic castration and compression of the digital age existed then. It was pure, brassy noise.

"You Don't Have to Go" was holding strong at No. 13 in March 1955 when *Billboard* optimistically reported that "it most certainly will move up." And it did. It went into the Top Ten on the R&B charts. By April 1955, it had spent five weeks on the charts. For his entire dramatic climb, Reed was going toe-to-toe with such heavyweights as the Penguins' "Earth Angel," Ray Charles' "Come Back," Johnnie Ace's "Pledging My Love," "Sincerely" by the Moonglows, and fellow Chicago harp player Little Walter with his traditional-based/Willie Dixon–penned "My Babe."

Maybe Chess was *not* right after all. Perhaps Leonard's busy office had kept him from devoting the kind of time he would need with a new artist; or perhaps his incredible radar for talent thought Reed only a blip. "Leonard Chess was record man," explains Mickey McGill of vocal group the Dells, a onetime Vee-Jay and Chess Records recording artist. "Leonard Chess told his producers that all of your jobs are on the line. He'd tell them that they needed to grab an artist and make a hit record, or else they were fired."

By this time Vee-Jay was giving Chess a good run for its money. The label had moved out of its garage-chic offices on 47th Street and eventually landed on South Cottage, just across the street from Chess. (Vee-Jay would later move to South Michigan Avenue and was again close to Chess, which had moved its operations in the late '50s.) Vivian Carter and Jimmy Bracken had built a formidable label with up-and-coming talents like Jimmy Reed, the El Dorados (who were basking in the success of their singles "I'll Be Forever Loving You" and "My Loving Baby"), the Spaniels, Jay McShann with Priscilla Bowman (with "Hands Off," a No. 1 R&B hit), the Kool Gents (with the future bona fide pop idol Dee Clark), and veteran Floyd Jones, who was keeping it real and representin' (in contemporary terms) by recording the politically charged "Ain't Times Hard," a remake of his Tempo-Tone single. The disc was popular among black audiences. Of Floyd's Vee-Jay remake, *Cash Box* magazine proclaimed: "Many here call this diskery one of the peppiest in the biz."

This music business was serious. So to beef up their bottom line and run more efficiently, Vee-Jay hired administrative and A&R execs with industry experience and business acumen, such as Ewart Abner and Al Smith, both from the recently folded Chance Records. Abner became the manager of the label (and "public relations deluxe," Calvin Carter would say), and Smith was in charge of finding Chicago musicians who could record for Vee-Jay and tour with their talent. House tenor sax player Red Holloway remembers Ewart Abner well. "He was a nice dude," Red says. "He was also eccentric. Abner was wearing earrings and shit—basically before anybody did that kind of thing. People used to think he was a faggot, 'cause he was wearing the bracelets and the earrings and, of course, now everyone is doing that. But that was back in the 1950s. If you were wearing an earring, you were a sweetie pie."

"Calvin and Abner made a good team," explains Jerry Butler, once of the Impressions. "Calvin had the ear and Abner had the business acumen. Abner knew how to structure the deal. Abner knew how to schmooze and to entertain and cajole and get folks smiling in his favor as he went around to the different radio stations where the product was being played. Most of the disc jockeys, especially those in the African-American community, loved Ewart Abner. He would come to town with a bag full of money and a lot of good times. And so they loved to see him coming. They would love to play his music whenever he sent it to them."

Al Smith was charged with putting together bands for Vee-Jay tours, coordinating bands for rehearsal and recording sessions, and all-around pre-production activities. "I'm trippin' here, but Al Smith, when I think back, was a bass player," says Chicago sax player Von Freeman, who had toured as part of Al Smith's bands. "He was the kind of cat who ran a band really well."

"I knew Al well," explains Butler. "When we were recording 'For Your Precious Love' we rehearsed in Al Smith's basement. Al was responsible for contracting most of the musicians for the recording sessions and those same musicians played just about everything."

With a new committed crew, new marketing schemes, and a growing roster of talent, Vee-Jay was basking in the glow of chart success.

Reed would further bolster their reputation when he recorded "Pretty Thing" and "I'm Gonna Ruin You," the latter being a very un-Reed-like song with stops. Ray Scott was again on drums, Dave Ship on bass. "I'm Gonna Ruin You" was a twisted overture to violence—one for which Reed unconvincingly plays a tough-guy role in the face of infidelity. Though Reed growls ever so slightly in spots, you get the sense that he is making empty threats. Even the music and his harp playing belie the message of the song. It's a plucky little number that has a sense of joy. Reed was just not good at trying to convince people he was a hard-ass. Now, if Howlin' Wolf had sung that song, it would have been a different story. In fact, one of Wolf's songs can serve as an example. Where Reed sang, "Send you to get butter, you brings back lard," Wolf's line would have been, and was, "I asked her for water, she brought me gasoline."

Reed's voice hadn't fully developed as an artist by the time of "I'm Gonna Ruin You." While "High and Lonesome" was a witty take on love, loss and betrayal, here Reed was thoroughly entrenched in the macho blues tradition of singing about cheatin' women and how exacting revenge rectified a broken heart.

Audiences responded. By May, Reed and Vee-Jay had another hit on their hands. Making a much smoother transition from the recording studio to the radio, "I'm Gonna Ruin You" was on the charts in less than two months after its recording. Of the single, with B-side "Pretty Thing," *Billboard* remarked: "Southern territories have been the first to respond to this disc, with excellent reports now coming back from Atlanta, Nashville, Durham, and St. Louis." The platter was also doing fine locally in Chicago, as well as Detroit, Cleveland, and Philly.

If any of the Vee-Jay recordings were superior in the marketplace, it had in some small part to do with where the music was recorded. Vee-Jay, like other local Chicago labels (including competitor Chess Records and Mercury Records), used Universal Recording Studio. Everyone from Nat King Cole and Ella Fitzgerald to Count Basie, Sam Cooke, Chuck Berry, Muddy Waters, and Duke Ellington came through Universal's doors.

Like Sigma Sound in Philadelphia, Muscle Shoals in Alabama, and Stax Records studios in Memphis, Universal was part of a scene in its own right. Though Chicago is rarely seen as having a "sound," Universal was a vital part of the engine that made that musical city run.

Reed, who was recording at roughly six-month intervals for Vee-Jay, was benefiting from the work of sound engineering visionary Bill Putnam and his disciples at Universal. Putnam shouldered the title of the father of modern studio recording, as he mastered such techniques as overdubbing, the use of isolation booths, the tasteful execution of reverb on recorded tracks, 8-track recording, and half-speed mastering. Though Putnam wouldn't stay in Chicago to see Jimmy Reed get big, the engineers who followed in his footsteps, Bruce Swedien and Murray Allen, were at the helm for some of Reed's best songs.

"In those days we pretty much went straight to mono, so in the control room it was me and Calvin Carter," explains Allen, the sound engineer who went on to buy Universal. "Jimmy Reed would be in the vocal booth, and the band would be out in the studio. Everything was done pretty much first takes. Even today, with the multitracks, you'd never get it on first takes the way things are. In those days, people were a little more efficient.

"Most everything Vee-Jay did, they did at Universal," Allen continues. "Vivian and Jimmy Bracken were very loyal to Universal. All of the Jimmy Reed material was done in Studio B, which was a fairly decent-size studio with a vocal booth—a gorgeous room, echo chamber. Studio B was the same studio we'd do people like Muddy Waters in. We also had some 3-track machines, but for Jimmy Reed we never used them. We just did it all straight to mono. The console was a homemade console that Bill Putnam made years and years ago. It was rotaries, which means it wasn't even sliding faders—it was rotaries. Eight-input console is all it was, with rotaries. It was all tubes."

Though Abner and Smith were making things happen on a business and personnel level, Calvin Carter was still keeping his nose in the recording end as Vee-Jay's production maven. "Calvin was easy to work with," Allen says. "He hired good musicians, and was a talented producer. We did Jerry Butler, Gene Chandler, and so many people on up and down the list. I remember one session we did with a huge band— huge string section and brass and everything else—I forget who the artist was. We got done and it was going all to mono (the early days before things were released in stereo), and we got done with a take. I asked, 'Should we play the take back?' He said, 'No reason to play the take back. I heard it. Let's just master it so we can get it out tomorrow.' We used to cut things, make the master that night, and go into the pressing plant overnight and be on the street the next day."

In July Reed, bassist Milton Rector, WC Dalton (on guitar), Henry Gray on piano, and a new addition for the Reed sound, drummer Earl Phillips, were present for a one-day session at Universal. The crew churned out "I Ain't Got You" (which went unreleased at the time but eventually showed on Jimmy's 1959 LP *Found Love*), "She Don't Want Me No More" (vaguely pointing in the direction of Chuck Berry, being led by Reed's patented high-end, first-position harp squeal), "Come On, Baby," and "I Don't Go for That." Each song created the illusion and atmosphere of a smoky Chicago nightclub. (You can almost hear the beer being poured, the chatter of the crowd growing with each passing song, and the clinking glasses.)

"I Ain't Got You" is one of the most effective Reed tunes to grace Universal's recording reels. The deceiving lead harp lick (Reed draws and blows air through his *B flat* harmonica) is the very essence of the Jimmy Reed formula and mystique. It sounds so simple, yet so juicy, so accessible, and so unforgettable.

Reed's direct language is very effective here. Jimmy says: "I got a Eldorado Cadillac/with a spare tire in the back/I got a charge account at Goldblatt's/But I ain't got you." Reed explains how lucky he is: he has a mojo, winning numbers, a closet full of clothes, a tavern, a package store, and even a harem of girlfriends at his beck and call. He has it all, just not the woman he wants and needs.

An amalgam of noise produced by the bass and drums creates such a roundly raw sound, its uncanny beauty is not lessened by the fact that it happens to be one of Reed's most rockin', raucous tunes. (Indeed. The song penetrated racial and generational lines, as it was covered by such artists as the Yardbirds with Eric Clapton—famously in *G*—and by Aerosmith. The song was also recorded by Vee-Jay labelmate and harpman Billy Boy Arnold, which, not surprisingly, is the closest of the three to Reed's. Arnold's harp attack is much more intense; his solo is rife with stutter notes and tremolo, achieved easily by playing with your hands and not holding the harp in a rack.)

"We would use an overhead mike...for the drums," explains Allen. "It was sometimes a Shure mike on the bass drum. We used to use the Western Electric 639 on the bass drum—I always remember that. On the guitar we would have a mike on his amp. On the bass we'd put a mike on the bridge—an Altec pencil mike—a condenser mike, and we'd wrap it in a lot of foam and stuff in the bridge for the bass. For the piano—I think we had a couple of C12 mikes. Everything had a good sound because it was all live and we didn't close-mike as much as they do today. We got a little bit of the room sound and the room sounded very good. That was important. The artist didn't work that close to the microphones. Jimmy was maybe about three feet away from the microphones. Nowadays they sing right into it."

The helping hand(s) of Louisiana native pianist Henry Gray—perhaps best known for his work with Howlin' Wolf around the same time—adds the right amount of incessant, repeated notes (like a stream of rain or tears) for that extra little bit of excitement. Earl Phillips' crushing beats and Dalton's and Rector's rhythm guitar/bass riff (*E*, slide up to *G*, *G sharp*, *A* to *B*, back to *E*) weave through and virtually frame the entire song. On harp, Reed slides up to *B*—from *A*—where it seems he'll make himself cozy by releasing bluesy tension, but thinks better of it and instantly cuts himself off. The song resumes with the band coming back full blast into the mix.

Everything came together perfectly for "I Ain't Got You." Calvin Carter (who is curiously credited with having co-written the song) knew just when to fade out a track, and he outdid himself here. As the tune rumbles to its "off into the sunset" conclusion, it is as if we are viewing a film of the band onstage, and the camera pulls back in increments—the music and its players become increasingly small with each passing frame, with the forlorn lover Reed repeating, hypnotically so, "but I ain't got you...." Reed's voice reverberates as the song glows to its virtual end and fades. "I believe that was Calvin's thing," says Chuck Barksdale, who was a production assistant for Calvin Carter and is still a member of the Dells. "That was his methodology of recording Jimmy Reed: using a lot of echo sounds, and I think that was happening with the general sound of records during that period. Whenever Calvin would master or mix the record, he always kept Jimmy like he was almost back in the canyon, sort of. Whatever it was, it was successful."

"I think we probably used a [Neumann] U47 on Jimmy Reed," adds Allen. "That was typically used for vocals. Jimmy would be in the vocal booth, and the band would be out in the studio. They were separated, but there was a lot of windows so they could see each other. Jimmy didn't use earphones, so we had a little speaker and he'd hear the band from the speaker and sing to that. The band did use earphones if they wanted to hear what he was doing."

With a few hits under his belt, Reed had joined the "Blues-O-Rama" show with the Cardinals, Little Walking Willie, the Buddy Johnson Rock 'n' Roll Unit, and others, touring the country and doing strong business, as *Billboard* reported. Jimmy was supporting his newly released "She Don't Want Me No More," with a rhythm that will "sell operators, particularly in the Southern areas," *Billboard* remarked, having made it a "best buy" of the week during the fall of '1955. However, it was the single's B-side (the uptempo, near–rock 'n' roll "I Don't Go for That") that clicked with listeners as the song reached *Billboard's* R&B chart, peaking at No. 12 and staying on the chart for two weeks.

Of "I Don't Go for That" *Billboard's* weekly R&B record reviewer wrote: "Reed has few peers when it comes to the funky Southern blues idiom. This is a good one and this really wails. With the solid beat provided by the band and those wild harmonica and guitar sounds in the background, jukebox operators are going to see the possibilities of this disc at once."

With stardom came notoriety, legend, and even exploitation. Reed was making his way through the South—places like Atlanta, Dallas, Birmingham, and New Orleans. Jimmy and Eddie could make friends quickly, especially with club owners. One such club owner was Jack Ruby, who shot and killed JFK assassin Lee Harvey Oswald on national TV. "Eddie Taylor told me that Jack Ruby was someone they knew well," says Mark Brumbach, a piano player who performed with both Reed and Taylor. "Ruby was someone that booked a club in Dallas that they played. You have the making of a great movie there, with that information. I'm telling you Ruby was a Jewish guy on the West Side of Chicago. Rubenstein was his real name. Eddie Taylor knew him very well."

It's easy to see why information like this, whether verifiable or not, has remained somewhat underground. Adult gentlemen's clubs or strip joints hired musicians, and many times those musicians were required to be behind curtains. The fact that these were *black* musicians playing in Texas makes it even less likely that many white people actually *saw* them, let alone knew their identities.

Ruby was born Jack Rubenstein in Chicago in 1911 and lived near Maxwell Street. It is quite possible that Taylor and Reed may, in fact, have literally rubbed elbows with Ruby. Even more significant is that Ruby managed a young musician by the name of Little Daddy Nelson for a short period of time.

Unfortunately for Reed and Taylor, doing business with Ruby may not have been a bed of roses. As the *President's Report on the Assassination of President Kennedy* (1964) spelled out for inquiring minds, Ruby could be violent toward musicians in his employ. In 1951, when guitarist Willis Dickerson told Ruby to " 'go to hell,' Ruby knocked Dickerson to the ground…pinned him to a wall and kicked him in the groin. During the scuffle, Dickerson bit Ruby's finger so badly that the top half of Ruby's left index finger was amputated. In approximately 1955, Ruby beat one of his musicians with brass knuckles; the musician's mouth required numerous stitches."

"I can see Reed and Taylor being ripped off by Jack Ruby—at the end of the night not being paid," Brumbach says.

As Reed was doing a kind of anachronistic and faux Forrest Gump act—a country boy falling in with pivotal historic figures—some others were attempting to jump through the door he had opened. One artist, J.B. Lenoir, whose music the *All Music Guide* called "Jimmy Reed on coffee," did indeed share some similar qualities with Reed. Like Reed, his blues rocked as much as it dragged and his boogie rhythms and high-pitched voice, especially on songs like "Eisenhower Blues," does conjure Reed. Though Lenoir made greater use of saxes (on his Parrot label sessions), his loose shuffle—one of many "loose" elements in his songs—was similar to Reed's, but not as pronounced. Lenoir, of course, was far from being a clone: he was recording before Reed and was distributed by such labels as Chess, JOB, Parrot, and, later, Reed's own Vee-Jay.

Despite his influence and hits, Jimmy Reed was watching his home life being dismantled. Being on the road left Jimmy and his family vulnerable. "Daddy was on the road and the twins [Rose and Roslyn] were born, and we had a bad situation with the landlord," Loretta Reed explains. "Actually, he put us out with two babies. We were kind of in the street and finally when John and Grace Brim found out about it they came and took us and brought us to their home. We lived with them [in Gary, Indiana] for a couple of months until we found another place. It wasn't a long time."

But it was long enough to be something of a humiliation to Reed. It was also something Reed never really talked about. In fact, his secrecy and vagueness in connection to the episode had caused confusion over the years for writers and researchers who caught snippets of misinformation and filled in the gaps with their own imaginations, not knowing anything of the Brims' hospitality. (Many had thought Jimmy and family were living in Gary, Indiana, for a good deal of time while Papa Reed was employed by the South Chicago steel mills.) It was just one of the many impossible and apparent contradictions of Jimmy Reed's growing stardom.

Ewart Abner was boasting about his new artist signing in the pages of *Cash Box* magazine in late 1955. "Vee-Jay Records has just signed veteran John Lee Hooker, whom Abner calls, 'one of the best country blues singers around.' First release is expected shortly."

Abner was so enthralled with Hooker, so careful not to damage the merchandise, that he and Calvin Carter drove in their Oldsmobile to Detroit, Michigan, to personally escort Hooker to Chicago. With such precious cargo, nothing was left to chance. Hooker told *Living Blues:* "When my [Specialty] contract expired, Abner called me. He said, 'Well, look, we're coming to get you. We ain't gonna depend on you comin' on your own 'cause you may not get here. We're gonna drive there and pick you up.'"

Vee-Jay was salivating over the prospect of having another genuine down-home blues hitmaker to complement Jimmy Reed. On the strength of singles like "Crawlin' King Snake," "Hobo Blues," and the multitracked vocal showcase "I'm in the Mood" (which Hooker maintained was inspired by Glenn Miller's 1930s song "In the Mood"), not to mention his 1949 smash, the electrified acoustic, no-chord vamp "Boogie Chillen" on the Modern label, John Lee Hooker was far and away the genre's bestselling artist and surpassed his contemporaries Lightnin' Hopkins and Muddy Waters.

Backed by drummer Tom Whitehead, Hooker settled into the coolness of Universal's Studio B as Jimmy Reed, Eddie Taylor, and bassist George Washington prepared to record. Committed to tape were "Time Is Marching" and the song that would eventually back it on single, a rather misguided tune named "Mambo Chillen"—a Latin twist to Hooker's late '40s hit "Boogie Chillen" (so recorded to plug into the current mambo craze). "Mambo Chillen" is a bit silly and a waste of time (though perhaps we should cut Hooker some slack here, as Calvin and others at Vee-Jay—most probably Abner—wanted a quick hit with Hooker), but "Time Is Marching" certainly ranks among the best of Reed's early recorded harp playing. There are some incredibly thrilling moments here as Reed's quivering and sinuous harp lines weave around Hooker's dark and deep voice.

Unfortunately, the best of the sessions were over. Guitar-less and free to blow without his harp rack, Reed uses both tremolo and vibrato in "Unfriendly Woman," manipulating the harp with his throat and hands. But it's to little effect. Reed sounds tired and uninspired here. His delivery, while rarely injecting a sense of urgency in the music, is quite uncharacteristically forgettable, and this fact was perhaps just one of the reasons why Vee-Jay chose not to immediately release this track after it was recorded.

"Wheel and Deal" (think "Boogie in the Dark" minus the candy-coated and infectious rhythm) instantly became a rarity—for good cause. Hooker was trying to establish his musical identity by forcing Reed's persona through his art. For some reason, for some magical and even intangible reason, the songs that are patterned after Reed's hit-making style just don't cut it. Vee-Jay knew this, and they were also cautious about flooding the market with Hooker, whose older sides were still readily available for most anyone who wanted to buy them.

Despite these less-than-stellar results, Vee-Jay continued to steer Hooker in a Jimmy Reed way, by having him record "Every Night" (a takeoff of "Every Day I Have the Blues" by the Count Basie Orchestra featuring the vocal talents of Joe Williams), which boasts a walking bassline and in-the-pocket drumming. The music plods along predictably, and lumps towards the finish line at just under three minutes. Despite the feel of the music, ironically, of Vee-Jay's dynamic duo only Taylor is present for the session. Jimmy is nowhere to be found.

Hooker would go on to record such evergreens as "Dimples" and "Boom Boom" and other crucial Vee-Jay sides with Eddie Taylor in tow. Hooker grew so attached to Eddie Taylor that nary a note was recorded without Jimmy Reed's right-hand man. As Hooker told *Living Blues* in 1979, "I'd tell [Vee-Jay], 'Well, if I can't get Eddie, I'd rather just wait until I can get him, you know.'"

Eddie, of course, still and always had time for his main gig with Jimmy Reed. Aside from being an in-demand guitarist, Taylor was loyal, perhaps even to a fault. "[Eddie Taylor] was Jimmy Reed's main man," Hooker also told *Living Blues*. "I mean on records, you know; he made 'that sound.' I guess everybody know that he made 'that [Jimmy Reed] sound.'"

The trouble was, *not* everyone knew, at least not how much of a driving yet stabilizing force Taylor had been to Reed and his music. However, in January 1955 Eddie took center stage as a guitar hero, singer, and songwriter with the recording "Bad Boy," which is essentially a "Jimmy Reed" slow-to-mid shuffle (or should it be an "Eddie Taylor" shuffle?) in *A*. (Prior to this session, Taylor had cut Sonny Boy Williamson I's "38 Pistol Blues," but it had gone unreleased.)

Reed accompanied Taylor on the session, and his signature first-position, high-end harp squeals are integral to the quality and level of interplay between the instruments. It's the kind of interaction that easily rivals anything Reed recorded under his own name with Taylor. Because Taylor hadn't had the pleasure of being backed by a guitarist of his own caliber, the track represents the unprecedented fruits of Vee-Jay's greatest blues duo. One wonders what the Reed–Taylor unit must have sounded like on the Chicago streets and in Gary, Indiana, when they were really blowing in the early days. If this was any indication, it surely must rank among some of the very best electric Chicago blues.

Response for the record was positive, so Vee-Jay kept its collective fingers crossed that they had another star in Taylor. On one hand, it made good business to separate the two. On the other, busting up the combined unit of Reed–Taylor was a dangerous prospect to the integrity of Reed's music. That was a risk Vee-Jay was willing to take, as it would with many other artists, most notably the Impressions, when Jerry Butler was forced into being the breakout star. Some of the Impressions never recovered from the debacle. In breaking off Butler from the Impressions, Vee-Jay thought it would have two hitmakers. Between Vee-Jay's wish and the music industry's acceptance of the idea, a rift separated Butler from the Impressions. It created a tense situation, one that was not conducive to open, free music, and things were never the same.

But that is what record companies do, and did. Dollars and cents rule, not artistic balance, which might, ironically, bring greater returns in the long run. So then, why not spin off Taylor as a solo artist? If Vee-Jay was whispering in Eddie's ear, one would have to question how hard Eddie's arm needed to be twisted.

And throughout, Jimmy was drinking more and more, before and after the gigs. Being on the road was hard for Jimmy. "Prior to [Daddy] getting into the music business, I don't remember my father ever being drunk," says Loretta. "I don't remember him really drinking and that was something that was important to me. I always felt the music was something that took him away from me, because of the fact that everything about him changed. The other part was that Daddy didn't like being away from Mama. He really didn't. That was very hard for him."

"When Daddy came home, it was time to party," Jimmy Reed, Jr. adds.

Drummer and harp player Frank "Little Sonny" Scott played with Reed and Eddie Taylor in Gary in places like Pulaski Bar, and roadhouses and juke joints outside Gary, and Johnny's Place on Roosevelt in Chicago (when he was also gigging with Freddie King). Scott remembers Eddie and Jimmy very well and the high stress level of some of those gigs.

"We worked together real good," Scott says. "We were not only good at playing together but we were all friends. I sold Eddie Taylor his first car—an Oldsmobile. We had a regular thing for a while. It was on the weekends. I'd drive—I had a Buick Special then—I would drive Eddie and Jimmy over to the show at Pulaski on Virginia and 19th.

"The thing about Eddie was that he could get angry real quick," Scott continues. "He didn't like nobody to mess with his guitar too much. He be shinin' it all and wiping it off and Jimmy Reed would get into it, you know? I was the one who had to keep it together. Eddie would get angry with Jimmy Reed and then grab his guitar in the middle of the set. He didn't care if it was the middle of the set—he'd grab his guitar and quit it. We couldn't do too much without him and I had to talk with him [to get him to stay]. See, Jimmy was drinking and that would aggravate Eddie. Jimmy would eat up all his money on drink and I'd have to lend him some of mine. It was all right playing with those guys, but they did a lot of arguing and fussing."

After being on the road with Jimmy, and having recorded some more with Hooker, Eddie had scheduled studio time on December 5 with Jimmy on harp and second guitar, and Vernell Fournier on drums for "Ride 'Em on Down" and "Big Town Playboy." (These songs were released as a single, which sold a reported 37,000 copies.) Taylor also recorded "Do You Want Me to Cry?" and "I'm Sitting Here" with Howlin' Wolf guitarist Hubert Sumlin and piano man Johnny Jones. (Taylor would reprise his role as leader in July 1956, with George Meyweather, Jimmie Lee Robinson on guitar, and Earl Phillips on drums for the tracks "You'll Always Have a Home" and "Don't Knock at My Door.")

On the same day, with some of the same personnel (Taylor and Fournier), Reed himself cut "Ain't That Lovin' You Baby," "Baby, Don't Say That No More," and "Can't Stand to See You Go," the greatest of which is the first.

"Aint That Lovin' You Baby" is one of the most rockin' and feel-good songs of Reed's career, yet he manages to interject such concepts as resurrection, decomposition of human remains, inhuman endurance, murder, and the nightmarish scenario of being stranded in the middle of an ocean. How was this possible in a two-plus-minute number, and why have so many people glossed over the lyrics?

The origin of the song is a strange one. When Reed and a young travel companion named Cody (who popped up in many conversations about Reed) were on tour, making appearances on a multi-act bill with the likes of LaVern Baker, the Spaniels, and others, Reed had some car trouble outside of New Orleans. It was four o'clock in the morning: *what garage would be open now?* Luckily for Reed and Cody, a mechanic was indeed open at the crack of dawn.

Reed explains on the 1965 LP *The Legend—The Man:* "The boy I had with me, he was helping me drive. Fact of business is, I had to go 13 miles to get hold to a telephone to call back to the cumpneeeeey in Chicaaago to get them to wire me some money so I could pay for the car being fixed. They had one mechanic there and I was the first one there, 'cause I got to the place, I should say, about four o'clock that morning. So, he just went on start workin' on my car…. [He] fixed that car and only charged me thirty-two dollars…. I got a cab and went 13 miles to get this money."

Before Reed ever got the money and the car was fixed, he and his travel companion were holed up for a few hours in the early morning, sitting and talking. The young man was concerned that they would be stranded. "[He] said, 'Gee. It doesn't look like they're gonna send us that money.' He said, 'You know the way I feel…I'd do anything to get hold of my baby. I'd just do anything to get where my baby at.' I said, 'Man, you shouldn't say it like that. Anyway, shucks. Man, I don't know.' He said, 'I guess I'd rob—I'm just [liable] to kill somebody or steal me somethin' to get to my baby,' and [he] kept on like that word for word. I told the guy, I said, 'Man, look, this don't sound like it's true.' [He said,] 'They could drop me out in the ocean and I'd swim to the bay, and I'd crawl back to my baby.'"

And "Ain't That Lovin' You Baby" was born. Reed puts to music nearly the exact words he had heard his young friend use: "Let me tell you baby/Tell you what I would do/I would rob, steal, kill somebody, just to get back home to you…. They could drop me in the ocean, I'd swim to the bank, and crawl home to you/Ain't that lovin' ya baby."

It is a very Western, even Judeo-Christian, ideal: redemption and winning against impossible odds. It's "Hollywood endings" at their best: being the receiver of good fortune and witnessing something miraculous; about things being put in their rightful place, either by a higher power, human will, or plain damn luck. This is perhaps what sets Reed apart from many other blues, rock 'n' roll, and rock artists. His "serious" takes on love were concrete and stone believable. (Reed genuinely believed in the strength and power of the human spirit.) His words were not hollow, even when talking about the most fleeting feeling. But Reed is perhaps, and always was, his most sincere when speaking of love. If the Police's misunderstood meditation on relationships, "Every Breath You Take," was speaking to the creepy side of possessive love, then "Ain't That Lovin' You Baby" is a cross between spirituality, obsession, and unflinching devotion.

Punctuating Reed's points are quick "breakdowns" that interrupt the constant flow of the music and represent the relentless manner by which the singer is making his way back to his love. Throughout, drummer Vernell Fournier halts the rustling of his snare and hi-hat (he opens his hi-hat cymbals on the third beat of nearly every eighth-note pattern—a faux vaudevillian pattern) and comes to an abrupt stop on the word "back" of the line "get back home to you." Fournier is, and the band with him, quiet for a whole measure (you can faintly hear Fournier counting time with his sticks), as if straining their instruments to hear Reed's tale, as Jimmy's solo voice reverberates. Fournier then picks up on the *four* of the next measure (just before the next *one*) and thumps along as Reed sings, "Ain't that lovin' you baby."

This stop tactic is especially effective on the last verse. Though the band drops out of the mix nearly entirely, this silence funnels into the music's overall heaviness. When Reed sings, "They may kill me, baby/bury just like they do/my body a rot, but my spirit's gonna rise an' come back home to you...," Fournier stops on the word "spirit's" (on the *one*) and continues with a galloping fill on the *two* of the next measure. Funny enough, it also sounds as if the bass drum is playing four beats to a measure for a good deal of the song. Hearing the kick, at all, in a Reed song is a rarity, and the listener can on occasion hear Fournier hitting the beater up against his kick-drum head while the band is in total silence (as a timing mechanism for himself, no doubt).

"Ain't That Lovin' You Baby" exemplifies how different Reed's music is when compared to fellow Chicago bluesman Howlin' Wolf, whose seminal, trademark song "Smokestack Lightnin' " (recorded in January 1956, a month after "Ain't That Lovin' You Baby") was fitted around a variation of a one-chord Delta vamp. By contrast, Reed employs a recurring, not repetitive, theme—a hook—to drive home the point of the song. Reed's music is so steeped in the verse-verse-refrain framework, the basis of 12-bar blues, that he might be more closely identified with "pop" artists.

Jimmy wasn't doing rock 'n' roll, and his music wasn't completely countrified blues, either (though it bore a resemblance to driving rhythms heard in Robert Johnson tunes such as "(I Believe) I'll Dust My Broom," "Sweet Home Chicago," and "When You Got a Good Friend"). Like "The Father of Country Music" Jimmie Rodgers before him, and Jimi Hendrix, who'd arrive at the dawning of the psychedelic '60s, Reed in his music conveyed a sensibility that appealed to whites and blacks that truly knew no boundaries.

The song also represents the existentialism apparent in Reed's approach to life. For Reed, all his actions—even his mistakes—were valid and equal in the human experience. They should be weighed as such, and even celebrated. This philosophy certainly helped Reed get through his life, especially later on when he knew he was at fault.

For the time being, however, Reed had no regrets and was taking joy in his life. He was a kind of Dionysian pied piper, a minstrel singer on his way to the top, finding comedy and song in everything. "Ain't That Lovin' You Baby" was set to peak at No. 3 on the *Billboard* R&B charts and "Can't Stand to See You Go" (Reed's vocal range and jocular nature here struck a chord with listeners) would make the Top Ten.

"There's a mistake in the intro [in "Can't Stand to See You Go"], one of the rare cases where he uses a guitar intro," producer and Jimmy Reed fan Jim Dickinson told *Blues Access*. "Usually he used harmonica. There's this guitar figure for the intro and whoever's playing guitar screws it up and you hear Jimmy Reed laugh. I loved it because of that. You hear this riff, riff, then 'hahahahaha,' and the next start, and finally he starts to sing."

Jimmy Reed was hot and living high on the blues world. He would grow even hotter in short order, but he'd stumble over indestructible obstacles along the way.

Chapter 3
You've Got Me Dizzy

Jimmy often had "spells" that his wife and friends thought were caused by his dangerous and excessive alcohol consumption. But Jimmy didn't bother to see a doctor: *They wouldn't do me no good anyway.*

Jimmy would drink for a couple days at a time, then stop for a day or two (as he saw fit), and often experienced what he thought was some form of the d.t.'s. The d.t.'s, or delirium tremens, consist of severe hallucinations, seizures, confusion, vomiting, and other symptoms that occur when an alcoholic is deprived of alcohol. Maybe he was kidding himself, maybe he had lost track, maybe he was being optimistic in the face of these incredibly frightening episodes, but Jimmy began hitting the bottle even harder. Strangely, he thought the episodes would subside through drink.

James "Red" Holloway was a saxophonist and member of the Vee-Jay house band in those days, and A&R exec Al Smith rang him up to tour with Jimmy Reed on occasion. Red remembers at least one time when Jimmy's drunken state nearly put the kibosh on the gig. "I remember we were playing down in Texas and this place was in Fort Worth for this policemen's ball," Holloway says. "Jimmy Reed got drunk, O.K.? So, like he acted like he is not going to go on stage, you know? So, the police said, 'If you don't go on stage, we're gonna have to throw you in jail.' And when they said 'jail,' boy, he straightened out real quick."

"I remember I used to run with Jimmy Reed when he recorded," recalls harp player Bobby Rush. "Calvin Carter was a personal friend of mine who was about six years older than I was. Maybe seven. When Jimmy Reed got ready to record he might take me into the studio with him. I didn't know then what I know now. I was Jimmy Reed's *cover*. 'Cause when Jimmy Reed was too drunk to blow his harp and do his thing, he had me because I could blow a harp—just like Jimmy Reed. Jimmy was sometimes too drunk to know he was in the world, and that's the truth. Calvin would say, 'Hey, Bobby, can you blow this note like Jimmy?' And we'd get the session done."

Whether from the alcohol, or general carelessness, or simply his lack of education, Jimmy placed little regard in committing his words to memory. Song lyrics he'd "write" would vanish from his mind as quickly as they flashed. Luckily for Reed, he had Mary Lee "Mama" Reed.

Whenever he had an idea, he ran it by Mama. Not only would she give the song a thumbs up or thumbs down, she was capable of writing down the lyrics for Jimmy. Rather than forget his words and waste time and money in the studio, Reed had Mama in tow nearly each time he entered Universal. She'd sit next to Jimmy in the vocal booth and feed him words he forgot. This was not a very scientific process, but an effective one. Mary is heard on some of Jimmy's records, sometimes as a second voice.

"You can hear it on the records—Mama telling Jimmy the words," guitarist Lonnie Brooks says. "You can hear her. On the records you could hear her telling the words. I saw it. They was cutting records in the studio and I walked up and I thought they was rehearsing, but they was playing."

"One of the most outstanding things about those Jimmy Reed sessions were that Jimmy Reed's wife would be in the booth with him whispering the words in his ear," Phil Upchurch, Vee-Jay house guitarist confirms. "Sometimes you could even hear her on the record. While he was singing one set of lyrics she was whispering the next in his ear. That is a pretty amazing thing to watch, but that is the way they did it…. He probably couldn't read and that was probably the reason for her doing that. He needed to know the songs but he hadn't committed them to memory yet."

"Sometimes Daddy would forget the lyrics and Mama would be sitting there beside him to whisper the lyrics in his ear while he was singing," explains Jimmy Reed, Jr.

"Other words, behind every great man there's a great woman," says his sister Rose Reed.

"Nobody wanted Daddy to come into the studio without Mama," adds Loretta Reed, "because when she went [into the studio] the takes were easy and everything was fine. I remember being in the studio with them one time and I said, 'You're doing this [song] over and over.' The recording engineer said, 'Let me tell you something: your father does the least takes of anybody who comes to this studio. It doesn't take long for him to get his stuff together.' They wanted Mama there, believe me."

"I remember one funny story," notes Universal recording engineer Murray Allen. "His wife would always be in the vocal booth with him. She was a help in those situations. I remember once she didn't show up. Reed was in the vocal booth by himself and he said, 'I can't sing, because she knows all of the words!' Calvin said, 'Hold on a second. When you work in the nightclubs, the bars, you are on the stand by yourself and she is not there and you know all the words.' He says, 'Hey, come to think of it, you are right. Calvin, you are smart. That's why you're the producer and I'm *just* the singer.'"

On June 11, 1956, Reed, Eddie Taylor, Earl Phillips, Lefty Bates (most likely) on second guitar, and Mama Reed (for moral support) stepped into the Universal studio to cut three songs: "When You Left Me," "My First Plea," and "I Love You, Baby." Having both Eddie Taylor and Earl Phillips on these tracks, the Jimmy Reed triumvirate was solidified. The Reed/Taylor/Phillips core band, which was nearly set to take flight, was a unique occurrence in the history of blues and rock 'n' roll. Somehow, their musicianship occupied the same headspace and heartspace. One person's musical personality supported the other and they at times melded. Like three of a perfect pair (to steal a phrase), to rip one of the elements away and force it to live on its own would only result in the total collapse of the Reed musical universe.

A Harlem-born drummer, Earl Phillips came to Chicago some 13 years earlier from Nashville, Tennessee. Phillips had a whip-like percussive touch integral to the Reed sound. Phillips even slipped into jazz but seemed more at home in the blues idiom (at least it was the genre that gave him the most work through the 1950s). Phillips' sensitive touch balanced incredible power. His work with Howlin' Wolf (on classic sides like "Smokestack Lightnin' " and "Forty Four"), Billy Boy Arnold, John Lee Hooker, and Dee Clark among others, showcases his in-the-pocket playing and lethal sense of timing. When Phillips busted out the grooves, it was as if he was releasing a whip, letting it unfurl until it came back—and "snap."

"When You Left Me" tells the tale of a woman who thought she was too good for Jimmy. He buys her a Ford; she wants a Rocket 88. She wants out of the relationship, fast—and gets out. She leaves Jimmy in the cold, enters the world at large, and learns a hard lesson about love and life. When she comes back to attempt to rekindle the relationship with Jimmy, he ain't havin' it. He sings: "And the last time I saw you, you was heading back down the road."

Reed references "Rocket 88," the Jackie Brenston song (which was based on an earlier song called "Cadillac Boogie"), which is a double entendre, referring literally to a circa 1950 Cadillac and an Oldsmobile Rocket V-8 engine (and so dubbed a "Rocket 88"). But unlike that early rock 'n' roll gem, here the *speaker* is the victim.

On "My First Plea" (released as a single and then included on Reed's first full-length record, *I'm Jimmy Reed*) Reed's voice bears a striking resemblance to Sonny Boy I's, and his harp phrasing is expelled in bunches. Instead of long-winded squeals, here he squeezes out quivering lines that play with the timing of the Eddie Taylor groove. Reed speaks these memorable yet cryptic lines: "Don't pull no subway/I'd rather see you pull a train/You know I love you dear baby/Girl you know it's a cryin' shame."

The song was released as a single with B-side "I Love You, Baby" featuring a squealing and grainy vocal performance plus strong and simple tones blown on harp. To see the lyrics written out one wouldn't think much of the song. "You got me runnin' in circles, baby/You got me jumpin' through loops, pretty child/I want to tell you what I do believe, baby/I believe that I'm losin' cool." Not the stuff of legend, for sure, but the perfect marriage of music and words that ignites excitement. Reed had the ability to talk about the most mundane things and play music that seemed created in a haze, yet his songs connected with people.

Reed was a folk artist. People loved to hear him, especially in the deep pockets of urban black life such as in South Chicago and Gary,

Indiana. The *Chicago Defender* took notice of Reed, Vee-Jay, and the many haunts around Gary, some of which Reed had played. It seemed in the first several years of the 1950s Gary had become quite a hotspot for nightlife. "Things are always jumping when it is time to relax and have fun, and most of the Steel City cats and kittens know how to kick up their heels and blow their wigs," the *Defender* wrote in June 1956.

Reed often played Gary's Pulaski Bar on Virginia Street and 19th Avenue, just a couple blocks south of the most hoppin' place in town: the red-light district known to locals then as "The Border" (aka Central District, more or less the heart of town). Bill Hill, Gary jazzman and historian, remembers seeing and jamming a bit with Jimmy Reed at Pulaski Bar. "He used to play over there at Pulaski," Hill says. "We were at Dobbie's Bar that was counter-corner from Virginia, right? We played jazz and we were hip. But Jimmy was drawing these crowds when he would be playing on weekends, you know? A lot of our crowds would be watching out the window seeing people going to see Jimmy. They'd ease out of our bar and see Jimmy instead. We look around and they are all over at Pulaski. I went over there one time, man, and it was like, 'What is the attraction?' I couldn't understand how he was attracting all of these people—and women. Because, I mean, we were playing *real* music. We thought we were so hip. And this man…*twang, twang, twang….*"

Chuck Berry might have been the first great rock 'n' roll poet, speaking of chicks and stick shifts, but Jimmy Reed made a more universal and perhaps more adult brand of popular music. His musings—no matter how convoluted—are on love, adultery, and troubles in a mature man's everyday life. Some of the biggest names in blues couldn't touch Jimmy Reed. True, pianist Ivory Joe Hunter's mixture of blues, soul, and doo wop might have reached both the pop and R&B charts (most notably the 1956 smash "Since I Met You Baby"). But his soft, heavenly, more densely layered music came from a vastly different place than Jimmy Reed's down-home, gutbucket approach. True, both made forms of dance music, but, for better or worse, there was immediacy in Reed's music that just did not exist in Hunter's strolling rhythms.

Reed's music isn't gimmicky, either. Not like Screamin' Jay Hawkins, who laid down some nasty voodoo shit such as "I Put a Spell on You" and the completely hysterical and stomach-turning "Constipation Blues." Hawkins, in effect, was a bit of a frustrated opera singer who turned his flair for the dramatic and theatrical into pure schlock gold. (Hawkins got a boost when Creedence Clearwater Revival covered his one and only famous track, "I Put a Spell on You.")

Jimmy Reed seemed to be a universe unto himself. On recorded tracks like "Honey, Don't You Let Me Go," the music and words are so idiosyncratic, he proved yet again that he was not very much like any other artist—blues or otherwise. It could have been his songwriting, maybe his singing, his harp playing, Eddie Taylor's and Earl Phillips' contributions, or the equipment he used (Marine Band harps on an Elton harmonica rack and Kay guitars). Maybe it was all of this.

"Honey, Don't You Let Me Go" is like Reed's greatest hits rolled up into one. He gives a rundown of some of his most popular songs, strung together as one very twisted thought. He sings: "You look like you're high and lonesome/I believe you wanna roll & rhumba/afore you do somethin' smart/let's go boogiein' in the dark…. Said I don't mean maybe/Ain't that lovin' you baby/Honey, 'fore you get a little speed/let's go rockin' with Reed." Reed always comes back with a chorus (of sorts): "You got me, you know/Honey don't let me go."

"Honey" was recorded in the follow-up session to his June recordings, which also included "You Got Me Dizzy" and an untitled instrumental (that went unreleased at the time). For "You Got Me Dizzy' (in *E*)—a conscious follow-up to "Ain't That Lovin' You Baby"—Reed is in second position, playing an *A* harp. When Jimmy returns from his harp solo, he enters what can only be categorized as *one* of the most hotly disputed song lyrics of all time (the entirety of the Kingsmen's "Louie Louie" must be at the top of that garbled list). Many had thought Reed was singing, "Wait a minute, baby/Don't you *give a fuck*?" In actuality, Reed says, "Don't you *vip or vop*," as in "Don't say 'vip' till I say 'vop.' In other words, "watch your step." (The phrase is not uncommon in the annals of swing and R&B; check out the Isley Brothers, Duke Ellington, Jimmie Gordon and his Vip Vop Band, and Martha Davis' "Vipity Vop.")

During the 1950s, Reed was one of many stars included in Vee-Jay's package tours.

As 1956 was drawing to a close and 1957 was on the horizon, big changes were set to unfold. As Jimmy needed more and more looking after when he was on the road, Vee-Jay co-founder Jimmy Bracken invited Al Smith to be more hands-on, and asked him to follow Reed on tour. Smith became Reed's personal manager—commencing one of the blues world's most co-dependent and least understood professional relationships.

Al Smith was born (according to one official document) in Kentucky on December 6, 1907, and had grown up with music, dancing in the streets of Rosedale to a Delta jug band. The Smiths, if this research is to be accepted, had moved to Greenville, Mississippi, only to be forced out by the great flood in 1927. The Smiths found themselves in Pace, Mississippi, where his mother, Ollie Smith, opened a roadhouse. It was there that Al had a front-row seat to blues talent, which inspired him to play bass.

As he got older and more adventurous, Smith moved to Mobile, Alabama, and enrolled in The Merchant Marine. Upon his discharge, he headed north to Milwaukee, Wisconsin, where he became a cook. By 1943 Smith had found employment in a Chicago munitions factory, and by 1945 he'd put together a jazz ensemble. When that fizzled, Al moved on to leading an R&B group. Eventually, Smith was to be the house band coordinator for such labels as Parrot, States, and Chance Records. When the Chance label sank, Smith was offered a job in the A&R department of Vee-Jay Records. He took it.

Vee-Jay house musician Red Holloway remembers Al Smith more for his organization skills—his slick ways—than for his bass playing. "Al was a talker," Holloway says. "He could talk the paint off the walls, man. I remember when we were in Texas and we were speeding and the police…I mean in those days, the highway patrolmen had to be six foot three or something. They were *biiiiig.* So when they stopped us, they said, 'Boy, don't you know you were speedin'?' Al said, 'Well, where I come from, Illinois, we don't have straight highways and they are so straight down here.' Anyway, he talked the police out of a ticket. He was a great organizer, a better organizer than a musician. He'd slap that bass around and not know what he was doing. He was just playing anything. Someone would have to tune his bass. But we couldn't tell anyone. He'd never really play it or play it correctly, but he didn't want people to know he couldn't tune the bass. I used to have to tune his bass. He'd say, 'Tune it up.' I'd tune it for him, but I'd be thinking, 'What do you want it tuned for anyway?' He seemed to know what I was thinking and said, 'Just in case someone wants to play.'

"And we had a good band," Red goes on. "We had Quinn Wilson on bass, Lefty Bates on guitar, a baritone sax player named McKinley Easton, guy named Harlan "Booby" Floyd on trombone; we had either Paul Gusman on drums or Al Duncan. We used Al a lot in the studio, too. Al Duncan could play those New Orleans beats and shit. He was on a lot—*a lot*—of sessions. We recorded for United, Chess, Vee-Jay, all of these companies. And Jimmy had his regular guitar player—Eddie Taylor was there. It was a regular band. See, I was part of the house band for Chance Records. When Jimmy Reed and Vee-Jay Records started going pretty good, Al was talking with the owner, Jimmy Bracken, and so he started doing work for Jimmy Bracken. Al left Chance… and I started recording for Chance. Al was asked by Jimmy Bracken to put a band together to go on the road with Jimmy Reed. So, Al asked me to go on the road with him. Al was a good coordinator, but he was a bass holder. He didn't even know how to tune his bass. In those days the bass was so hidden that he could just hit the bass anywhere and it wouldn't matter that much. They didn't have no amplifiers. So, then we started going on the road and down in Mississippi and various places with Jimmy Reed."

"Here's a story for you," says Earl Lavon "Von" Freeman, saxophonist who also toured with Jimmy Reed. "Al Smith decided to get the station wagon washed. We were out in the country and we had all of that sand and stuff [stuck to the car]. We were in Georgia somewhere. Real down-home. We went into this great big beautiful car wash. June Bug—that was the driver—drove around to enter the car wash. Now, June Bug wasn't the brightest bulb, but he was loyal and a very good driver who never seemed to need any sleep. So, he was perfect for the road. So, June Bug drove into this garage, at least we thought he was. The garage had a door that was up, so June Bug had forgotten that the bass was tied up to the top. So, when he was driving in there, he got stuck, and the bass—and if you know anything about the bass, it is a very delicate instrument, you can hit it too hard and it might explode or something. It is that fine wood. Man, when we heard this loud noise—it was the bass—we all got sick. We were running around saying, 'June Bug, what have you done now?' That bass collapsed and it was cracked. The strings were down and the bridge was down and it was cracked. We were going to this big gig and then we had to tell Al. Wouldn't you know it, we told Al, and Al Smith was a very relaxed man, he just simply said, 'Really?' He said, 'What happened?' 'The car's clean but the bass…' So, as we were going to the gig we said, 'How are you going to play?' He said, 'Not to worry.' Man, he went on to that gig and sounded good. How that man played that bass, I just don't know. He somehow took the bow of the bass and used that as the body so it was straight up and down—and he attached the strings to it. He just played it that way. It was just amazing. People were coming up looking…but he was getting a sound out of it, man.

"Personally, I think Al played bass different from anybody I had ever met," Freeman continues. "When he played the bass, you might say, 'Did he have any schooling on this thing?' But, boy, he would always get the money. We had to play without him and you did miss him. Why? He played in a very unorthodox way. He had a sound, see? Most bass players I had been with had happy hands and all primping for the ladies or whatnot. Man, he just leaned over that thing and got a sound out of it. We played some great big barns and he would be all over that place with sound—and there was no amplification, either. He was short and wide and he looked just like that bass. He'd be pulling on it and sweating over it. He gave people their money's worth."

Al may have been good at keeping and picking a band, as well as pulling bass tricks out his ass, but looking after Reed was no easy task. One urban legend tells of Al Smith, who needed to run errands before a show, leaving Jimmy in a locked hotel room and barricaded from the outside (read: from the liquor store). When Al returned Jimmy was stone drunk. Somehow he had managed to grab a young man's attention on the street, throw down a twenty-dollar bill to him, and via the hotel room sheets receive a bottle of whiskey through the window. Al was dumbfounded.

Jimmy liked to play cat-and-mouse with Al Smith. He resented being looked after. He didn't need it. He didn't want it. And being Jimmy's caretaker was harder than Mr. Slick Smith had imagined. Sometimes, it seemed, Reed would vanish into thin air. According to musician Mike Henderson, Jimmy once said: "A promoter who wanted me on this show said to me, 'You can play the show but you can't drink.' You know, I would get to drinking and then I wouldn't show up. That whiskey start tasting good and they'd be looking for me and they couldn't find me."

Von Freeman remembers one incident on a north–south tour through Connecticut, upstate New York, Maine, and most of the Deep South. "Al had a station wagon and, man, we were all piled in," Freeman says. "Jimmy was driving in one of those Park Avenue Mercuries. I didn't even know that Mercury made a thing like that. It was like a Lincoln Town car. A great big Mercury—he loved them. One time we played a dance in Texas—a very successful dance. It was big, what with a crowd waiting at the door to get in to see him perform. Before the show, Jimmy is going out the door and we got word that Jimmy was bouncing off a few cars out there in the parking lot —this big ole parking lot where people were parked just indiscriminately. They just parked everywhere and Jimmy was banging on a few cars and we got word. When we went out there he had banged a few, maybe as many as ten, cars here and there just trying to get out of that lot. We were thinking: 'Man, they are going to kill us out here.' Instead they were saying, 'Man, I am not going to have anything done to this car, 'cause Jimmy hit it.' I crashed, man. I just fell out and the whole band just fell out laughing. And Jimmy was laughing, and said, 'Man, I have to get out of here.'"

There's no doubt that Jimmy was a handful, but Al Smith was a multidimensional manager whose motivations for helping Reed were murky at best. He seemed to be part angel, part devil. "Al Smith had a little business savvy," Jimmy Reed, Jr., says. "He knew how to take Daddy on the road, how to get him recorded, how to handle some of his negotiations, and so forth. He also knew how to take care of his own business at the same time."

"If something happened, Al Smith was Johnny-on-the-spot," Loretta Reed admits. "He was right there. He came, you know? If you said, 'Call Al,' he would come. But Al was like everybody else to an extent in the music business. The bottom line is the dollar, and if he can see a place where he can make money at the expense of Jimmy Reed, he would do it. Al was a good guy who was a music man."

When Reed wasn't on the road, he was in the studio. In early 1957, he recorded "It's You, Baby," "Honey, Where You Going," "Do the Thing" (a song that would be tailor-made for the Louisiana market—more about that in a moment), and "Little Rain."

The clicking and popping noises heard on "Little Rain" are not wood-blocks played by Earl Phillips. In actuality, the sounds are Reed's heels. He's stamping his feet to mirror the droplets of rain slapping and tickling the pavement. (In one instance, it feels as though Reed is pulling himself out of time as he speeds up to double time. Phillips, great timekeeper that he was, never falters. He presses on, literally without skipping a beat.) The song is based on a big, slow, loping beat that seems simple upon first listen but, like many Reed songs, has hidden complexities. Taylor mutes his strings at the end of each *F-G-A-C* key cycle. On the turnarounds, Taylor never plays the same riff twice, even when the notes are virtually the same. Reed scratches his high *E* string, and notes lightly fall over the track (as heard in the right channel), in keeping with the concept of "little rain." The boys at Universal outdid themselves on this one, generating an incredible presence from well-placed room mikes. The atmosphere of the song is perfect—as if the band were playing in a dark, empty alleyway, or a cavernous, deserted baseball stadium, with a gentle sprinkling tickling their instruments and feet.

"Little Rain" reached No. 7 on the R&B charts, while "Honey, Where You Going?" (the song's flip side) proved to be a hit for Reed in March and April of 1957. "Honey" is another uptempo blues with odd stop breaks (Taylor inherently seems to know exactly where the cutoff is), chilling harp shrills, and lead vocals (which are "pitchy" in spots), spurred on by studio reverb. The mood of the track is so chilled, it sounds as if Reed is blowing harp in the middle of an icehouse—with vibrato to boot. (Unlike tremolo, which is produced by cupping and uncapping your hands around the harp, vibrato is produced by Reed's diaphragm and throat—common for harp players who use a rack.)

The hits spilled over, and the Jimmy Reed 3—Reed, Taylor, and Phillips—were joined by classically trained multi-instrumentalist Remo Biondi, perhaps best known for his work with swing drumming great Gene Krupa. In an April session, Remo and the Reed 3 were very productive: they garnered instant classics "Honest I Do," "Signals of Love," "The Sun Is Shining," "State Street Boogie," "Baby, What's on Your Mind?," and "Odds and Ends." (For the last, Biondi sat in on violin.)

The thunderous pounding of three eighth-notes (on what *sounds* like a muffled snare drum) kicks off "Honest I Do," one of the most identifiable and catchy Reed songs ever recorded. Reed squeezes out—literally—a killer harp riff in the song's intro. He states the melody with a distinctive high-pitched wheeze, utterly knocking out the listener. By blowing through holes seven through ten of his diatonic Marine Band harp (tuned to *A*) and bending the notes by raising the middle of his tongue up close to the roof of his mouth, Jimmy Reed creates pure pop gold.[i]

"Honest I Do" was a Top 40 hit for Reed in 1957.

Remo Biondi's glassy, punchy echoing lick along the *A* scale interacts with Reed's harp lines and vocals in a call-and-response motif, as Jimmy chops chords on acoustic guitar (which sound like light upstrokes), Earl Phillips unfurls his whip to slap his snare head (while maintaining straight eightHs on the hats), and Eddie Taylor builds the shuffle/foundation, brick by brick, note by note. To get an idea of just how well-oiled this band is, isolate one of these elements as you listen, and you'll find a band so in sync, so in total harmony, so intent on hearing each other in the studio that it's hard to imagine the blues being any sweeter.

Through the reverb, Reed's sincere words penetrate, but they are, as in years past, deceiving. Why does he feel so bad at the end of the song? Is it love's pain? Is he guilty of some act against his woman and now tormented by her unwavering loyalty and devotion to him? We must stop short of saying that the lyrics aren't coherent from start to finish and realize that each verse is, in a sense, a separate thought—and that "Honest I Do" is a collection of thoughts that are thinly connected by Reed's love for his wife. As the song kicks in, Reed sings, "Don't you know that I love you? Honest I do," only to be followed up by "Please tell me you love me/stop drivin' me mad," then closing with "When I woke up this morning/I'd never felt so bad." What Reed did, and did so well, was take a seemingly simple song (simple at first blush) and give it a perspective through his sincerity. Reed is passionate about *something,* and to understand the words in their entirety perhaps it requires the listener to get into the right headspace. The lyrics are less gospel than hieroglyphics to be deciphered and interpreted.

Reed dedicated the song to Mama Reed. As he says on *The Legend—The Man,* "I'll get up in the morning and I don't know whether the Boss Lady has done…fixed me some breakfast early or not," Reed explained in his charming Southern drawl, "and I happen to get up and walk on in through into the dining room and happen to look around and there Mary Lee had set up all my food and sittin' up here all ready, hot coffee and everything. And I thought, 'Baby, you know I love you so much.' She say, 'Do you really mean that?' I say, 'Honest I do.' "

The aptly titled "Odds and Ends" was an anomaly for Reed. Biondi fingerpicks and saws his fiddle and Reed occupies the lower registers. (Eddie, of course, maintains the Reed groove.) It is the spookiest Reed song ever committed to tape, and Jimmy had remarked that the addition of Remo on violin gave his music more "fullness." As the wicked sonic twirling slows to a creepy, abrupt end, you are left thinking, "What did I just listen to?" There isn't much meat here, but the song's power to conjure macabre and angelic images simultaneously sticks with you.

Mama Reed, who was present at this session, remembered vividly for *Living Blues* how the song came together. "Whenever Jimmy's sessions were on," she said, "there was always a lot of people who wanted to sit in on it, and just watch and listen, you know. And one night, this white fellow, Remo Biondi, was there and he had his violin out. We had a boss session and got through with it, and was listenin' to the playback. And then Eddie and Jimmy stood up there and started on these guitars. They just started jamming, and then Calvin [Carter] told Remo to try the violin out. And it sounded good—very good."

Mama had boasted during and after the sessions that "Odds and Ends" was probably the first time anyone had mixed violin with the blues. It wasn't, of course. Charlie Patton's and Muddy Waters' work with Henry "Son" Simms comes to mind as well as the music of Henry Williams and Eddie Anthony in Atlanta in the 1920s. Nonetheless, you'd be hard-pressed to find a more intoxicating example.

Reed's harp playing on the tracks "The Sun Is Shining," "Signals of Love," and "Baby, What's on Your Mind?" slays: it's as if Gabriel himself took Reed's Marine Band and blew a few bars.

It's a pity, though. This session, and we would have to suppose every recording session Reed had with Vee-Jay, was tainted by the business deal he made.

According to documents obtained, Reed entered into a single-song publishing agreement with Conrad Publishing Company in April 1957

STANDARD SONGWRITERS CONTRACT

Agreement made this   22nd   of   April   , 19 57 , between

CONRAD PUBLISHING CO., Inc.   Illinois, An Illinois Corporation.

(hereinafter called the "Publisher") and
JIMMY REED
EWART G. ABNER, JR.

Jointly and/or severally (hereinafter called "Writer(s)"):

Witnesseth:

In consideration of the agreement herein contained and of the sum of One ($1.00) Dollar and other good and valuable consideration in hand paid by the Publisher to the Writer(s), receipt of which is hereby acknowledged, the parties agree as follows:

1. The Writer(s) hereby sells, assigns, transfers and delivers to the Publisher, its successors and assigns, a certain heretofore unpublished original musical composition, written and/or composed by the above named writer(s), now entitled:

BABY, WHAT'S ON YOUR MIND?

including the title, words and music thereof, and the copyright registration thereof No. EU 475093/4-24-57 , and the right to secure copyright therein throughout the entire world, and to have and to hold the said copyright and all rights of whatsoever nature thereunder existing, including any and all renewals of copyright to which the writer(s) may be entitled hereafter.

2. The Writer(s) hereby warrants that the said composition is his sole, exclusive and original work, and that he has full right and power to make the within agreement; and that there exist no adverse claims to or in the said composition. The Writer(s) hereby further warrants and represents that he is not a member of the American Society of Composers, Authors and Publishers, the Songwriters' Protective Association, or of any other society or association which requires as a condition of membership the assignment of any right of any kind in said musical work and that no assignment of any of the rights herein set forth has been directly or indirectly made to any other person, firm or corporation whatsoever.

3. The Writers hereby warrant that the foregoing musical composition has been created by the joint collaboration of the Writers named herein and that said composition including the title, words and music thereof, has been, unless herein otherwise specifically noted, the result of the joint efforts of all the undersigned Writers and not by way of any independent or separable activity by any of the Writers.

4. In consideration of this agreement, the Publisher agrees to pay the Writer(s) as follows:

   (a) In respect of regular piano copies sold and paid for at wholesale in the United States of America, royalties of 3   cents per copy;

   (b) A royalty of 3   cents per copy of orchestrations thereof in any form sold and paid for in the United States of America;

   (c) A royalty of 50   per cent of all net sums received by the Publisher in respect of regular piano copies and/or orchestrations thereof sold and paid for in any foreign country by a foreign publisher.

   (d) The sum of One Dollar as and when the said composition is published in any folio or composite work or lyric magazine by the Publisher or licensees of the Publisher. Such publication may be made at any time in the discretion of Publisher;

   (e) For purposes of royalty statements, if a composition is printed and published in the United States of America, as to copies and rights sold in the Dominion of Canada, revenue herefrom shall be considered as of domestic origin. If however, the composition is printed by a party other than the Publisher in the Dominion of Canada, revenue from sales of copies and rights in Canada shall be considered as originated in a foreign country;

   (f) As to "professional material"—not sold or resold, no royalty shall be payable;

   (g) An amount equal to 50   per cent of all net proceeds received and actually retained by the Publisher arising out of (1) the manufacture of parts of instruments serving to mechanically reproduce said composition, or (2) the use of said composition in synchronization with sound motion pictures;

   (h) Except as herein expressly provided, no other royalties shall be paid with respect to the said composition.

   (i) Notwithstanding anything contained in this agreement, the Publisher shall deduct 10 per cent of all net receipts from all licenses issued by it to licensees in the United States and elsewhere, as collection charges for the collection of the proceeds of such licenses, before computing the royalties payable under Paragraph 4 of this agreement.

No.

BMT CLEARED

A 1957 single-song songwriters contract. Was it fair?

5. It is understood and agreed by and between all the parties hereto that all sums hereunder payable jointly to the Writer(s) shall be paid to and divided amongst them respectively as follows:

NAME	SHARE
JIMMY REED	50%
EWART G. ABNER, JR.	50%

6. The Publisher shall render the Writer(s), as above, on or before each August 15th covering the six months ending June 30th; and each February 15th covering the six months ending December 31st; royalty statements accompanied by remittance for any royalties due thereunder.

7. Anything to the contrary notwithstanding, nothing in this agreement contained shall prevent Publisher from authorizing publishers, agents and representatives in countries outside of the United States and Canada (and in Canada if said composition is printed by a party other than Publisher in Canada) from exercising exclusive publication and all other rights in said foreign countries in said composition on the customary royalty basis; and nothing in this agreement shall prevent Publisher from authorizing publishers in the United States from exercising publication rights and other rights in the United States in said composition, provided Publisher shall pay Writer the royalties herein stipulated. If foreign publication or other rights in said composition are separately conveyed, otherwise than as a part of Publisher's current and/or future catalog, then, but not otherwise, any advance received in respect thereof shall be divided in accordance with Paragraph 3 (f) and credited to the account of Writer.

8. The Writer(s) hereby consent to such changes, editing and arrangements of said composition, and the setting of words to the music and of music to the words, and the change of title as the Publisher deems desirable. The Writer(s) consents to the use of his (their) name and likeness and the title to the said composition on the music, folios, recordings, performances, player rolls and in connection with publicity and advertising concerning the Publisher, its successors, assigns and licensees, and said composition, and agrees that the use of such name, likeness and title may commence prior to publication and may continue so long as the Publisher shall own and/or exercise any rights in said composition.

9. Written demands and notices other than royalty statements provided for herein shall be sent by registered mail.

10. Any legal action brought by the Publisher against any alleged infringer of said composition shall be initiated and prosecuted at the Publisher's sole expense, and of any recovery made by it as a result thereof, after deduction of the expense of the litigation, a sum equal to thirty-three and one-third (33-1/3) per cent shall be paid to the Writer(s).

    (a) If a claim is presented against the Publisher in respect of said composition, and because thereof the Publisher is jeopardized, it shall thereupon serve written notice upon the Writer(s), containing the full details of such claim known to the Publisher and thereafter until the claim has been adjudicated or settled shall hold any moneys coming due the Writer(s) in escrow pending the outcome of such claim or claims.

    (b) From and after the service of summons in a suit for infringement filed against the Publisher with respect to said composition, any and all payments thereafter coming due the Writer(s) shall be held by the Publisher in trust until the suit has been adjudicated and then be disbursed accordingly, unless the Writer(s) shall elect to file an acceptable bond in the sum of such payments, in which event the sums dues shall be paid to the Writer(s).

11. "Writer" as used herein shall be deemed to include all authors and composers signing this agreement.

12. The Publisher shall have the right to sell, assign, transfer, license or otherwise dispose of any of its rights in whole or in part under this agreement to any person, firm or corporation, but said disposition shall not affect the right of the Writer(s) to the royalties hereinabove set forth.

15. This agreement is binding upon the respective parties hereto, their respective successors in interest, legal representatives and assigns and represents the entire understanding between the parties.

IN WITNESS WHEREOF, the parties hereto have hereunto set their hands and seals the day and year first above written.

Writer _____

Address _____

Writer _____

Address _____

CONRAD PUBLISHING CO., Inc.

By _____

Writer _____

Address _____

that said Reed was to be paid three cents per song regarding "piano copies" (or sheet music, per unit sold). The contract also stipulated that 50 percent of net proceeds received and retained by Conrad for manufacturing and reproducing the compositions was to go to the writers.

That might seem equitable at first blush, but there is more to the story. The contract in question was for the song "Baby, What's on Your Mind?" and explains that Reed *and* Ewart Abner, Jr., were co-writers of the song and were to split their royalties evenly. This meant Reed would see not 50 percent, but only 25 percent of any royalties. If we operate under the likely assumption that perhaps Vee-Jay A&R exec

Abner did not have as much to do with writing the song as championing the song, then we are faced with a problem—a financial one beyond the moral. How fair was this contract? (Abner is also credited through BMI with co-writing such Jimmy Reed tunes as "Honest I Do," "Honey, Don't Let Me Go," "Honey, Where You Going?," "Do the Thing," "It's You Baby," "Little Rain," "You Got Me Dizzy," "You Upset My Mind," "Signals of Love," and "The Sun Is Shining" with Calvin Carter as a third co-writer.) So, Reed would receive twenty-five cents for each dollar earned (net). And this would only be after collection costs for royalties are subtracted; in the text of the contract, it read that Conrad Publishing would take ten percent of the net proceeds and put it towards collection costs before royalties of any kind were paid out. Most legally advised musicians today are warned against such deals and are urged to have the company cover the costs of collecting royalties rather than have it come out of their pockets.

"Vee-Jay was no different from all the other record companies," Jerry Butler of Vee-Jay act the Impressions (and later solo artist) says. "None of them paid you well. They all ripped us off. Why? They knew that we didn't know. And anytime you are in a position where you are ignorant you stand a good chance of being ripped off. And that is what happened.... I remember we talked about publishing with the company, and when we did Calvin Carter, Jimmy Bracken, and Vivian Carter, they hit the ceiling: 'What are you guys talking about, publishing your own music?!!' 'Well, we hear that people published their own music and they made money off the music.' Well, as you can imagine, we weren't supposed to know that. As a matter of fact, Calvin Carter told Curtis [Mayfield] and myself not to write songs because he would get all of our songs from professional songwriters."

"I don't know if Jimmy [Reed] ever got a royalty check, but I know one thing: we never did," says Mickey McGill of the vocal R&B band the Dells, also on the Vee-Jay label. "They [Vee-Jay] had a lot of great acts but they didn't pay royalties. I think when the original 'Oh, What A Nite' started selling, they *loaned* us $500. They wired it to us in New York City. They bought us a station wagon, but they owned it. We could use it and pay the notes on it."[ii]

There's no evidence to suggest that any of Reed's other contracts were any different from the one he "signed" in 1957. While it is clear that Jimmy did indeed enter into deals he shouldn't have, he really had no other choice if he wanted to record his music. He couldn't read well, and he didn't understand about recouping and collection expenses and that the bill would be charged against his royalties. Reed just shrugged it off as another aspect of the business he either didn't understand or didn't want to be bothered with. He hunkered down and accepted what was handed to him.

Still, deep down, no matter how much he knew people were out to make money for themselves, he knew whatever transpired—fair or not—was as a result of his choice. "They didn't put no pistol on me and make me get into [a contract]," Reed told *Living Blues.* "I couldn't do nothin' about it or say nothin' about it, because all I was doin' was cuttin' the records and running here and there singin' them old blues and acting a fool."

Reed may not have been happy with his agreements, or his lack of royalties, but he also refused to see a lawyer. He thought they were the same as the record company: always with their hands out, ready to take a large chunk of the money he was rightly owed. He didn't "trust those cats," and so he was between a rock and a hard place.

Reed was beginning to see that this music business wasn't all it was cracked up to be. It was a business that seemed established for the express purpose of sucking your soul. "[M]y daddy was not an easy person to get along with if he had an idea that you didn't like him," Loretta says. "He did not like hypocrisy. If you thought you could smile in his face and stab him in the back, it wasn't going to happen. He actually read people very well. He pretty much knew who he could depend on and who he couldn't. Then he had business associates that he did business with, but you could tell that he really didn't put much trust in them. You know, he wouldn't put his life in their hands."

"And he had good reason to feel that way, too," adds Reed, Jr. "A lot of people, when they looked at him, portrayed him as a drunk. He was, in the eyes of some of the higher-ups in the music industry, an easy target."

"I really don't think Daddy liked music as a business," Loretta continues. "I think he loved to just play guitar. I remember him laughing and sitting down just playing the guitar. That is what stuck in my mind. I don't think he liked the rat race and the dog-eat-dog world of the music business. He was not that kind of person. It was hard for him to deal with."

Even the fans—who loved him—were unpredictable and seemingly, and inextricably, "out to get him." One night, Reed's touring band was warming up the crowd, but it appeared nothing was going to settle their restless behavior. "We escaped a lot of fights and a lot of shootings," Red Holloway says. "This one night we had to rush Jimmy out behind the stage and out the back door to the car. People would be running out the front. When you are young, you don't get scared that quick. If there was a shooting you have to make sure you don't get in the way of the bullet, that's all. Or so we thought. Anyway, if anything happened, we would always rush Jimmy off first. He was our bread and butter, you know? The guitar player might say, 'Wait, my guitar.' I say, 'Fuck your guitar. Get yo' ass outta here.'"

"We played the Royal Theatre in Baltimore, Maryland, on occasion," says Mickey McGill of the Dells. "The Royal Theatre, which was notorious for intimidating its acts, because when you would come on stage, these young guys at the Royal Theatre would tell you: 'You better sing good, man.' There would be whiskey bottles in the air. Back then they had a screen that would show a movie before the concert, and during the movie they were throwing whiskey bottles at the screen. You knew what you were in for. Jimmy Reed, when he came on stage, they were making so much noise, Jimmy stopped and said, 'Why don't ya'll leave me alone and let me sing my song?' That's all someone had to hear: a whiskey bottle hit him right in the forehead. It knocked him down. But I don't think he felt it. Seemed like he kept a lot of alcohol in his system."

Marvin Junior, McGill's band mate, also remembers the incident. "Reed had sung his song 'You Don't Have to Go' and then he played and sang another. Then some people in the crowd said, 'You Don't Have to Go'—trying to get him to play it again. He told 'em, 'Why don't you shut up and please let him do his show.' Somebody threw a bottle up on stage and hit him. That was the way it was at the Royal. I got hit with a bottle there once myself. They was just thugs. A lot of entertainers wouldn't work the Royal. All of us *had* to work it. For ushers, they had a guy with a dog walking up and down the aisles. It was horrible. Those were the things you went through in those days."

If his roadwork was any indication, Jimmy was in for a long year. But he never could have seen the curve that was about to be thrown at him. Those seizures he and his doctors had thought were the d.t.'s had been misdiagnosed. They weren't the d.t.'s at all. Jimmy Reed had epilepsy.

"The only people who knew were the people who were around him when he had a seizure," Loretta reveals. "It was not a big announcement. But it was traumatic for him as well as for us."

"There is a bad misconception about my father," says Reed's son. "They kind of label him a drunk. They more or less focus on his drinking habit. What they don't know is that my father had epilepsy. And the only reason he drank was because he was afraid of having those seizures."

Having epilepsy back in the 1950s was an especially frightening prospect. Like alcoholism, epilepsy was very misunderstood. Some thought Reed's epileptic seizures were manifestations of mental illness. It certainly wouldn't have been the first time people with epilepsy were mistakenly thought of as daft. As far back in recorded history as ancient Mesopotamia, epilepsy was referred to as "the falling disease" brought on by evil spirits. Even in researching this book, many sources didn't really have a good handle on what epilepsy is, labeling people who have it as "epileptics"—a term the medical establishment wants to abolish because it allows the disease to define the person.

Above all, epilepsy has suffered from bad public relations. And that skewed public image has a tendency to infiltrate even the thickest skins. Reed's self-esteem was tested daily. Reed wasn't exactly private about his disease (he did talk openly about it in later years), but the last thing he wanted was for someone to get the wrong impression of him, or get stuck with the lasting image of his body while seizing. Drugs could help treat it, but Jimmy had to keep on his toes. He had to take his medicine religiously, and he'd have to pack it with him when he headed out on tour. Reed would have been given lithium bromide (a common treatment for epileptic seizures, which contains bromine, a depressant), but this certainly wasn't a cure. Dilantin (phenytoin), a more powerful drug, was the alternative.

"Dilantin is the medication I remember," says Loretta. "When this first started, having the seizures, I believe his doctor at the time put him on phenobarbital for nerves. I know that didn't last long, because he wasn't taking it that long at all."

"He took his medication every day," Reed, Jr., notes.

However, the dosage of medication did little to stem the tide of seizures. These epileptic episodes frightened the family. "Speaking of my own experience, we were living at 212 West 68th Street," recalls Junior, who went on to record and tour with his dad as a guitar player. "Dad and I were rehearsing, going over a song that he was gonna record in the studio, and all of a sudden he got up and left out the room and went to the bathroom. He came back down the hallway and went into one of the bedrooms, and then one of the smaller children—maybe Malinda, Rose, or Roslyn—had come running in there and told us that he had fell on the bed."

"It scared me," Rose says.

"It scared all of us," admits Jimmy's son. "We didn't know what was going on."

"What scared me the most," Rose adds, "was my mom coming in and saying, 'I knew this was going to happen. Go bring me a towel.' We didn't know this was going to happen. Before that we had no idea."

"There was another occasion when we were on the highway headed to New York," Junior remembers. "We were scheduled to play at the Apollo Theater, and we stopped at a service plaza on the Ohio Turnpike. We went in to get breakfast. There was myself, Al Smith, Dad, and I think Albert [Brown], who we called our adopted brother. Our family would 'adopt' our friends who would spend time at the house. We sat down at the counter to begin eating and all of a sudden we noticed that Dad was looking kind of strange. Al Smith picked up on it right away. He just stood up and got him up and tried to walk him toward the door. This is what made me realize how painful this was for [Dad]. He was walking out the door, and I heard him let out a cry. I knew he was in pain. Well, I don't know if it was as much pain as fear."

Red Holloway remembers an episode in the South. "A lot of times when we were down South they were selling that white lightnin'," Holloway says. "People were dying from that. Jimmy had bought about two gallons of that and we showed him in the paper somewhere that about seven people had died from drinking that white lightnin'. He hated to, but he had to throw it out. Jimmy had epilepsy, so you had to try to stop him from drinking. There were times when I saw him have a slight seizure where he would kind of tremble, like. It was not a grand mal. I never saw him have a grand mal. He had one or two slight seizures when I was with him. He'd drink heavy and he might have a seizure. I think he had medication and maybe he didn't take it a day or something. You had to make him take his medication."

It was hard to know exactly when an epilepsy episode was coming on. Truth be told, for Reed there were a few signs, but in the early stages he might not have recognized them himself. An "aura" (also called a "predome") is a pre-seizure event that can occur hours or even days before a seizure sets in. Auras manifest differently in individual people, and in some cases act as a warning of a tonic-clonic seizure. Symptoms include anxiety, smelling or tasting something unusual, hearing musical notes, or vision disturbances.[iii]

Jimmy explained, as only he could, that his seizures attacked indiscriminately, but that physical and sensory reactions signaled a seizure was on the way. "I was on the point of view of having seizures on accounts of my nerve[s]," he told interviewer Norman Davis. "I could hear [a] siren blowin' like they had a big fire somewhere and hear a…fire department whistle…. And I see people running and start hollering, and I go to shaking for nothing, you know what I mean?… The next thing I know…I just done be out like a light."

"We all learned the signs," Loretta notes. "We learned to watch him and all of those things. He would get quiet, kind of to himself, and we knew that there was a possibility that he might have a seizure."

Rock music icon and admitted Jimmy Reed fanatic Neil Young, having survived a bout with polio at a young age, also suffered early in his life from epileptic seizures. "When you have a seizure," Young told biographer Jimmy McDonough in his book *Shakey*, "you go off…it kind of feels like you lose yourself for a while. Somehow you're still there. All of these things happen to your body, but you don't have any recollection of it—and it wasn't an accident, where someone hit you. It came from inside."

Reed's seizures could be violent. He'd have grand mal seizures, which affect the entire brain and cause the afflicted to fall to the ground and their limbs to thrash uncontrollably. His health was quite a handful for those who had to look after him. "I want to tell you, man, back when I was about 26, and I was raised on a farm, I could pick up 300 pounds," says Chicago guitarist Lonnie Brooks. "I didn't weigh more than 185 pounds. But that cat [Jimmy] was stronger than me. He could grab your hand and crush it. And he wasn't heavy, or as heavy as me. It took me years to find out how strong he was. When you had those fits, you could grab a person and you don't realize how much strength he had. He almost bit my finger off, man. I seen him gasping for air and fell down on the floor. I seen that he had done swallowed his tongue. I reached in there with my finger and pulled his tongue out. By the time I got his tongue out, he crushed down on my finger—with his front teeth. If it had been his back teeth he would have crushed it.[iv]

"I couldn't play," Brooks continues. "I found a way to play with other fingers because that one was so hurt. I did it with my right hand, my pointer finger…. Someone put a knife in his mouth to try to get my finger out of his mouth. He was cutting it off with the front teeth. I was sick there for a while after that. I had been with him for about six months. The manager said, 'You don't have to play tonight.' The other guitar player was with us said I should get a pick, so I played with a thumbpick. I used to play with my fingers. I didn't play with a pick. I couldn't move it. They put a splint on it, the doctor. But I saved his life. But he didn't even know I did that. He didn't even know he bit me. You could tell when he was going to have it. He would start to talk funny and his tongue would be dragging, you know. It sounded like he was drunk, but this was different. I know when someone is drunk, O.K.?"

"It was common knowledge that Jimmy had several [seizures] right there in the office," Jerry Butler says. "They would have to get sticks and things to keep him from biting through his tongue."

With Jimmy now diagnosed with epilepsy, Eddie Taylor had eyes on making a break for it and leaving Jimmy to fend for himself. Earlier in the year and in 1956, Taylor had left his options open. He had cut tracks with John Lee Hooker ("Dimples") and Elmore James ("The 12 Year Old Boy," "Take Me Where You Go," "Knocking at Your Door," "Coming Home," and "Cry for Me Baby," which features a scorching Taylor solo). And he was now playing with three fingerpicks—one on his thumb—and was able to approach the strings from three angles and create a three-pronged percussive attack. Eddie could do just about anything he wanted on the guitar. But he couldn't leave Jimmy high and dry. He rethought the consequences of such a rash decision: he felt responsible for Jimmy and he had to look after him, even if he felt it was not his job.

Despite his disease, Jimmy kept working like a dog. Touring was top priority—and entertaining the folks was what he did best. Von Freeman remembers: "I always like to tell a joke about Jimmy Reed: he is the only male entertainer who I ever worked with who made men cry and faint and carry on. I mean working men in overalls. It was the most amazing thing that I had ever seen—because I had never seen that—men fainting and carrying on. 'Jimmy, you are knocking me out, Jimmy,' I said. I've seen that with lady singers. But with male blues singers? Oh, man. We went around the country with him—he and Al Smith. We played a lot of barns—and I do mean *barns*. Great big ole cow barns—out in the pastures. People would just come from everywhere."

Holloway recalls an experience down South that defies logic. "Another time we were down in Mississippi and Jimmy Reed had been drinking and his car hit another fella's car," Red remembers. "So, we were in the town we were getting ready to play in, and this fella jumped out of his car and called him, 'You sonofabitch, you. This is my goddamn car. I'm gonna kick your ass.' So, Al Smith was in another car and he jumped out and said, 'We'll pay for it, sir. Just give us the bill.' The guy said, 'O.K.' Then Al said, 'This is Jimmy Reed. You just got into an accident with Jimmy Reed. We'll pay for it.' The guy said, 'Did you say Jimmy Reed? Jimmy Reed? Jimmy Reed hit my car? Hey, George,' or whatever this other fella's name was, 'George, Jimmy Reed.' Al said, 'Oh, we'll pay for it.' The guy said, 'Don't worry about it. Can we get your autograph?'"

"We were in Shreveport, Louisiana," says Butler, who remembers a similar—possibly even the same—incident. "Jimmy Reed got in his car and after the concert was over, after having too much to drink and driving down the street, he banged into a man's car. The man's neighbor saw the accident and ran over next door and banged on his neighbor's door and said, 'Man, Jimmy Reed just hit your car.' The owner of the car said, 'Where?' The neighbor pointed it out—'Right there on the front. See that big dent?' The man looked at the damage and told his neighbor, 'I ain't never gonna get it fixed.' That was the kind of affection people had for him. The owner of the car said he had braggin' rights. He could show people the dent Jimmy Reed put on his car."

Reed was idolized by a healthy dose of both white and black fans. America, amid Cold War scares and the so-called "global communist conspiracy," was truly dancing to its own drum. It is safe to say that no other nation in the world had produced the kinds of R&B and blues artists America did. And Jimmy Reed? Nothing could be more American than Jimmy Reed. When Jimmy Reed was first played on the radio, McCarthyism had reached new highs (or lows), and, in part, Jimmy and others helped those fears, worries, and troubles melt away.

In September 1957 people were eating it up. *Billboard* reported on the progress of the single "Honest I Do" (with B-side "Signals of Love"): "Reed sells a Southern-styled blues with primitive passion and deep sincerity." By mid-October, "Honest I Do" flirted with being in the Top Ten on the R&B charts (coming in at No. 11 and entering the coveted spot in late October), competing with such songs as Elvis' "Jailhouse Rock," Jerry Lee Lewis' "Whole Lotta Shakin' Goin' On," Sam Cooke's "You Send Me," Little Richard's "Keep a-Knockin'," the Everly Brothers' "Wake Up Little Susie," or uddy Holly and the Crickets' "That'll Be the Day." Like a steaming freight train, "Honest I Do" pushed on to the "pop" charts, where it shot to No. 32. (The song was in the Top Five of the Most Played R&B by Jockeys by late November, and remained in heavy radio rotation into December.)

Also in September the Reed 3 were at it again. They recorded a total of five tracks in the fall: "My Bitter Seed," "Ends and Odds" (an instrumental complement to the, well, odd "Odds and Ends," which was more easily drawn from the Reed template), "My Baby" (or "Down in Virginia," which went unreleased as a single), "You're Somthin' Else" (a jaunty little number nasally delivered over the standard Reed shuffle in the "You've Got Me Dizzy" mode), and a loping-grooved, mush-mouthed gem entitled "A String to Your Heart."

It seemed whenever Reed was not recording, he was on the road, much to his fans' delight. Drummer Robert Barry remembers getting the call to play with Jimmy—and says he'll never forget the road trip. "We went through Phoenix, Arizona, Los Angeles, San Francisco, Chicago, Philadelphia," he says. "We avoided Denver—they had something like a foot of snow. We bypassed Denver. It was a wild time [laughs]. The thing about Jimmy is that you had to keep the man sober. His alcohol consumption was…. Man, that was that a trip. We went from here, Chicago, all the way to Los Angeles. First we stopped in Arizona. Then from Arizona we stopped in Los Angeles, then San Francisco, and then Stockton. It was tragedy all the way. We had a few days to get to Philly. We was going to Philly but had a terrible wreck in New Mexico…. The driver did not know what he was doing and he almost got us all killed!"

Von Freeman had played with Jimmy's touring band for years. "[The audience] idolized the man," he says. "We'd be sitting up there—trained horn players, man—and they wouldn't even be paying attention to us. Jimmy hit one note on that harp, man, and they would go crazy. See, everything was centered around that one little vamp that he had. He played it differently—he had different tunings. He played a lot in A natural. As a rule, unless you play with blues cats, you rarely play in A natural—you play a lot in E natural. These are natural guitar strings. That was one of the things that made him different. And he didn't use those staples that were across his strings. Most times he just took his guitar and started playing…. We used to crack up. He said, 'Well, I like this jazz my band is playing. I am going get right with it. What was the name of that tune you were playing?' 'It is C jam, Jimmy.' 'Good, let's hit it. One, two, three, four…' Of course, he would be in E natural or A natural or something. I think he was screwing with us. We'd crack up. It was like, 'Well, you big-time jazz musicians, play these keys.'

"The truth is we were a hard band to keep up with," Freeman continues. "Al [Smith] knew how to pick the cats who could play well together. When we were traveling with him, we had the nucleus of a [jazz] band: trombone, trumpet, tenor, and guitar. We had Wayne Bennett—he was great jazz guitar player. It could be tough to get away with sometimes, and of course, you had some great groups down there already, like the Upsetters. Those were great bands, and when you go on the bandstand either before or after them, you had to have something that played with some harmony. A lot of people were calling us beboppers."

Freeman knew right away that blues was where it was at. No matter how accomplished he or the rest of the band thought they were, Jimmy was their meal ticket. "Everybody can't just throw together some lyrics and shuffle and sell it," he says. "He could do that, man. I can't remember a tune he ever wrote or did that didn't sound good. All the jazz cats knew the only way you made any money was working with blues cats."

"We worked with Jimmy Reed three or so years," Marvin Junior notes. "Because when artists had hits, they worked the same places we worked, if it were blues, or whatever it was. The audience wanted a variety on the show, anyway. Another thing: you did the circuit. You worked with entertainers and you made your way through all the theaters. You'd start over at the Apollo, then go to the Howard in Washington, then go to the Royal in Baltimore, then go to the Uptown in Philadelphia, then you do the Regal in Chicago, the State in Connecticut. And this went over and over again. After you finished the circuit you went back again. In one year we worked the Apollo 27 times. That was the way it was. That was the main work then. You didn't do many concerts. There was no such thing as a concert for our acts then. You did dances, but no concerts. The closest thing to a concert was at the theater."

Jimmy was traveling a good deal down South in his mother country, through Arkansas, Mississippi, Alabama, Louisiana, and Georgia. Jimmy's laconic harp blowing rang a bell with the South, and with Louisiana in particular. The so-called "swamp blues" and "swamp pop" music artists seemed to take Jimmy Reed's music and use it as a launch pad for their own style.

Lightnin' Slim (Otis Hicks) kicked off what is seen today as "swamp blues" in 1954 with the song "Bad Luck," which many blues historians consider as taking a cue from artists such as Sonny Boy Williamson I, Muddy Waters, and Jimmy Reed. Slim's "Bad Luck and Trouble" and "Nothin' but the Devil" could pass for cousins of Reed's raw early tracks like "High and Lonesome" and "You Don't Have to Go." In a larger and more simplified sense, it's all in the turnarounds and harp lines.

Slim's one hit (though we should be careful in using the term "hit:" the 1959 song didn't even break the Top 20 on *Billboard*'s R&B chart) was another in the Reed mold. "Rooster Blues," with its "I got to rock the night, baby" refrain, packs all the punch of Reed's raunchy, rockin' tune "I'm A Love You" (aka "I'm Gonna Love You") and the classic "Ain't That Lovin' You Baby"—right down to the timed musical gaps. Slim's 1963 track "Winter Time Blues" is nearly a carbon copy of the down-home boogie blues Reed might have recorded in the 1950s (and after). It should also be noted, however, that there is a darkness surrounding Slim's music, from within and without, even today that just doesn't exist around Reed's songs. Though Reed did, on occasion, scrape the earthiness of the more deep, growling blues singers, Slim set up shop in the gutbucket, conjuring John Lee Hooker regularly (check out "Have Mercy on Me Baby," for example).

In his book *South to Louisiana: The Music of the Cajun Bayous*, author John Broven tracks the development of Cajun music and swamp pop, and the impact of Jimmy Reed on Cajun artists. "The two influences were Fats Domino, obviously—the South Louisiana kids being so near to New Orleans—but the other influence was clearly Jimmy Reed," Broven says. "One thing that fascinates me, and I do this as an aside, because it does fascinate me, is just how many young white bands Jimmy had influenced. That was the Jimmy Reed sound—the sound of the South. It was just so many young bands from Billy Lee Riley in Memphis right through to people like Joey Long [Joseph Earl Longoria from Zwolle, Louisiana], Rockin' Dave Allan in Texas, and all of these, so many of these, young Louisiana bands. All they were doing was basically trying to copy Jimmy Reed."

Slim Harpo—called the most accessible of the swamp blues performers—was related to Lightnin' Slim through marriage. But that wasn't the only thing they had in common. Lightnin' Slim may have appeared to have shared only a small trace of commonality with Reed, but Slim Harpo was undeniably influenced by the Boss Man. Harpo's 1957 gems "I've Got Love if You Want It," "Strange Love," and "Wonderin' and Worryin' " were dead-on for Reed, right down to the lazy vocal style, laconic harp delivery, and unmistakable Reed lump beat (particularly the latter).

"Jimmy Reed was the best with that particular style," says Lazy Lester (Leslie Johnson), who has recorded as a solo artist as well as with Louisiana music icons Raful Neal, Lonesome Dundown, and Lightnin' Slim, with whom he had an extended recording run and successful partnership. "It rubbed off on a lot of us, really. It was so handy to play that particular style because there was so many things you could do with it…. Raful Neal was playing with me, and I know he was influenced by Jimmy Reed. He played a lot of Jimmy Reed. Plus Jimmy Anderson, over in Natchez, Mississippi, somewhere, he was just the spitting image of Jimmy Reed. He was a lot like Jimmy Reed."[v]

Although as a harmonica player Lester doesn't stay in the high registers the way Reed often did, the general flow does remind one of Reed. Still, no matter how lazy Reed sounded (he sounded absolutely intoxicated on some takes), Lester made a near equally grinding, grungy style of blues (occasionally with the swing of country music). Lester's playing falls somewhere between Reed and Little Walter, yet one of Lester's most recognizable tracks, "Sugar Coated Love," is in fact a hot-rodded "You Got Me Dizzy." And for all of the shots critics have taken at Reed's voice, when you cross-reference Lester's darker/near monotone vocals, you begin to get a sense of how in tune and more perfectly pitched Reed's vocals have always been.

J.D. "Jay" Miller, who recorded Cajun and blues artists in his Crowley, Louisiana, studio, established regional labels such as Feature and Fais Do Do. Miller licensed music to the Nashville-based Excello and others such as Dot, Nasco, and Decca, and as a result Louisiana artists like Warren Storm and Slim Harpo achieved wider acclaim and chart success. Whatever Miller was doing, it was working. Maybe a little too well. On more than one occasion, the record-buying public was having a hard time differentiating between more established names like Jimmy Reed and Louisiana artists.

Lester recounts a funny anecdote: "Jay Miller had a recording studio and record shop in the building he had in Crowley. A lot of people had heard a record by Jimmy Reed. They had heard but didn't know exactly what it was. They *thought* it was Jimmy Reed. They'd come in, 'I want that new record, "I Told My Little Woman."' I'd ask, 'When did you hear it?' They'd answer: 'I heard it on the Nashville station.' When I would hand them a copy of the record—it had an Excello label, you know—they looked at the label and it said, Lazy Lester. 'Lazy Lester?!', they'd say, 'I thought it was Jimmy Reed.' The kids then were into real music because everybody was listening to whatever we play."

Jimmy's records were heard on WLAC in Nashville—a 50,000-watt station that knew no borders, having seduced white teens with black R&B in states throughout the South and out West. What is remarkable is the number of white listeners Reed reached—he influenced a whole generation of young white musicians, more so than Muddy Waters and Elmore James. Perhaps that Southern, hypnotic, lazy feel was part of the Southern and Cajun culture, and people of Louisiana identified with Reed's music.

"Having worked alongside black farmers, listening to their music, adapting it to some of their recordings, we found it easy to incorporate Reed's style of simplicity, in words and music, to our own music," says Cajun artist Johnnie Allan. "Jimmy Reed was very popular in south Louisiana with the white audiences during his heyday. If you wanted to pack the dance floor, just play 'Honest I Do' and watch the belly rubbing. 'Big Boss Man,' 'Bright Lights, Big City,' and 'Ain't That Loving You Baby' were other audience favorites…. Can you believe this? I even bought an *E* harmonica and tried to emulate Reed's expertise. The simplicity of his words and rhythm had a close semblance to the sounds I wanted to perpetuate in my repertoire at performances."

In all fairness, Allan had a bit of a head start on some of the other Louisiana artists. He came from a musical family, one which boasted such talents as Joe Falcon (Allan's grandfather's brother), who has been credited with recording the first Cajun-French release, "Lafayette" (aka

"Allons a Lafayette," translation: Let's go to Lafayette). "I would join in family jam sessions on the back porch of our old sharecropper home and sing mainly hillbilly songs at the ripe young age of three," Allan says. "I'd memorized those songs from listening to our old battery-operated radio."

Whereas people of the Cajun bayous would play, listen, and dance to traditional rural Cajun music, Allan explains that he could sense a sea change in attitude toward music in his part of the country around the middle of the last century, as more artists and the public became aware—or more accepting—of rock 'n' roll, R&B, and country or hillbilly (cowboy) music. The blues was seeping into the very soul of these musicians, including people like accordionists/vocalists Nathan Abshire with his 1949 "Pine Grove Blues" recording (thanks to the persistence and business sense of Virgil Bozeman and George Khoury's sponsorship) and Clifton Chenier, the undisputed "King of Zydeco," who was combining Zydeco, big band, Cajun waltzes, and blues. "I could feel the winds of change sweeping the Cajun bayous in the mid-'50s," Allan says. "The R&B recordings of Fats Domino, Chuck Berry, and Little Richard among others were getting into my musical skin. My high school classmates would rave about this new genre of music they had heard the Saturday night before at a local nightclub. On an off weekend from playing Cajun music with Lawrence Walker and the Wandering Aces, I heard Earl King and Gatemouth Brown at Landry's Palladium in Lafayette, Louisiana, in 1956. I was hooked.

"I also remember seeing Jimmy Reed. The first and only time I saw Reed perform was at the Southern Club in Opelousas, Louisiana," Allan says. "Can't recall the year and month but 'Honest I Do' was hot on the local jukeboxes as well as radio stations. I can still visualize him sitting in a chair accompanied by his bassist and drummer, his wife providing him with constant whiskey drinks. Sad to say, the capacity crowd of about 600 patrons couldn't hear him past 20 feet from the bandstand due to an inadequate sound system. Luckily, I was privileged to have a listening spot at the side door to the bandstand…. Little did I realize that I would become a part of a new genre of music, which has since become known as "swamp pop" music.

" 'Swamp pop' is a term coined by British authors Bill Millar and John Broven to abbreviate what was before known generally as South

Louisiana music," Allan says. "Personally, I like the term since it gives our music a better identity. I give credit to the musicians, artists, songwriters, and studio engineers for creating this genre of music, though. We incorporated the varied styles of south Louisiana and nationally recorded music, and voilà—came up with our own brand now known as 'swamp pop.' It was easy for us since we grew up in an area steeped in rich musical traditions."

It was inevitable. Reed would soon collide with the swamp blues guys. Lazy Lester remembers being on the same bill with Reed on more than one occasion. "One show stands out—it was Scenic Theater in Chicago and I think Sonny Boy Williamson, Lonesome Sundown, Slim Harpo, Lightnin' Slim, and Magic Sam were all on the show," says Lester, who left the music industry for the better part of two decades—most of the 1970s and 1980s. "It was a big bill. During that time we all liked what we were doing, and we would do anything that would make us comfortable, you know what I mean?"

"I think Lester in his trip—with Lightnin' Slim, Slim Harpo, Lonesome Sundown, and others—went up to Chicago with Jay Miller's van," says Fred Reif, who represents Lester. "That was an experience that Lightnin' Slim put to a song for a Fly-Rite record that was never released.... I can tell you that from having dealt with Lester all of these years, one of Lester's biggest influences is Jimmy Reed. There may be some nights that Lester doesn't do any Lazy Lester tunes—they are all Jimmy Reed songs."

A whole new generation of Louisiana artists have been influenced by Reed, including Kenny Neal, guitarist/singer/harp player and son of Raful, who has always incorporated Jimmy Reed into his live sets, and Tab Benoit (born in 1967 in Baton Rouge), whom *Guitar Player* once called "the hottest thing to come out of Louisiana since Chef Paul Prudhomme."

"Jimmy Reed would be played on the radio down here—he was just everywhere," Benoit says. "I don't think you could get away from him. I didn't necessarily see him as blues—he was like a pop star, really. Jimmy Reed got that beat through an amalgam of, or a combination of, the different parts of the band. Even the definitive 'Jimmy Reed' beat, chugga, chugga, chugga, chugga, is often misinterpreted. People think it is some static line that repeats. It's hypnotic, O.K.? But it is more like cha chugga chugga chugga cha chugga. You know? There is a subtlety to it, and a rhythmic base that I think people down here in Cajun country were certainly attuned to and influenced by. For me, personally, I hear a kind of swing in his playing. You can hear it in the Texas shuffle. There is a Jimmy Reed influence in Texas. It was sort of a combination of the Delta thing, a shuffle and the jazzy West Coast swing, like a T-Bone Walker thing. That definitely influenced the musicians in Texas. Each area had its own take—from Louisiana, Mississippi, Texas—but I don't know if anyone really achieved that kind of laidback shuffle."

And Reed was influencing more than just musicians in Texas and Louisiana. At clubs in Dallas and other areas of Texas, teens were doing a dance called the Push to Reed's music. This is one of those instances that an artist's style helped to popularize a kind of dance. "The dance was a slowed-down Jitterbug and we moved to the rhythm of Jimmy Reed songs," says Barbara Logan of 230 Music. "You could hear him everywhere on the radio down here."

"What Jimmy Reed played was definitely laidback," says guitarist Pete Mayes. "People would do something called the Whip to his music—Houston version of that Push dance. We call it the Whip here [in Houston]."

Larry Petrisaan, a Texan dance instructor, explains some of the subtleties of the Push, a Texas interpretation of the popular West Coast Swing dance. "Every person I have talked to about this subject—Push vs. West Coast Swing—has a different opinion on it," Petrisaan says. "The West Coast Swing is done to blues, but you can do the Push to blues if it is a faster blues song. The way I look at it, it depends on the tempo. The Push and West Coast Swing are what we call a slot dance, which means it is danced in a slot. You go back and forth—like dancing on a diving board."

It is no wonder that Jimmy Reed was so closely identified with a dance. He was played on the radio and made so many appearances in the Lone Star State, he seemed like a permanent fixture to the scene, even from the earliest part of his career. Dick DeGuerin, a powerful

Texas attorney (as of this writing representing former House majority leader Tom DeLay), saw Jimmy at the Doris Miller Auditorium in Austin in the mid-'50s when he was just a pimply teen. The place was packed, DeGuerin remembers, and there was dancing in the aisles. "Everyone called it the Dory Miller Auditorium," he admits. "It was a completely black venue, and this was just after segregation had ended. We had one black high school and three white high schools and very little mixture. I had heard of Jimmy Reed because I had heard him on KBET in Austin. They had an hour or two at night where they would play R&B and blues. That was the only time you could get what they called then "colored music." There was a DJ that played it—Dr. Hepcat was his name. His name was Lavada Durst and his signoff was, 'This is Dr. Hepcat, Lavada Durst, in the cool of the evening wishing you a warm goodnight.' He'd play Little Walter and Jimmy Reed."

Though Reed often brought people together, especially in Texas, DeGuerin recalls one show in which an outburst of violence nearly caused total chaos. "The next time I saw him was at the Austin Coliseum," DeGuerin says. "I remember there was a riot: a lot of white folks and some black folks were there, and some big white officers were bullying their way around. It was not a pleasant deal but I remember Jimmy Reed was on the top of his game. The last time I saw him was at a black nightclub on East 12th Street in Austin called Charley's Playhouse. Charley's Playhouse was kind of like a little Antone's. It was pretty small but had a stage. One of the reasons, besides seeing Jimmy Reed, that white kids went in there was because we could drink and they wouldn't ask for ID. Nobody asked any questions. Jimmy Reed had a big following among white kids."

Even Reed had to point out the immense following he had in the white community. "That's where I really got my kicks," Jimmy Reed told interviewer Bill Scott. "Look like to me, if you ask me I got more kicks out of white, playing for the white people than I did playing for the colored people because it just looked like, there was something funny about it…. It looked like they sure did enjoy it…looked like the colored people enjoyed it to a certain extent they would, then they get so full of it…. Just like the man got you hired to come on to the bandstand and play. Well, you playing on time. If a cat done pay his money to come in there to hear a record and you done played it once but he only got to hear but half of it. Then he want you to go back up there and do it again, even if the [stage manager] tell you that you got to come down.... Now if you don't go up there and do it then, then [the audience member] either want to shoot ya or he gonna start somethin', which ain't gonna be right. You know what I mean? That's what I didn't like about it."

Reed scored another hit with "I'm Gonna Get My Baby," while tracks like "Caress Me Baby" (a rare two takes were recorded for this slow-burning groove), the harpless "The Moon Is Rising" (the counterpart to "The Sun Is Shining" recorded a year earlier), "I Wanna Be Loved," "Going to New York" (which would be backed with "I Wanna Be Loved"), "I Told You Baby," "I Know It's a Sin" (featuring a nicely delivered soul vocal line by Jimmy), a remake of "Down in Virginia" (a romping and noisy little number that, unlike its earlier version, was released as a single), and "You'n the Sack" were being pumped over radio stations and record players in the Midwest and South.

"Caress Me Baby" is an archetypal Reed track. It's all here: the first-position, high-end harmonica shrieks; the dips, the blown and then drawn-bent notes shifting directions; Eddie Taylor's deliberately unspectacular and immaculate bottom-end groove; Remo Biondi's violin finger plucks; and Reed's incredibly simple but soulful lyrics— "Caress me baby, like the wind caress a tree/I want you to *loooooove*, love me, baby, like soft, soft summer breeze."

Reed was fascinated by the vibe and allure of the Big Apple, and in a brilliant pre-"Bright Lights, Big City" inspirational moment, the blues standard "Going to New York" was born. Reed had toured the South, the West, and Midwest, but New York—New York was a magical place. Getting to New York, *playing* New York, was the ultimate musician's showcase. The Big Time. To win over the jaded crowds with his music: what else could be better?

Having played places like the Rockland Palace and the Apollo Theater in Harlem in the 1950s (and Carnegie Hall and Brooklyn's Brevoort Theater later in the 1960s), Reed was familiar with New York by the time he had written this tune. Still, making the trek through Ohio, into the eastern corridor of Pennsylvania, through Philly, and up to New York always held something special for him. "I said, 'I'm gonna go to New York,'" Reed explained about the song's origin on *The Legend—The Man*. "I know I'm gonna have to go later…sooner *or* later. So, I'm gonna try my best to see can I make it up so I go to New York for somethin'…. I said, 'I don't care what anybody says. I'm not gonna rob and steal. I ain't gonna kill nobody to get to New York.' I said, 'But I'm goin' to New York. I'm goin' if I have to walk.' I'm gonna go to New York!"

Earl Phillips' playing is both subtle and heavy-handed. His left hand (playing grace notes on the snare) at times mirrors his right (stating the time on the hi-hat) so as to create a pitter-patter tapping. Phillips also plays the "hits"—hitting the accents—the musical spikes and dips created by Taylor and Biondi. Phillips uses all of the snare, and rim shots emanate. He plants his sticks dead center as he simultaneously pounds a floor tom for throaty resonance, and subtly changes the complexion and texture of the music by using the side stick during the opening verse. (Phillips also smashes what must be the trashiest-sounding crash cymbal in recorded blues history. Its short decay splatters all over Reed's harp solo.) With mathematical precision, Phillips follows, beats-for-notes, what Taylor and Biondi are playing on guitar right up until Reed begins singing at the song's opening. Phillips' beats also weave around Reed's vocals, sometimes landing squarely on the words.

Because of these tracks and the volume of hits Reed had amassed by the late '50s, Jimmy Reed was, for all intents and purposes, becoming as popular as a rock 'n' roll star. Elvis, Sam Cooke, and Chuck Berry all shared the R&B charts with him, and he was booked on national tours, independent of the Vee-Jay label's cavalcade of package tours. "Teddy Powell was a promoter who promoted all over the New York area and that would be cities from Buffalo, Newark, all over New Jersey, down to D.C., all over Virginia," says saxophonist Grady Gaines, bandleader of the Upsetters, perhaps best known for their association with Little Richard and Sam Cooke. (Gaines also claims to have appeared on the Clarence "Gatemouth" Brown classic "Dirty Work at the Crossroads"). "Henry Wayne was another promoter in Atlanta. Teddy Powell was the promoter in New York. Then when we changed territory—down into the Carolinas, Georgia, Alabama—it was Henry Wayne. They had territories, those promoters did. The same tour might have five or six promoters. We were playing behind all the acts on the tour, and sometimes we had ten to 15 acts on the bill. We would tour all over the country. It was like 45 or 55 days at a time, and certainly Jimmy Reed would be on some of those shows. We were playing armories and tobacco warehouses and big auditoriums and the biggest hall in the town we were coming through.

"On those tours, everywhere we go—playing to mixed crowds—Jimmy would tear up the house," Gaines says. "He held his own. Our main act would be people like Sam Cooke, maybe Little Willie John. But we played for all of them. Everywhere Sam Cooke would go, we would go, and he would be the headliner. They had people like Solomon Burke, Bo Diddley, the doo wop groups, and quite a few of them. Those were the types of people on the tour. Sam Cooke would be headlining and on other dates Jackie Wilson would be headlining. It was mostly people who had at least one hit record—whether it was doo wop groups or Jimmy Reed. They had it mixed up where it would be a variety of artists so if you came there would be something for everyone. We knew what the people liked, but we didn't know how big it was. That was the way it is a lot of the time."

Gaines says that he and the band would rehearse with Jimmy before the show went on, but Jimmy Reed, because he couldn't and wouldn't write out specific musical passages for the band, ensured his act didn't become stale. "He didn't hardly have no music," Gaines says. "If he wanted you to solo, or take a solo, or play some horn lines behind him, he would tell us. But as far as written music, he didn't have none of that. Jimmy might have had his rhythm section with him but he would use the horns out of the band. Whatever he needed, we were there to give it to him."

Jimmy was reaching both blacks and whites and his crossover was compared to Little Richard's, whom Gaines knows well. "Once I got in Richard's band, Richard really liked the way I played and I liked the way he played," Gaines says. "The way he played and the way I played sort of married one another, you know? It fall right together.... The music Richard was doing before he crossed over, before we recorded 'Tutti Frutti,' he wasn't doing that kind of music. He was doing mostly soul and blues-type music—we would call it rhythm and blues. And once we did 'Tutti Frutti,' that crossed him over all the way, and he knew the direction to go to stay there, where he would have a much wider audience. As far as the blues, though, the way I see it, Jimmy Reed was just as great as Muddy Waters. I know Muddy was first and I love Muddy, too. But all the local traveling bands, every band, big or small, black or white, all of them was playing Jimmy Reed stuff. Every little band in town was playing Jimmy Reed. Jimmy Reed was Jimmy Reed. And it was *black* music, you know?"

Jimmy Reed thought he was going to die. Al Smith and Calvin Carter kept shoving the paper in his face and he kept throwing it back at them. It was sheet music—music they wanted Jimmy Reed to record, to *cover*. Jimmy hated to record music written by anyone else. "Jimmy never wanted to do anybody else's tunes," Mary Lee Reed said in 1975 to *Living Blues.*

But it was a bit more than that.

The name of the tune was "Take Out Some Insurance," a catchy tune written by Charles Singleton and Waldense Hall.[vi] It scared the hell out of Jimmy. "Mama, every time any someone do a song like that, I don't know, they usually don't live long."

Nonetheless, on March 26, 1959, Reed went into the studio with Taylor, Lefty Bates, and Earl Phillips to record the song. Despite his reticence, Jimmy nails it. His laidback, mush-mouthed delivery soft-pedals the heaviness of the subject matter: "If you leave me baby/you say you won't be back /that would be the end of me/'Cause I'll have a heart attack.... You better get some insurance on me, baby/Take out some insurance on me, baby...'Cause if you ever, ever say goodbye, I'm gonna haul right off and die...."

Phillips' pitter-patter shuffle and his inconceivably laidback, laser-sharp approach (check his in-the-bucket feel in the stop break, which has his beats falling on the *four* and the "and" before the *one*) and the deep, soft bottom end plucked out by Taylor, along with Lefty Bates' splash of chords, opens a wide pocket. It is really one of the more effective, subtly raucous tunes Reed has ever recorded in his career. The song is in the key of *A* and Reed is using an *A* harp (first position) to accomplish the "feels so right" mood.

Jimmy was a deeply spiritual man, and he had been raised as a religious spirit. To him, recording such a song was tempting fate. And up until that point, it had been a mixed bag of success for Reed: he was scoring hits—not making money off them, but scoring them—and he had a pocketful of cabbage from his constant touring for a bottle of whiskey anytime he wanted it. Yet he was increasingly unreliable because of his drinking, and his epileptic seizures made him the object of ridicule, or so he thought. It was hard to say he was lucky, but for outsiders it must have appeared so, at least on the surface. But Reed was having serious doubts, and "Take Out Some Insurance" threw them up in his face.

"Jimmy was wild and drinking," says Little Arthur Duncan, who knew Jimmy Reed and Little Walter and soaked up jam sessions they'd have at Willie Foster's place on Chicago's Richmond Street. "He would get drunk in intermission and they would be looking for him and he would be in the bathroom somewhere laying on the floor. So, that wasn't interesting to me—to see, you know, how musicians do when they get drunk. Alcohol brings out real life in people. You might talk to me and I might seem like a nice guy. But the minute I start to drinking, I will tell you what I think about you that has been in my mind all the time. And that is what would happen to Jimmy sometimes."

Eddie Taylor used to tell a story about Reed when the two were touring through California. Jimmy was sitting on his amp and he was playing. Apparently, Jimmy had been happy (in a sense) before he ever got on the stage, and as he was playing he started to drift backwards. Eventually Jimmy tumbled over his own amp, sending his feet over his head. His shoes fell off and everyone onstage could see that he had worn socks without toes on them. When Eddie looked to his right, he did not see Reed standing there but Jimmy's feet with his toes wiggling up above the amp.

Reed sent himself, literally, head over heels. Even though he had already achieved a kind of popularity in his career, the next few years his fans would go head over heels for his music. The question was: Did Reed have the endurance to hold on to his fame, and was he clear-minded enough to stay straight? Some doubted it.

It was no secret that when Reed was on the road he might scope out women. If he had a good show (what he perceived as a good show), a good woman, some money in his pocket, and a big bottle of whiskey or wine, he didn't really need much else.

In 1959, however, Mama, perhaps having heard some of the stories about her husband when he was touring the country without her, decided to join him on his next tour.

In Dallas, at the annual state fair, with Big Tex's 52-foot-high freakish smile welcoming visitors, Jimmy was losing his focus. "I used to work for my father at the state fair in 1959," says Benno. "That was the first time I saw Jimmy Reed, inside the Cotton Club revue tent. He had on shoes that looked like a checkerboard, and asked his wife, 'Mama, where's my harp?' [She answered] 'Jimmy, yo harp is around yo neck!'"

Later in the show, Jimmy's problems appeared to continue. "Jimmy stepped up to the mike and, you know, just sort of had a burp-puke," Benno says. "He turned around and noticed the bass player was laughing at him. The bass player had a cigarette in his mouth and Jimmy told him, 'Hey, no smoking on the stage, *goddammit*."

Incredibly, Reed was able to maintain his stature as a viable artist and songwriter. Perhaps it was his support system, or some divine presence guiding him, but nothing seemed to stop him. Either way, when he broke out "Baby What You Want Me to Do," Calvin Carter knew he had a massive hit on his hands. (He even recorded two alternate takes of the song.)

Just before the take of this song, you can hear a debate over the title break out in the studio between Mama (staking her claim), Calvin, and Jimmy. No one can convince the other of the best fit. Calvin asks, "What's the name of this?"

"Ahhh..." Mama says, quite unsure.

"'You Got Me Doin' What You Want Me,'" Calvin decides.

"No," Reed mumbles.

Mama and Jimmy talk over one another, and she offers, "'Baby, What You Wanna Let Go?'" Unflinchingly, Calvin shouts, "'Baby, What You Want Me to Do.'" Mama and Jimmy aren't swayed and both speak at once. But Jimmy overpowers her with "'Baby…Baby, Why You Wanna Let Go?'"

"Yeah…" Mama says softly.

"You could even make it 'Why Let Go?'—make it short," Jimmy offers.

Calvin drops the issue and the tape rolls.

And Calvin wins, of course, but it is interesting to note that the words "baby, what you want me to do" are never sung. It is even more fascinating to know that Jimmy claimed Mama Reed was the inspiration for the title, having actually cited those very words as the impetus for recording the song. It is no surprise, then, that Mama has graduated to a full-fledged singer on this track, not a whispering coach—a *vocalist* who is harmonizing with Jimmy. She had earned it.

The song, in *E,* seems simple enough on the surface, but there are hidden complexities: Reed is in second position on an *A*-tuned harp and there is a funny chord change in bars nine and ten, twice flipping from the II chord to the V chord, where the standard blues pattern would go from V to IV.

There isn't a blues or rock 'n' roll band that doesn't know the lyrics: "You got me peepin'/you got me hidin'/you got me peep, hide, hide, peep, any way you wanna let it roll…. You got me doin' what you want me, baby why you wanna let go?"

By the year's close, Jimmy, Mary Lee Reed, Lefty Bates, Eddie Taylor, and Earl Phillips recorded "Please Don't," "Found Love," and "You Gonna Need My Help." Reed had been consistently charting hits from 1955 through the end of the decade, capping it off with Top 20 R&B hit "I Told You Baby" in early 1959—a track that was recorded on September 11, 1958, and would not be released on any of Reed's subsequent Vee-Jay LPs. It would be a sign of even greater things to come for Jimmy Reed, the songwriter and musician.

Though its title is neither spoken nor sung in the performance, VJ-333 became one of Jimmy Reed's biggest hits.

Chapter 4
I'm Mr. Luck

"Baby What You Want Me to Do" had reached the top ten of *Bill-board*'s Hot R&B Sides chart, and was still riding the charts into late February 1960. It peaked at No. 37 on *Billboard*'s Hot 100 pop chart for the leap-year issue date, and rival *Cash Box* listed the song for 12 weeks straight, beginning January 30, 1960. Reed sought to follow up that success by recording "Hold Me Close" (most notable for the appearance of Vee-Jay artist Curtis Mayfield on guitar and true harmonizing by Mama) in mid-March 1960, and in late March he followed that session up with one of his signature tunes.

The latter session, which occurred on March 29, 1960,[i] yielded "Come Love"—a slow- to mid-tempo dance number (with Mama's backing vocal adding a nice high-end dimension, singing the high *A* and *B* to Jimmy's lows of the same), "Meet Me," and what would become a signature Reed tune, "Big Boss Man."

Countless bands—rock 'n' roll and blues—have covered the song onstage and on record ever since its first appearance on Vee-Jay (B-side "I'm A Love You," aka "I'm Gonna Love You"). I mean, who doesn't recognize the refrain: "Big boss man, can't you hear me when I call? Well, you ain't so big, you just tall, that's all."

"You tell me what working person in America can't relate to 'Big Boss Man,'" quips blues singer Janiva Magness, who explains that she used Jimmy Reed's song "Found Love" in her wedding procession.

Is there a blues band on Earth that hasn't played "Big Boss Man"?

The genesis of "Big Boss Man" is a curious one. Al Smith and Luther Dixon are credited with writing the track, but Reed's input is undeniable and essential. When Smith wanted Reed to take his music in a different direction, the idea was to speed things up a bit—and get Jimmy doing things that he might not have done otherwise. In this respect, Smith achieved his goal. But at the outset, he wanted Jimmy to go way out. This was never going to happen.

In fact, years later Jimmy commented to guitarist Mike Henderson that with a buzz surrounding a certain song called "Try Me" by James Brown and the Flames, Al Smith wanted Jimmy to sound more like the soon-to-be Godfather of Soul. "They were trying to get me ahead," Jimmy told Mike. "They got me into the studio and they tried to make me do it a certain way—like James Brown—and I said, 'Nah, nah, nah, let me do it my way one time and see what you think of it.' " Well, Jimmy did it his wayand it stuck. No other version was needed.

The very structure and substance of the song seems to belie the song's writing credits. Reed referenced his incident on the McMurchy farm as a foundation for the lyrics, he told interviewer Norman Davis: "Al Smith...he say, 'You ought to do a song about [the] boss man,' " Reed said. "And when I got through with it, I made it, because so many things happened to me."

As further proof of Reed being the true writer of the song, Reed told record producer Calvin Carter the story that launched his diatribe about the boss man. "I don't know if you ever had a boss man," Reed said, "but I once had one.... That's just a guy be out in the field workin', Calvin, and you out there workin'...and the guy ridin' the horse, you know, up and down the field. He sitting up on the horse with his legs crossed lookin' at everybody just choppin' cotton like mad and all that. You thirsty and the water boy went [over] here somewhere and you can't find him, and you hollerin' at 'im, 'Hey, Mr. So and So.' You keep on calling, you know what I'm sayin'? Then you turn around and say, 'Well, now I *know* you hear me when I call ya. I'm right up on ya.' "

And Reed's words bear this out, as he sings: "You got me workin,' boss man/workin' 'round the clock/I wanna little drink a' wadder, but you won't let Jimmy stop."

And the song is in fact zippier than Reed's usual droning but infectious rhythm. Boasting three guitarists, a bassist, a backing vocalist, and a drummer, the session was graced by Willie Dixon on bass, drummer Earl Phillips, Lefty Bates and Lee Baker (Lonnie Brooks) on guitar, and Mama Reed on vocals—oddly enough, both backing and lead.

This was a common occurrence and in actuality doesn't undercut the perspective that Reed had a major part in writing the tune. Regardless, Mama did indeed speak the lyrics, so loudly in fact that she is a second vocal on the track. Red Holloway, who was part of the Vee-Jay house band, was in attendance for the session (though he didn't play on the song). "I was there," Holloway says, "and his wife would whisper him the lyrics—and she did for that song. I didn't record on the song, but I remember being around the studio when it happened. You know, we were the house band, so I got to see a lot of these types of things."

No doubt that Mary Lee's voice is heard on the track, in the background. She is in a support role, but perhaps not in the same way that some might think. While there is no doubt that she is coaching or supporting Reed on some of the lines, the fact is there are points where she drops out of the mix. Reed is heard alone, singing before she does. It almost sounds like *Jimmy* is coaching Mama on some of the lines.

Still, Mama's importance to Jimmy's writing technique should be undisputed. In fact, Mama was such an entrusted matriarch that she was practically a built-in writing partner and sounding board. Jimmy would sing his songs to her even before playing them for Calvin Carter, the engineers at Universal, or Al Smith. Close associates have imagined Mama's influence was as simple as this:

Well, Mama? What do ya think of it?

I don't like that one, Jimmy.

Well, I ain't gonna record that, then.

If he tried out all of his songs on Mama, then she had to know which one would be best to record and which one was a hit. She was right a lot of the time. Some speculate that Mama was the real talent of the Jimmy Reed experience. "Nothing Daddy ever did was done without Mama's approval," says Loretta Reed. "They worked so hard together. I mean, he was never by himself putting anything together. She was always by his side. I remember the rehearsal where we had to get up and go to school in the morning and they were up practicing and getting ready for that next session. She was always there, and that's why you started hearing her sing on some of those tunes. They decided to just leave her in [the mix]."

"The guy had that thing going for himself and he couldn't read and write too much," says Eddie Kirkland, John Lee Hooker's right-hand guitar man early in the Boogie Man's career. "His wife was a great writer, man. She was a blues writer, period. Everything she wrote for Jimmy, man, made money. I don't think [Reed] would have been as big in the music business as he was if it wasn't for her. He was a great harmonica player and a good guitar player, but you had to have someone write those songs for ya or know how to write those songs."

During the early summer of 1960, Reed went alone to the studio to record a slew of songs with Earl Phillips, Lefty Bates, and Phil Upchurch. Their combined efforts produced "I Got the Blues," "Sugar Sugar," "Got Me Chasing You," "Down on the Road," "Want to Be with You, Baby," "Jimmy's Rock," "Tell the World I Do," "You're My Baby," and "Ain't Gonna Cry No More"—all of which went unreleased at the time.

Reed was cutting songs so often that the only thing that kept his sessions from being just another day at the office was his sense of humor. "Reed was a funny guy," Phil Upchurch remembers. "He kept us in stitches. Calvin Carter would be in the session and Jimmy would have Calvin in tears rolling down his face. Jimmy Reed, man—some guys are just born funny, you know what I mean? He had this nasally Southern drawl, you know. [Imitates Reed] 'Now, Calvin, you know I can't get loose without my juice.' Or something like, 'Calvin, I'm gonna go to New York if I have to walk.' He would say things so humorously and they would wind up working themselves into songs."

Amid Reed's consistent hit-making success, "Found Love" hit *Billboard's* R&B charts at No. 16 in June 1960 (it lasted three weeks on the *Cash Box* singles charts), while the song "Hush Hush" scratched itself into *Billboard's* Top 20 R&B singles chart in October 1960 and earned a six-week occupancy on the *Cash Box* singles charts. "Hush Hush" was classic Reed. Like "Big Boss Man," Reed had a way of speaking his mind without coming across as an insensitive ass. Over the familiar loping groove, Reed sings: "Hush, hush. You just yakety yak all the time…if you don't stop yakkin' you gonna drive me outta my mind." His complaint is real, but the effect is comedic.

When in August 1960 Reed's second LP, *Found Love,* was released, it became the first blues record to crack the LP charts. *Cash Box* listed the LP 11 times on its charts, peaking at No. 35, over a 12-week period starting August 20, 1960. The album included songs such as "Baby, What You Want Me to Do," "Big Boss Man," "Going by the River (Parts 1 and 2)," "I Was So Wrong," "Where Can You Be?," "I'm Nervous" (from the same March 1959 session as "Take Out Some Insurance," which had gone unreleased until the issuing of the *Found Love* LP), and "I Ain't Got You," a song that was recorded in July 1955 but, like "I'm Nervous," was never released before it appeared on *Found Love*.

Found Love was simply a powerhouse record. It was a kind of greatest-hits album—having outsold Jimmy's hit-laden debut LP, *I'm Jimmy Reed*—without being labeled as such. It is also interesting to note that *Found Love* offers a smattering of influences and musical variations. The title song, for instance, is a kind of "Going to New York" vamp, one in which Reed blows and holds a harp note (a high *E*) for 17 seconds. Reed's playing here is very reminiscent of Sonny Boy Williamson I's style (in first position, in *E*), and the song features Eddie Taylor and Lefty Bates on guitar, Earl Phillips, and Mama Reed.

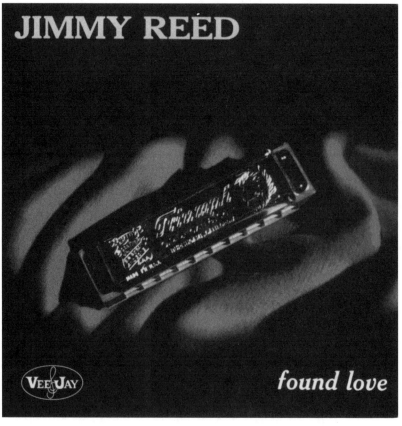

Reed's 1960 LP Found Love introduced Reed to many listeners.

"I'm Nervous" reprises a cheatin'-woman theme for Reed, accented by his distinctive descending vocal line: "I'm gettin' nervous, girl/you tryin' to give me a runaroun'." He shows some real vocal range, his voice falling from a steady, low-pitch mumble to an even deeper, throatier, muffled tone that is nearly smothered by his closeness to the mike.

We also hear the slow galloping beat of "I Was So Wrong" (courtesy of guitarists Upchurch and Taylor, while Phillips' near-comatose feel flips the accented backbeat from *two* and *four* on the snare to *one* and *three* during the harp solo, to no ill effect); the chunky, walking basslines of "Going by the River (Part 1)" (featuring Taylor, Bates, and bassist Marcus Johnson); and "Where Can You Be?" (a striking change of pace, with Upchurch's curt, short, and truncated bass rhythms mingling with the classic, gently rocking Reed boogie).

Despite the fact that Chicago blues was being systematically wiped off the map by commercial rock 'n' roll music, Jimmy Reed pushed on in the face of shifts in public taste and the recording industry. But Reed was not insulated from the perils of the business in the early '60s. He had lost his good friend, for a brief time.

Eddie Taylor needed a break. Never seeing eye-to-eye with Jimmy (about most things), Taylor had grown tired of playing second fiddle to Reed and the long, grueling touring schedule, which didn't seem to be getting him anywhere. He could just as easily stay in town and earn money. Of course, it wouldn't be as much money, but it would have to do. It wasn't good-bye forever, but good-bye for now. So, while Reed played clubs like DeLisa in Chicago and Tenkely Hall in Indiana's East Chicago, Eddie "Big Time Playboy" Taylor was scheduled to perform with his own band.

Jimmy shrugged it off. He had gigs to do—at the Brevoort Theater in Brooklyn, New York, in the fall of 1960, and other East Coast dates, and then back into the studio in December. Reed and crew (including Taylor) recorded "Close Together," "You Know You're Looking Good," "Laughing at the Blues," and "I'm A Love You." "Close Together" was a noisy, jangly, atmospheric gem with Mama Reed's coaching vocal accompaniment and Lefty Bates' near-dissonant chords fighting Eddie Taylor's "lump." And "Laughing at the Blues" is the perfect Jimmy Reed song: the very title sums up Jimmy's musical outlook (though not his mental outlook), which also sums up the feeling his audiences had come to expect from him.

"I never did name any one of my records a blues," Reed told *Living Blues* quite incorrectly, though the sentiment is what's important. "After all, everybody else called my sounds what I made the blues. I always felt good behind 'em. I didn't feel like I was playin' no blues."

In early January 1961, Reed, Phillips, Bates, and bassist Quinn Wilson were set to record with John Lee Hooker for what would be the Vee-Jay LP *The Folklore of John Lee Hooker* (originally released as *The Country Blues of John Lee Hooker*). Charles Shaar Murray, Hooker's biographer, described the record as a "Frankenstein patch-job." One would be hard-pressed to find a better, more suitable description. These tracks were recorded in between Hooker's contract negotiations with Vee-Jay, so the LP is composed of songs from different sources. (Songs that led off each side of the original LP, "Tupelo" on the A-side and "The Hobo" on the B-side, were recorded at Freebody Park at the Newport Folk Festival in June 1960.) Some of these tracks are solo studio pieces and some with a band, while others are live as a solo act or with a band. One track is very nearly traditional Euro-folk mixed with a bit of blues ("Take Me As I Am"). And the album's title is fitting, since Hooker was retooling his image as a "folk singer" at this period. (For some of these tracks, Hooker was playing an *unamplified* acoustic guitar.)

Hooker's new "direction" as a "folkie" was met with mixed reaction, and some critics thought the album lacked the fire of earlier sides. Perhaps, but to suggest that there was anything safe about his presentation is to ignore the ever-present Hooker anger that surfaces in a song like "I'm Mad Again"—a revisit of the Specialty side "I'm Mad" (the Motor City bluesman had re-recorded this tune under different names throughout his career). "I'm Mad Again" portrays Hooker as the victim of his woman's infidelity. He trusted his friend, even brought him into his house, only to discover his down-on-his-luck buddy has made his wife a two-timer. But Hooker won't be the sucker for long. He's got a plan to get back at 'em he just doesn't know when. He's mad with his buddy, mad "like Al Capone." (Hooker's taunting, self-satisfied, and maniacal laugh is worth the price of admission alone.)

Reed appears on one song on harp and guitar, and he *might* appear on "Want Ad Blues" as a guitarist, not as a harp player. This would make sense, since the structure of the song is consistent with a Reed rockin'-boogie beat.

Vee-Jay has Reed credited to four songs on this record (including "I'm Mad Again"), but this seems unrealistic given the fact that the sound is just too empty. Where's Reed in the mix? Could it be that his playing mingles so seamlessly with Lefty's, Quinn's, and Hooker's that it is nearly invisible? What would be the point of that? It is easier to believe that Reed appears on only two songs: "Want Ad Blues" (a Hooker romp in *E* in which he sings about trolling the newspaper for love) and "Hard-Headed Woman."

In the latter, Reed's harp playing is weak and marred by barely audible crybaby tremolo. However, that can be accounted for very easily. Hooker's fast-paced boogie (fast-paced as compared to Reed's own loping grooves) wouldn't have meshed well with Reed's upper-register honking—a trademark that Reed, entrenched in his well-proven style, wouldn't have tossed aside. Besides, whenever Reed blew the harp, he usually stole the songs. So, Reed sounds *consciously* restrained; he barely makes an interesting attempt at going toe-to-toe with Hooker amid his mumbles, yelps, screams, and biting commentary. (One would think this would be a fertile field for creative harp blowing but, alas, it isn't.) In short, there could have been better interplay here, and it's a lost opportunity.

If the Hooker sessions were more of a distraction than a career push, then Reed got back on track within a matter of weeks. By February of 1961 Reed's "Close Together" was a No. 12 hit on the *Billboard* R&B singles charts (it also garnered a four-week stay on the *Cash Box* singles charts, having peaked at No. 77). On its heels was "Big Boss Man"—recorded nine months earlier—which rocketed to No. 13 on *Billboard's* Hot R&B Sides chart. ("Big Boss Man" also scored on the magazine's Hot 100 chart, reaching No. 78 in mid-June, while staying on the *Cash Box* singles charts for three weeks beginning June 10.)

More chart success and record sales would follow. In March of 1961, a Jimmy Reed LP entitled *Now Appearing* included most of the tracks recorded during the June and December 1960 sessions, but not the ill-fated "Sugar Sugar" and "That's It." *Now Appearing* broke another barrier for the blues in the pop world when it squeaked under the No. 50 mark of the *Cash Box* album charts. It came in at No. 49 and stayed in that position three of the four weeks it registered.

On the record's cover, Jimmy Reed's name was lit up on a faux venue marquee in sharp contrast to the dark-night backdrop. Reed's blues was definitely attracting attention, and Reed seemingly could do no wrong. Every batch of songs he recorded had at least one song the public saw fit to make a hit. Perhaps one of the reasons that Jimmy Reed's song was so popular—besides the fact that he struck a nerve that every 9-to-5er can relate to—was the manner in which he said it. The "pop" chart was just a synonym for "white mainstream" audience. Reed was able to cross over in a way that eluded other Chicago bluesmen like Howlin' Wolf, Muddy Waters, Little Walter, and others in the Chess Records label crew.

One can only speculate how hip-hop acts like 50 Cent and the Game would have been received in decades past: Would they even exist without Reed and his Chess brothers? Reed was a *black* entertainer, plucking words from his soul. He never came off as angry in his music—and this is key. While Muddy was busy being the "hoochie coochie man," and the wild-eyed, thick-necked, iron-fisted Wolf was knocking at your back door, and Sonny Boy Williamson II was the archetypal disinterested, heavy-drinking, cantankerous blues bastard, Reed didn't outwardly appear to be strapped by all that Delta angst. After all, his major "protest" song is *pleading* with the boss man to hear him.

The fascination with Wolf, Muddy, and even John Lee Hooker is their *mannishness,* the inherent *meanness* in their delivery. In short, they presented themselves as badasses, whether this was true or not. Conversely, Reed rarely forced misogynistic nightmares onto the audience, nothing even close to the heaviness of "I'm a man/I made 21...." Reed didn't attack the listener and his fans with his music, and because of this he may have been more acceptable to a wider, whiter audience.

Reed could have been the guy who sidled up to the bar and drank a couple of beers with you—and often was. He was certainly different from other so-called bluesmen, both musically and as an individual. "All of them—Muddy Waters, Howlin' Wolf, Little Walter, Sonny Boy—they were in some way associated with Chess Records," explains Jimmy Reed, Jr. "Chess Records at that time was *the* blues label. Daddy was a national and international star." "His determination was to play the music he wanted to play," adds Loretta. "It was like when he first went to Chess Records. They wanted him to be part of the group, which he never really was."

"It was Jimmy Reed and T-Bone Walker and Martin Luther King for me, really and truly," blues-rocker Steve Miller told *Blues Access*. "The music definitely broke down barriers way before the law did or before Martin Luther King did. Guys like Jimmy Reed were making people think. A lot of people weren't thinking of it in terms of race and segregation, they weren't thinking about it at all, except they liked the music and danced to it and they got down to it."

Reed's follow-up recording session was fruitful. The batch of songs recorded produced two bona fide hits and provided the guts of one of Reed's most beloved LPs, *At Carnegie Hall*. (More on that in a moment.) As usual with Reed, a strange circumstance blossomed into a hit record. Dazzled by the streetlights of many a Southern city while he was on a brief tour, Reed was struck with lyrics; words and images just seemed to manifest. He could hardly see in front of him as he sped down the road in his car, saying "these lights sure is bright." And the basis of a song emerged. He couldn't get the experience out of his head, and when he returned to Chicago Reed explained to Mama what had happened to him on the road, according to *The Legend— The Man*:

"I'm gonna write me a song about these bright lights and all that," Jimmy told Mary Lee.

Mama looked at him quizzically and suspiciously. She didn't know what Jimmy was talking about and thought perhaps he had lost his mind (again) and was letting his slobbering mouth, one that had been thoroughly washed with alcohol, run a bit too long.

"What'cha mean? These lights 'round here in the house?"

Jimmy answered: "No, but in some city I come through the lights were so bright till you couldn't hardly see how to drive...." Mary immediately knew the direction the song should take: "Name that song 'Bright Lights and Big City,'" she told her husband. Jimmy would later give complete credit to Mama for her contribution. "So, she jumped in there, just like Al [Smith] done did about this 'Boss Man' thing. And she started helpin' me write that thing, word for word—'Bright Light [sic] and Big City.'"

It should be no surprise given Mama's contribution that her voice is as strong and transparent on this song as any other (save "Big Boss Man"). At times she overpowers Jimmy's voice and even fills in gaps in the vocal lines when Jimmy drops out of the mix periodically.

Jimmy had "Mama" Reed to thank for this smash hit.

"The bright lights, big city—they've gone to my baby's head...I've tried to tell the woman, but she don't believe a word I say."

While the lyrics create a small confusion and even contradiction at times, the main gist is Jimmy is trying to warn his woman against the seduction of the big city, but she just won't or can't hear him. Maybe she is too far gone with the notion. Or, perhaps there is still hope, as Reed sings: "I still love you, baby, 'cause you don't know what it's all about."

The harp solo follows the basic flow of the chorus, which runs along, roughly, a I-V-IV (G6-Dm7-C) chord sequence, passing through the III chord (B flat). Reed was playing a B-flat harp in first position here. It is nearly childish in its simplicity, but that is its strength. It's irresistible, and lulls the listener.

Google the song title and marvel at the amount of hits you'll get. "Bright Lights, Big City" is so associated with Jimmy Reed that even if he didn't coin the phrase (historians and etymologists can correct me, but the concept, if not the exact term, has been around for hundreds of years, as far as I can tell)—then he certainly cemented it in the psyche of American popular culture. A diverse cross section of American and European artists would take a stab at the song—from Them (with Van Morrison), Neil Young, and the Animals (for a gritty and manic take), to Count Basie and his Orchestra and Bill Cosby (on his 1967 half-serious/half-spoof record *Silver Throat*). "Bright Lights, Big City" was also chosen as the title of Jay McInerney's 1984 fiction masterpiece (which, in 1988, was turned into a major motion picture starring Michael J. Fox and Kiefer Sutherland). The title was quite fitting, given the main character's desperation and search for substance in the alluring and wicked big city (New York City, in that case).

But none of these works captured the same coolness, sense of omnipotence, and maturity that Reed portrays through his song. He's been through the big city and knows how treacherous, dangerous, and seductive it can be.

In the spring of 1961, Reed was on tour yet again. Among other East Coast venues, he made a stop at Carnegie Hall in New York City. As

Jimmy had done dozens and dozens of times before, he was out on a multi-act bill. On May 13, he happened to be sharing the stage with Muddy Waters, Big Maybelle, Oscar Brown, Jr., and Jimmy Witherspoon (shades of the Spirituals to Swing concert of 1938 organized by John Hammond, Sr.). Advance tickets, being hawked at record stores around the city, ranged from $2.00 to a whopping $3.85!

A flier from a star-studded 1961 Carnegie Hall show.

The quality of the performances at Carnegie Hall that night is lost to time (though Reed's playing couldn't have been anything less than adequate, as he was invited back). It is stunning to learn that *no* professional recordings of the performance exist. That's shocking on two levels: given the stars at that show it would have been a coup for any label to have waxed these performances, and Jimmy Reed's *At Carnegie Hall*—soon to be released—was, by its very title, supposedly recorded at the May 13 show. It wasn't. In fact, the track listing for this double album was built on prior Reed hits and freshly recorded songs never put on LP before.

Calvin Carter always maintained after the performance that the record was indeed cut at Carnegie Hall. Being the business and marketing man he was, Carter knew that any leaked info casting doubt on the record's authenticity would seriously hurt sales. Vee-Jay knew they would have a hit if they combined Jimmy Reed's best music with the excellence associated with Carnegie Hall, packaged with album artwork (soon to be iconic) featuring a hollow-bodied electric guitar leaning against an empty chair on a concert stage. Vee-Jay got their hit, but it was based on an illusion that traded on the respectability of the Reed gig at Carnegie Hall.

"We didn't say 'Jimmy Reed *Live* at Carnegie Hall,'" Carter told interviewer Mike Callahan. "I thought we could get to use the name, because at the time Carnegie Hall was a very big name in the music business for all your classical and opera stars...."

Carter expressed doubt that anyone would come to see Reed: "I doubt if we could have got ten people in New York to see Jimmy Reed in those days; we could sell him in Newark [New Jersey] and other places, but we could not sell him in New York."

These assertions were blatantly false in every respect, of course. Jimmy played the Hall more than once, whether Carter ever admitted it or not. Furthermore, as of this writing, Carnegie Hall has no record of the tracks being recorded there (a thorough check of the Hall's booking ledger revealed this). Since there is no paper trail, it is unlikely that the record was actually recorded in the Hall at all—live or otherwise. Though not entirely impossible, it is highly probable that Jimmy Reed did, as later liner notes state, record *At Carnegie Hall* in New York's Bell Studios and Chicago's Universal *to re-create* his Carnegie set.

Carter was right about one thing, however: the marketing ploy worked, and its timing couldn't have been better. The song "Bright Lights, Big City" was included on the Carnegie Hall LP and spent seven weeks on the *Cash Box* singles charts (after having fallen off for three weeks) beginning in mid-September 1961. *Billboard* also tracked the song's success: it peaked at No. 58 on the pop charts, after being on the charts for six weeks, and it lingered on the *Billboard* Hot 100 singles chart until the early months of 1962.

The flip side of the "Bright Lights" single—"I'm Mr. Luck" (which also appears on *At Carnegie Hall*)—is almost as intriguing. It reveals Reed's unique shade of masculine cool, a restrained one in which he acknowledges his magic touch (and hopes you will, too), as well as his struggle to overcome adversity. It was bragging, but Reed didn't beat it into you. He asked for one simple acknowledgment: tip your hat to him and call him "Mr. Luck." (The title is as much soaked in bittersweet irony as pure fact. Despite Reed's personal problems, he was having unparalleled success as a blues entertainer.)

At Carnegie Hall, released in September 1961, crawled its way up the charts to a respectable No. 41 at its peak. *Cash Box* charted its course, and showed the LP as appearing eight times, falling off the chart once for only one week and then re-entering at a higher position, from early October 7, 1961, through nearly the end of that fall. While it is difficult to track sales of the record, sources have noted the LP sold nearly 500,000 copies.

Reed's success was stretching across the northern border of the US. Toronto was a staple on the chitlin circuit, and many of America's premier blues talents came through town and were being played on local radio there and throughout Canada. "Probably my greatest and most influential album was *Jimmy Reed at Carnegie Hall,*" says David Clayton-Thomas, best known for fronting Blood, Sweat & Tears. "The double set with the chair and guitar on the cover. And that was a priceless album. Playing in garage bands in my late teens and early twenties, having a working knowledge of 'peepin' and 'hidin' and 'Big Boss Man' and Jimmy Reed material was really important. We were playing a lot of that

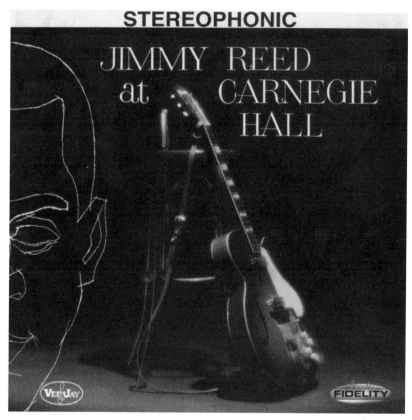

At Carnegie Hall has become one of Jimmy Reed's most influential recordings.

stuff in our sets. Every guitar player learned to play the basic Jimmy Reed lick. The basic dah-da-da-dah, da-dah da-dah, you know what I mean? The first lick that a young guitarist could learn because he could play it with two fingers, you know what I mean? So, Jimmy Reed was very influential."

"The first time I had heard Jimmy Reed I was living in Toronto," says Downchild Blues Band's Donnie Walsh, whose songwriting talents Dan Akroyd and John Belushi tapped for their 1978 Blue Brothers record, *Briefcase Full of Blues.* "I was maybe 16? I went to my girl-friend's birthday party, and I got there a little later than most people— it was like everybody was already there. Do you remember the old stereos? There was one of those in the living room.... All the guys were standing around the record player playing Jimmy Reed's *At Carnegie Hall.* I had never heard him, or anything. I went, 'What the hell is this?'

I wouldn't let anyone play any other records all night…. Then I went out and bought that album. I had one of those old record players—which was good, and portable—and it would stack records one on top of another. The first one goes down and plays and then the second one goes down and plays all night. I had that on every night and every waking hour and every waking moment I wasn't at work."

If *At Carnegie Hall* marked a kind of high point for Reed musically, medically he was starting to show chinks in his armor. According to *Living Blues,* Mama said Jimmy had "about 12 seizures in a row" while he was cutting the songs for what would become *At Carnegie Hall.* Reed was even on his medication—as long as people like Mama, Eddie Taylor, and Al Smith were around. But if they weren't, of course, or if they believed that Jimmy was telling the truth about taking his medicine (even if he wasn't taking his prescribed dosage), then he'd have the violent episodes.

Because Reed's epilepsy medicine was a depressant, when combined with alcohol it made the poor man dazed at times.[ii] Many Reed fans had no knowledge of his medical problem; they thought some of his whacky behavior could be chalked up to alcohol abuse, or worse. The truth is, Reed preferred to stay drunk most of the time because he thought it would keep his epileptic seizures at bay.

"[Jimmy] would swallow his tongue and you could tell when he was going there [about to have a seizure]," guitarist Lonnie Brooks explains. "He was lisping and you could tell he was going there. When he would drink he would come out [of it]…. The drinking kept him straight—or so he thought. When he would drink, he thought that would calm him down." (But in fact, according to a paper published in the medical journal *CNS Drugs* in 2003, "the seizure threshold is raised by alcohol drinking and declines on cessation of drinking.")

Reed undoubtedly saw the conundrum that was his medical situation: if he continued to drink he would be in a perpetual stupor and surely unable to perform at 100 percent; if he didn't drink at all, so he thought, he would suffer from the worst seizures of his life. (Reed wasn't too far off the mark; he was susceptible to *alcohol withdrawal seizures* if he quit drinking cold turkey.)[iii]

Reed made the rounds in the Chicago public and Veteran's Administration hospitals—Edward Hines, Jr., Downey, Provident (on the South Side), and St. Luke's. After doctors examined Reed they asked if he would commit to being checked in for a longer period of time. He declined. He had shows to do, records to cut. Jimmy Reed may have been "Mr. Luck," as he sang in a song celebrating his music chart success, but his act was starting to suffer. One show in Texas was a perfect example of Reed being out of sorts:

Three friends caught his show at a Houston nightclub called Van's. "The nightclub was on the far north side of Houston," remembers David Burns. "The place had a horrible reputation. That was the very first place I carried a gun to. Not because I was afraid of Jimmy Reed, but because I was well aware what frequently happened there—the melees, and innocent bystanders being injured. I was not up for that. I would never be an innocent bystander. I'm gonna participate one way or another."

"Van's is what we might call a honky tonk around here," Charles White says. "The type of place you'd hear country music. It was in a redneck neighborhood—it was a white nightclub. Early '60s in this part of the country was in the more agonizing part of the civil rights movement. There was a lot of hostility, and segregation of the races in liquor joints was pretty much a doggone rule. You wouldn't dare take a woman in that place because there was no telling what might happen."

As Dave Burns, Charles White, and Art Dietz remember, they were packing in more ways than one. "The counterculture was stirring—so some of the recollections may not be as clear as they should be," admits White. "We were drinking beer and I think maybe even Charles brought a bottle," remembers Burns. "We were drinking beer—at least I was—and enjoying everything. People were dancing and having a good time.

"Actually, I wasn't old enough to be in the bar that night," Burns reveals. "Things were somewhat lax in those days. If you weren't dressed in a beanie and knee britches they would let you in and sell you a beer."

Reed was scheduled for two performances that night (at 8:00 P.M. and 11:00 P.M.), and though they were partying already, long before

Reed showed, the crowd in this honky tonk with a reputation was becoming antsy…and angry. Where was Jimmy Reed?

"Jimmy didn't show and he didn't show and he didn't show and he didn't show," Burns says. "The owner kept going around saying it was his fault and that the man who was handling his booking said he'd be here. Knowing Houston traffic, it was bad even then, I said, 'We don't know that he is not over there in the daggum hospital because of a car wreck or something.' The owner said, *'He better be.'*

"I think [the owners] had given him the money up front," Burns continues. "The owner had sold a lot of tickets and people wanted their money back. He was three hours late and he still hadn't showed."

"If I remember anything it was way later than it was supposed to be," chimes in Art Dietz. "I was in no shape to even know what was going on other than that."

Finally, Reed showed up, and the crowd that was becoming a little less civil by the moment started to quiet down. " I think it was nearly four hours before he showed up—*late*," Burns says. "When he finally showed up, that man was wasted."

It is worth noting here that Reed's lateness and demeanor could very well have been due to his epilepsy. Without solid evidence—only Burns' assertion that it appeared as though Reed might have been medicated—it seems logical to think that Reed might have had seizures before the show and taken something to combat them. It must be remembered that the drugs Reed was taking for epilepsy were depressants. Mix that with disorientation, a whirlwind ride over to the nightclub, and perhaps alcohol, and it might appear as though he was heavily drugged.

"I didn't know about his epilepsy, but it looked like he was totally wasted," says White. "I do know that he was very, very late. All bars closed at midnight then and there was no 2:00 A.M. law. No one o'clock on Saturday. Bars closed at midnight —that was it. So, he completely missed the entire first performance and he didn't show up until just about the time his second performance was supposed to start, which was right around 11:00 P.M. As it turned out, the 8:00 P.M. show started a little bit before 11:00 P.M. And it was not a real long show."

"The performance was good," Burns notes. "I was surprised, because the way he was acting—it was surprising that he sounded exactly as he did on the record. It was not a long set, but it was pretty satisfying, which was exactly what he had done on the records. He was pretty out of it, but he still did a good job.

"I remember when we left, that place was about to shut down," Burns adds. "I remember telling the guy at the door that when the second show started we had to go. It was pretty obvious at that point, though, that there wasn't going to be a second show."

Reed showing up late for performances was not unique. When he went on the road in the early '60s, he would take with him the jazz band Al Smith had assembled a few years earlier: Von Freeman, Wayne Bennett, drummer Phil Thomas, a trumpet player named Shaky, and Al, who was the bass player and bandleader. For several different reasons Jimmy would sometimes be late to the venue, and the crowds could be brutal when Jimmy wasn't around. The band would play jazz to entertain the audience and stretch out, which they were not always allowed to do in the sets with Reed. "The people would be angry and asking for Jimmy Reed," said piano player Jodie Christian in conversation with the late Charles Walton. "One time the people were about to attack the four of us but Jimmy showed up in time to save us."

Working Chicago's jazz clubs, Christian had no idea that this bluesman was crossing over and touching so many people, white and black. But Christian and the rest of the band would soon learn, as Reed became increasingly popular each time they went out on tour. Despite the crowd response, some in the band felt like men without a country. They were jazz guys and some, Christian in particular, didn't know what they were doing out on the road with someone like Reed—in the South no less, where the civil rights movement was just in its infancy. "Each time we went out on the road with Jimmy Reed we, the band members, would say this would be the last time," Christian said.

Von Freeman had a different view. "Me, Jodie Christian, and Phil Thomas—we're all like beboppers, really," Freeman says. "I be sitting up there—a trained horn player, man—and they wouldn't even be paying attention to you. Jimmy hit one note on that thing, man, and they would go crazy. Essentially, when we were traveling with him all through the South, we would just be merely playing the way we were playing in Chicago. Al [Smith] didn't mind, because with Jimmy, the fact is, the way we played enhanced him, really. He'd come up there with a differ-ent thing altogether—a lot of backbeat and shuffle. Jimmy liked it. Jimmy told me numerous times. He said to me: 'I like the way you play that jazz.' I'd say, 'I like to make this money the way you make it.' He cracked up, you know. He said, 'You could do it if you wanted to.' I said, 'Not really.' He could make those hits, man. A lot of people turn their head up at that, but that is a gift."

The band would stay together for a few years. They would travel up North (northern New York and western New York, such as Buffalo), Connecticut, and Maine, as well as the Deep South. All it would take was for "Svengali" Smith to say the magic word, and the band members would assemble at a moment's notice, pile into Smith's station wagon, and hit the road.

Smith knew the crowds loved the band, and if they got a whiff of something funny about Reed, whether a medical condition like epilepsy or a disease like alcoholism, they didn't seem to mind. Veteran piano player Walter Price remembers Reed coming through Houston and Lake Charles and Opelousas, Louisiana, and garnering the usual reac-tion from the audience. "There would be times when he would be so loaded, but people loved him anyway," says Price. "That didn't make no difference. The places were packed—wall to wall—you couldn't get nobody else in the places."

Richard Banks, a Houston-based guitar player, remembers dancing to Jimmy Reed music at Brick Hollow Country Club in Dallas in one of his swings through Texas in the early '60s. "There was a program on WRR-AM radio in Dallas at night, 'Kats Karavan,' and the theme song was 'Ends and Odds'—the instrumental version of 'You Don't Have to Go.' So, from a young age I was aware of Jimmy Reed…. He had such a strong impact on the white kids at a time when there was disfavor among our parents for black music in general. I think he was the most popular black musician who played anything approaching true blues, of the time. He followed a straight 12-bar blues progression pretty reli-giously, but he had the variations for 'Honest I Do'—he did a couple songs with that progression…. It was kind of a I-V-V-I kind of thing. At that time a lot of young bands played Jimmy Reed songs—it was just something you *had* to cover."

Banks, like so many other young music enthusiasts who would turn professional musician—particularly in Texas—saw Reed at a local club. "I remember the venue well, it was Lou Ann's in Dallas," says Banks, who is on the board of the Houston Blues Society. The place has now burned down, unfortunately, but I actually saw Jimmy there on several occasions. Jimmy always had Mama Reed with him, and yes, she was whispering words in his ears. She was standing right next to him onstage and telling him the words. He was playing that old Kay guitar he used to play. He could have afforded a Fender, I think…. Or maybe it was a good guitar. But I don't think anyone *then* thought it was a good guitar. I don't think anyone *today* thinks it is a good guitar. Apparently, he just liked using it."

"When I was 14 my band backed up Jimmy Reed at Lou Ann's," explained Steve Miller to *Blues Access.* "I never really did get to talk to him. I didn't even think he was even going to be able to play [because he had been drinking so much]. He was almost unconscious before he hit the stage. He had this black guy with him [Al Smith], who was sort of his roadie who ran the band, and we were just little kids wearing seersucker suits and Ray Charles sunglasses, trying to be cool."

In 1962 Vee-Jay released *The Best of Jimmy Reed,* a single LP that matched song for song the "B" record of the previous year's double LP *At Carnegie Hall.* To support the record, Jimmy was on the road once again, and making a few swings through his favorite areas: Texas and Oklahoma. Though road manager Al Smith was not with him on this trip, Mama Reed kept Jimmy straight—as straight as could be expected.

Johnnie Wood, a Dallas-based bass player who had played with Freddie King, Roscoe Gordon, and others including jazz artists like Sonny Stitt and Marcel Ivery, remembers working with Jimmy. "I was with Lattimore Brown at the time, so we basically would back Jimmy up when he came through," says Wood. "We did this a number of times. We played the Empire Room, the Zanzibar, the Longhorn Ballroom. Then he would go to Tyler, Waco, they loved him up in there, too. Then some up in Oklahoma…Tulsa, Oklahoma City, Norman—the college up in there. I think he was around here [in this area] for a few months one time, right around the time of that greatest-hits record, and then he left and went back to Chicago.

It was nothing but three pieces up there, man. Bass and drums, and him," Wood recalls. "I'll tell you one thing: everywhere we went it was crowded, it was loud, and I think the best people in town came out. Jimmy performed well. As a matter of fact, as soon as he started playing they would run to the dance floor.

"Jimmy was a real nice guy," Wood continues. "He would come by the house just about every day. In fact, every time we'd look up, there was Jimmy. You know, he'd have a little nip, then hang out with the guys. We weren't gigging or nothing, but he'd come over to the apartment and hang out with us. He weren't a ladies' man too much—his wife was with him. I told Jimmy and his wife, Mary, that I started with a blues band in my teens and all we did was play Jimmy Reed stuff, Howlin' Wolf and all these guys, Muddy Waters. I would take that music home, listen at that bass, and got goddamn pretty close. So, it wasn't nothing to me to get right on it. So, [Mary Lee] liked me."

When it was time to head back into the studio, the Jimmy Reed recording band was morphing. Drummer Earl Phillips had been replaced by session and touring great Al Duncan, and a young Jimmy Reed, Jr. (he was only 13 at the time of the sessions), was making his first appearances on record with his dad. Junior, or Boonie, as he was called (a nickname given to him by his parents; he admits he doesn't know what it means), was a shoo-in.

Jimmy, Sr,. already had Mama on the sidelines and in the studio with him, and Junior was just the next in line to carry on a family tradition. Instead of tapping Eddie Taylor again, Jimmy thought the time was right to give a chance to his son, who had made his stage debut with his dad when he was just nine years old. Besides, Eddie was playing more and more with his own band at Pepper's Lounge in Chicago, trying to get something started for his solo career as a separate entity from Reed—or, more specifically, sidestepping listeners' perceptions of him as simply a player in Reed's backing band. (In the near future, Taylor would frequently work with Floyd Jones and eventually find his way to the stage with Paul Butterfield at places like Silvio's in Chicago.) Al Smith, overseeing the musicians on the session as he had for years, knew he needed a good replacement for the Chicago rhythm guitar king Taylor, and gave the green light to Junior for the session. Junior had internalized Reed's music for years, and who better to pick up where Taylor left off than a blood relative of Reed's? With Lefty Bates as a guide, this band could do no wrong.

Enter Al Duncan. Duncan was known around Chicago as the groove man, the guy who could lay it down without frills and still inject a pleasing, rhythmic lilt. He had played with the Impressions, Little Walter, and John Lee Hooker, and although Reed had played with Duncan on the road, he was not comfortable recording with him at first. "See, nobody give [Jimmy] the beat like Earl Phillips," Eddie Taylor once said.[iv]

So, it was Reed, Lefty, Junior, Phil Upchurch, Mama Reed, and Duncan who were on the 1962 sessions—three over a number of days—that created "Good Lover," "I'll Change My Style" (words and music by David Parker and Manuel Villa; often appears as "I'll Change That, Too"), "Let's Get Together," "Down in Mississippi," "Take It Slow," "In the Morning," "Back Home at Noon," "Kansas City Baby," "You Can't Hide," "Too Much," and "Oh, John." ("Down in Mississippi," recorded in the same session as "Take It Slow" and "Good Lover," would appear on a Vee-Jay best-of compilation, *The Boss Man of the Blues Jimmy Reed…With More of the Best,* along with "Oh, John" and the burning-throated "Too Much," written by Oscar Boyd.)[v]

"I'll Change My Style" is perhaps the least Reed-like of all the tunes he ever recorded, but it was still a major hit with fans. The organ acts as a rudder for the entire tune, backed by the horns that labels like Stax would make their trademark just a few short years later. The song kicks in with Reed singing a cappella in the left channel (the right is dead until the organ kicks in). Upchurch's bass is unmistakable and very necessary, whereas in the past the basslines on Jimmy's tunes could have easily been played by six-string guitar.

Reed sings like a wounded bird: "I'll change my walk/even change my talk/if there is something about my kisses that don't please you/tell me, oh, tell me and I'll change that, too."

What is remarkable about these sessions is that some of the songs have a "bop" (though not as in bebop) and less of a "lump." For anyone who said Jimmy's music didn't progress, here was living proof. The rhythm chords were accented completely differently from those of the earlier Vee-Jay material.

"Take It Slow," with its standard Jimmy Reed turnaround (*A–A sharp–B*) and Mama Reed backing vocals, possesses a kind of trashy beauty. Al Duncan swings on a ride cymbal to state the time, which is very uncharacteristic of a Reed tune. Former drummer Earl Phillips would normally use the hi-hat throughout the verses and chorus to push the song along. Here, it is the drummer who holds the song together and plays what resembles a Reed "lump," rather than the rhythm guitarist. Junior softly cuts chords. (It should be noted that the guitars *do* play the classic rocking Reed rhythm at points, with varying degrees in volume and frequency.) The tune was an obvious run-up to a future and superior Reed hit, "Shame, Shame, Shame," recorded a year later.

On "In the Morning" Jimmy showed his irritation with this band. The song revs up, quickly, in a "Big Boss Man" mold, and Jimmy is playing taut squeaks. A very peppy Reed indeed. Jimmy doesn't like what he hears. "Ho' it, hold it. Eh, too fast. It's too fast. We gotta put it between there," we hear him say. Mama Reed mumbles something inaudible and her words are cut short. It's difficult to tell if she was being supportive or trying to push Jimmy in a different direction, as Calvin and no doubt Al Smith would have liked to do. As it turns out, Jimmy Reed is just Jimmy Reed. The Boss Man wins, and the song reverts to the slow groove. The idea to put the beat somewhere "in between" what was originally played and what was normally heard and felt as "Jimmy's" tempo doesn't come into it. It's the same ole Jimmy. Not a very remarkable song, aside from it being cut from the traditional cloth of a 1950s R&B vocal with heavy echo.

"Oh, John" was one of those inspirational tracks that had an idiosyncratic exchange between Jimmy and Calvin. "Oh, John" is perhaps one of the most misunderstood songs Reed ever recorded. Besides being convoluted, it is extremely difficult to understand what Reed is singing. Jimmy told Norman Davis the story of how he made up the song, and why:

"I was headed to the studio that morning," Reed said, "that was, I should say, about ten or eleven o'clock…. I am gonna get me a hit before we go in there." And he did, but not before meeting a man named John, who was sitting in the corner of the bar Jimmy had ducked into before going to the recording studio. Reed was wondering what he was doing at the bar, why he was alone, and why he wasn't with his "old lady." Apparently, Big John wanted to talk about his wife—how much he despised her—but Jimmy didn't want to hear any of that. So he left, leaving the man to his misery.

When Reed arrived at the studio, with his new friend John still fresh in his mind, he started to recite lyrics about this man's life—a life he barely knew. Jimmy Reed had a song, a believable song with deceptively deep lyrics.[vi]

With little prodding from producer Calvin Carter, Jimmy went into an impromptu version of what would become the signature tune "Oh, John." Jimmy built an entire story of a relationship deteriorating right before the couple's eyes. Before the song is cut, you can hear a verbal exchange between Calvin and Reed (one of several such exchanges on this LP):

Calvin: "Very good. What's the next one, Jimmy?"

Jimmy: "You name 'em, I'll play 'em." [laughs] "If you name 'em, I'll play 'em." [slightly off mike, with guitarist noodling]

Calvin: "Just do anything—anything come across your mind."

Jimmy: [laughs] "Say, hey John. I missin' talkin' trash 'bout your ole lady, but I don't wanna."

Calvin: "O.K. Stand by."

The band knows immediately what to do and "Oh, John" shows Reed at his most vocally pathetic (with the exception of the borderline baby-talk of "Let's Get Together"). This is not a degradation of his style of individualism. In fact, it is the opposite. Though the province of the song is muddy at best, somehow we get a clear picture of what is happening, which showcases Reed's ability to tap into an adult situation, see the irony of it, and even make light of it. Reed is commenting on a love broken, but all he can say to John is: "John, call on the telephone/Now, John I know your lady ain't even home.... You should've been home with your lady."

"Kansas City Baby" was yet another example of Jimmy feeling his way through a new recording lineup. Al Duncan expresses interest in Jimmy doing a song, an "Oklahoma thing," which is appropriate, since Duncan was born in McKinney, Texas (Reed would eventually record this song a few years later as "Texas Is Doggone Big," aka "Crazy 'bout Oklahoma"):

Reed: [insultingly] "Say somethin'."

Duncan: "Oh, come on, come on let's go…"

Reed: [insisting] "I say, say somethin'."

Not even Mama could penetrate Reed's mood: she pleads with Jimmy to do a particular song, obviously something other than what Jimmy has in mind. A chorus of voices pleads with Jimmy to record one song or another. All the while Jimmy seems to chide the session attendees by ignoring their pleas. A few seconds later Calvin barks, "Kansas City." Jimmy concurs: "Kansas City…Kansas City, here I come." Mama seems unimpressed and lets out an "Ahright."

Calvin: "I want you to go 'round that long trail to Kansas City—don't go down that highway to Kansas City.…"

Reed: "They just pulled in!"

The song truly is the long way around for Reed. The groove is played slower than the norm, with Jimmy throwing himself into the storyline.

A more appropriate title for the song "You Can't Hide" could not be had. The song appears to be taking shape out of the hazy, sonic fuzz of a practice session. Almost. Here again, Reed is irritated with the session players, despite Mama and his own son Junior being present. Still, Jimmy, of all people, finds himself in the wrong key. He abruptly stops the music. "Whoa…I was singin' in G. I'm sorry," he says. (The root of the song appears to be in E.) His misstep doesn't stop him from laying into his band. "What they supposed to do is let me…" Jimmy sputters, "let me turn it around and when I turn it around then they come in. Then, then I be ready to go to work. You know what I mean? That's where it's at."

Mama laughs as Jimmy discourages: "We might not make this." Calvin explains that Reed might pull off the take. "You might get lucky, Jimmy, you never can tell." "I'll take a shot at it, sure," Reed says.

And he does give it a try, but to no avail. The pain of the studio theatrics and dramatics, unfortunately, are not really worth the end result. Duncan is, at best, feeling his way through the song (he even skips a couple of beats to get right with the song during the passing of the intro to the first verse), and Jimmy is obviously winging it and laughing his way through the take, rehashing "Baby, What You Want Me to Do" in the process. Ultimately, he (quite uncharacteristically) comes across as rather ungentlemanly. With devilish chuckling and lines like "I got love

I ain't never used…you can run…but you sure can't hide," Reed is truly in rare form: uninspired and borderline nasty.

The 1962 sessions, yielding such key songs as "Let's Get Together," "Take It Slow," and "I'll Change My Style," produced only one bona fide hit: "Good Lover," which landed at No. 77 on the pop charts in June 1962. "Good Lover" was released on the LP *Just Jimmy Reed,* and it is easy to hear why it was a hit: the Reed boogie is more pronounced than what would surface on slightly later songs, and Jimmy is self-effacing enough, saying he can't shower his woman in luxuries but he has the goods as a natural-born lover.

Scoring hits was just commonplace now for Jimmy. "Aw Shucks, Hush Your Mouth," recorded in late 1961, cracked *Billboard's* Hot 100 chart in January 1962. *Cash Box* lists the song as scoring a six-week stay on their charts. "Aw Shucks" is a more uptempo and perhaps more enjoyable song than 1960's similarly titled Reed hit "Hush Hush." It certainly sounds as though Reed had more fun tracking this one.

With his continued success, Jimmy became a bicoastal act in 1962 and hit all the points in between: Club 99 (in Joliet with old friend John Brim), the Empire Room in Dallas, and numerous clubs in the San Francisco Bay Area. On top of that, he was being asked to attend some very exclusive parties. One Jimmy Reed urban legend involves his and Eddie Taylor's attendance at a party in the Hollywood Hills. Stories of this party have been circulating in the blues community for decades, with surprising consistency. (I attempted to double check the following account, but to no avail.)

"From the stories Eddie Taylor told, Jimmy was just an unbelievable alcoholic," says harp player Mark Hummel. "One story, a famous one, about Bette Davis. He was apparently at a Hollywood party. He had so many fans. He was rubbing shoulders with fans who never figured they would meet Jimmy Reed. I think Eddie said that they played the Hollywood Palladium. Then he probably got invited back to someone's house in the Hollywood Hills or something, and he was talking about this party—John Wayne, Bette Davis, and Joan Crawford. Eddie told us that one. Jimmy and Eddie were in a limo and I guess Jimmy had to go to relieve himself. So, he pulled out his dick and it was like a windshield wiper across the windshield. Bette Davis kept saying, 'You poor dear.' Eddie said Jimmy was in the back trying to piss in whiskey bottles."

"Eddie told me this 35 years ago," explains Chicago piano player Mark Brumbach. "He told me about Hollywood stars giving parties with Jimmy Reed playing. He was a big star. There is a famous story. [Jimmy had] a bladder control problem. According to Eddie Taylor he was always reaching down there and putting a little vise grip on it if he couldn't run to the bathroom. Eddie Taylor told me of a time when he and Jimmy were in this limo with Gary Cooper and Joan Crawford and everybody is shoved together. Jimmy Reed was more or less on Joan Crawford's lap and peed his pants. I think it is interesting that Hollywood stars would throw him a party. It spoke to how far he went."

"Eddie told me a story about playing for John Wayne at a party," says Austin nightclub owner Clifford Antone said in a 2005 interview. "It was in a limousine with John Wayne and Bette Davis. They hired him for a party and then they all got into a limousine and Jimmy needed to relieve himself. He did it right there in the limousine."

While most people express remorse at recounting stories of Jimmy's incontinence, some are perhaps unaware that it is not only a symptom of being drunk, but of an oncoming tonic-clonic epileptic seizure. Despite being medicated and taking his pills with a large glass of water each day, Reed was experiencing his seizures more and more, and his alcohol intake wasn't helping matters. Neither was his constant touring schedule. "Daddy became ill and all of this stuff started happening," Loretta recalls. "Like I said, I really don't remember him drinking before music came along."

Reed's difficulties in performing became common occurrences. Drummer Mile Clark, renown for being a member of Herbie Hancock's Headhunters, gigged a few times throughout the '60s and '70s with Reed, most notably in Fort Worth, Texas. Clark's experience was further proof that Jimmy's health was sliding. "We played at a little barbecue joint just outside of Fort Worth, Texas, for three nights—the name escapes me," says Clark who was only 15 at the time. "What I remember most about the show is that the music really swung and Jimmy had passed out. I can't tell you exactly, but as we were playing Jimmy just went down. His wife happened to be there with him and helped him get up. He just passed out cold. I was a young kid, underage, trying to keep a low profile, and I didn't think much of it at the time. I just thought he'd tripped or something. I wasn't quite sure what happened then, but now I don't think he tripped at all."

The world was becoming an increasingly dangerous place in the early '60s, but you'd never know it from the songs coming out of the Vee-Jay hit factory. By October 1962, US President Kennedy's demands that the Soviets dismantle their nuclear sites in Cuba had been met, and the world had skirted certain disaster. But Vee-Jay and Jimmy Reed seemed impervious, and the future looked bright.

Gene Chandler and the DuKays had kicked things off at Vee-Jay with his 1961 crossover No. 1 hit "Duke of Earl" (it went on to become a gold record, selling one million copies), Dee Clark struck a No. 2 hit with "Raindrops," Gladys Knight & the Pips scored a Top Ten hit with "Every Beat of My Heart," Jerry Butler (now a solo artist, no longer with the Impressions) scored a No. 11 with "Moon River" in 1961 and a Top 20 with "Make It Easy on Yourself" in 1962, and Betty Everett crossed over with "You're No Good" (a song originally selected for label darling Dee Clark). Plus, the Four Seasons had signed on with Vee-Jay and released one smash hit after another: "Sherry," "Big Girls Don't Cry," and "Walk Like a Man," million-sellers all.

"We were pretty hot," Calvin Carter said of the label years later. "There was a No. 1 record in England and they asked if we wanted it, and of course, we wanted it. It was "I Remember You" by Frank Ifield. We took the record, and as a throw-in, they had a group [the Beatles] they didn't want, and asked if we would take them, too."

On February 7, 1963, Vee-Jay Records released the Beatles' first US single, "Please Please Me" and "Ask Me Why" ("Please Please Me" went to No. 1 in Britain in March). Of course, we all know how huge the Beatles were, but the mop-topped Fab Four had American record labels confused about what to do with them at first. Ewart Abner and Calvin Carter may have heard something in the Beatles that caused Vee-Jay to ink a licensing deal with British label EMI, but the Beatles were certainly an afterthought at Vee-Jay, at least initially. (The band's name was even misspelled, as the Beattles, on the single's label.)

"I don't think anybody thought that much of the Beatles going in," says Jerry Butler. "The Beatles were a cute little group from England that had tremendous exposure by coming to America. The first place they landed was on the Ed Sullivan show. And they were heralded as the new hot item, with the pageboy haircuts, and the cute little smiles, playing rhythm and blues music. Nobody going in could get from 'Can't Buy Me Love' to 'Eleanor Rigby.' Who could have guessed?"

In the mid-'50s, Capitol Records was bought by EMI, but Capitol retained the right of first refusal for US releases by British artists. By 1962, seeing that Vee-Jay had scored hits with numerous R&B artists, EMI took a chance and allowed the US label to release a Frank Ifield single. As it turned out, Vee-Jay had a hit with Ifield and broke the native Australian in America. Capitol had never had that kind of success marketing an overseas talent in America. So, when the Beatles cut "Please Please Me" and "Ask Me Why"—and Capitol passed—EMI sent Vee-Jay to the rescue. Vee-Jay then issued the single on behalf of EMI.

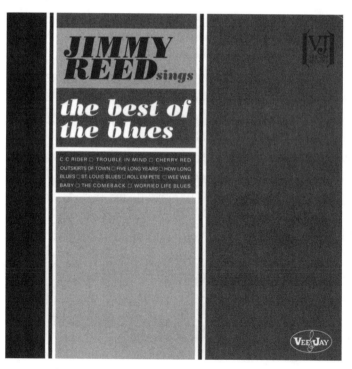

Most tracks on The Best of the Blues *betray Reed's discomfort covering other artists' songs.*

The rest, as they say, "is history."[vii]

Seemingly unconcerned about the shifts in pop music and the industry, Jimmy continued with his own brand of blues. In March 1963, Reed recorded "Shame, Shame, Shame"—a fun song in C, despite it coming about when Reed imagined Mary Lee leaving him and how lost he'd be without her. "Now, she really didn't leave me, but I was just picturing how I would feel if she did, " Reed said with a laugh on *The Legend—The Man.*

Reed is one of the few singers in American pop music who can simultaneously sound indignant, self-pitying, and joyous. It is still a bit of a mystery how he pulled off this oxymoron when he sings, "Well, I tried to tell ya, baby, runnin' make no sense…now you got me, baby, up against this fence…and ain't that a shame, shame, shame…shame, shame the way you do."

"Shame, Shame, Shame" made it to No. 52 on *Billboard's* Hot 100 chart, and *Cash Box* reported the song having parked itself on the singles

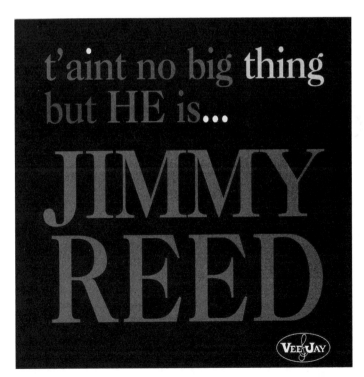

A textbook of the Jimmy Reed sound?

chart for nine weeks straight (beginning April 1963). It was also a true "crossover" hit, as in "across the pond" in the United Kingdom, where it crashed into the Top 50 singles chart.

The year 1963 also marked the release of three Jimmy Reed LPs, the best of which was *T'aint No Big Thing, But He Is...* "Shame, Shame, Shame" appeared on this record. In fact, *T'ain't* was composed of tracks taken from the "Shame, Shame, Shame" session (with Lefty Bates and son Jimmy, Jr.), which also included "Cold and Lonesome" and "There'll Be a Day." Additional tracks recorded in a July session with Eddie Taylor on guitar also wound up on the LP: "Mary-Mary," "Upside the Wall," "Baby's So Sweet," the "Baby, What You Want Me to Do" soundalike "I'm Gonna Help You," the semi-twisted love song "Up Tight," "Mixed Up," "I'm Trying to Please You," and the song that spawned the LP's title, "Ain't No Big Deal."

Taylor was as clean and solid as ever, the drumming was neat and relatively quiet, and Reed seems to be laughing in the studio and giving shout-outs to Eddie. And Reed can clearly be heard playing lead guitar on "I'm Gonna Help You." But aside from that, the LP boasted very little new or fresh material. Reed sounded tired—more than his usual. It was as if he were thinking that as long as he dragged his mouth across the harp keys and played in tune (and most of these songs follow a I-IV-V template), it really didn't matter what he played. Few fans would argue with Jimmy in 1963, but the result is a generic batch of largely forgettable songs with little of his lyrical play.

Some critics saw Reed as in a rut and drained of creativity. They may have had a point. Reed's schedule was almost inhuman. From the road to the studio, then the studio to the road. And given that Reed's basic musical premise varied only slightly, it was only a matter of time before critics saw the Boss Man's grooves as less than boring. "Side one has 'Shame' and 'There'll Be a Day'...and was quite rightly a big success," wrote Graham Ackers in *Blues Unlimited* in 1964. "The rest of the first side is a disgrace. The words, which used to be delivered with an attractive drawl, are now slurred beyond recognition; guitars and drums seem to be forever chasing one another. Side two has five tracks which are a slight improvement, but none escapes mediocrity and two are really terrible."

But, ironically, it was Reed's monotony that made his music so identifiable. If any musician wanted to hand another musician a textbook for how to "play a Jimmy Reed," he might fork over *T'ain't*. That isn't to say that these tracks didn't have some subtlety. The song "I'm Trying to Please You," for instance, stands out, if for nothing else than that it would sound great through deep subwoofers.

The Vee-Jay LP release *Jimmy Reed Sings the Best of the Blues* is exactly as the title suggests: Jimmy Reed covering well-known and beloved blues. The lead song, "St. Louis Blues," was written in 1914 by the father of modern blues, William Christopher Handy, and was later sung by Bessie Smith, in 1929. Handy's composition was equal parts ragtime and black spiritual. While Reed certainly rekindles the feelings of the original (and even some of the melody), this track, and most if not all of the record, is pure Reed. Ordinarily this would be a good thing, but *Sings the Best of the Blues* shows, more than any other record, how frightened Reed was of being like everyone else—to his own detriment. While no artist should ever be compared to another, this collection makes it difficult to do anything but.

"St. Louis Blues," for example, varies little from Reed's own material. The same Reed shuffle is present, and is far from the tricky and more sophisticated 1956 Big Joe Turner version. Reed adds little to the blues canon we hadn't already heard. Other tracks, like "The Comeback" written by Memphis Slim (and which he re-recorded in 1959 for Vee-Jay), were shoo-ins for coverage. "C.C. Rider" (a huge hit for Chuck Willis in 1957; Ma Rainey had recorded it in 1924 as "See See Rider") seemed like a logical choice. Willis was king of "the Stroll." Perhaps it was thought the trademark Reed shuffle would draw some connection to Willis' schtick. It doesn't.

The most convincing songs to come out of this session were Eddie Boyd's "Five Long Years," "Roll 'Em Pete," and "Worried Life Blues," of which Bill Dahl wrote in the liner notes: "The downbeat sentiment in [Big Maceo Merriweather's] signature song not only fit Reed like a glove, it prompted a punchy 1960 cover by duck-walking rock icon Chuck Berry for Chess."

In "Five Long Years," unlike some others in the set, we can believe that Reed has some personal stake in what he is singing. The concept of the song—working five long years in a steel mill—at least had relevance in Jimmy's personal life.

"Roll 'Em Pete" was penned by Kansas City hollerin' bandleader Big Joe Turner and pianist Pete Johnson when a boogie-woogie craze swept the nation in 1938. Turner would reprise "Roll 'Em Pete" in 1958 with King Curtis on sax as a jazzy rockabilly rave-up. We certainly get a heady dose of Reed's absolute heaviness, in every way (from his mental state to his slow, deliberate vocal delivery), and this is a thoroughly reinterpreted classic. In fact, it is hard to imagine it is even based on the Big Joe Turner version at all. Where Turner sang with abandon and devilish alacrity, Reed's words ring morbid and barren as he sings, "Honey, you so beautiful, but you got to die someday...."

By the LP's conclusion, the eleven tracks tend to run together and leave the listener drained and confused as to its purpose. Most of the tracks are not recognizable vis-à-vis the originals or later recordings of the songs. The question inevitably arises: Why did Reed do the record?

More or less forced by Vee-Jay, coaxed by Al Smith, and egged on by fans, Reed had no choice but to record a standard "blues" record, even though he completely hated the idea of covering other people's songs. As the liner notes state, Vee-Jay maintained that the record's alternate title could have been "*By Popular Demand: Jimmy Reed.* The mail, telephone, and all other media of communication have brought requests for many years that the Boss Man of the Blues record the great blues classics of our time." That might be true, but Calvin and Al should have seen the wisdom in *not* submitting the inflexible Reed to such personal torture and listeners' displeasure—despite Vee-Jay's assertions. And the fact that the material chosen for the session was diverse only makes it all the more sad that Reed seemed unwilling (he certainly was capable, in this writer's opinion) to lift the shuffle-pattern template in order to perhaps breathe more life and vitality into these tracks.

With the folk boom in full swing in 1963, Jimmy Reed's music faced yet another shift in American popular culture. Singer-songwriter and trendsetter Dave Van Ronk had made New York City his stomping ground since the mid-'50s (he practically founded the Greenwich Village cof-feehouse scene) and would influence a young Bob Dylan. Dylan had moved to the Village in 1961 and within two years began recording some of his most powerful if not most subversive material, such as "Blowin' in the Wind," "Masters of War," and "A Hard Rain's A-Gonna Fall." Pete Seeger, a folk vet who was being rediscovered and played banjo and 12-string guitar, was recording and touring the country with such consci-entious tracks as "This Land Is Your Land," "We Shall Overcome," and "Turn! Turn! Turn!" It can be argued that Seeger, also an original mem-ber of the Weavers, spun some of the most humanistic folk music ever performed, short of his personal heroes Leadbelly and Woody Guthrie. Seeger played concerts throughout the country—sometimes for free—offering such working-class-hero anthems as "John Henry" and "Talk-ing Union." Perhaps more than Dylan, he was a man of the people as much as for the people. And that describes Jimmy Reed to a T.

While the folk music of the day was more globally conscious and politically charged than Reed's music, we can't ignore that Reed *did* hit upon universal themes in his blues love songs. Like his folkie counter-parts, he was able to touch people and speak a language they under-stood. It was unadulterated, and perhaps less of a threat to the status quo and establishment.

As if on cue, Vee-Jay announced that it was going to broaden its horizons and tap into the folk market. The September 7, 1963, issue of *Billboard* reported: "Vee-Jay plans to step up production in the folk field with albums to be released soon by Hoyt Axton on Horizon and the Big Three on FM." Vee-Jay's president, Randy Wood, even described the Big Three as a "Weavers-type group with a fine, down-to-earth sound."

You couldn't get more down-to-earth than Jimmy Reed. Vee-Jay wanted more roots music—of every color and stripe—and knowing there was very little the label could do to get Jimmy to change his format, they figured on letting the Boss Man do his thing. His odd mixture of electric and urban/down-home blues was working. Why mess with success?

Without further ado, Jimmy headed into the studio in July with Eddie Taylor, Jimmy Reed, Jr., and Al Duncan. Jimmy had a good band back-ing him once again, but he did little with the talent that surrounded him. If Eddie Taylor (who had one hand in tradition and one in the future) had been allowed to break free for just a moment, this release may have showed a side of Reed that few had seen, or would ever see again.

If *T'aint No Big Thing* and *Sings the Best of the Blues* were not Reed's strongest hour, at least they didn't compromise who he was. To Reed's credit, he never went in for very many trends. That would soon change with the folk boom. The ill-advised instrumental LP *Jimmy Reed Plays 12 String Guitar Blues* was nonetheless tailor-made for the folk market. Later, Chess Records would try to cash in on the fading trend with releases from Muddy Waters, Sonny Boy Williamson, John Lee Hooker, and Howlin' Wolf of previously recorded material called *The Real Folk Blues*. The criticism of these records has always been that there is nothing particularly "folk" about them, save their titles. We could very nearly say the same for Reed's instrumental LP, if it were not for the fact that he was, in the larger sense, a folk artist.

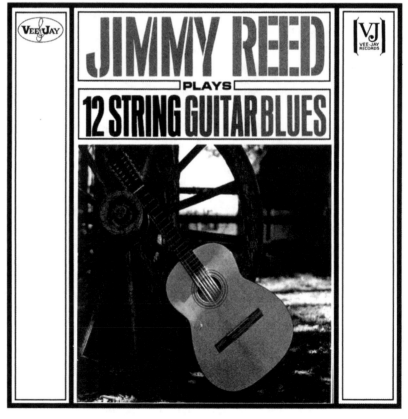

"Jimmy Reed lite."

12 String Guitar Blues presents such prior hits as "Bright Lights, Big City," "Big Boss Man," and "Hush Hush" with a sprinkling of originals ("New Chicago Blues" and "Blues for 12 Strings"), sans vocals. Reed plays his 12-string guitar in place of the vocals. Critically this is a move backwards for Reed, but aesthetically perhaps there is nothing wrong with having "elevator Jimmy Reed music" in the world.

If the listener didn't know any better, and since the tracks fade in and fade out at interesting points and the overall sound is so familiar, it is almost as if Reed were playing to his original song mixes. For example, Lefty Bates' guitar solo on "Blue Carnegie" seems identical to the one that appears on the 12-string LP, except that it gets chopped off by a fade-out. It is doubtful a new band came into Universal with the express purpose of recording new foundation tracks for an easy-to-produce, cost-effective, and get-it-finished-and-on-the-store-shelves record like *Jimmy Reed Plays 12-String Guitar Blues*. Rather, Reed sat in Universal's vocal booth and did his thing (blow harp and play 12-string) in time with the original track. The engineers took care of the rest.

One of the few redeeming qualities, as the liner notes to the original LP point out, is that Reed shows another side of his musicianship. The specter of Huddie Ledbetter rises, conjuring up a folkie atmosphere for the session. As the liner notes read: "…the 12-string guitar is the perfect instrument for interpreting the blues. The instrument is a most difficult one to play as the motion that is required to ordinarily strike one string, results in the simultaneous sound of two strings."

While it has been said many times that Reed's music is repetitive, there had always been in his recording career (up to this point), quite inexplicably, a depth. No such thing here. This is Reed "lite," and the music is as innocuous as Reed's art would ever get.

Reed's latest LPs may not have been complete successes, but the road still loved him no matter what he did. Jimmy continued to drink heavily and please crowds in the process. Often when he came through Detroit, as he did in 1963 to play the Prince Hall in Motown, he visited his friend John Lee Hooker. It was an oasis from the relentless gray of hotel rooms and blur of similar musical venues and theaters across the country. Zakiya Hooker, John Lee's daughter, remembers Reed coming over to the Hooker household often, and being left with quite an impression. Even during a rough patch in his career, both in the studio and in his personal life, Jimmy seemed regal.

"Jimmy was a very memorable man," Zakiya says. "I remember him as a child. We lived on the west side of Detroit, Michigan, on Bangor Street…. My dad always had people over the house. When people came through they would stop by. I remember Jimmy being a thin, fine-featured man. It really struck me, the way he carried himself, the way he walked. Whenever he would come he would have Big Mary with him, his wife. She was a big woman who didn't take no guff from anyone. She was in control. And when they come, they were always sharp as a tack. I always saw him to the nines. He drove this big Cadillac—big white Cadillac. I remember he came by and he was wearing a snow-white suit. Mary was dressed in white also. Jimmy had red shoes, red shirt, and a beautiful white Cadillac. To me, Jimmy was truly one of Daddy's most colorful friends. Jimmy was truly the most fabulous one to me. He epitomized Hollywood entertainer. He was da bomb."

Even Jimmy's critics had to acknowledge how little negativity (usually) the alcohol had on the audience's reaction or his performance. *Blues Unlimited's* Neil Patterson remarked on an August 1963 show at Detroit's Prince Hall: "Jimmy swayed around his microphone; slurred his singing even more than usual with the prominent bass sound to produce a hypnotic effect, all of which made even more effective the orgiastic squeal of his harmonica. So, Jimmy had hit the bottle, but the only consequence was to enhance his mannerisms in tremendous fashion."

In Texas, it was the same story. "I was in high school in the early '60s in Houston," says Ernie Gammage, who would go on to form the band the Sweetarts in Austin, Texas. "I would surreptitiously drink beer and listen to Jimmy Reed records. I was excited to see Jimmy—the only time I ever saw him—at a club called Menuti's in Houston. The club was purported to be run by the Mafia. I mean the name was not something you'd find in that neck of the woods and it was not in the greatest spot in town, either. Plus, I was not of drinking age and there was no way I should have gotten into that place legally. The walls of the place were all red, but you didn't get this really warm feeling.

"But the night I saw Jimmy," Gammage continues, "a guy came out on stage and made an announcement that Jimmy was going to be late.

He said Jimmy had to be taken to the hospital because he had apparently mixed beer with a screwdriver and needed medical attention. Anyway, finally Jimmy arrives, still pretty loaded, but not so much that he couldn't perform. I remember the strap on his guitar came undone and I went, 'Oh, my god.' It looked like it was going to plummet to the ground, when his guitar player—I think it was Eddie Taylor—reached over and grabbed the guitar by the neck without it crashing to the ground. It was quite remarkable because it seemed to be this guy had an attitude like this was something that happened all the time—like he was ready for it. Still it was like he was meant to do this show. It was almost as if he was fated to perform, as if he were conquering adversity."

There's plenty of blame to go around for Al Smith (among others) for not getting Jimmy to this and other shows straight. But one has to marvel at Smith's chutzpah to attempt to transform Reed's public image when word was spreading of the bluesman's alleged drunken live performances. Smith convinced prospective bookers that Reed was in shape to perform. What's a manager to do when an artist's main means of income is touring? Artists lose sight of the overall picture, become paranoid, and then blame their managers—"the suits"—for pushing them too hard, for working them too hard. In the Al Smith–Jimmy Reed partnership, Smith did overextend Reed in the face of his growing medical problems and alcoholism. But it was Smith's duty to ensure that Reed was paid and the only way he could make that possible was to continue to push him.

"[Al Smith] did drag him around, didn't he?" muses Chris Strachwitz, founder of Arhoolie Records in California. "When Jimmy was on, he was great. He could sing. But other times, he was just pitiful. I saw him once at Sweet's Ballroom in Oakland in, I believe, 1957. I had just gotten out of the army and I remember Reed was a big hit. It was a show put on in conjunction with KWBR. It was a typical rhythm and blues show hosted by DJ "Jumping" George Oxford. Reed was totally bombed out of his mind. He looked like that, anyway, but he managed to pull it off. He did his thing O.K. 'cause, I mean, his whole sound was so drunk anyway. [sings/mimics "Baby What You Want Me to Do"] That was just a totally drunkard song."

Strachwitz has a nightmare tale of a show he promoted at Berkeley Community Theater in 1963, billed as a "concert of blues and gospel music." Despite the packed crowd (admission was as low as $3.25), it was "the worst concert ever put on at Berkeley," he says. "I will never forget it. It was Jimmy Reed and the Reverend Gary Davis. It was almost show time and guess what? No Jimmy Reed. The Reverend was sitting in the dressing room and the union sent a guy who was saying, 'You need a piano player, and I am the piano player who is going to play.' I said, 'Listen, I don't need any piano player.' I rushed down to my car and went to the California Hotel in Oakland, which was about a mile or two away from the venue. And I stormed into the hotel and I asked where Jimmy Reed was. He was in room so and so. As I walked in, there was Al Smith standing next to the bed and Jimmy Reed was laying on his back on the bed and I asked, 'What is going on? Is he going to make it or not?' Al said, 'Oh, yeah. He had one of his epileptic attacks and bit off part of his tongue, but he'll make it. He'll be there.' So, anyway, I drove back and I keep selling tickets. My partner was in the ticket booth still selling tickets. Anyway, I think a kid came in and he said 'My name is Johnny Hammond. If you need somebody to fill in I would be happy to do so.' I said, 'Thanks, but I better wait till Jimmy Reed gets here. Anyway, hang around.'"

Hammond—son of legendary producer John Hammond, Sr., who is often cited as having discovered Billie Holiday, Charlie Christian, Count Basie, Bob Dylan, and Bruce Springsteen, among others—had been performing country-blues. (He would go on to record "Big Boss Man" in 1965 for his *So Many Roads* Vanguard LP with the help of Charlie Musselwhite on harp, drummer Levon Helm, guitarist Robbie Robertson, organist Garth Hudson, Mike Bloomfield on piano, and bassist Jimmy Lewis.) Hammond wanted an identity apart from his dad, and even traveled from New York to the West Coast to soak up the growing L.A. folk scene that was centered around clubs like the Ash Grove on Melrose Avenue.

Blues was in Hammond's heart (and blood), and he remembers having seen Jimmy Reed for the first time in 1957 at the Apollo in New York's Harlem. It was a seminal moment in Hammond's early development as a blues enthusiast who'd eventually become a notable blues performer. Reed's double-action harp blowing and guitar playing, and his electric but strangely folksy feel, made a lasting impression on the young aspiring musician. "Jimmy Reed is ingrained in me," Hammond says.

"His style, his feeling, I just absorbed it as fast as I could. That feel he had, it is a zone thing—he was a natural. His songs were pure magic."

When Reed still didn't show that night at the Berkeley Community Theater, Strachwitz gave Hammond the nod. San Francisco Bay Area guitarist Mike Henderson recounts the story Hammond told him about the show: "After I played with Jimmy Reed the first time, John Hammond told me a great story," Henderson says. "He told me, 'It was a show in Oakland and they were putting on this big show.... Jimmy was late getting there and the audience didn't care for [me] anyway. It was an all-black audience and they were saying, 'Get that white boy off the stage.' I kept doing my set and the promoter said, 'Jimmy ain't here. He's gonna need ten more minutes.' I walked back out on the stage and they were booing me like they did when I left the stage. I sat down and started doing a song. It was getting so loud that they couldn't even hear me. They were screaming, 'Where's Jimmy? We want Jimmy.' A promoter comes over and he said, 'Jimmy is here.' I grab the stuff and get off the stage. They bring Jimmy Reed out and everybody goes nuts cheering. Jimmy sits down in this chair and he starts rockin' and rockin' and rockin'...right through the bass drum head—he fell backwards. He was out of it. The promoter comes in and asks if [Hammond] can play.... [Hammond says] 'No, no, no...I am not going back out there.' "

"Finally, when Jimmy showed up it was just horrible," Strachwitz recalls. "He couldn't stand. It was a disaster. They almost booed him off the stage [laughs]. I had to go up onstage and say, 'Stick around, the Reverend is coming up.' "

"What I remember from that night is that the unannounced act was John Hammond, Jr., who performed solo acoustic, playing country-blues Robert Johnson style," notes Bay Area drummer and blues maven Lee Hildebrand. "I remember the audience was shocked to see a white guy doing Robert Johnson—nobody had ever seen that before. Then Jimmy Reed came on without harmonica. *No* harmonica. That whole element of his music was missing."

"Then Johnny Hammond *did* come on for a little intermission set and I guess it charmed some folks and disappointed some others," Strachwitz explains. "Anyway, the Irish piano player decided to sit out. We had another guy sit in. When the Reverend was ready, I announced, 'Now, here is the Reverend Gary Davis,' or whatever I said. He came on, then he started talking about the Israelis marching across the desert and this and that. I finally had to go out and tell him, 'Reverend, sing a *song*.' He wound up going back to his preaching, which just seemed like babbling to me."

"The Reverend Gary Davis spent more time telling dirty jokes than singing and playing religious songs," says Hildebrand.

"We finally had to yank him off the stage," Strachwitz says. "The night was just a disaster. People wanted to get their money back. I saw my partner in the ticket booth and noticed a bunch of money laying all over the floor. I went in there and just stuffed it into a bag and said, 'Get the hell out of here.'"

What do you make of this story? Reed was obviously incapacitated— and his condition had once again been "misdiagnosed" or misread by the public at large. Even his fellow performers didn't realize that Reed had had a seizure just moments before he was scheduled to hit the stage.

This creates an interesting dynamic between Al Smith and Jimmy Reed, which involved a bit of cheerleading, pep, push, and practicality. Al was playing bass in the band that night, and he knew that no matter what performance Jimmy Reed turned in, folks would pay to see him. "Jimmy Reed was such an idol. Jesus Christ," Strachwitz says. "He was a huge hit back then. The kids back in the late '50s loved the sound of the George Lewis band. The kids in the early '60s loved the Jimmy Reed sound. It was a kind of sound that no matter how primitive, or how basic, it just appealed to people. Jimmy Reed may have been a totally hopeless character, but the kids loved his sound."

Reed was building a mystique, consciously or not. Some wondered what shape he might be in to perform at other shows. Reed was leaving a trail of absent-minded performances in his wake. What some on the outside didn't understand was that Jimmy's absence didn't always boil down to his alcoholism. "What [Strachwitz] told me some years later was that Jimmy was very, very sick and had been in the hospital prior to that concert in the Bay Area," Hildebrand says. "I think it might have been Jimmy's manager, or somebody, who insisted he perform rather than cancel. The man was really sick and he played and sang and he wasn't very good."

For years there have been stories of Jimmy Reed being a no-show at some very high-profile, important gigs. One urban legend has him missing a key date on the *Ed Sullivan Show*. "I think he might have [been invited to play]," muses Loretta Reed. "It certainly was possible. He was a crossover artist. Then again, Daddy pretty much did his gigs. That was how he took care of his family. If he was invited and didn't go to the *Ed Sullivan Show* it would have been a very good reason. It didn't have to be, well, 'He is too drunk to perform.' There were people who were with Daddy and could keep him from getting drunk if that was the case." Adds Jimmy Reed, Jr., "People would have been there to keep Daddy sober. They would have made sure he arrived to the show on time."

Nevertheless, Jimmy was getting a reputation as an unpredictable musician who might not show. The artist Li'l Jimmy Reed, a Jimmy Reed clone for all intents and purposes, got his start because of just such a Reed mishap at a show at Louisiana State University.

"I grew up in Baton Rouge, Louisiana," Li'l Jimmy Reed (aka Leon Atkins) says. "I remember WLAC in Nashville was playing Jimmy Reed, and my daddy loved "You Don't Have to Go." I was living right across the street from a nightclub. I used to go to sleep with the nightclub right across the street and they would be playing some Howlin' Wolf. Slim Harpo. John Lee Hooker. I would stay up listening. I couldn't go into the club —I was too young. Then someone played Jimmy Reed and he had the place rockin'. I liked Jimmy Reed because of that beat, you know. Dancing style. So, my daddy bought me a guitar on a Monday and by that Saturday I was playing it. I started to blow harmonica first. But when I started to play guitar I put the harmonica down. Finally I went to the store and I bought me a harmonica rack. I put the two together. In about two days I had all the Jimmy Reed tunes."

Atkins never met Jimmy Reed, but was called to fill in for him. His reputation for imitating Jimmy Reed preceded him. "I played with his band that night [at Louisiana State University]," Atkins says. "I never got a chance to see him. It was like I walked through the front door and he was being brought out the back door or something. He was not up to playing, so since they had paid to see Jimmy Reed, I played everything that Jimmy Reed played. I think back then they paid me $100 and the auditorium was packed. Me? I was just learning Jimmy Reed back then. I didn't know what key to play in. I didn't know what to play. They looking at me…. Boy, let me tell you something: I turned those players out. I didn't know none of those guys. They were all set up on the stage when I got there. I don't remember Jimmy ever coming back to Baton Rouge after that."

Reed would later say that the pressures weighed on his nerves. Compounded by his drinking and epilepsy, the man was a stone-cold, run-down mess. His fraught mental state and medical condition sent Reed careening. And it all came crashing down in the fall of 1963.

Though the specifics of the incident are cloudy, Reed had what he and Mama would later refer to as a nervous breakdown. He was admitted to Downey V.A. hospital. "One time I passed out and stayed out for niiine [sic] days," Reed told interviewer Norman Davis, "…and they fed me for nine days through a needle."

As horrible as it was, it was inevitable. The last several years had been a whirlwind for Reed—from hit records and constant road travels to session recordings scheduled like clockwork. It was enough to exhaust anyone. There is only so much a body can take, and as Vee-Jay's frontline bluesman, and a true pop star, Reed had to be the banner guy. But it was a role he was just no longer up for—if he ever had been.

Irony of ironies: in the fall of 1963 Vee-Jay released nine FM label, five Horizon label, and 14 Vee-Jay label records, a portion of which were Jimmy Reed records. As Reed was languishing in a hospital bed, LPs bearing his name were on the shelves, buyers unaware of what had befallen their blues music idol. And this from the Vee-Jay president, Randy Wood (who replaced Ewart Abner): it would be an "excellent fall."

Years later, Reed seemed to laugh about his hospitalization and even mixed a bit of tall tale with the horror of his collapse, as he told it to Norman Davis. "You know when I woke up? The morning they killed Kennedy. You know who I was talking to when I woke up? President Johnson…. I never seen him in my life, but I was talking to him then."

We have explored how Reed seemed to rub elbows with Hollywood celebrities, VIPs, and historically significant public figures, but making contact and speaking with the newly sworn-in President of the United States on the day JFK was assassinated?

A dream, perhaps, or denial of his own problems. One thing was for sure: he swore off alcohol. At least for a time. Alcohol had become "demon rum" and to meddle with it was playing right into the devil's hands. As he did on occasion, Jimmy asked for the help of God, the love of Jesus, to get him through.

"I told one of them nurses, 'If the Lord let me get up out of this bed, and get me back out there in the street…I ain't never gonna touch another drop of liquor,'" Reed said. "'Jesus, you just let me get up from here and I'll prove it to ya.'"

Jimmy was serious. He wanted to back up his claims—and felt he could. "I made a promise I wouldn't touch that stuff," Reed said.

Slowly Jimmy was recouping and regrouping. It would be seven months before he returned to the studio. In the meantime, he was playing around town with Eddie Taylor and getting his feet wet again. He was also beginning to listen to another songwriter for ideas: female drummer Johnnie Mae Dunson. "Jimmy never really had a band," Johnnie Mae says. "He'd meet different guys and would play with them, but never did take responsibility for a band."

Johnnie Mae is one of the most embattled women on the blues scene. Stories have been told of her carrying around large ledger books full of lyrics and unheard songs just waiting to be recorded. She claims to have helped a lot of people and to have offered her music to them; she also claims to have been ripped off, sidestepped, and disrespected. For Johnnie Mae, life has always been a fight.

"I wasn't even supposed to live past 14 years old," says Johnnie Mae, who contracted rheumatic fever at an early age. "God bless my mother's soul. God answered her prayers [and healed me]. She said, 'Please don't take my baby away from me. Please spare her life and let her live.' She said that many times when she was down on her knees. Every time I think about it, tears start to come down…."

After taking up haircutting as a vocation, Johnnie Mae went north to Chicago where she would often perform on Maxwell Street. While some people were encouraging, others, who found it hard to swallow that a woman—and a drummer, no less—was leading a band, just didn't cut her a break. Pretty soon, however, Johnnie Mae's songwriting talents became evident, even if she isn't given the credit or royalties she perhaps deserves. "I wrote that Muddy Waters song 'Evil,' and when I confronted Chess about it, they took it off the air," she boasts. (The BMI Web site lists McKinley Morganfield, aka Muddy Waters, as the author of the song.) "I could have written three songs in just the time I am talking now. And that is what they can't stand about me. God gifted me. He knew I wasn't going to be able to work on no job. That is why he gifted me with a mind to write and sing."

Larry Hill, Eddie Taylor's stepson, remembers seeing Jimmy, Eddie, and Johnnie Mae perform on Maxwell Street, some 20 years after she had arrived in Chicago. "My dad, Johnnie Mae, and Jimmy were all friends," Hill continues. "The first time I saw them all playing was on Maxwell Street…. I can remember a time on Maxwell Street when Jimmy was playing but people didn't believe it was him. They said, 'That's none of Jimmy Reed,' and my dad and Johnnie Mae Dunson stood up and said, 'That *is* Jimmy Reed.' They said, 'That's Jimmy Reed?' 'Yes, that's Jimmy Reed.'

"There were a lot of great musicians on Maxwell Street," Hill continues. "Good Time Matt Murphy, John Lee Hooker, Jewtown Jimmy Davis, Floyd Jones…Jimmie Lee Robinson. I got exposed to watching them. The scenery was exactly as it was in the early '20s and '30s. The whole sector of Maxwell Street, which was littered with businesses owned by Jews and African-Americans, had all kinds of music, bought and sold, sandwich shops, and all kinds of clothing shops."

Slowly but surely, Reed resurfaced and hit the road again in the South. As usual, he was traveling light. He was alone, except for Al Smith. Jimmy would often use local bands who were familiar with his music to provide him his orchestra for the night or nights. He made swings through towns like Birmingham and Montgomery, Alabama, being backed by an up-and-coming guitar talent named Clarence Carter.

Carter grew up as a blind child, and listened to the Jimmy Reed records his stepfather bought. Reed was one of the first blues performers Carter began emulating as a young artist. "I was playing with Jimmy when he'd come through town, but I had played with Betty Everett and Solomon Burke before him," Carter says. "We even played with John Lee Hooker—once. Whenever these artists would come through town and needed a band, I would get the call."

It is interesting to note that Carter has been blind from birth and that he graduated college in 1960. "Everything I have learned to do, I've learned without sight," Carter says. "I grew up in Talladega, Alabama, and I think everybody knows now that they put that racetrack down there. At that time [early '40s] it was just one of those small towns, that if ain't nobody ever told you about, you would never know. That was where the blind school was located.... My thing with Jimmy, when he used to come to Montgomery, he would come down and play and if he didn't have a band, they would have to get a band to play with him. Most of the time they would get my band."

Clarence Carter and his backing band (which included piano player/organist Calvin Scott) were familiar with Reed's tunes—and it was a tight band. "Reed would play local clubs in Montgomery like the Derby Supper Club and Tijuana Club," explains Carter. "They knew that whoever we was supposed to play for, we would know the music. If I go a place now to play, most likely the musicians I am playing with I will have to send them the tape or CD so they can learn it. When I was playing with different artists, if I knew I was going to play for these artists I would go to the record store and get their records. But with Jimmy Reed—I knew his stuff, see?

"When Jimmy got there, I already knew what he was going to play," Carter continues. "It makes for a good experience because when the person gets there it makes it seem like you have played with him forever."

Carter and his band blew through versions of some of Reed's live favorites such as "Big Boss Man," "Baby What You Want Me to Do," and "Bright Lights, Big City." (When Jimmy would return to the Derby and Tijuana clubs in the mid-to-late '60s, Carter and crew would tackle Jimmy's 1965 song, "I'm the Man Down There," which Carter would eventually re-record himself.)

Carter has some vivid and amusing anecdotes about Reed during his limited touring with the Boss Man. "I remember we were on the road and we were in Memphis and I heard this knocking on my door early in the morning," Carter says. "I said, 'Who is it?' A voice said, 'Jimmy Reed. Let's get some breakfast.' 'Well, Jimmy,' I say, 'I haven't gotten up yet.' 'Well, why don't you go on and get up?' He was an absolute character. He didn't know I was mystified by sitting and eating breakfast with Jimmy Reed. I don't think he ever, as far as I know, realized how much he was an effect on me."

In Alabama, the band and Jimmy were staying just outside Birmingham at the A.G. Gaston Motel—perhaps best known for its connection to the civil rights movement. Besides being the embattled home base for Dr. Martin Luther King and his staff, the Gaston was also the site of infamous bomb threats during the tense days of desegregation.[viii]

Carter remembers one incident at the Gaston that has stayed with him. "The Gaston had two floors," Carter says. "Jimmy was up on the second story there. I had already gone down to the car and Jimmy was on the second floor and they were telling him, 'We got to get in the car. Jimmy, get down here.' But for whatever reason he just didn't want to use the stairs. Jimmy was saying, 'Why can't I just step down right from here?' 'Jimmy, you are on the second floor. You can't step down.' To me, this was something…. Here I am listening to a star saying, 'Why can't I step down from up here?' I knew that he had been in the bottle. I knew he had had something to drink. Personally, my experiences with Jimmy Reed were quite exciting to me, and he always treated me real nice."

As the pressures of the road mounted on Jimmy, he hit the bottle harder and harder. Although business associates and the fans could tell he wasn't sober on the job, somehow they were satisfied enough with his performances (or maybe just thankful that he had showed up) to continue booking him and paying good money to see him. But behaving with an alcoholic as if nothing is wrong can be disastrous. It can make that person feel insulated and invincible—free of life's consequences.

Back in the 1950s and 1960s, alcoholism wasn't seen as the disease it is today by the public at large. It was thought of as a character flaw or deficiency—a sin, even. And Jimmy Reed was far from the only blues harp player with a drinking problem at the time. Charlie Musselwhite, though now clean for years, explains how alcohol abuse/misuse and the Chicago club scene walked hand in hand: "[Drinking] is a Southern tradition. A lot of people I knew drank a lot. That went for all the hillbillies. That's just what people did—they made their own liquor and drank it. Then if you happened to be a musician and you were in nightclubs every night, you would be around alcohol constantly. I was lucky enough to figure out how to quit. I could drink all night and go to work the next day without having a hang over. I could drink as much as two quarts of gin a day. Quitting was, and is, a long process. Slowly I cut down when I realized that I wasn't cutting it anymore. I felt claustrophobic. I didn't live without alcohol and I was never onstage sober."

"I think that no matter what, there is no doubt that Jimmy Reed had a hard life," says guitarist/songwriter Doyle Bramhall, Sr. "We can't forget that Jimmy had epilepsy, too. Back then there was not a whole lot of talk about it—epilepsy. I know people were put in hospitals because of epilepsy, as if they were crazy. People might say that Jimmy Reed was just a drunk, but it was not all that. He was just misunderstood. He drank, probably because he thought it helped. Up to a certain point, alcohol probably did help, until it hurt him. Back then you were scared to talk about things and you didn't know the repercussions. I remember seeing Jimmy in Austin—he was late for the show. Somebody went over to pick him up and he was laying outside his hotel room having a seizure. He wound up coming, but it was about an hour and a half later. I remember that happening because it was like, 'Where is Jimmy Reed?' We all thought he was just drunk. Come to find out he was having a seizure."[ix]

On a road trip through Memphis, DJ Gary Burbank, then a self-described third-string drummer for Stax Records, had the opportunity to see many sides of Reed the night he shared the bandstand with him. His tale is so sad it bears repeating, if for nothing else than to serve as a cautionary tale.

"I got a call from a booking agent whose name was Ray Brown and he said that there was a gig at the Cadillac Club—it was a place outside Memphis in Shelby County," Burbank says. "It was a big place, but at the time, because of the laws, you couldn't serve drinks to people. So, people would bring in their own bottles. Anyway, I remember I got there early for this gig, a couple of hours or more. I'm out there and setting up my drums and the bass player, can't remember who it was, is getting himself set up. After setting up, I went outside to smoke a cigarette and this big, long Cadillac pulls up. And people start getting out of it and there is this one guy in a white suit and, man, he is reeling all over the place. So, I'm thinking, 'That's Jimmy Reed.' People are helping him and a manager, Al Smith, walked up to him and I introduced myself. He said, 'That's Jimmy, but make sure you don't give him anything to drink.'

I said, 'That's good, but I think you are too late for that.' [Smith said,] 'No, that is kind of residual.'

"We go into the place and we are setting up and Jimmy Reed, Jr., is lucid and together," Burbank continues. "Jimmy is kind of crazy. But he is one of my heroes, right? I mean Muddy Waters and Robert Johnson played better than Reed, but Jimmy had this real gutsy, wonderful feel that spun off into rock 'n' roll. Anyway, I am then sitting behind the drums, we are about to do a sound check or something. Jimmy walks up to me and stands over the drums. You ever see a picture of his hands? His hand would cover my snare drumhead, man. He looked at me and said, 'You the drummer?'—even though I was sitting behind the drums. 'Yes, sir, Mr. Reed.' 'O.K. You can hit that'—pointing to my snare. I said, 'O.K.' Then he pointed to my hi-hat and said, 'You can hit that.' I said, 'O.K.' Then he pointed at my bass drum and said, 'You can kick that. Now, if you touch any one of *dees udder* drums, or *dees* cymbals up here, I'm gonna bust you 'cross the head with this goddamned *geetar*.' I said, 'Yes, sir, Mr. Reed.' He didn't know me from Adam, but I was scared shitless."

Burbank knew what Reed wanted and for most of the night gave him that "chung-cha, chung-cha beat," as Burbank hums. "That was what I did all night. A couple times a night I might have gotten off the hi-hat and ride to kick something in and I'd get a stare. The times I would come off that hi-hat and do a little lick, it would get a little look. Then it was right back on the hi-hat. He was aware of not only what he was doing but what everybody else was doing. To that end, I remember we were playing at one point and the place is full, right? Jimmy Reed is rockin' and all of a sudden in the middle of one song he just stopped and started yelling and turned to Junior, his son, and said, 'Oh, Junior, you mutherfucka!!' Junior just stops and puts his head down as if to say, 'Oh, damn.' 'Don't you turn my amplifier down!' Jimmy said. Everybody in the audience was kind of embarrassed and laughing nervously. So, Jimmy, Sr., walks over and turns the amp up again. You see, Junior had snuck over and turned down his amp, you know? Jimmy was so loud, and Junior just tried to get it together a little bit. So, we stopped and then it resumed: 'boom-clat, boom-clat.' "

At the end of the night, as the band was waiting to get paid, Burbank experienced something disturbing that sticks with him. "Suddenly they couldn't find Jimmy Reed," Burbank says. "We're looking everywhere. Finally someone found him. The tables had these really big, long, red tablecloths. Jimmy was under a table. He was sitting under there and he was having 'the spiders out of the bottles,' he called it—the tiny bit of beer in the bottles left on the tables. Even though it was kind of nutty and wild, it was just that wildness that made you not want to turn your back on him—you might miss something. I remember just being mesmerized by him. I remember after the gig I wanted some sort of recognition about doing good, but nothing. Junior did say something to me, however. Jimmy never said a word. He was too busy finding the spiders in the bottles."

By the summer of 1964, America was an ever-shifting place. The civil rights movement was igniting, the country was being sucked into deeper involvement in Vietnam, the space program had achieved greatness, a US president had been assassinated, and race riots raged in Alabama. And playing in the background of it all was "the sound of young America:" the Motown Sound.

With such premier talent as Little Stevie Wonder, Marvin Gaye, and Smokey Robinson, Berry Gordy's revolutionary Motown label was not only giving listeners what they wanted, but perfecting the *business* of music. Diana Ross and the Supremes alone had No. 1 hit after No. 1 hit, with such crossover pop tracks as "Where Did Our Love Go," "Baby Love," "Come See About Me," "Stop! In the Name of Love," and others throughout the 1960s. It seemed Motown had learned a thing or two from Vee-Jay by appealing to whites as well as blacks.

"Motown brought about a lot of change," says Jerry Butler, who'd later record with Motown. "Vee-Jay was basically considered a 'race record' label, whereas Motown was considered the music of young America. Just the title tells you something. Rhythm and blues, blues, jazz, and gospel would be more accurate in describing what Vee-Jay did. Motown was purely *Motown*. It really did not get off into the other genres. There was no John Lee Hooker, no Muddy Waters, no Jimmy Reed, no Lightnin' Hopkins, Memphis Slim, or Howlin' Wolf, because Motown was not about that."

Motown proved that vocal-oriented R&B music could be brought to the masses by tight song structure, hooks, incredible production, and image. "It was focused to be music for everybody as opposed to being *black* music, even though most of its artists were African-American," says Butler. "The economics of the music business had changed."

The connection between Motown and Chicago—and the blues— is clear. "Motown was a kind of 'lite' version of what was in Chicago at that time: R&B, religious, soul, blues," says the Dells' Mickey McGill. "At that time Motown was recording in Chicago. Motown was a Chicago label in that sense."

"We laughed when we saw Motown," explains singer Mavis Staples. "We just saw them as Chicago sound, but lighter."

Despite all this, Jimmy Reed still had an effect on the public. Inexplicably, Reed's music continued to soak into every seam of the American popular culture—and counterculture. Haight-Ashbury would be ground zero for the first group experiments with psychedelic drugs, as well as the explosion of the hippie movement of youth, art, literature, music, and culture. And the Grateful Dead—a band that perhaps more than any other embodied the spirit of '60s San Francisco—would later cover Reed's material, including "Big Boss Man." (In fact, songs like "Boss Man" and "Baby What You Want Me to Do?" became so identified with the jamband that some Deadheads still think they are Jerry Garcia originals.)

As youths were tripping, copping, and dropping out, Reed was also speaking to bands who didn't know the secret to passing an electric Kool-Aid acid test. Groups like the Bay Area–based Beau Brummels, who some considered one of the first American responses to the '60s British Invasion, were also taken with Jimmy Reed.

" 'Ain't That Lovin' You Baby,' like most of the songs recorded for the Beau Brummels' first album, probably got done in no more than three takes," says Sal Valentino, the Brummels' lead singer. "Sly, that is, Sly of the Family Stone, produced the Brummels' first album. He found my voice and singing interesting and liked the idea of my singing [the Jimmy Reed song], and Tom Donahue and Bob Mitchell, Autumn Records owners still AM DJ-ing, felt it was a good idea and convinced Ron Elliot—the Brummels songwriter—that it was a good addition to the first album. We probably did that song in three takes.

"Why did we do it?" Valentino posits. "It was right at the time, in the pocket, and easy to follow—a little like the song 'Money.' I don't know why it got to me. I liked what it said…. I'm glad I heard [Jimmy's music], and was thrilled when I first heard him. I would think that he was heard on AM/Top 40 radio with a hit, as it were, around the turn of the '60s, maybe as late as 1962. Then again it might have likely been heard in North Beach around the crossing of Columbus Avenue and Broadway Street. The topless dancers were about to happen in San Francisco and a band backing George and Teddy at the Condor might have been using [Jimmy's music] as well…. Les Welch and the Preludes could have, and maybe even Joe Piazza and the Continentals also. I started singing 'Ain't That Lovin' You Baby' long before any of the Brummels heard Jimmy Reed or even Slim Harpo."

Quite rightly, however, Reed knew that he still had something to prove. B.B. King, Freddie King, and even white boys like Paul Butterfield and Michael Bloomfield were playing scorching, city-slicked urban blues. Reed's countrified electric blues were no match for their "uptown" sophistication or high-energy records and live shows. B.B. was rocking the Regal, Freddie was influenced by Eddie Taylor (but taking a fingerpicking style to new heights), and Reed knew, deep down inside, that they all had something. But he would never admit it in public. He called hitting all those notes "playing jazz and all that junk," even if the artist in question was firmly planted in the blues genre.

The blues was moving on, and Reed seemed destined to be stubbornly tied to his own style. That's why when he was scheduled to record a new list of songs, it was a brilliant move by Reed to pull in Johnnie Mae Dunson as his songwriter. Reed had always been perceived as a ghettoland philosopher, and less—or not at all—as someone who could dazzle with clean, flawless technique and unbridled passion. Reed's music was starting to become stale, and Johnnie Mae's images of life and love were a much-needed shot in the arm. (Black soul singers and crooners like Lou Rawls, Sam Cooke, and Nat King Cole often garnered the tag of "sepia Sinatra"—golden throats that could move through gospel, blues, R&B, you name it. While Reed didn't have their vocal or even musical range—their ability to shift their voices at the drop of a dime—he was infinitely closer to their artistry as musical interpreters than the bluesman of the dog.)

Over two sessions in July and August, Reed and his band cut more than a dozen tracks, many of which were issued as singles and comprised Reed's next LP, *At Soul City.* Four of those songs are credited to Johnnie Mae. Other credits for the sessions are sketchy (a number of people I interviewed were not sure of the lineup; even various compilations shrink from committing themselves). The original production/recording engineer notes (now in Vee-Jay's storage facility along with the master tapes) offer no clue. Johnnie Mae admits that she did not play drums on the record, and by ear it is most probably Al Duncan on drums. Others on the sessions were Phil Upchurch on bass and Eddie Taylor with Jimmy Reed, Jr., on guitars. (Howlin' Wolf's right-hand man, Hubert Sumlin, is sometimes listed as a second guitarist on these sessions.)

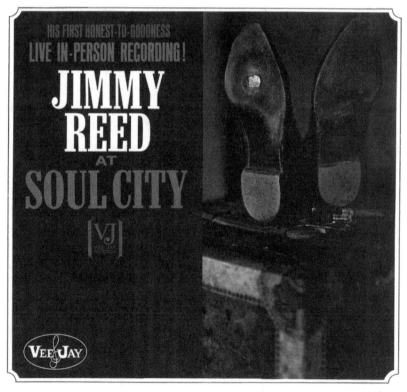

Vee-Jay slyly marketed this studio LP as a live recording—which it was not.

One of the strongest Johnnie Mae songs to come out of the *At Soul City* sessions, "I'm Goin' Upside Your Head," returned Reed to form. Reed had complained about songs being too fast in the past; he was not able (or willing) to keep up with the band. Not here. It sounds like he's playing "catch me if you can" with the band. It's virtually double-time of the typical Reed "lump," and Reed obviously did not put up any resistance toward it. His harp solo is enough to convert the disaffected. Reed's metallic and ear-piercing high-end squeals in *A* (on an *A* harp), has all the vibrancy of a red-dressed dancer pounding the juke joint floor on Saturday night.

"I Wanna Be Loved (Crazy Love)," another song written by Johnnie Mae, is a mush-mouth masterpiece full of raucous shuffling. If ever there was a song that *sounds* live on this record, it is this one. The listener really gets the sense of the engineer using the room's atmospherics to their full effect. The sound has depth, with just the hint of wetness. Though some of the technical notes have been lost to time, it would seem that the tracks were very dry when recorded—not a lot of studio panache involved. That is why it seems to be that vibrations and sound waves bouncing off the walls were adding to the shimmering effects of the track. Simply put, it sounds like it was recorded with Reed live on the stage of a concert hall, with just the right amount of echo and reverberation.

Calvin says to Jimmy in the preamble to the track, "We're rollin,' Jimmy. Don't worry about it. Be relaxed." Of course, Universal—where many of the Chess Records and Vee-Jay tracks were cut—offered plenty of controls. Some of Chicago's most important homegrown blues and jazz was being recorded in this state-of-the-art facility on East Walton. Still, as if testing the boundaries of natural sound, the resulting "I Wanna Be Loved" is a noisy, mid-tempo gem that has a steady rockin' and rollin' feel that even dips into dissonance at turns. The rhythm guitar and Reed's voice are a bit hot for the recorder, but given the frenetic nature of the song, it's appropriate—and works—in ways the producer and Reed probably hadn't even realized.

Here Reed's harp shrieks as loud as a steam engine's whistle. Duncan plays a traditional eighth-note swing pattern and a constant four-on-the-floor beat with his kick. The song fades out at what feels like an appropriate instant as if mirroring the song's general concept of not wasting time. Vee-Jay's producer Calvin Carter was less interested in having each element of the band being heard than in making sure Reed's instantly recognizable sound was front and center. Who could blame him? Still, it would have been nice to hear how and where Duncan placed his bass drum beats in relation to Reed's vocals and how he conversed with the very beats he was playing on his snare, hats, and crash cymbals. As it stands, only some of Duncan's kick beats poke through the cloudy production.

The Johnnie Mae instrumental "The Devil's Shoestring, Part II" (Part I was not recorded) is not your typical Reed song; we hear Jimmy take the guitar lead. While not a great lead player, it is good to hear him giving it a go here with a snap in his fingers as he scratches the strings. There's a bit of rockabilly and a ton of "hillbilly" in these lines, from the bassline to the guitar phrasings (think Chuck Berry). Lightly picked guitar floods the right channel; it is so light and so ethereal it sounds like a Henry Gray piano line.

With the Reed original "Help Yourself" (in E; Reed's harp solo is in second position), Jimmy proved that he still could write a great hook and have it differ, just enough, from the usual 12-bar-blues type of format he was accustomed to. (With its self-empowering theme, the song became a live favorite of Reed's.)

Here Reed sings he was a little too strong to ask for help from anyone else. Without a doubt that describes his outlook on life, and was unquestionably why some of his mental and physical ills persisted. He wanted to do things himself without being guided by anyone else. Like many of his so-called "simple songs," the title "Help Yourself" is deceiving. It may seem like a preachy type of ditty, but in fact it is very introspective. Though Reed explained once that he did not write this song in reference to anything specific in his life, it is hard *not* to think about his epileptic seizures, alcohol consumption, self-doubt, and, frankly, the strain that all of these various character traits put on his family, managers, and friends. (The song would subsequently become a staple of Jimmy's live shows.) Though it wouldn't exactly jibe with Reed's real-life condition, his lines explain that he did manage to help himself. He sings, "You can help yourself, baby, all you gotta do is try sometime…I wanna tell you, people, almost didn't help myself…my doctor told me, he said, 'Jimmy, you can help yourself.' You don't have to go 'round…worryin' everybody else."

At Soul City includes other Reed originals, such as "Heading for a Fall," sometimes titled "Things Ain't What They Used to Be" (which also appears on later records, as do "Left Handed Woman," "A New Leaf," "Wear Something Green," and "Fifteen Years"). "Heading for a Fall" is vaguely in the "Big Boss Man" mold, and despite the dire prediction in the title, the song is lifted—thanks to choppy chording accents and Reed's ironic, rosy vocal hooks.

In keeping with the idea of freshness, Reed's "Goin' Fishing (Ain't Got No Pole)" must have tickled his rhythmic fancy. Throughout the take, Duncan is splitting the traditional backbeat (two and four on the snare) between his snare and the sidestick. Duncan doesn't play elaborate fills, per se, but he certainly makes use of many of the sound sources available to him for this tune. He pounds a dozen eighth-note beats on his snare and hi-hat, then subtly tosses in sixteenths on his hats to nix any chance of the song sinking into a heavy monotony. The kick drum isn't always audible but Duncan infuses a balance of fierceness and elegance in his drumming style that would have been better served by better sound quality.

To psych Jimmy up for "A New Leaf," Carter tries to prep him for a definitive take. You can hear Carter say, "Let's make it a record this time. Let's make it a smash. We talkin' 'bout 500,000 records now, Jimmy. Let's do it." Reed replies, "All right."

But Jimmy didn't need any pep talk. He knew he was on target in this session, more so than he had been for the last few. Appropriately enough, the tune concerns itself with shedding old ways and habits, and the singer is looking for a brighter day: "I've been travelin' a crooked path, somehow lost my way."

Most of these tracks were placed on Jimmy's LP *At Soul City,* which was released in the fall by Vee-Jay (the company was working FM, Horizon, and Vee-Jay labels in their fall line), and promoted by the label as Reed's "first honest-to-goodness live in-person recording." The title, similar to the one that was chosen for the *At Carnegie Hall* record, is a bit of a misnomer. Vee-Jay, besides the wording above the title, doctored the record in other ways. The songs on the original Vee-Jay LP 1095 (and some of the issued singles) had an audience overdubbed for effect. The later CD versions did not include an overdubbed audience, though the original liner notes (reprinted for CD) state that "This compilation of Jimmy Reed is a fine study of the man singing in live concert—it will become a standard of authenticity and soul of performance." Once again Calvin Carter, the newly appointed vice president of A&R and publishing (perhaps with the assistance of Vee-Jay president Randy Wood and vice president of sales and promotion Steve Clark), made quick work of this LP, his fingerprints all over it. But while the Carnegie record was a commercial smash, *At Soul City* was not.

The cover of the LP depicts two crossed feet sporting shoes—with worn soles (and one with a hole in it)—resting on a travel trunk. A stitch of newspaper peeks through a hole at the bottom of the left shoe. Johnnie Mae notes that feelings about Jimmy's empathy and depth gave inspiration to the title. "I gave it that title," she says. "He had a lot of soul, Jimmy, and I was talking to him about that. I was thinking about him, and how it concern his tunes."

By the fall of 1964 Jimmy was scheduled to play England at the end of October through November, at the same time the classic American Folk Blues Festival was sweeping through Europe with such star-studded names as Howlin' Wolf, Lightnin' Hopkins, Sonny Boy Williamson II, Sunnyland Slim, and others. Reed's music was so popular in Europe—England, specifically—that he really didn't need to be part of this packaged festival or "blues tour." And he seemed to be outside a certain blues clique—an artist who did his own thing and had crossover potential. He certainly was thrilling listeners on the other side of the pond.

"In the early '60s Jimmy's LPs were starting to be released in England," explains author and Reed fan John Broven. "I wouldn't say as much or more than Muddy Waters, but Jimmy Reed, certainly along with Chuck Berry and Bo Diddley, helped to spark the British blues boom. All of a sudden, from nothing in 1960, there was a pretty good catalog of Jimmy Reed material by 1963–1964."

England's newest hitmakers, the Rolling Stones, had taken their name from a Muddy Waters tune, but their sound was as much Jimmy Reed as it was Muddy. They covered Reed's "Honest I Do," and their song "Little by Little" seemed to be a take on the classic Reed–Taylor heartbeat feel. The Stones were picking up on that beat and they were getting as close to it as any Brit band could in the early '60s.

Dave Williams, blues writer and music historian, had grown up with Jimmy Page of Led Zeppelin fame and was also friendly with Brian Jones of the Rolling Stones. The three had met and eventually went to the first American Folk Blues Festival when it came through England. "Reed's music was much more melodic than some of the other blues artists," Williams says. "I think they were easier to cover by white rock 'n' roll artists than the really early hard blues of Muddy and Wolf. People like me and John [Broven] were perhaps the definitive Reed enthusiasts in Britain in those days. We had no money in those days, and I remember I had this Jimmy Reed record and Brian was begging me, 'Please, can you record this for me? Please, can you record this for me?' Reed was very influential over here."

"Some people said that all of Jimmy Reed's music was the same," Broven explains. "When [Reed fans] heard this, that really got our hackles up. We couldn't convince the other side, just as much as they couldn't convince us. I think it was John Peel who gave us the memorable quote, 'It's all such great music to fuck to.' "

Having looked at the charts and the interest Jimmy was garnering overseas, Vee-Jay knew it was time for a tour. Calvin Carter asked Vee-Jay artist John Lee Hooker if there were any good bands in England who could back Jimmy. " 'Well, ma-ma-ma-ma backing band is good, the Ground Hogs,' " relates Ground Hogs guitarist/songwriter T.S. "Tony" McPhee.

It was true. The band was the perfect fit for Hooker. Aside from naming themselves after a Hooker song ("Ground Hog Blues"), they were not stymied by the Boogie Man's less-than-conventional song structures and changes. "With Hooker we learned to expect the unexpected," says McPhee. "It was difficult to play with John, but we knew that he would change in the middle of a bar. The fact is we had a great drummer, Dave Boorman, who just did a backbeat that was necessary for John Lee Hooker—and Jimmy Reed."

McPhee had been studying Reed's music, and the Reed "lumpty-lump" guitar lick was the first he had played on guitar. McPhee remembers it being a whirlwind month with Reed on the road. When I met the guy, he was exactly as I thought he would be," McPhee says. "He was very laidback and nothing fazed him. But I could tell that Al Smith, who was traveling with him, was a kind of black godfather to him. He always caught Jimmy off guard. I remember this hilarious moment when Al was trying to find Jimmy and Jimmy had locked himself in the bathroom. Jimmy couldn't get out—he had locked himself in the bathroom. He had tremendous charisma."

The Hogs had just gotten off a month on the road with Hooker, so they were primed and ready. "We knew exactly what [Reed] needed," McPhee says. "The only problem with Jimmy was that he would come to the stage without his guitar being in tune. See, with Hooker, his guitar was always around and generally in tune. But Jimmy always carried it with him, so I could never get hold of it. It was one of those things that you just say, 'Oh, my god! I hope this is not too far out.'

Jimmy with the Ground Hogs: (from left) Tom Parker, Tony McPhee, Dave Boorman, John Cruickshank, Reed, and Pete Cruickshank outside the Twisted Wheel in Manchester, England, 1964.

Reed backstage during his 1964 tour of England.

"At the time I had read that he had a lot of problems with drink. The first thing he said was that 'I am on the wagon. I don't drink anymore.'"

But McPhee began to wonder. "We did the first gig—the first of two gigs that night —and there was a support band that did sn opening set," he recalls. "After we finished our set and started to break down our equipment, I walked into the dressing room and Jimmy was there telling the support band about how much he enjoyed playing with them. These guys were looking at him like…[laughs]. They didn't know what he was talking about."

The Hogs jumped around England quite a bit backing Reed. Some of the gigs, as best McPhee can remember: Saturday, November 7, at the Flamingo in London; Friday, November 13, at the Crawdaddy in Richmond; Saturday, November 14, at the Rikky Tick club in Windsor at 7:30 P.M. and a second Rikky Tick club in Guildford at 9:30 P.M. Sunday, November 15, they were at the Rikky Tick in Windsor again for a special 6:00 P.M. performance (there was also a later performance that night at the Rikky Tick in Reading); Wednesday, November 18, the band was at the Flamingo; Saturday, November 21, it was the Twisted Wheel in Manchester; Monday, November 23, they hit the British Legion Hall in South Harrow; and Friday, November 27, the band returned to the Flamingo. (Before the Ground Hogs signed on, Reed had appeared on television on October 30 on *Ready, Steady, Go,* for which he lip-synched and mimicked his playing style for the songs "Shame, Shame, Shame" and "Ain't That Lovin' You Baby"; he was also at the Noreik club on Halloween and the Flamingo on November 2, and played with Them, featuring Van Morrison, at the Bromel Club on November 25.)

Writer Cliff White, in his diary of the month that Jimmy Reed was in England, described how Jimmy, he, and Al Smith had one liquid breakfast. Jimmy swore he was off whiskey: "I quit drinking whiskey altogether," Reed told *Melody Maker* in 1964, "but sometimes I take a cold beer."

"Hooker used to drink a bottle of whiskey a day," remembers McPhee. "The thing with Jimmy is that he always sounded drunk."

If Reed had fallen off the wagon, it didn't seem to affect his music. "I remember seeing Reed at the Rikki Tick club in Guildford, about 30 miles southwest of London," Broven says. "I went with a few of my friends who were devoted Jimmy Reed fans and there was no question that we were going to see him at the Rikki Tick club. But by then we had heard rumors that he was an alcoholic, he was this, he was that…. Honestly? We were genuinely excited to see him. There was some concern as to just how he would perform on stage…. Well, the thing that hit me really from the get-go was what a good guitar player he was. He was really driving the whole thing along, basically on rhythm guitar. It wasn't an amateur playing. He was playing some very nice figures—and some solos, but here was a man who was in command of his instrument."

Broven happened to speak with Reed that night and he and his friends introduced themselves. "Two things that struck me was what a very pleasant man," says Broven. "No front to him at all. He didn't give the impression of being an aloof or unapproachable artist. Maybe because of the reception he was getting, he was treated like a hero and quite rightly so. The other thing that struck me was how small he was. He was quite small in stature. One had seen the photographs of him on the cushion and so on, but really he was a very tiny man and that was the only thing that struck me. There appeared to be no signs of his touted alcoholism or even his epilepsy."

Dave Williams remembers a slightly different Reed on the 1964 tour. "I saw Reed in a local dancehall here in Guildford," Williams says. "I even got the chance to go upstairs and speak to him and he was, unfortunately, drunk, in a nutshell. But what was very surprising was that his playing didn't seem to be affected in any way. Reed could actually play lead guitar—it wasn't just rhythm and chords—with some relatively intricate fingerpicking."

Confirming this is a bootleg recording I received of one of Jimmy's sets, recorded at Wallington Public Hall in South London. Reed's voice here is deeper and darker here than on his records of the time, and his harp playing is as lazy as ever—as if someone propped him up, still half in a daze, in bed and shoved a harmonica in front of him and demanded he slide his mouth across the holes. Incredibly, the music never falls apart, and the band is solid, yet loose. "We had a great drummer who did this great backbeat which was totally necessary for Jimmy, you know?" McPhee explains.

Cuts "Shame, Shame, Shame," "Baby, What You Want Me to Do," and "You Don't Have to Go" are exceptional, with an extended solo by McPhee in between songs. And while this is a warts-and-all sonic snapshot, it reveals a very accessible and inspirational set, and underscores Jimmy Reed's impossible combination of the light and heavy to joyous results.

"I was disappointed not to get here when I was in the Service," Reed told *Melody Maker* in November 1964. "So far, I think it is going to work alright.... I want to do what the people want to hear, and that is about as far as I can go with it."

Despite his comments to the contrary, Jimmy was consuming vast amounts of whiskey then, and he had plenty of drinking buddies. For some, they had never seen, met, played with, or drunk with the man. When Jimmy arrived, it was a party backstage. And everyone wanted a piece of that fame (even then fans knew he was something of a living history). Jimmy never had any outward disdain for the backstage atmosphere, and it would be increasingly hard for him to stop, to just say "no," as it were, and end the party. In each town, in each country, there would be eager young fans that wanted the opportunity to be in the man's presence. An old story and an occupational hazard of the entertainment industry: no one wants the party to end and as long as things are going fine, the money is coming in, and the shows are being done, "don't rock the boat."

Reed continued to tour through 1965, exciting crowds in Detroit at the Blues Unlimited Club and New York City at the Apollo Theater. But in some respects it was a relatively slow year for Reed. Only one recording session was on the docket, which bore the fruit "When Girls Do It," "Don't Think I'm Through," and "I'm the Man Down There." The latter is an answer to the Willie Dixon–penned, Sonny Boy Williamson II–recorded song "One Way Out" and G.L. Crockett's "I'm a Man Down There." (The Allman Brothers Band would cover "One Way Out" in the '70s to great success.)

In the Sonny Boy and Crockett versions, the singer has trepidation in facing a new girlfriend's man coming upstairs. (Although it *is* hard to imagine Sonny Boy being afraid enough of any man to consider slipping out a window rather than leaving through the front door.) Drummer Fred Below goes Latin for Sonny Boy, and ironically, Crockett copped Reed's style and vocal drawl when he recorded his own version to a basic, Reed-esque *B, C sharp* to *D, E, F* to *G* shuffle.

Reed's reactionary tune, an obvious dig to copycats and newcomers (and a send-up to his influences), kicks off with an amplified acoustic guitar and immediately that familiar lump unfolds and chugs, enveloped by his signature lead turnaround. Within the tune, Reed states, once and for all, who all the cats should have been afraid of all the time: Jimmy Reed, *the real man down there*. He's the man coming upstairs who's going to catch the other man with his cheating woman. "You're messin' with JR, baby, and you ain't messin' with no fool," Reed warns. "I'm that man down there/And I'm tellin' you, boy, don't you walk down that stairs...."

In the liner notes to *Rhino's Blues Masters: The Very Best of Jimmy Reed*, writer Cub Koda mused: "The lyrical text and rhythmic grooves of the two songs [Reed's and Crockett's] have fused together over the years (much like Ann Cole's and Muddy Waters' versions of "Mojo"), and the result has endured as almost a modern-day folk song of the idiom."

With this side, Reed answers once and for all a burning question.

Though a cloud of mystery has always surrounded Crockett (some have cited the existence of only one publicity shot of the man), he was in fact living on the West Side of Chicago for a time. He scored a Top Ten R&B hit in 1965 with his "I'm a Man Down There," but then, in 1967, he died before he could amass any kind of catalog. His recorded output wouldn't even pack one side of an LP.

Crockett's legacy is that of a one-hit wonder, but little did Jimmy Reed know that his own days were numbered as a recording artist for a label he helped put on the map. In June 1965, Ron Kass was asked to fill in on the short term for exiting executive vice president of Vee-Jay Lasker. The outgoing Lasker had joined Vee-Jay in late summer of 1963 and effectively opened West Coast offices of the label when he replaced president Ewart Abner. Both Lasker and Randy Wood lived in

California, and rumors were circulating that the entire operations of the label would shift to the Golden State.

"The Lasker appointment fans rumors, neither confirmed or denied by Vee-Jay, that the label may be moving its headquarters to the West Coast," *Billboard* reported in October 1963. In essence, Vee-Jay did move. All the important decisions were now being made in Santa Monica, California, though a Chicago office was still being maintained.

This separation between Chicago and California rocked the label, creating allegiances, political inner turmoil, and bad business decisions. "I didn't have much of a working relationship with the California office," Calvin Carter explained. "I stayed in Chicago and tried to keep that alive. We were making money, and all they were doing out there was blowing it."

Things just hadn't been the same for Vee-Jay since the early '60s. Former president Abner left the company to form his own firm, Dart Record Sales, under suspicious circumstances that, at this writing, are still not fully known. Vee-Jay and Kass tried to figure out ways to better improve their foreign distribution systems, but it would soon be all for naught. Vee-Jay label founder Jimmy Bracken bought out the West Coasters and brought operations back to Chicago in October 1965, literally overnight (as Calvin Carter would later say).

Word on the street was Vee-Jay had seen better days. They were running on fumes. Wood was the last California domino to fall when he, too, was shown the door. Bracken then pulled the ole switcharoo and made a strange announcement that he had *rehired* marketing wunderkind Ewart Abner as the label's general manager. This did little for the company, aside from raising red flags in industry circles.

The boom that most people in the industry had predicted would drop on the Chicago label was waiting patiently for the right moment to swoop down and cause total financial ruin. Vee-Jay's days as a viable ongoing concern were virtually over. The only commercial home that the unflappable, unyielding, at times obstinate Jimmy Reed had ever known was about to perish.

Chapter 5

The ABCs of the "New" Jimmy Reed

The last song Jimmy recorded for Vee-Jay, "Don't Think I'm Through," was less a prophetic statement about love and relationships than a declaration of his perseverance in the music industry. Vee-Jay was crumbling around him and Jimmy Reed was actively looking for a new record label, with the help of manager Al Smith.

Jimmy was in deep water professionally, but Reed-mania was still going strong. Frank Frost recorded "Big Boss Man" and "Baby Scratch My Back"—the latter originally done by Reed protégé Slim Harpo. Otis "Smokey" Smothers, who arrived in Chicago in the 1940s, was playing a Reed-esque shuffle in Windy City clubs. (Smothers was also signed to the Cincinnati, Ohio, label Federal, for which he recorded slow-to-mid-tempo shuffle-laden tracks with Freddie King on lead axe in 1960.) Federal hoped to carve a piece of the down-home, "Jimmy Reed-style" blues pie, and gave Smothers a shot. (You might think you are actually listening to a lost Jimmy Reed session when hearing Smothers' "Come On, Rock Little Girl," "Honey, I Ain't Teasin'," and "I Can't Judge Nobody.") As for Freddie King, he was familiar with the style—a style he had loved when he heard Jimmy Reed (and other down-homers like Lightnin' Hopkins)—and insinuated himself into the Smothers session. Furthermore, King's guitar playing was also, by his own admission, brought along by none other than Eddie Taylor. King told *Living Blues* magazine: "I was taught to use the picks by Eddie Taylor and Jimmy

Rogers. I used to use [three picks], but then Eddie Taylor, he showed me how to get the speed out of it. He's fast, man, Eddie is."

None of this impressed the Chicago chapter of the union. By February 1966, the American Federation of Musicians cancelled Reed's membership for the Boss Man's failure to pay the balance on a claim to the University of Florida in Gainesville (to the tune of $150) and a nearby nightclub called the Branch Inn ($205). These claims had been hanging over Reed's head for a few years.

Reed had empowered Al Smith to handle the paperwork and to see to it that he and his son Boonie were reinstated in the union. "This matter would have been clean [sic] up earlier but I've been to [sic] ill to look into this matter promptly, however I hope I shall be forgiven this time," wrote a negligent Jimmy to the musicians union. Smith saw to it that Reed's union dues were always paid, despite some of his checks having been returned and marked "N.S.F.," which was true on this occasion.

Personally, Jimmy was also leaking money. He'd be on the road and literally drop money out of his pockets. Von Freeman remembers having two jobs when he would go out with Jimmy Reed: one as a sax player and the other as a money catcher.

"My side job while we were playing all of these places was to pick up the loose money Jimmy dropped," Von explains. "Sometimes I would pick up fifteen or twenty dollars—all in one-dollar bills. Jimmy had a wad of money in his pocket, and because he was always spending money, he'd reach into his pocket and he'd drop bills. So, it was my job to follow him around and I'd pick up the bills for him."

Besides the few luxuries Reed allowed himself—a big white Cadillac, jewelry, and some nice clothing—he had very little in the way of savings. His mind was not on the tomorrow, it seemed. There were times when Smith would have to hide money from Jimmy—squirrel it away just to make sure it was sent home to his family for expenses rather than get blown on alcohol or frivolous items. But, as Smith would later say, what could you do? "Jimmy is a grown man." If he wanted his money, you had to give it to him.

"He would get drunk if you looked at him," says Houston-based guitarist Pete Mayes. "When we was playin' the Apollo, his manager—Al Smith—came across the street to get him something to eat, and while his manager was gone, someone had slipped Jimmy one drink. All you had to do was turn your back and Jimmy's drunk. I'll never forget that when we pulled into Birmingham, Alabama, one time, we pulled into a motel and Jimmy Reed was about drunk walking up and down throwing twenty-dollar bills on the ground. His son, Junior, was walking behind him picking them up. Junior went into the motel and wanted to put his lay-out bag on the bed. Before he could, Jimmy Reed jumped on the bed. The son cussed a little and said, 'Jimmy, get out the bed!' You know what Jimmy said? You know he had that song out, 'Ain't That Lovin' You Baby.' So, Jimmy looked up at Junior and said, 'Now, ain't that lovin' you, baby.'"

It seemed financial problems abounded in the Reed universe. In May 1966, Vee-Jay had officially gone bankrupt, having filed for Chapter 11. In August 1966, Vee-Jay was declared bankrupt, but had been under Chapter 11 for months in the hopes of reorganizing the company on more secure financial footing. That day would never come. The company had been carrying nearly $2 million in debts with $1.5 million in back taxes due, and back in 1963 an audit of the company revealed that Vee-Jay officers owed the company over $200,000. (Many theorize the exorbitant amount was tied in with Abner's alleged gambling habit.)

"They had some problems—they never paid their taxes," explains engineer Murray Allen. "They claimed somebody had stolen some money from them and so forth—that kind of thing. You have to remember Jimmy Bracken came from shining shoes and they used to sell the records out of the back of their cars. Then it became a major label with major artists. But they forgot that they had to pay income tax, you know? All of a sudden they are out of business."

"Vee-Jay would have been bigger than Motown," says Bruce Spizer, a tax attorney and author of *Songs, Pictures, and Stories of the Fabulous Beatles Records on Vee-Jay* and *The Beatles Are Coming: The Birth of Beatlemania in America* (498 Productions). "You had the Four Seasons and the Beatles, and even if the Vee-Jay attorney had not screwed up, a court may have ruled that Vee-Jay put out the *Introducing the Beatles* album but technically didn't have the right to because they had exercised their right of first refusal."

"What happened was, Ewart Abner, he was with Chance and went over to Vee-Jay and he wasn't paying taxes," says Red Holloway, who was part of the explosive '60s jazz band that Brother Jack McDuff had put together. "And he wasn't keeping records for Vee-Jay as far as royalties that needed to be paid. So when Uncle Sam came in and it was known that they didn't pay their taxes, they took everything, as they usually do."

"Vivian was a radio personality and Jimmy Bracken was not a 'record man.' O.K.?" explains Chuck Barksdale of the Dells. "When they brought in Ewart Abner and made him the president of the record company, it was pretty much their demise, in my eyes. He had a terrible gambling habit…. It eventually cost the company to just go into bankruptcy. I was there, along with Bobby Miller, along with Barrett Strong from Motown. We were there the day they padlocked, literally, the doors on the Vee-Jay office [at 1449 S. Michigan Avenue]. Other words, no one could get in through these doors—they have been locked by order of the IRS. That tore us apart, and we were working at the company in the A&R department. The three of us, along with Wade Flemons. It literally tore us apart because we…there used to be a place across the street that was called B&G's restaurant and that was where we would always meet and have coffee and have a little tea and egg sandwich or something before we would go over there and go to work, then we saw the people padlocking the place. We said, 'Oh, man,' we went over there and read the sign saying the place was closed down. That was the end of Vee-Jay as we knew it. Even though they moved to California, that was probably the worst move they made in their lives. They went from 'sugar to shit,' as the old saying goes."

Rumors spread. To this day, the reasons many give for the label's demise are simply conjecture spliced together with some fact. Some cite the frivolous expenses used for promotional campaigns (one story tells of Vee-Jay flying in blonde Swedish models to a radio convention in Los Angeles as a marketing gimmick), others say losing a bitter battle over the Beatles cost them so dearly that their cash dwindled down to nothing and they were incapable of paying royalties. Still others thought that onetime Vee-Jay execs, with offices in California, had their eyes on the Hollywood soundtrack pie.

The Dells' Marvin Junior offers his point of view: "I'll tell you something that isn't very well known. Vee-Jay wanted to get into soundtracks, Hollywood soundtracks. But the people out there, they weren't having it," says Junior. "Vee-Jay was the largest black-owned record label, before Motown came along, but they grew too quickly and they got too big. When they moved out to California, that was the beginning of the end. [Their competitors] cut their heads off out there. They weren't going to have a black-owned label coming in and working on the same turf—soundtracks. So you had all of this stuff about back taxes and bribes and everything else being investigated. Vee-Jay was being taken out. Its head was cut off, you understand?"

"To be honest, we were not sorry to see them go," says Mickey McGill, Junior's bandmate in the Dells. "We received a number of checks from Chess when we went over there, but never anything from Vee-Jay. Chess loved us. Vee-Jay started to get greedy. There are some other reasons, but I won't get into them now. They wanted to get into pop music—a more commercial or 'white' sound. They saw the success of Motown and thought they could copy it."

From the evidence, Jimmy Bracken and Vivian Carter were shocked at their own sudden demise and stunned into paralysis. After having lived in California for a time, the Brackens had to sell their house and head back to the Midwest. "[Vivian's] was a rags-to-riches story," explained Carter family friend Yjean Chambers in 1989. "When she came back from California, she had an unusual adjustment to make. She felt some rancor toward the people who helped do her in, but I wouldn't call it bitterness. She was analytical about it."

Were forces out to get Vee-Jay? Carter, who suffered diabetes, amputations, and a stroke in her later years, began her final descent in the early '80s. Her business and life partner Jimmy Bracken had died in 1972, and Carter spent her twilight years in a nursing home before she died in 1989, alone and with very little money to her name. The saying "only in America" comes to mind when thinking of Vivian and Jimmy Bracken. It was a wild ride, and they rode it to extravagance at times (throwing expensive parties for friends and flying around the world), only to see the company they had built being methodically dismantled by the powers that be. But in the process, they burned a path for other black labels to follow. Gordon Keith, who first recorded the Jackson 5 on Steeltown Records (a label he founded), called Vivian "the mother of black recording companies."

"This is not facts, but it seemed like it could have happened," explains Barksdale. "By us being in Chicago and Lake Michigan, Jimmy [Bracken] wrote a message that said, 'To whom it may concern: Whoever picks this message up and you want to start a record company, these are some of the mistakes you cannot make...' and then listed them. He stuck the message in a bottle and put the top on it and the bottle floats across Lake Michigan. On the shores was a guy named Berry Gordy who was looking for ideas to open up his own record company. That is called put a message in a bottle, baby."

Keith agrees: "If there had not been a Vee-Jay Records, there would not have been a Motown Sound to begin with."

"If you look back, you will find that most of those [indie] labels were run by guys who were not attorneys, not accountants," says Vee-Jay artist Jerry Butler. "They were street guys. Jimmy Bracken owned a shoeshine stand. But he and Vivian parlayed that into a record shop, and that into a record label. They were not accountants, and by the time we get to 1961, 1962, all of a sudden the industry is flooded by sharp executive types who were, in fact, lawyers, CPAs, marketing experts—and the music, as well as the way it was promoted and marketed, started to change. Vee-Jay was a victim of its own success. I think they got so enamored with having some of the first product in America on the Beatles, that they kind of overran the store.

"Did they fail? No. They went *bankrupt*," Butler explains. "Why did they go bankrupt? Because they owed more money than they could get in. Now, it wasn't that they weren't owed the money—they couldn't collect it. Because what happened was they went to the pressing plants when they found out that they had all of this Vee-Jay product with the Beatles on it and they put all of this money out into the street because the pressing plants and the studios said, 'We want our money now.' And so they paid them. Then they put the product out to the distributors and the distributors said, 'Well, we will pay you in 30 or 60 [days].' And so suddenly you go from selling a half-million records on all of the artists to a million and a half records on one. Get my drift?

"So, all of a sudden you have a lot of money out there on the street that you have to collect. Except you are not set up to collect it. Because you never expected it to be that big. Now, this is just my opinion of what happened," admits Butler. "You may go and find statistically that all of this is incorrect. From my point of view, that was part of the reason why Vee-Jay went down. They owed a lot of money to the pressing plants, to the studios, the people who were marketing and promoting this product. And they were owed lots of money by the distributors. But when the distributors found out that Capitol EMI was suing Vee-Jay for releasing this product after the time that they had allotted for them to release it, the distributors said, 'Let's wait and see what happens.' They were also in the record business in a town that was not a big record company town. If Vee-Jay had been in New York or Los Angeles some five or ten years later, they could have borrowed the money to keep them going. But because they were a small black company, based in Chicago, where most of the people thought the music industry was a joke, where would they get the money? To prove my point, about 1967 or 1968, most of the record companies were purchased and moved to either New York or Los Angeles...

"You must look at the Four Seasons," Butler continues. "They were a deal rather than an artist on a label. It really was a record production deal more than the Four Seasons being on Vee-Jay, like I was. Vee-Jay called all the shots as to how much money I was going to make, when I was going to record, how I was going to be promoted. With the Four Seasons they didn't have that same luxury. The Four Seasons were brought to them in a deal with the producers and everybody else built into the deal. And so, I even heard Abner say this, 'They had promised Vee-Jay several albums or one or two albums after they left and went to Mercury.' And when they got it, it was a live album, geared toward Las Vegas—a lot of show tunes—and not the kind of product Vee-Jay needed to compete with 'Big Girls Don't Cry.' So, it was not the same as if they were on Vee-Jay and that was the whole nine yards."

If Yankee Stadium is "the house that Ruth built," then Vee-Jay was, at least partly, "the house that Reed built." He was there at the label's near inception. And, just as future Yankees would surpass Babe Ruth in certain statistical categories, so, too, Reed was not always the bestseller. But he was the heart and soul of the label and his greatness was synonymous with Vee-Jay's. He was also perhaps the most consistently commanding presence the label ever had.

Still, Jimmy, as he had done throughout his life, seemed to be taking the label's crash in stride. Besides, how much was Vee-Jay doing for him anyway? He had always made his money by playing for the people, on the road, not cutting records, from which he'd see only a few royalties.

By the spring of 1966, all Vee-Jay employees were released from duty and the phones cut off. The Boss Man was shielded from the fallout of the label collapse when he hooked up with Vee-Jay affiliate Exodus. In May 1966, Reed cut two singles for Exodus: "Knocking at Your Door" with flip side "Dedication to Sonny" (also appears as "Tribute to a Friend") and "Cousin Peaches" with "Crazy 'bout Oklahoma." These four sides are among Reed's most memorable of the entire decade of the '60s.

Reed's bizarre but memorable tribute to his idol.

"Dedication to Sonny" is as idiosyncratic as any of Reed's music from the past. A tribute to Sonny Boy Williamson II, who had died a year to the month before the song was recorded, it is one of those occasions that we can clearly hear someone (most probably Al Smith) feeding Reed the lines. Softly Smith speaks the words to Reed, who repeats them, often with a twist. The line "he has passed on to the other side," for example, is spoken and Reed makes it his own by saying "he has *done* passed on the other side now." It's amazing not that he was fed the lines, but that he was able to keep himself in time.

Reed talks with a slight lilt in his voice: "…and Sonny Boy? This is for you…from *Jimmah* Reed." The words must have meant something to Reed at the time, though the rants sound arbitrary and quite bizarre. "They are scratching their back, clipping their toenails, running buck and barefoot.…"

Reed takes the song in a few wacky and different directions, speaking off the top of his head. Reed wants the listeners to "sit back and relax" and "listen at me play these blues." Wherever his old friend "Sonny Boy Williams" [sic] is, Reed "know he is swingin' " and hopes that he is "enjoying hisself." It is borderline comical, but the power with which Reed blows the harp isn't. He captures Sonny Boy's ferocious playing, as if channeling him. Reed lives in the lower registers and his harmonica voice is rife with warbles and vibrato (a Sonny Boy trademark). He accomplishes this furious vibrato through manipulating his breathing to push alternating strong and soft gusts of air through the harp's holes.

The flip side, "Knocking at Your Door," is equally amusing, i.e., not revealing, and remarkable for no other reason than its witty imagery and neat rhyme scheme: "I ain't gonna leave, baby/Honey, don't you have no doubt/Honey, if Jimmy Reed can't get in, ain't nobody comin' out." Like a mealy-mouthed big bad wolf, Reed is huffing, puffing, and blues shufflin' in attempts to shake something loose. As the song lumbers to its conclusion and fades, Reed is left behind frustrated.

Reed is back on the prowl for his next track. It seems he finally heard Al Duncan's pleas and recorded "Crazy 'bout Oklahoma" (legal title "Texas Is Doggone Big")—an ode to a certain part of the female anatomy. "The girls' legs so *biiiiig* they look like Willie Mays' baseball bat…they got some long, tall ones down there, and, *man,* they really know where it's at," Reed sings. (Willie Mays often used a 35-inch, 36-ounce Adirondack white-ash bat during the late '60s and early '70s. That's a hefty piece of lumber.) The guitars are very nearly in dissonance with one another, and the drumming is classic Al Duncan falling-off-the-table. The only thing holding the song together is Jimmy's harp playing and the humorous way he stuffs too many words into his vocal phrasings: "I'm crazy 'bout Oklahoma/Honey, Texas so doggone big/You know Oklahoma got 'the oil, baby/Texas got the money to buy it with."

"Cousin Peaches" was a nickname he was given down South when he was growing up. It was an affectionate name that Reed would later use to refer to other people who came in and out of his life. As the song says, "I'm just a poor country boy lookin' for a home to call my own." Reed seems to be wearing his country background as a badge of honor, and he is more proud of his Mississippi past than overwhelmed by the big city, despite singing self-deprecating and sad lines like "I may look like I am happy, [but] everything I do is wrong."

There was more truth in those words than hype. Through Reed's clownish exterior, he was hurting. He wasn't comfortable in his own skin. Knowing he had something different to offer the world than being a hardworking, verbally abused farmhand, Reed had escaped the South. But to what end? The city was full of jobs where the frontline was blazing hot furnaces and shrieking livestock. He had worked and escaped those jobs, had a steady relationship (though it had its rocky points of infidelity, too), and in many ways was living the American dream. He even became, for all intents and purposes, a "rock 'n' roll star." He dealt with his rise to fame the only way a simple man could: by hiding inside himself. If that meant taking substances to do it, so be it.

In some of the quieter moments Jimmy let his guard down. "Jimmy Reed sat down and talked to me about many, many things," says Johnnie Mae Dunson. "The man was all right, but he was sick—sicker than anybody knew. Jimmy Reed had some God in him, I'll tell you that. I had faith and he had belief."

Von Freeman remembers: "He was a very down-to-earth guy, and he liked his wine. He would buy you some wine and you could talk with him for two or three hours with him. He made sense."

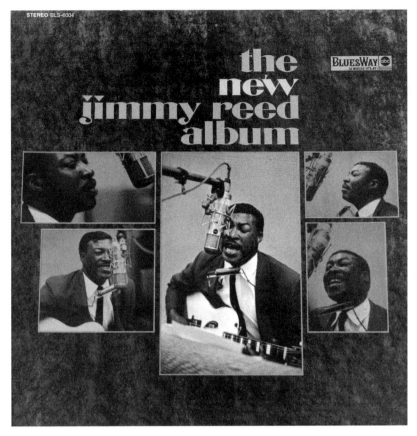

BluesWay presented Jimmy an opportunity for change and a fresh start.

Jimmy was fully aware of his shortcomings. He and Mama hadn't had the best of times lately. They had been arguing and getting on each other's nerves ever since they were married, but Jimmy was praying that he could be a more steady man. "I'm very proud of myself that I was able to stay with my wife for 21 years," Reed is quoted in Sheldon Harris' liner notes to *The New Jimmy Reed Album.* "My father went all the way through…stayed with my mother until he passed. And I'd appreciate it very much if I am able to do just like my father did."

"When I was in my twenties, not really grown up, I was cocky and still wild, you know?" says D.C. Bellamy, who would later do pre-production work with Jimmy. "I loved Jimmy Reed. From sitting in that room with him, I got to study him as a man, not as someone who drank.

When he walked around he never carried a guitar case. When he walked into that room, that guitar was around his neck. He'd get out that car and the guitar would be around his neck. We, today, if we have a problem we go to see a therapist to go to talk to somebody. This was his therapy: music. This was what got him further up into life, this music and instrument, that anger and sadness and even joy—that was Jimmy Reed's entire life. If it wasn't for the music I don't know if he or others would have made it as long as they did."

"We'd talk and drink together," Red Holloway adds. "He never really hurt anybody but himself."

Byther Smith worked with Jimmy in the local Chicago clubs and in places like Minnesota and Texas. "He was a trusting soul," Smith says. "To me, he was a nice guy, because the first night I worked with him, he didn't know me from anybody else yet he told me to pay the band. He told me to keep his money until he was ready for it. He would get drunk but he was trying to be careful."

"Overall, Jimmy was just a country guy," explains Doktu Rhut Muuzic (formerly Roy Hytower), who would record with Reed. "He never was like a city guy. He did never wear his celebrity. He didn't act like a star—though it was a thrill for me, having grown up listening to him, to have played with him. His whole family was just regular folks. It just seemed like nothing was really a big deal for him. Even going on tour. A lot of times Al Smith or someone would say, 'Come on, Jimmy. We've got some tours lined up. We have to go on the road.' It was no big exciting thing. The celebrity thing was not part of his makeup. He was real, and there wasn't anything phony about him. People liked that. They knew he had a drinking problem in spite of that."

By June, Reed's recording career looked dire (ironically, though, he was on the charts again, at No. 39 on *Billboard*'s soul chart with "Knocking at Your Door"). Reed guitar man Eddie Taylor had seen enough. He was leaving his options open. Not waiting around to see what happened with Vee-Jay, Eddie walked into Chicago's One-derful Studios with his old friend Floyd Jones (aka "Frog Mouth Floyd" because the corners of his mouth nearly reached his ears). They were joined by Big Walter Horton on harp, Otis Spann on piano, and Fred Below on drums.

Eddie re-recorded his big "hit," "Big Town Playboy," and his other signature tune, "Bad Boy," with killer rolls from Spann that spiral across the tune. Taylor even performed "Peach Tree Blues," a variant of the Big Joe Williams song "Peach Orchard Mama."

Taylor shared top billing with guitarist/bassist Jones, flip-flopping lead roles (Jones plays bass on the Taylor tracks) for this Testament label LP, one in a series called *Masters of Modern Blues*. While there are some fine moments here (Jones' remake of "Hard Times," which he had first recorded in the late '40s), the session wasn't making Taylor rich, nor was it as powerful as the liner notes would have you believe. It is a dark, non-cathartic, hypnotic effort on which the band meshes well. (Listen to the sympathetic musical interplay between Spann, Taylor, and Horton.)

Rolling Stone reviewed the record and the two others in the series: "Technically, the recordings lack (by just a hairbreadth) the punch and presence Chess was able to get in the 1950s, but they do have the advantage of authentic and well-mixed stereo." The record was a fitting "tribute," the magazine read, "to the Chicago *band* sound at its peak."

Indeed. The record is a great snapshot of the development of Delta blues into the Chicago blues style—of longtime friends who operated on silent communication. The players here aren't so much pushing one another but allowing their musical antennae to scope out fertile sonic ground.

Perhaps much more importantly, this LP was one small step in the right direction for Eddie's solo career. As Pete Welding's liner notes conceded: ". . . though Jones has made a larger number of recordings than his close friend Eddie Taylor, the latter has been known to a large number of blues fans through his prolonged association on record and in personal appearances with the popular Jimmy Reed."

Reed, however, was still without a real recording label home. In its absence, he hit the road, Mama Reed and Al Smith in tow.

Milton Hopkins, a distant relative of Texas acoustic bluesman Lightnin' Hopkins, remembers touring with Jimmy Reed around this time. Hopkins first hit the road with Johnny Ace and Willie Mae Thornton in the early '50s, carrying nothing more than a brown paper bag that held his meager belongings. Fifteen years later, he was playing on the same bill, as a member of Grady Gaines' Upsetters, with Jimmy Reed. "We did two dates in San Francisco at the Fillmore," Hopkins remembers. "We were in San Francisco and we were between the second floor and the lobby, there was a little stairwell taking you to a little lounge up there. We were getting ready to check out and go to Sacramento, and Jimmy, who was on the second floor, fell down those stairs. He slipped. We thought he had broke his ass, but when he got through rolling and tumbling…he came up and looked up and said to everybody, 'Now, ain't *that* lovin' you, baby.'

"We did from time to time go up to Buffalo or Schenectady, New York," Hopkins continues. "We worked a club up there and Jimmy Reed was always on the bill. I remember one time we were in Memphis, Tennessee, at a place called Sunbeam Butler's, dancehall, on the bill with Jimmy Reed. Al [Smith] refused to switch over—he played upright bass. Even when Al didn't have a band, when Jimmy went out, Al was always there. Bass player and a drummer was always there and sometimes they had an extra guitar player, horns, piano player—the full complement. Most of the time if they didn't have a band, they would have Al Smith and a drummer who would come in when Jimmy Reed was doing his set. His wife was there, too. Jimmy had some help. His wife would be up there whispering the words to him."

Hopkins remembers Reed as someone who was always buzzed on life and on drink. "Jimmy was always happy. He and Aretha Franklin and all those guys used to get together and have some hellacious parties. I have no idea what the deal was or what he was drinking, but he was drinking. When I went out [on the road] with Willie Mae Thornton—she loved Old Crow. She would have a half-gallon of that stuff any time. I don't know why [Jimmy] drank like that, but he was always aware of his audience. He could feel what they wanted and do a good show. Some of them songs people would hear nothing but the first couple of words. A lot of the time you had 400 or 500 or 600 people in a hall—and they didn't have the types of PA systems that they have now—and people would start hollering, jumping up and down, boogieing and screaming. They wouldn't hear nothing but the first couple of lines because it got so loud in there. But they didn't care."

The Upsetters were scheduled to record with Reed, but the session never materialized. Instead, Hopkins recalls playing clubs in the Deep South with Reed in the 1960s, memories of which are priceless in and of themselves. "Hollandale, Florida. That was where this one club was," Hopkins says. "The Palms in Hollandale. That is where all the gangsters went, you know. All those people up in New York would go down there in the swamps.... They used to have bungalows down there for those guys. The promoters would put us up in those things during the off-season. They had three- and four-room bungalows, way back in the boonies. And, of course, there were gators down there, and we saw them, man. And there was only one way you could get to and from the bungalow: boat. We was all young fellas and it was all new to us, it was all fun and games because we didn't know any better. Can you imagine having to use a boat to get to your room, through a swamp full of alligators? But we did it. We just stayed away from the gators and they never did bother us too much."

By November 1966, with the help of Al Smith, Reed would finally find a new home at a newly founded record label, BluesWay, a subsidiary of ABC. Though the Vee-Jay troubles were now a million miles away, ABC-BluesWay was a monster of a different color.

A bit of history: Jay Lasker, formerly of Vee-Jay, founded Dunhill Records with Lou Adler and Bobby Roberts. Dunhill was eventually swallowed by ABC Records, and ABC opened BluesWay. Pretty soon BluesWay had an array of blues artists, some of whom were lucky enough to get called to the big time: ABC Records. The problem was, the ABC and BluesWay staffs were overworked and busy with promoting artists on its jazz label, Impulse! The ABC "blues team" was nothing more than a one- or two-man operation at any given time. There just was not enough time and manpower to properly devote to all the new material being produced by the label.

"I was making in the neighborhood of 40 albums a year," explains producer Ed Michel. "I was working 50-hour days in my home studio when I wasn't out in the world recording. I was running BluesWay as a side issue to running Impulse!, which was my main job, and recording for ABC as well."

"The big guys were getting paid for how many records they were putting out," explains John Dixon, who worked for BluesWay and Impulse! as assistant national promotion director. "They would get a dime an album. There was no concept of quality; it was all about how many records can we get out this month. They got paid for records pressed and shipped—it had nothing to do with returns, or anything. It behooved them to find anything they could move that could be pressed and put it out. That was the deal Jay Lasker had with ABC. So, they would ship anything out. That is why they bought Duke Peacock and you'd have 15 Peacock records come out one month by all of these gospel artists. Some were great and some were just very, very average. I was on the West Coast and my time was taken up with John Klemmer and Keith Jarrett and that kind of thing. They were getting airplay and they were touring and that kind of stuff, so...."

BluesWay's promotion budget was zilch, making it even more difficult for an artist like Jimmy Reed to break through with a new record. "It is hard when you have 13 or 14 albums on BluesWay and there is no money behind it," explains Dixon. "They didn't give you any money to do posters. They may have given you money to do ads and stuff, but it was more like we would put out 23 albums and see what happens."

"BluesWay was very much a stepchild label," Michel admits. "Any artist who sold well enough to be noticed on BluesWay would be moved over to ABC, the parent label. When someone corporate decided a release was needed, I was told to come up with some new albums and repackage some older ones. Nobody saw it as an art project."

What this meant was manager and now producer Al Smith had to have more control as a producer to achieve a greater sound. A question, however, is raised about just how much Al was looking out for Jimmy in this ABC–BluesWay deal, and how much he was looking out for himself. "I would almost bet that nobody, including Jimmy, had a deal with Al Smith, not BluesWay," says Dixon. "It was a production deal. They gave Al Smith $50,000 and he gives them ten albums. It was not like you sign, you get an advance, and they agree to promote your career.

With BluesWay it was just a master purchase deal. If the company has no money in it, they are not going to promote it. That's it. Could be a fluke and some little station starts something out of nowhere and suddenly you have a hit out of one of those things. But, it was just another record to be pressed and shipped out the door, with no sense of direction or commitment to the artist."

The harsh reality was that BluesWay didn't treat or do anything new or different to their blues artists than any other label. With the exception of Ray Charles and B.B. King on ABC, most of the time these R&B, soul, and blues artists were putting out records in obscurity.

Nevertheless, there was a sense of optimism surrounding Jimmy's new digs. To that end, Jimmy went into Columbia Studios in early November 1966 to record what would become his first BluesWay LP, *The New Jimmy Reed Album*. Besides five guitarists (Lefty Bates, Boonie, Jimmy, Jimmy Gresham on bass, and an uncredited sideman on the first six songs—undoubtedly Eddie Taylor), the band also included Al Duncan on drums. Smith brought back Duncan to relax Jimmy and make him comfortable with the groove laid down by a drummer he had grown somewhat accustomed to in the past. No one could be Earl Phillips, but Duncan could do the job.

Recorded over two sessions, the record did produce two singles: "Two Ways to Skin a Cat" with B-side "Got Nowhere to Go," and "I Wanna Know" with B-side "Two Heads Are Better than One." The latter sounded as though it had been brewed from the classic Reed stuff. That instantly recognizable loping guitar rhythm, the familiar (maybe all too familiar for some) harp solo, and the trashy cymbals (along with a creamy coat of cymbal hiss) give the record a kind of raw charm. Also notable is the fact that "I Wanna Know" and "Honey, I'll Make Two" (the first song on side two of the LP) were co-written by Reed family friend and musician Johnnie Mae Dunson.

Reed's attempt to re-record his classic sides for the LP fell far short of what the need camp might have hoped. In all honesty, BluesWay couldn't care less. With that kind of attitude, it was up to the Reed camp to provide all the marketing strategy. The record label's lack of interest was Smith's advantage. Smith was smart as a whip: he knew that this new label would present him the opportunity to not only stress

Reed's new material and its fuller, more orchestrated sound (in Smith's opinion), but present an entirely "new" Jimmy Reed.

Reed certainly did get and need an overhaul. For one thing, on a purely superficial level, he was wearing a hairpiece these days, having slowly lost his hair during the late '50s and the early '60s. Smith used Reed's down-but-not-yet-out appearance to his advantage by packaging Reed as "Jimmy reinvented." More importantly, Smith was trying to sell Reed's music as fresh. "We worked hard on the rhythm patterns," Smith explained on the liner notes for *The New Jimmy Reed Album.* "On this album each instrument is doing something different. It's hard to work four guitars. Jimmy and I worked on the road seven, eight years together to work this sound."

As far as Jimmy was concerned, this BluesWay record was not much different than any other he had done. He thought he was as creative as ever. "It's kind of hard for me to keep count of all that I did write," Reed explained to *Living Blues.* "I guess it is just a mother wit thing, because as I ride along maybe I see a sign say something funny on it and I get to thinking about that, and I go from there and I just write that into a sound. Words just start coming automatically after I get the idea."

For Mama Reed, *The New Jimmy Reed Album* was simply Jimmy's best, and it was no surprise: Reed, who had become a father for the eighth time weeks after recording tracks for the new LP, dedicated the record to Mama.

The problem of presenting a whole "new Reed" is that with a man who had been known for "repetitive" music—no matter how cozy or comfortable—it becomes impossible to break the mold he had created for himself. As long as he was reaching the audience, Reed didn't feel he should have to learn new tricks.

Simply put, the whole idea of a more "orchestrated" Reed sound never truly materialized. Besides some subtle differences, not much had really changed as far as Reed's musical presentation. Critics noticed this too, and said so, but mostly their criticism was sharpened by their affection for Reed's Vee-Jay releases. They just didn't hear the same kind of fire and wit in the BluesWay record.

But many of the musical hallmarks of Reed's Vee-Jay material are indeed present on *The New Jimmy Reed Album,* and so some of this criticism begs the question: If there were only subtle differences between the Vee-Jay classics and this first BluesWay LP, why the negativity?

There was a glimmer of hope, however, for the "new Reed." Jimmy's first single for ABC, "Got Nowhere to Go," peaked at No. 125 in January 1967. That wasn't exactly earth-shattering—it was well off the *Billboard* Hot 100 charts—but it was within the radar of public consciousness. This came virtually simultaneously with Otis Redding's untimely death, which brought about a posthumous No. 1 hit (on both the pop and R&B charts), "(Sittin' on) The Dock of the Bay." In general, Stax was busy dominating the R&B and soul worlds in the mid- and late '60s with acts like Sam & Dave, the Bar-Kays, Albert King, Carla Thomas (daughter of Rufus, and once rejected by Vee-Jay), and Isaac Hayes. But Jimmy Reed's vital signs hadn't leveled. He still "had it": a consumer audience, a viable career, and raw talent that connected. Fittingly, Reed said in the liner notes to *The New Jimmy Reed Album:* "I only want my rhythm and my sound to be something the people [can] really feel."

Reed didn't show it much in public, but privately, to close friends and family, he revealed he knew what he had accomplished over the past 14 years of his career. "My dad would play his name card in a minute," says John Lee Hooker, Jr. "You know, 'I'm John Lee Hooker.' He'd walk up to the hotel clerk, 'You got my room ready?' Clerk would say, 'Sir, who are you?' He says, 'You don't know who I am?' 'Well, no-no, sir.' 'I'm John Lee Hooker.' She say, 'Oh, my goodness, Mr. Hooker, I am sorry.' She would *act* like she knew [laughs]. And Jimmy was the same way, '*I'm Jimmy Reed.* You ain't never heard of me?' I think that is why they loved each other. They had a great sense of themselves. You know, Jimmy'd walk up to me and say, 'You know who I am, boy? I'm *Jimmah* Reed.'"

Reed took advantage of his resurfacing and continued visibility by making a swing through the West Coast, beginning with the Calderon Ballroom in Phoenix, Arizona, on December 29, 1966, and working venues such as the Fillmore Auditorium in San Francisco (February 10–12, 1967) and the Berkeley Community Theater in late March 1967. And indeed, he still had it.

"I worked with him in Houston, the Apollo in New York, and Cleveland, Ohio," says Pete Mayes. "I was Junior Parker's bandleader for about four years and we worked shows in Cleveland, Ohio, with Jimmy Reed. We backed him up. I worked with him with my band in Houston at Jimmy Menuti's place more than once. He'd come through maybe two or three times a year, or more. Menuti's was predominantly a white audience. Menuti's was an old theater that had been turned into a club. So, it had a balcony and a bottom floor. He made a dance club out of it and a bar. It was big. You know what I think it was that got the crowds going? Jimmy was no phony—he wasn't trying to put on no show—he was just Jimmy and they loved that. I seen him right here in Houston, sober—on a package show here in Houston at the Coliseum, with the Impressions, Archie Bell, and stuff like that. There was a package show with Jimmy Reed and they called him 'Cous.' " They would say, 'You gotta watch ole Cous—he'll steal the show.' And he would—and he did. He'd go out there and do his stuff. They would be applauding Jimmy more than anyone in the show."

Jimmy certainly had a way about him. He could get away with shit that no one else could. "I remember once we were at Menuti's in Houston and it was almost like a black-tie affair," Mayes continues. "The people were all dressed real well—they had coats and ties and the ladies had on long dresses and things. This one lady, a white lady—Jimmy drew a lot of white people—this lady hollered up to Jimmy and said, "Caress Me Baby." Jimmy looked at her and staggered back and said, 'I will caress ya allright.' You know, he could get away with that because of the way he was. But if I did that, they'd come out and lynch my ass."

There was always an endearing quality to Jimmy, no matter how loaded or off he was. A famous story for case in point goes like this:

Firebrand southpaw guitar slinger Otis Rush, opening for Jimmy Reed, is sweating it out, really busting his ass to warm up the crowd. His sonic dips and bends had left them stone-faced, and they are seemingly incapable of mustering anything more than some polite applause. Otis shakes his head, unplugs his guitar, and storms off the stage. When Jimmy Reed comes out from behind the curtain, however, it is like the greenhouse effect in super high-speed action—the iceberg of an audience is instantly melted. But before Reed can even play a note, he stumbles over himself and nearly does a flip before the crowd's anticipatory eyes. Thinking it is all part of Jimmy Reed's act, the place goes nuts. Otis leaves, wondering what he had to do to connect with the crowd, *and all that muthafucka have to do is walk across the stage.*

John Lee Hooker, Jr., remembers Jimmy as a blood uncle. "He used to sit me on his knee," Hooker says. "He used to talk to me and sit me on his knee and then he'd say, 'Boy, go get me some water.' You know, with that drawl—'Go get me some *whadda.*' Then he'd say, 'You know who I am?' I say, 'Yeah.' 'What's my name?' he'd ask. I'd say, 'You Jimmy.' He said, 'I'm your *Uncle* Jimmy Reed, and don't you ever forget it, boy.' He was a really kind and soft-spoken man. I remember sitting on his little skinny knee, 'cause he and my dad were skinny to me. They could have been brothers. They wore their hair straight back. You can talk about somebody who can do an impersonation of Jimmy Reed, ain't nobody do it like my dad…. He and my dad were so much alike. I used to see them sitting up wherever they were, laughing and telling stories."

Michael Powers will never forget a stop Jimmy made in Bayonne, New Jersey, where Powers was helping his father run the family business. Bayonne is a port city and many black sailors would flood the local stores, nightclubs, and restaurants to listen to good music, eat soul food, and enjoy some R & R. As Powers was attending to daily chores, he heard this otherwordly harp and guitar playing emanating from across the street, from the alley. Drawn by the sound, Powers left his duties behind, floated into the alley, and watched the music-making man, accompanied by a woman on tambourine. (Powers believes that it was Mary Lee Reed.)

Powers approached the man and saw his giant fingers (giant to the 15-year-old Powers) stretch across the fretboard of the guitar neck. He was blowing into his harp, which was fastened to a rack, and stamping his feet on a drum. "I have never seen anyone really play that way before," Powers insists. "I asked what he was playing, and the man told me, 'a barre chord.' Well, I had no idea what that was. So, he showed me how to form the chord with my fingers, where to place my fingers. After that, I ran home, picked up a guitar that my mother Doris had bought me, and tried to learn what it was that this man just showed me. It took me a while, but I got it down. It was a total chance meeting that kicked off my musical search. The name of the man responsible? Jimmy Reed. And he took the time out to teach me. Who was I?"

Meanwhile, in Chicago, Eddie Taylor was inspiring young players as well. W.C. Handy Award–winning and Grammy-nominated guitarist James Solberg (he'd play with Luther Allison after his early blues education in Chicago) was an aspiring rock guitarist when he was bitten by the blues bug. "I was playing in rock bands and stuff and I was hanging out in Chicago and sticking my ear to the back doors of these clubs," Solberg says. "That's how I met Eddie Taylor. He said, 'What'cha doin' out there, boy?' I told him, 'I just want to hear the blues.' He said, 'C'mon in.' When he found out I was a guitar player we just started messing around together a lot. I started playing with him and Big Walter Horton, Johnny Young. Eddie Taylor and I would stay up all night and we would mess around and he would show me some stuff. He was amazing.

"Back in those days," Solberg notes, "even up to our early twenties, guys my age, you could go to some bars in Chicago and see Muddy and Wolf still setting up on the floor—there wasn't even a stage. Not that I wish that on anybody, but…. They welcomed us and took us under their arms. We learned how to play music from generations before us. Even if you were playing something that seemed modern, it was based in music that was carried down from generation to generation. It had depth."

It seemed that even though Vee-Jay had all but vanished from the radar, the label's problems hadn't. By March 1967, a former Vee-Jay officer was on trial for bribing an IRS agent. And Jimmy Bracken had to open a new Vivian's Record Shop in Chicago after the original shop in Gary was seized by the IRS, while Vivian continued to broadcast "Vivian Says" from WGRT. Former Vee-Jay president Ewart Abner signed on at Motown as vice president of international management at the insistence of Motown founder Berry Gordy. (Abner would eventually become president of Motown and Stevie Wonder's manager for a decade.)

By July 1967, former Vee-Jay employees Randy Wood (Abner's presidential successor) and accountant Betty Chiapetta bought Vee-Jay and resurrected the label name. Vee-Jay seemed to be back, but then again, so was Jimmy Reed—with a new label.

Jimmy's next LP for BluesWay, *Soulin'*, was unlike his first. It contained previously released material from his two Exodus singles ("Knocking at Your Door," "Dedication to Sonny," "Crazy 'bout Oklahoma," and "Cousin Peaches"), three tracks he cut for the Vivid label ("Peepin' & Hiding"—a remake of "Baby What You Want Me to Do" with some nice sympathetic harp and guitar tones—"Buy Me a Hound Dog," and "Feel Like I Want to Ramble"), and unused material from the November 1966 sessions that became *The New Jimmy Reed Album*, including "Don't Press Your Luck, Woman."

The latter song was straight out of the pages of 1960s soul. Jimmy sings about being a "natural soul brother" from way down on the farm. He's blowing harp in second position here, and Al Duncan charges the song with extra zing thanks to a kind of boogaloo beat (a twist of R&B and Latin where Duncan seemingly maintains a steady eighth-note pulse on his hi-hats, as crisp snare attacks and kick-drum rumble battle for sonic supremacy). Despite a repetitive nature, "Don't Press Your Luck, Woman" is rife with unexpected stop breaks, unexpected left-turn harp lines, and catchy chordal lines by Eddie Taylor and Jimmy Reed, Jr. However, in all fairness, if the song were even a half-minute longer, that repetitive rhythmic pattern would surely become irritating and drive the listener up a wall. Everyone—from the audio engineers on up to Al Smith—knew just when to cut this baby off.

Reed had a new, complete LP, and he hadn't done any real work for it for the better part of a year. And perhaps that was a good thing. Jimmy's seemingly bottomless energy was starting to peter out. If *The New Jimmy Reed Album* lagged a bit and fell short of expectations, then *Soulin'* played as the title would indicate, with a nice sense of dynamics that perhaps eluded the first BluesWay LP.

Things appeared to be on track for Reed: he had a strong LP hit the market as the year was drawing to a close and he was on the road. But by November 1967, he had unwittingly undone everything he had worked for throughout his entire career. He and Mary Lee Reed signed a contract with Arc Music that effectively conveyed copyright ownership for the Reed catalog to Arc.

JIMMY REED

Dated: November 30, 1967

ARC MUSIC CORP.
1619 Broadway
New York, New York 10019

Re: Arc Music Corp. -w- Jimmy Reed - Letter
Agreement dated December 13, 1965

Gentlemen:

This will confirm the understanding between you and us modifying
the letter agreement referred to above (hereinafter referred to
as the "Agreement"):

1. In consideration of your paying to me the sum of Ten
Thousand Dollars ($10,000.00), receipt of which I hereby acknowledge,
I, for myself, my representatives and assigns, do hereby release
and forever discharge you, your successors and assigns from all
obligations which you now or in the future may have to me or my
representatives and assigns with respect to the Compositions (as
that term is defined in the Agreement) including, without limita-
tion, your obligation to account for and pay me or them writer royalties during the original and renewal terms of United States
copyright in the Compositions. I further release you, and your
successors and assigns, from all claims, debts, demands, remedies,
and causes of action whatsoever which I or any person deriving
rights from me, ever had, now have, or may in the future have with
respect to the Compositions.

2. I hereby acknowledge that all writer royalties and
all other compensation due to me as of the date hereof with respect
to the Compositions have been paid to me, and I agree that all
accounting statements previously rendered to me by you shall be
binding on me and not subject to objection by me for any reason.
I further acknowledge that I have had an opportunity to examine
your books and records with respect to the Compositions.

3. I hereby confirm the representations and warranties
made by me in the Agreement, and in connection therewith I hereby
indemnify you and your successors and assigns against any loss,
liability, damage or expense (including attorneys fees) incurred
or suffered by you or your successors and assigns by reason of the
breach by me of any of such representations or warranties.

4. Except as modified herein, I hereby ratify the terms
and conditions of the Agreement.

If the foregoing accurately sets forth our agreement, kindly confirm your acceptance thereof by causing this letter to be counter-
signed below.

Very truly yours,

Jimmy Reed

JIMMY REED

ARC MUSIC CORP.

By: *[signature]*

STATE OF *[Illinois]*)
                       SS:
COUNTY OF *Cook*)

On this 30 day of *Nov* 1967, before me personally
came JIMMY REED to me known, and known to me to be the individual
described in, who duly acknowledged to me that he executed the
same.

[signature]
Notary Public

Consented to insofar as my
interests are concerned.

Mary Reed
MARY REED

A flawed 1967 Arc Music contract.

Some background:

When the Vee-Jay officers had needed money, they had asked Chess Records for a loan. "[The Chess brothers and Vee-Jay] came up with a deal to give Vee-Jay the loan with Conrad, its publishing company, as collateral," wrote Nadine Cohados in her book *Spinning Blues into Gold: The Chess Brothers and the Legendary Chess Records.* "The loan was actually made in the name of Arc Music."

Chess did not suppose Vee-Jay would make it through the financial storm, and they had pegged it right. Vee-Jay couldn't pay back the money it had borrowed, and as of November 19, 1967, Arc Music had acquired the complete catalogs of Conrad Music and Tollie Music, Inc., which included the Reeds' compositions.

Jimmy was given just $1,200 for the transfer of copyright ownership for his entire catalog. Mary Lee seems to have been given $1 (a legal transaction). Still, there was at least one major problem with the contract. Jimmy and Mary Lee received nearly identical agreements from Arc, with the exception of one subtle though troubling point. A portion of Mary Lee's agreement read: "I will use my best effort to obtain *from my wife* her assignment to you (in writing, the form of which shall be approved by you)...."

Neither the Reeds nor Conrad or its confederates were careful enough to realize the wording was incongruous. Nevertheless, the contracts were signed by Phil Chess, the Reeds, and a notary in mid-December 1965.

By November 30, 1967, this flawed contract with Arc Music was revamped and updated. Jimmy Reed was paid $10,000 and he signed off on an agreement that acknowledged he released Arc and its successors and assigns "from all obligations which are now or in the future may have to me or my representatives...including, without limitation, your obligation to account for and pay me...writer royalties during the original and renewal terms of the United States copyright in the compositions." Reed had signed away his rights to collect royalties in return for one lump sum of $10,000.

While this was a decent sum of money back in the 1960s (it could easily have paid for two cars and a healthy down payment on a house), what Reed gave up was far, far more valuable. Effectively, he and Mama had relinquished all rights to Jimmy's compositions—presently or any time in the future. With no idea his catalog could eventually be worth virtually an incalculable amount, Reed—and his family—would come to regret signing this agreement.

Jimmy didn't have time to think about how he was getting screwed—or even if he *was* being screwed. He needed to get back on the road. By early 1968, Reed was swinging through the West Coast again. He played a two-night stand at the Concord Coliseum in Richmond, California, and a weeklong engagement at the Golden Bear in Huntington Beach, California—a hip nightclub that opened initially as a folk bar, the original owner, Delbert Kauffman, told me. The spot soon became a favorite of blues artists throughout the country, and anytime Reed or John Lee Hooker played there (and they were booked together frequently), the place, which was charging a two-drink minimum and a $3 or $4 ticket price, would be packed to the rafters.

"Jimmy Reed and John Lee Hooker in those days would draw more people than anybody," says drummer Richard Innes, who first performed with Reed at the Golden Bear when he was all of 19 years old. "That includes Muddy Waters and Wolf or any one of them. You know that? I've seen the line down the road a block-and-a-half long waiting to get into the Golden Bear to see Jimmy Reed. They would have two shows a night and they would clear the house after each show. I don't know why he was so popular. I've seen a lot of blues guys but I never saw anyone draw like that."

On this weeklong engagement (perhaps as early as February 20–25, 1968), Jimmy was with Eddie Taylor and he needed a drummer, so Innes, who was playing with harp player Rod Piazza at the time, obliged. Piazza seems to remember that Innes was never paid a dime for his drumming skills, but Innes recalls differently. "I got $16 for the gig—that was my pay," Innes says. "That is what everybody got. I was playing with George Smith and Rod and I made $20 a night. So, I am pretty sure it was $16 a night. In those days they would book an act for three or four or five nights. Not like now. Whether it was Paul Butterfield or Janis Joplin or Jimmy Reed, they would be there for four or five nights at least."

Reed drew crowds so large for his Golden Bear performances that long lines formed just to get into the club.

"Every night when Jimmy would walk on stage he would say, 'No cymbals: just bass drum and snare drum.' Every night," Piazza distinctly remembers.

Innes, who would later join the Fabulous Thunderbirds, knew he had a tough assignment. "It is real deceptive to try to cover Jimmy Reed," he suggests. "Have you ever heard anyone cover a Jimmy Reed song as well as Jimmy Reed? You know why? Tempo. They can't get Earl

Phillips' tempo, man. It is so simple, yet so few people can do it. I am not going to say that I can actually do it, but I can come close. If you want to get any young modern drummer to play that tempo, you are going to look for a long time. It was so far behind the beat that most people can't conceive of it. Earl Phillips was one of those guys who fell through the cracks. He made some great records with Howlin' Wolf, too, but a lot of guys don't realize that without that drummer, it wouldn't feel like that."

Reed stuck to his big hits and did a great version of "Down in Virginia," Innes remembers. He also recalls being dazzled by Eddie Taylor's command and ability to hold the music together. "It really was no problem doing just 45 minutes or an hour—the length of a set—of merely his hits. He had so many. He was blowing the harp in the rack, harness is what he called it, and Eddie playing the main guitar part, though he could do both the rhythm and the lead at the same time, damn near. Eddie Taylor would play all the fills. Then some of the leads were played on harp, you know? He blew those fine. I never heard him screw up a harp solo, ever. But Reed would play over bar lines and still make it work. He could play over changes and his timing was pretty good. Unlike John Lee Hooker or Lightnin' Hopkins—13 or 15 bars or whatever—Reed's changes and his time were all right. And, of course, Eddie Taylor held it in there without ever being lost. If it was 14 or 15 bars or something, Eddie would make it work."

The music was working, but one night at the Golden Bear, around this same time frame, Reed was having tremendous trouble maintaining. "I remember I came off the stage and they wouldn't sell Jimmy no alcohol backstage," Piazza says. "So, Jimmy was giving me $2 and he said, 'Here. Go get two beers. You drink one and I'll drink the other one.' I didn't care. I didn't have any money. So, I go up there and get the two beers…. I don't know what else he might have been drinking, 'cause when we got there he was already feeling good. He saw George Smith and said, 'Hey, Snake, what's happening?' And George said, 'Hey, Snake.' They called each other 'Snake'—don't know why. I kept on drinking until it was time to get on stage. Jimmy was out of it. The guy who ran the place had a heavy Greek accent and said, 'Rod, you must *goh beck* on. Rod, you must *goh beck* on. Take a hammer and hit me in the head if I ever book Jimmy Reed again.' Meanwhile I know I was the guy feeding him these damn beers, you know?"

This incident was a far cry from Piazza's first exposure to Reed a few years earlier. "Reed's records were brought home in the 1950s by my brothers," Piazza remembers. "They were ten or 12 years older than me, so when I was seven and eight, right in there, I started hearing R&B records. Joe Turner and Jimmy Reed and that kind of thing...I would always play the records when I would get home from school, until one day I was walking home from school and was thinking that I wanted a guitar. So, I convinced my brother and my mom to get one of these $3.50 or $4 guitars. It was an old, used acoustic. So, I got that, started fooling around on it and playing the guitar. Then my brother took me to see Jimmy Reed and we went backstage. I was feeling really out of place. I remember my brother saying to Jimmy Reed, pointing at me, 'This young man is trying to play the guitar.' Jimmy said, 'Well, it looks like you need someone to go along with it.' So he gave me one of his harps.... So I started messing with that and the guitar. That's really where I got my first blues band—the Dirty Blues Band. It wasn't called that then, but it would become that and we signed with ABC-BluesWay."

Back in Chicago, the world was about to lose one of the greatest harp players that the blues—or any genre—had ever known. Though Walter Jacobs (aka Little Walter) had plenty of people to look after him and make sure his temper was in check, he was too far gone for help. He died of complications from injuries he received in a street brawl. "Those guys all got along like brothers," explains guitarist/vocalist Jimmy D. Lane, son of the late guitar great Jimmy Rogers. "I remember they all had to go and babysit Walter. They had to make sure he didn't do this or that. Walter was a hothead. He was mean onstage, no one could touch him on that harp, but he could start a fight right away."

Walter was beaten so badly, Lane explains, that when he went to see Rogers and Muddy at a club they were playing, the doorman didn't recognize Walter. "They stopped playing and they took Walter to the hospital and they stitched him up," Lane says.

Walter died on February 15, 1968. He was less than three months shy of 38 years old. In the years just prior to his death, Walter was on a downward slide, exacerbated by alcohol. His playing, once brilliant, was sloppy and uninspired. His behavior, never fan-friendly, ran hot and cold. Walter was irritable, untouchable, and inconsolable. "What my old man had said was that Walter had lost it, right before he died. That he couldn't play like he had played on those records anymore. I know my dad would not lie about that. It came in some form of proof when I heard a recording of Little Walter and Otis Rush. I heard Walter blowing and I think he did 'Watermelon Man.' I heard this and it didn't sound anything like Little Walter. They recorded it shortly before his death, and it confirmed what my old man had told me. Walter had let the alcohol take him over and he couldn't do it anymore. It was disappointment and a lot of the things he brought on himself."

"I knew Little Walter pretty good," says Charlie Musselwhite. "He was a scrapper. He had his good days and bad days. Towards the end it seemed like he got confused—I don't know how else to say it. It was some kind of mental thing. It seemed like he didn't know how to play or something, or didn't want to. Then other times he would be just blasting. It was incredible, exactly what you wanted to hear. The last time I saw him his band was playing onstage and he was sitting on a chair in front of the stage staring at the floor with his harp in one hand and looking miserable. The band was playing and they looked embarrassed. I pulled up a chair next to Walter and asked him, 'Are you O.K.?' He just grunted and so I left him alone. It wasn't long after that that he died. It might have been a mixture of drinkin' and not understanding what alcohol does to ya and not knowing how to deal with it, and the fact that his whole career was not going well, and being depressed about that. I'd see him sometimes and he would be really depressed. Other times he would be laughing and joking, He'd ask me to sit in and buy me drinks. Sometimes he would wait for me at the bus stop to make sure I got on the bus safe. Sometimes he would give me a ride home."

"One thing is for sure," Lane says. "If you look up blues harmonica in the encyclopedia there is a picture of Little Walter."

It was a tough time to be a prominent black—famous or talented—in America. As soon as an African-American rose to any position of power, it seemed the fates (and other more tangible forces) conspired against him. A span of four particular years became almost unbearable: "Mr. Soul" Sam Cooke, whom Reed had shared bills with in the past, was shot in 1964; Malcolm X was assassinated in 1965; Stax label artist Otis Redding died in a plane crash in 1967; and Dr. Martin Luther King was assassinated in 1968. More than any other, though, Little Walter's death was as a cautionary tale for Reed. In a weird way, it shifted him into the enviable position of the most famous Chicago harp player. And while Reed certainly respected Walter's playing, he also knew that his own style was completely different. As Jimmy was known to say, "I'm playing my own guitar and I'm blowing my own harmonica."

Reed had work to do, including cutting a new record for BluesWay entitled, appropriately enough, *Big Boss Man*. The LP starts off with a jumpin' little number. For a 43-year-old man with problems inside and out, Reed is surprisingly in control of his voice, singing seemingly without a care on "Give Up and Let Me Go." Underscoring the point is the lyrics' question, "Why be mad when you can be happy?"

Big Boss Man isn't overly conscious of itself, nor is it particularly meaningful in the Reed catalog. But with contributions from Al Smith (his voice can be heard faintly in the background on occasion, feeding Reed the lyrics) and Mama in the writing department (most notably "Run Here to Me Baby" and "My Baby Told Me"), and the tight backing band, *Big Boss Man* is at best pleasant, at worst vapid.

So, *Big Boss Man* is largely forgettable fluff, yes. And it doesn't expand on the Jimmy Reed sound any more than the previous BluesWay releases (and the songs tend to flow into one another, even more than usual), but it does have the distinction of presenting a tight band. *Big Boss Man* boasts the Al Smith Blues Band (sans bassist Smith): guitarists Lefty Bates and Eddie Taylor, Jimmy Tillman on drums, Phil Upchurch on bass, and Wayne Bennett on "lead" guitar. Eddie, once again, builds the foundation (Reed is keenly aware of Eddie's contributions as he yells "I hear ya, Eddie" at the closing of the Al Smith–penned "When Two People in Love") while Bennett circles around with the subtle/burning riff comments.

Al Smith came out and said that the way Jimmy plays guitar (as he put it, "playing two different things on two strings at the same time") has largely to do with the influence Eddie Taylor had on Reed. "Credit for this sound should go to bass [his word] guitarist Eddie Taylor...that's where [Jimmy] got it from. Jimmy always said he owed a lot to Eddie."

While Tillman's touch on the skins is much lighter than Al Duncan's or Earl Phillips', its fault is that it never drives these songs. Granted, it never gets in the way either, but the drums, so important to the Vee-Jay Reed, was a cog in a more formulaic machine. Reed had had his personal problems with Duncan—mainly that he was *not* Earl Phillips (who was?)—but his style did help pick up where Phillips left off. In Tillman's defense, it can't be overstated: playing the Reed laidback groove, whether we are talking guitarist or drummer, is no easy task. It is a skill, a sensibility. Still, there's something missing here: a true spirit and feeling of propulsion, of truly being in the moment, which can partially be blamed on the drummer and partially not. Reed was used to creating in a rush of emotions and thoughts, and Calvin Carter would race to get Reed's spontaneously combustible lines on the tape. Here, for the most part, it just sounds as if Reed is simply in a rush.

The paradox of Reed's music is its trademark laziness and its ability to hold the listener entranced, even electrified. Reed had a knack for setting listeners at ease and wrapping them in a bed of sonic comfort. Of course, in the case of *Big Boss Man,* bits of minimalistic musical pieces are seemingly patched together. Jimmy Reed's countrified vein is tempered by a more electric Chicago blues style, which collides (as it had done on other BluesWay releases) to make a larger, 12-bar blues sound. "Larger" is, of course, a relative term, but when you dissect the parts that make up the "Reed sound"—much like you'd dissect the music of Howlin' Wolf or Muddy Waters—you find that each person, each instrument, each little splash of chords adds that much more to the sonic painting. *Big Boss Man,* even with lesser-grade material, does fit together pieces as if they were a musical puzzle. The drawback of this approach is that it's less a singular musical vision than group effort.

Furthermore, Reed's personality is toned down a bit here, whether consciously or not, and the songs just don't pack much of a punch singularly or as a set. The only song credited to Reed is a painfully dragging remake of the 1963 hit "Shame, Shame, Shame." A shame, indeed, as the original was such a seminal track; the band here (in a rare case) turns in a tired and virtually tiring performance. Cashing in on the hits may have backfired in this case. There is just not enough energy to sustain a classic such as "Shame, Shame, Shame."

Perhaps the most successful song is "When I Woke Up This Morning," a song that recalls Eddie Boyd's "Five Long Years" as well as Reed's days in the South Chicago steel mills. One gets the sense of how far Reed has come, and how far he still needs to go to get right with himself and the larger world around him. It is almost too painful to read between the lines, but one has to, in order to understand. He explains that he spent ten years in a steel mill, bringing home the bacon, only to wake up alone and wondering if his woman is cheating on him. While the classic Boyd song has the man being "put out" by his lover, Reed's song approaches the relationship from a "pre"-breakup perspective, the discovery and realization phase. His own hands haven't gotten dirty, and the song, likewise, never sinks to the truly nasty. That is its flaw.

Ultimately, *Big Boss Man* is a transitory work, a step on the way to a larger goal.

And where Reed was headed, personally or musically, was becoming obvious. It was hard to break his stubborn mold. By 1968, it had become transparent that Al Smith was Reed's mouthpiece, bandleader, and father figure, sometimes working from behind the scenes to keep the integrity of the Jimmy Reed image intact. "Jimmy is so great, his mind is so fantastic, that in a split second, he gets the words, times it and sets it...all the while he's singing. Jimmy's really a fast thinker," Smith says in Sheldon Harris' liner notes to *Big Boss Man*.

The concept of maintaining the Jimmy Reed brand name, which was, to a degree, fading and somewhat damaged, is something Smith wrestled with constantly. Some might say that he wasn't fooling anyone—except perhaps Reed on occasion, and that was only given the "right" circumstances.

Fans who were not aware of Reed's drinking exploits by 1968 were seriously in the dark. Reed enthusiasts had heard and largely ignored the rampant rumors and off-color stories of Reed and his wildly inconsistent shows and bizarre behavior. To laugh off the problems Reed was having with himself and his inner circle—to buy a cover story, in essence—or to brush off these problems as simply indicative of a "bluesman" or the "blues way of life" is to further fuel the addiction of stardom and its inevitable downward spiral.

But Smith held on, for better or worse. And while there is almost something noble about his fighting the good fight for Reed (and himself, of course), given the fact that so many songs on *Big Boss Man* are credited to Smith (whether justified or not), one gets the sense that Jimmy was being propped up. The songs "When Two People in Love" and "I've Got to Keep Rollin'" were officially credited to Al Smith, but BMI lists Reed and Smith as co-composers. As blues maven Dick Waterman told me once, "Al Smith was a piece of work."

As it had become apparent with Jimmy Reed's work, Al Smith was taking credit for many of the songs on John Lee Hooker's new BluesWay records. Hooker was far from impressed or thrilled. "So many people got they name on my records, say they wrote," John Lee Hooker intimated to biographer Charles Shaar Murray. "Jimmy Bracken, his name on, saying he write this. Al Smith, Calvin Carter—all them gone now—he wrote this. How can anybody say they wrote John Lee Hooker's songs? I write all my songs."

Though Reed had often said that no one put a gun to his head to make him do the things he did over the years, he most surely placed a tenuous trust in Smith and later questioned his own ability to think straight. "I don't never remember signin' for him to be my manager," a defiant Reed told *Living Blues*. "Now, if he become my manager, it had to be in and through me havin' one of those seizures, or something or other. You know what I mean?…Well, my head shook up and tore to pieces till I didn't have no better sense but to sign it. But I never remember signin' for him to be no manager of mine, nothin' but a road manager, back in the '50s."

"Sometimes it was like Al was the best Daddy could get," explains Loretta Reed. "They had been together, they knew each other, they had gone through hard times, they were on the road a lot together. If your choice in managers is picking someone who you don't know and the guy you know, you'll take the guy you know. That was it. Daddy took Al. We all just took Al."

If Reed was losing control of his life and career, he was also losing touch with his best friends and musicians. Jimmy's constant drinking and Eddie Taylor's dutiful picking up of the pieces was starting to wear Eddie thin. Already irritated by a lack of respect he was getting as "Jimmy's guitar player," he quietly began to take mental notes of all the proceedings around him. Every time Reed was incapacitated, it'd be another reason why Taylor would never work with him again, once he got his own thing started up.

The cracks in the strained relationship were starting to bust at the foundation of this friendship, and Eddie soon could not help him. He often sank to outright disgust at his musical partner's behavior and lack of self-control.

For years Eddie had felt he was living in Jimmy's shadow. When each man was asked separately about who originated the "Jimmy Reed sound," the Jimmy Reed feel, they each took credit for it. Eddie Taylor's stepson, Larry Hill, a musician himself, offers a perspective: "Jimmy was an extraordinary harp blower, O.K.? Jimmy was not a fascinating guitar player. My dad showed Jimmy Reed how to play. People shouldn't be confused that when they hear this great guitar playing on record, that it is Jimmy Reed. No, it is not Jimmy Reed. It is Eddie Taylor. But Eddie Taylor was more than a great guitar player. Eddie Taylor had the history and that was why so many musicians resented him. You can't find too many musicians who go back to the time of Babyface Leroy, Charles Brown, and Robert Johnson and Bukka White and Charlie Patton. In Memphis, down on Beale Street, when B.B. King had the radio show— there was Honeyboy Edwards, there was my dad, and a lot more other people during the time of the Depression."

More and more, playing with Jimmy was becoming a chore, not a treat, for Eddie. Yet, Eddie was increasingly confused and continued to question why he was charged with taking care of Jimmy. "Things started going bad around 1968, 1969," claims Hill. "He was just like a big brother [to Jimmy Reed]. He had to carry it for many nights. A lot of times Jimmy couldn't do the show and he would have to get Jimmy's pay. He would have to collect Jimmy's money. Most of the time he would have to keep Jimmy straight to do the show. He took care of Jimmy in so many ways, man. Jimmy did a lot of mischievous stuff, too.

That would cause the relationship to split up. [Eddie] got tired of the situation of having to put up with a lot of crap."

John Lee Hooker, Jr., remembers one such incident in which Eddie had to carry and save the day. "First I want to say that Jimmy was very talented," Hooker says. "My dad was an alcoholic at some point and they both used to drink. But, Jimmy just went overboard. He had to be carried. He'd have to be carried to a car or room because he would do it to the extreme. It is really sad that they didn't have the help they have now back then. They had them, but the help wasn't as prevalent as it is now. I know it was an embarrassment to his family. My dad wouldn't get drunk where you would have to carry him. I guess you could say that my dad held his.

"Anyway, I was doing a talent show at the Fox Theatre in Detroit," Hooker, Jr., continues, "and I wanted my dad to back me up behind my little new song. And he wanted to because he was proud that I was put in the talent contest down there. He wanted to be there, but he had other commitments in Europe. What he did was call Jimmy. 'Jimmy, back my son,' I believe is what he said. 'No problem, John. I'm Jimmy Reed. You can count on me.'

"I was just so happy," Hooker, Jr., recalls. "'Oh, the great Jimmy Reed,' I was going around the house braggin'. 'The great Jimmy Reed gonna back me up.' I got down to the Fox Theatre and I was waiting on Jimmy. And here come Jimmy and he don't look so good. Then I see Eddie Taylor holding Jimmy by the arm. I said, 'Oh, I'm in trouble now.' Eddie Taylor said, 'Don't worry, Junior, I got it.' Eddie was the one who backed me. Jimmy was just out of it. Bless his heart. I didn't win the contest—I lost. I didn't win the contest."

Al Smith needed to shake things up a little. He needed some new blood for Reed's musical transfusion, if possible—and he needed it quick. Enter D.C. Bellamy. A native of Chicago's West Side who grew up around people like Reed soundalike G.L. Crockett, Bellamy often plays Jimmy Reed's music when he performs today. There's a good reason: he got to jam with Jimmy often in Chicago. He says he admired the way Jimmy wrote music, even before he ever knew him.

"I do 'Baby What You Want Me to Do,' and I stop and tell this story," Bellamy says. "A lot of people know it is a great blues song, but some don't understand what the song is saying. I didn't realize it myself until I had a girlfriend. She was cheating on me, and so I thought I would try to catch her one day. So, I was in the window, peepin' out the window, and every time a car would pull up to the street, the headlights would come through the window and I would have to jump behind the curtain and hide. This feeling had dawned on me that this is Jimmy Reed. This is the story that he is telling in this song—'You got me peepin'/you got me hidin'.'" This is more than a great blues song—it was a song about his life.'"

Bellamy had been playing with Betty Everett on the road (he was attending sessions for Curtis Mayfield when he was as young as 11, Bellamy says), and Al Smith had seen him perform in Detroit. Impressed with how the young Bellamy was able to take control of a band (and put them together for Everett), Smith asked Bellamy to stop down to the sixth floor of the Universal Recording building to see him in his office. After speaking with Bellamy, Smith was further convinced when his partner, Ed Winfield, who was road manager for Betty Everett, talked up Bellamy. It was settled: Smith offered Bellamy a job as a pre-production guitarist for Jimmy Reed, and whenever Bellamy wasn't on the road he'd spend time with Jimmy in the office, working over material.

"You have to understand: I grew up on Jimmy Reed music," Bellamy says. "This was big. The only blues artist allowed in the house was Jimmy Reed. There was Elvis, there was Johnny Mathis, Harry Belafonte, and a lot of different classical things, but Jimmy Reed was the only blues artist."

In retrospect, since Bellamy didn't actually record with Jimmy, his importance was split between babysitting an often troubled star for a few hours and making sure Reed got down to thinking seriously about music. Smith didn't know it, but Bellamy, who had dealt with alcoholism in his family, was the perfect fit to handle Reed and his reputation as a drinker. "Jimmy would be drunk sometimes, and you could smell it on his breath," Bellamy says. "His daughter, Malinda, would always be with him. That was one thing I thought was great because I was glad that he was not driving. I don't even know if he knew how to drive. She was taking him everywhere he needed to go. But I will tell you one thing: Jimmy wouldn't make one mistake. Remember, I am a younger guy and I am watching him. Not only am I a younger guy, but I am a young admirer of his and he doesn't even know it. He doesn't have a clue that I have been listening at his music since the '50s. Because I am considered a young guy, I must be playing and interested in only 'Motown music,' right? He didn't have a clue that I grew up with him. There were songs that I remember hearing. He would start singing and not make one mistake at all."

Beyond the obvious, Bellamy's job was important—so important that there could be no fooling around with Bellamy's paycheck. "Al Smith had two checkbooks when he hired me," Bellamy says. "Al was told that if he wanted to hire me, the only way he could was to write me a check out of the 'right' checkbook. When I used to go across the street from where I would do the business with Uni [Universal] and Al Smith, on Michigan and 13th Street was a check-cashing place, a currency exchange. I would walk into the currency exchange, and all of the checks that Al Smith had written were tacked up on the wall."[i]

Bellamy is sure of something else: his experience with Reed and Smith was different from the other musicians who would come through the office. "I had heard Al talk business with people, right in front of me," Bellamy says. "He'd reach into his briefcase, and he carried a .357 in his briefcase—you know, back in those days, artists were hard to handle. Artists would get cocky and go crazy. I'd seen Al Smith do that with artists. But I never heard him raise his voice to Jimmy Reed. Jimmy was mild-mannered and nice…. He'd never talk business with Jimmy out in the office area where people could hear him. If he did talk business with Jimmy, it was in private. I never saw anything out of the way between Jimmy Reed and Al Smith, but I have seen Al Smith at his worst moments. He could get very ugly."

When Reed showed up to work with Bellamy, it was all business: they'd practice songs or make some up and then the man was gone. "I was like, 'Man, what does he have goin' on? That man is fast.' It was every single time. I don't know if he was rushing to get the hell out of there, but I never saw him make one mistake. We weren't recording, but I was getting his music ready for recording. I would simplify it so everyone would know how to play it. Every now and again Jimmy would go off into Delta blues. Some of the musicians, as good as they were, they would try to count the change instead of feeling it. This is what I would try to rectify. I was only in the office two or three days a week.

"In dealing with Jimmy Reed behind the scenes I learned a lot about the man," Bellamy continues. "First of all it was a joy to work with somebody that I grew up with—he was the second person I worked with that I grew up with, listening to and admiring. I started working with him when I was in my early twenties. Jimmy Reed used very few 7 chords. His music basically, and usually, was done with major chords. Blues are 7 chords. The blues scale is a dominant scale, where you use dominant chords. The way he would blend rock 'n' roll and blues together was just magnificent to me. Occasionally he would dabble into the Delta blues spectrum of the blues. Like, he knew exactly what he was doing, and when he was doing it. Music was just like breathing."

As the Vietnam War was escalating and thousands of young men were being shipped off to boot camp, music festivals like the Flower Fair in Dallas were being organized to celebrate life, music, and peace. Thanks to entrepreneur Mark Lee, the organizer of the Dallas event, bands like Strawberry Alarm Clock, the Doors, the Turtles, Mitch Ryder, and Jimmy Reed were all on the same bill in April 1968.

Eddie Taylor soldiered on, and tried to maintain a united front for fans. "Jimmy at that time didn't really tour with a band," explains musician Wally Wilson. "It was just him and this kind of heavier-set guy with a Gretsch guitar. I think it was Eddie Taylor. It had to be Eddie because he had the stuff down pat. He knew all the parts and played them perfectly. Anyway, I was originally a bassist who had turned keyboardist and Jimmy needed a bassist and a drummer. There was no way I was turning down this chance to play with Jimmy Reed [laughs]. I was playing bass instead of the bassist in our band, L'Cirque. Anyway, the set was not the greatest at all, we didn't practice—why would we need to? We all knew the songs, but Jimmy was not exactly on top of things…. I could tell that Eddie was just fed up with him and really didn't take care of him. I think he'd had it with him."

The tension was palpable, and to add insult to injury, before Jimmy ever went on, no one knew where he was. "It was our time to perform and we couldn't find Jimmy," Wilson says. "Where was he? We searched everywhere and then finally I found him, in the bathroom. He was in the bathroom playing his harp. I didn't go in right away, but stood close by just to hear him play the harp. He was an incredible harp player. I don't think people really realize. When they think of Jimmy they think of his playing in the high registers, but he could play, man. If he wanted to, he could sound just as good as anybody—play in the lower registers. So, I stood by listening to him and it was incredible. When I went in to get him I found him on the floor blowing his harp. He was in there because he wanted to hear the sound of the harp notes reflecting off the tiles. Finally, I said, 'Jimmy, we have to go.' And that was it.

"We just loved Jimmy Reed in Texas," Wilson continues. "They used to do this dance, the Push, here in Texas to his music. I remember that clearly. I mean, Jimmy Reed would be played in all of the white joints. He was just as important as Lefty Frizzell. I was thinking about why he was so big at the time, why he made it to the top of the radio, the white radio, and was played by every band and on every jukebox in the '50s and '60s (at least in Texas, which is all I knew about) when Wolf and Muddy didn't make much of a dent. I am in the music business here in Nashville. I write and publish and produce hit country songs. I picked up a guitar and started playing 'Hush Hush,' and it hits me, that the difference in Jimmy Reed's stuff and, say, Muddy was that Jimmy had real melodies and real lyrics done to a 12-bar blues format. His melodies are much more pronounced and sing-along than most of the work of Willie Dixon and his protégés. This is what propelled him to the top of the charts. His songs are also very close to the country and western music that was popular at the time. Texas crowds took to it like a duck on a june bug. And it greatly influenced every Texas musician, then and for years to come."

"If it weren't for Jimmy Reed, several of my bandmates along with myself would have never got into music in the first place," says Kenny Daniels of Kenny and the Kasuals, also on the Flower Fair music festival bill.

Jimmy was something else. He had a six-night engagement at the Cheshire Cat (in Atlanta, Georgia) in August 1968. The Musicians Union was hounding him for payment of a little over $35 for failing to pay work dues to locals in conjunction with two performance runs (one in California, the other at the Cheshire Cat) and for not divulging those musician's names and addresses. As a result of ignoring payment pleas, Reed was suspended from the union.

That didn't stop him, though. Jimmy kept on rolling, playing across the country for anyone who would have him. And by the fall, he was off to Europe again as part of the 1968 American Folk Blues Festival (AFBF).

Reed knew he was loved in Europe and thought he would be running into welcoming arms. He decided to be daring and took only Eddie Taylor (who had played AFBF in 1966 and 1967) and drummer J.C. Lewis with him. The trio was to perform as in the Vee-Jay days of old, when Taylor, Reed, and Phillips made a formidable and memorable musical team.

Reed was, at least initially, readily welcomed back, but his lack of fresh performances soon had the blues police itching to pull the trigger. Reed tried desperately to make it through lame versions of "Big Boss Man," "Two Ways to Skin a Cat," and a crowd favorite, the usually lulling "I Know It's a Sin." But nothing was working, and nothing was saving him from his descent—not even having the wonder guitarist Eddie Taylor at his side. It was no use: after nearly ten minutes, Reed skulked offstage and headed for the green room where he chased curious fans and press away. He wanted to be left alone. That temper, rarely shown, mostly hidden just under the surface, had gotten the best of him and was now raising its ugly head.

"Jimmy clearly was not a well man—he was a disheveled figure who was on for about ten minutes and they literally had to drag him offstage," explains British writer John Broven, a Reed enthusiast for over five decades. "All of a sudden that image of him that I had built up since 1964 that he had been so wronged…I could see that perhaps there was something behind the continual stream of rumors that we were hearing. What I'm saying is that those BluesWay records showed him to be in good form, and it was almost, as far as I am concerned, as if that public deterioration started right there and then. That 1968 tour—it was as if he almost never recovered. It seems to me that it marked some sort of definite decline from which he never really came back."

But to hear Broven describe it, Reed's display was not a total devastation of his reputation. Ironically, the same fans who were disappointed in Jimmy were also quite sympathetic to his plight, self-imposed or not. "If Jimmy had been like that on the first tour, then his legend would have been truly punctured," Broven says. "We, all of us, were great fans, were understanding of the situation. It wasn't as if we went home and said we weren't going to play a Jimmy Reed record, because we understood that something wasn't quite right physically. Also, I think there has been a lot of confusion over being drunk or having an epileptic fit and as I understand it, epilepsy was part of his problem. I got the feeling that it was more than just alcoholism."

Still, fans, even years after the fact, feel cheated by the performances. "Nobody seemed to be able to hit their stride, you know?" Broven notes. "Obviously Eddie was trying to hold it together and it wasn't a fair assessment of the Jimmy Reed/Eddie Taylor sound by any means. It was to be the reincarnation of the Vee-Jay days. Of course, it wasn't to be. Jimmy did three numbers and that was the end of it. Yes, it was disappointing."

It is surprising Eddie stayed with Reed as long as he did. But then again, Reed was a busy man, and that kept Eddie busy as well. Perhaps out of a sense of duty, or loyalty, or friendship, or all three, Taylor returned for yet another Jimmy Reed LP. Titled *Down in Virginia,* after the 1958 song of the same name, the LP was recorded in late 1968 and released in 1969.

By this time, there was no denying—or hiding—that there was a formula to the Reed sound. The "formula," the effort of the Eddie Taylor–Jimmy Reed–Earl Phillips–Al Duncan team, creates a kind of conundrum. It's a thin line between rehash and an individual, idiosyncratic "sound." Though some songs on Vee-Jay might have been part of an established or consciously engineered Reed template, the passion exuded and the slight variation of hooks written by Reed (or, in some cases, someone else) surpassed any similarity of form from song to song. The sheer freshness of the sound then was enough to keep listeners satisfied and not feeling a sense of repetition throughout.[ii]

In the case of *Down in Virginia* the template *is* the thing. With the exception of a few songs, it seems Jimmy is just plugging himself into an established mode. (Most critics could perhaps overlook the similar rhythm and chord progression of these tunes, but when songs are presented in nearly the same way, you have to wonder why.) Reed instinctually, habitually warms up with similar harp melodies for most of the songs, usually in the beginning of the tune or just after the first verse.

The most outstanding elements of *Down in Virginia,* rather, are the lead snippets by Wayne Bennett, who takes more chances on this LP than on *Big Boss Man.* And, to be perfectly honest, there are some great sympathetic moments between Eddie's rhythm guitar, Upchurch's churning bass lines, Reed's harp, and Bennett's warm-glow solos. The feel is much more "jammy" here than even the earlier BluesWay releases. But since there aren't any breakout tracks (though "Jump and Shout," "The Judge Should Know," and "I Shot an Arrow to the Sky" are delightful), the playing time feels brief, which is not odd for a Reed LP or single—or a bad thing, given the circumstances.

Would some of the BluesWay LPs have been improved if Jimmy had taken more time in the production process? Perhaps not. Jimmy was a conduit and never worked too long over one thing or another. Though he did pre-production work (as we've seen), he bounced ideas off Mama Reed and used Al Smith (and sometimes other writers) as a resource. The notion of sitting in the studio for a week and getting things just so was foreign to him—and most blues musicians of the era. Jimmy didn't operate that way.

So that leads us to the question: Had Reed become uninspired? Had his muse left him? What is worse is that while Reed's mind is not working the way it once did, he seems not to care about pushing himself. He truly is popping himself into the framework that he, Eddie Taylor, and, yes, Al Smith had created for him. (In fact, Al made it extremely easy for Jimmy to just come in and do his thing.) Except for working with Mama—his only true savior—the music doesn't seem to interest Jimmy. Songs seem to cut in, as if the band had been playing when the tape was rolled to capture whatever magic might materialize when Jimmy happened to be ready—or able—to conjure it up.

Even though Jimmy's records had sunk to the depths of monotony, his music had deeply penetrated the American psyche. This was never in sharper focus than in June 1968 when Elvis was filming his now-famous "comeback" television special. Initially it was to be a Christmas special, but Steve Binder, the producer of the event, worked with Elvis to show a side of the King that was rarely seen by the late '60s.

After producing a Petula Clark and Harry Belafonte special (one of the first times white and black people touched each other on prime-time American television), Binder, having worked on the *T.A.M.I.* show and *Hullabaloo,* was assigned to produce the Elvis special. The Elvis Presley camp had seen the Clark and Belafonte special, which aired in April on NBC, and knew the 23-year-old Binder could bring the fresh approach to Elvis' material that the King desperately needed. Elvis hadn't appeared on TV in eight years.

"Initially I had turned them down, saying I was more of a West Coast guy, being into the Mamas & the Papas and the Beach Boys," recalls Binder. "I was amused by Elvis, but I was not really much into his music. I was in the middle of this conversation [with the Elvis camp] and my partner, Bones [Dayton Howe], walked through the office and said, 'Steve, am I hearing right? Are they asking you to meet Elvis Presley?' I said, 'Yeah.' He said, 'You have to. I engineered some of his dates and you guys would hit it off great. At least think about it.' So, Elvis came over to my office and we hit it off great from the get-go."

From June 20 to 30, Elvis virtually lived at NBC Studios in Los Angeles, contending with a rough shooting schedule and "Colonel" Parker running interference. The Colonel wanted an Elvis "Christmas special"—as this would air in December—but Binder and Elvis saw something more. The shape of the second performance (the so-called "Sit Down" section) was completely unplanned. "After ten- and 12-hour production days, people like Charlie Hodge, Scotty Moore, Lance LeGault would go into Elvis' dressing room and unwind. That is when Elvis did all of these great blues songs," Binder says. "They'd spend 20 minutes doing ["Baby What You Want Me to Do"] at a time. Elvis had told me that when he first grew up he didn't see or know any white people. He lived among the sharecroppers in Mississippi and everything he did was, to him, what everybody did. So, his roots were blues and black blues. It was then that I saw the real Elvis. That was what I was really trying to capture. When you do a big production show, you are so involved with all the frills in terms of sets and costumes, then all of a sudden I am watching this guy unwind in this raw, powerful, pure enjoyment. It was pure talent, and I said that is where I want the cameras. I wanted to go into the dressing room."

Not if the Colonel had anything to say about it. And he did. "Obviously, the Colonel was always playing one-upmanship without any logical reasoning behind it," Binder remembers. "I hounded him for three days or so to film in the dressing room until finally he came to me and said, 'O.K., I'll tell you what you can do. You can re-create it out on the stage if you want to. But I am not going to let you put it into the show unless I see it and approve it.' I bought into that and said, 'Fine,' even though it wasn't the same thing. And as great as it was, even as I am talking to you now, it was probably one hundred times greater in the dressing room. We went out on stage and that's when we did the improv acoustic sessions. I wouldn't let anybody take any amplifiers on stage. I even had D.J. [Fontana] play drums on a guitar case.... It was a gut reaction: 'Let's just try to make this as authentic as possible.' "

Billy Goldberg, hired by Binder to be the musical director, brought in the greatest studio musicians in Hollywood. Elvis was wary of having too many musicians at first but, after doing practice runs, came to like it. Still, to Binder and many others the real power of the show has always been the "Sit Down" section, which originally was a misdirection. "I could see the pure joy in Elvis' face," Binder says. "It never dawned on me that this—the Elvis playing roots music—was real, the *real* Elvis, and this was where his soul was. That was all stuff he played for himself as a musician. Bones described Elvis' studio to me as a stack of old blues records and old 45s. Elvis sat and listened to them for hours and hours, listening for certain licks. I think when he did the Jimmy Reed songs, he was tapping his internal library."

When the show aired in December, Elvis had recorded two Reed songs: "Big Boss Man" and "Baby What You Want Me to Do." Both versions are extraordinary, and Elvis' voice on the latter soars, balancing the right amount of darkness and light. (As the band was revving for one more practice go-'round, Elvis says, "Uhhh, get dirty, baby," and that is exactly what they do.) The Colonel, as always, got his way in the end—by hook or by crook. "After I had turned in the show to NBC, he had to get one Christmas song in the show. He threatened NBC with not letting them broadcast the show without a Christmas song," says Binder.

"One of the unplugged versions he did was 'Blue Christmas'—I never programmed it, he just did it."

"Jimmy Reed has a relaxed way of singing blues and playing harmonica that compels you to listen to him," bluesman Hawkeye Herman says. "Here is the major point in why Jimmy Reed crossed over: he didn't have that intense Mississippi angst…. That is why Elvis liked it. 'That's All Right,' Arthur Crudup's song, and the Jimmy Reed tune, has a rhythm that points the way to rock 'n' roll."

Elvis playing Jimmy Reed tunes had an impact on a generation.[iii] Richard Young of the Kentucky Headhunters remembers seeing the Elvis 1968 special. "The first time I really heard 'Big Boss Man' was probably when Elvis did it on TV," Young says. "I probably heard it before then, but that was the first time I really took notice. You have to understand, I grew up on a farm and my dad was raised by my grandmother. She also took in a black farm worker whose family was working on the farm in Wisdom, Kentucky, but had left the area. Jakey stayed behind to help. My grandmother basically raised my dad and Jakey together, and he was like a second father to me. Jakey loved Jimmy Reed. Jakey was living in his own house on the property. He would come home from work, open a quart of whiskey, and light up a cigarette while listening to 'Bright Lights, Big City,' 'Ain't That Lovin' You Baby,' and 'Big Boss Man,' too."

Despite the boost from Elvis, Jimmy Reed was still slugging it out in clubs. By the New Year, Reed was fixing to head down South again. In March 1969, he was in Austin, Texas, to play at the Vulcan Gas Company. Faced with the opportunity to bring Jimmy Reed to Austin, co-owner Don Hyde immediately booked his idol. It all came about by chance. "I had been booking a number of Chicago musicians through Al Smith," Hyde says. "I had booked [John Lee] Hooker a few times through Al and I had talked to him on the phone a lot. We always did really well with the acts that we booked through him. We did very well with almost all of the Chicago blues artists we did. Al said, 'Why don't you book Jimmy?' But I didn't know he was still doing shows. I asked if he was indeed still even doing shows and Al said, 'Yes.' So, I booked him."

A 1969 Vulcan Gas Company handbill advertising upcoming Jimmy Reed performances.

Though the blues had been somewhat eclipsed by the British bands like the Beatles, the Stones, and the Animals, Texas' heart still beat for squealing harmonica and 12-bar arrangements. College fraternities throughout the state booked blues acts, even at the height of the British Invasion. Hyde was only in his early twenties, but his club was one of the first clubs to book black and white bands together. "One of my house bands was Johnny Winter before he was signed—he played there every other week for me for about a year and a half," Hyde says. "I would book Johnny Winter and John Lee Hooker with the Conqueroo, which was basically white kids studying the blues and rock 'n' roll."

Al Smith, forever the businessman with his profit antennae up, computed that it was quite strange that a club—in the middle of Texas, no less—owned and operated by young whites could lure black talent to the Lone Star State and draw sizable crowds. Smith, a South Side of Chicago man through and through, was curious as to what exactly was happening down there, and what the club's secret was.

"He wanted to check it out for himself, so he got Jimmy in the car and drove him down to Austin himself," Hyde says. "We booked Jimmy for two nights, Friday and Saturday. We sold out both nights."

Though Smith's reputation had preceded him, Hyde maintains that he never had a problem with Smith, and, in fact, saw a very professional side of him. "I really liked Al. I never really had any problem with him. He was a real old-school music manager type. He had dressed to the nines. We were all just in cut-off shorts and sweatshirts and sandals. Jimmy and Al were both dressed to the nines and Jimmy had a suit that made him look like a million bucks. Al Smith was the same way, cuff-links and a handkerchief in the jacket pocket to match the necktie. Al was trying to convince me to go back to Chicago with him. He wanted me to be his protégé. He thought a white kid in Chicago could do something, you know? Both nights he was talking about Chicago and wanted me to consider working under him as a booker for a while. It was one of the few things I regretted, because I couldn't do it at the time. It wasn't in the cards for me. It would have been interesting to tutor under him. He was a real old-timer and knew his stuff and had a real style. I hit it off real well with him. I was open to stuff, and Al probably figured he could get a lot of work out of me and teach me a few things—and I'm sure he would have."

The Vulcan held nearly 1,000 people. It was similar to a big warehouse, Hyde says, and people were standing and sitting on the floor just to hear Jimmy Reed. Jimmy brought his guitar and that was it—no band, no nothing. He'd use a pickup band, as he did so many nights in the past. And to great success, remembers Hyde.

"We had a backing band for him—a drummer, guitarist, and bass player," Hyde explains. "White kids who had played around the clubs in

*Al Smith (right) and club co-owner Don Hyde at the Vulcan Gas Company,
March 1969.*

different house bands. There were not very many musicians in Austin at
that time who really knew what they were doing. They were mostly just
getting started. Playing behind Jimmy and John Lee could be pretty
problematic. I just remember the look on the guys' faces when they
would play with Hooker—it was a complete question mark, total panic
and question marks. Like, What the fuck is he going to do next and what
are we supposed to do now? There may have been a little of that with
Jimmy, not as much, but it went over well. The second night, Saturday,
Jimmy had done a wonderful set, and we stayed open until 2:00 A.M."

Bill Bentley, journalist at the time in Austin who would become a
Warner Brothers label exec, went to the Vulcan Gas venue and has vivid
memories of Reed playing there. "The Vulcan in Austin was our equiv-
alent of the Fillmore in San Francisco," Bentley says. "It had a lot of rock
and blues, and an audience mix of hippies and college kids. The night I
saw Reed play, he used a local group for backup, but they were all excellent players with a great feel for blues. Around the end of the set, a drunk
college kid dressed in typical fraternity gear—blue jeans, starched white
button-down shirt, and a razor-cut hairstyle—came to the front of the
stage and started screaming at Reed to play the fraternity's then-national

anthem, 'Louie, Louie.' After a minute of this, Reed, who was sitting down and only about five feet off the ground, quickly kicked the frat boy right in the head, knocking him back and shutting him up. The college kid was dazed but, to his credit, didn't leave. And Jimmy Reed never played 'Louie, Louie' that night."

But BYOB is less of a rallying cry than a danger warning when considering a Jimmy Reed night. Hyde had heard all the rumors about

Reed backstage at the Vulcan, March 1969.

Jimmy's drinking and knew the shows could easily slip into disaster. Literally just before booking Jimmy, he had been warned by promoters in Houston that he could be unreliable, or would fuck up, goof off, get drunk, and ruin the show. "But you know what? Al was on him every minute Jimmy was not onstage," Hyde explains.

"We didn't even have a liquor license in that club," Hyde admits. "We never bothered to get a license because the local authorities were so heavy on us that they would have shut us down under the slightest pretense. In those days people could buy their own beer and come into the club. They might buy a beer at the package store and sit there and drink it."

Still, Jimmy did manage to outwit Smith at least once. Constantly irritable when his drink was taken from him, and constantly playing cat-and-mouse with Smith, Jimmy got the best of him that night. "The second night he finished his set and Al turned his back on him for what couldn't have been more than five minutes to settle up with me," Hyde recalls. "I was paying him in cash for the weekend. We were counting the money and in the three to five minutes that Al had his back turned to Jimmy, some fan had come back into the office area and had given him a bottle of wine. He drank about two-thirds of a bottle of wine in about three minutes. He hadn't had a drink the entire time he had been there. He was as sober as a judge. No alcohol at all until that point. Just drinking that amount of alcohol in that amount of time it was like Dr. Jekyll and Mr. Hyde. He went completely over the edge—completely blotto. He said, 'I love it here so much, this is my new home and I'm never going to go anywhere else from here on in. They love me here.' Then he said, 'I'm not going back with you, you sonofabitch,' pointing at Al. 'I'm not going back anywhere with you. These people love me.' This went on for a good three hours. We finally got him out of the club at about 5:00 A.M. and got him to Al's car and went back to the hotel I put him in.

"I thought all of this was strange because I was out the whole weekend with them, even took Al and Jimmy to dinner," Hyde continues. "Al was just as sweet as could be. Al was never sharp with Jimmy. He treated Jimmy like a child, almost. He was very soft-spoken and patient with him. The way he'd get Jimmy to change his mind would be through soft-spoken opposition. You know, 'No, let's not do this. Let's do this instead.' It was never about ordering Jimmy around. He was always very respectful to him. When Jimmy got ahold of that bottle that night, Al never lost his temper, though it almost seemed as if he was about to cry. He was never mad at him. Al was really a caretaker, it seemed to me.

"The only other person I saw react to alcohol that fast in the same way was Sam Peckinpah," Hyde says. "I worked with Sam the last ten years of his life. Sam and Jimmy were a lot alike. Sam, with four fingers of sherry, was just impossible. That was very much like what Jimmy did. They were just in such advanced stages of alcoholism that a good belt of anything flipped them over into this other thing."

Drink was causing Reed to lose everything—his dignity, his money, and, slowly, his life. "The last time I saw him was around winter, late 1969," Lazy Lester says. "I remember it was colder than hell. I was in Chicago. I was working for a furniture company. Anytime I had a chance, I would go and stop by one of the clubs and listen to the music—they had music every Friday and Saturday. They had music every day. I'd stop by and I would get out my truck and when I turned the corner, coming down, the first thing I saw was Jimmy Reed up there with them old white shoes on, shirt was supposed to be white, but it wasn't white no more. And his shoes were so crooked he was standing on the ground, and the back of his feet were on the ground. Oh, it just hurt me so bad to see him like that."

And the Reed musical house was in disarray: Eddie Taylor had finally gone his own way, largely due to Jimmy's drinking habits. "I said to myself one day, well, at least I told a friend, my friend Eddie Taylor, I say, 'It is one thing everybody said, I drink too much, 'cause I don't think this [liquor] bother me,'" Jimmy told interviewer Bill Scott on KTIM in San Rafael, California. "'When I quit drinking this liquor they'll be pushing me to my grave, and you'll be liable to be looking down in my face. And then I might stop—then. But other than that, I ain't gonna stop.'"

Those who didn't know Eddie very well might get little or no reaction from him when asking why he was being seen around town and on tour without Jimmy. It wasn't exactly a secret, but it was not exactly something Eddie always talked about. "My dad got tired of the situation of putting up with a lot of crap," Eddie's stepson Larry Hill says. "Jimmy got drunk. That was a big responsibility. It wasn't one of his responsibilities to keep Jimmy straight, but he did it. But there is a breaking point to everything."

"To me, Jimmy Reed was everything that people—white or black—liked about the blues," says producer Bruce Bromberg. "You could hear that riff a zillion times and never get tired of it. The time I saw him, it was a sad spectacle. He was dead drunk. He had on a toupee and he fell off the stage. Eddie Taylor was playing with him—I did work with Eddie Taylor later and Eddie just stood there and looked disgusted at him. I'm sure Eddie wished he was somewhere else…. I had to drive 50 miles down to Orange County to see the damn thing and it really broke my heart. I'm sorry to report that I never saw Jimmy Reed in his heyday."

A brilliant musical partnership was broken, but it wasn't as if leaving Reed left Taylor destitute. He *did* have gigs around town—and the world. While Reed was getting offers by the boatload as a star performer, despite some of his onstage antics, Taylor was more of the Chicago blues handyman. He was the necessary ingredient, the good rhythm guitar player that a local band might need to complete its sound. It was well known around Chicago: if you wanted the sound to be perfect, call Eddie. He was the go-to guy.

Taylor was playing with John Lee Hooker in Europe and England, Carey Bell at places like Jo Jo's in Chicago, and Muddy Waters at various spots. (He had played with Muddy at the Zanzibar club some 16 years earlier and he was now reprising his role as rhythm guitar player in that solid band.) Eddie was smart. He hadn't jeopardized his solo career completely by staying with Reed so long. All throughout he played with his own band, when he could, at places like Pepper's Lounge in Chicago. He had also managed to appear with old friends Floyd Jones and Elmore James, and gained the respect of high-profile newcomers like Paul Butterfield at such clubs as Silvio's and Big John's.

Eddie might be gigging and recording, but that didn't mean he could sit back and wait for the phone calls. He had to hustle to make his money, playing small joints for little pay—a lot of small joints. Taylor demanded excellence from himself and his musicians. He was one of perhaps a half-dozen blues guitarists at the time who could rightly be called a perfectionist. The trouble with Eddie Taylor was not that he couldn't play—but that he *could*. Not very many blues artists were in his class, not even the more experienced black players who had been around the music and traditions all their lives.

Drummer Steve Cushing, who would in later years play with Taylor, recalls a gig that illustrates Eddie's predicament. "Eddie and I were playing with Jimmy Walker at a concert given by the Jazz Institute of Chicago, like a festival," Cushing remembers. "One year they hired Eddie Taylor, Jimmy Walker on piano, and myself on drums. One of them was playing everything in A and the other played in E. And there were songs where they just wouldn't change and you had two instruments playing in two different keys. It was unfortunate. Jimmy Walker was over 80—it could be excused. But Eddie was just so fed up that Jimmy couldn't play in any other key and just would play everything in the same key all night. When we got through, the woman who was a representative of the Jazz Institute took special pains to take me aside and let me know that we were the worst blues act that they ever hired in the history of their concerts. Poor Eddie Taylor. Here is one of the half-dozen greatest blues guitarists in the world and he gets stuck with that!"

Eddie never made a habit of speaking in depth about one thing or another with guys he'd play with, and he behaved gentlemanly for the most part, but he also possessed a certain tenseness lying just under the surface. "Eddie had a hot temper but he wouldn't necessarily tell you anything was wrong with you or anything," Chicago blues drummer Twist Turner intimates. "He just might be annoyed with the band and be on the stage and kick the nightstand over. You never knew with Eddie."

Blues composer, producer, and authority Dick Shurman saw Eddie a bit differently, without the hostility. "Eddie just felt he hadn't gotten his due for his contribution and ability," he says. "In a way he was right, but on the other hand sometimes it is not all just bad luck. He didn't have a star's personality. He was a taciturn, reserved person and he didn't strut his stuff like a star. One guy I knew called him 'The Man from Plaid'! He and Louis Myers [guitarist in the Aces] always had a love-hate relationship. I have this one tape of them on tour in Europe together. Louis sings a song he had written that I had never heard him do before, and it was something about 'I'm mad, and I'm not gonna take this anymore....' I asked him about it...and he told me he wrote it about Eddie. He had had enough. It was mutual."

"Louis was a very talented guy and he was better than everybody else in the world, but he was stuck on the South Side and nobody knew him," Cushing explains. "After I left Magic Slim I was trying to get Louis Myers gigs on the North Side, including myself and the band. That was what white guys did. The only way white guys got to play with the really accomplished players was to make themselves useful and get the black guys work. Maybe they would put up with you…. During the time he and I were looking for gigs and running all of these North Side clubs, we went into a place called Orphan's on Lincoln Avenue. Eddie Taylor and his band were playing there. As we walked in a song ended, Eddie got on the microphone, and said, 'I want you all to give a round of applause to one of the greatest guitar players in the world, Louis Myers.' Louis started yelling at him, 'You stop that black-on-black shit, Eddie Taylor.' Louis understood exactly what Eddie was doing. But Eddie was totally insincere. Eddie was saying that he didn't believe it for a second. I was just amazed to stand back and watch that happen. I think in his heart of hearts that Eddie would have told you that if he didn't think he [Eddie] was the best blues guitar player in the world, he was among the top three or half-dozen. You would never hear him say that kind of thing, at least not to us."

Eddie Taylor.

But rough times affected even "the greatest blues guitarist in the world." Things were tight, and even someone of Eddie Taylor's caliber would find it difficult to get good-paying gigs every now and again. There were also times that he could have helped himself, but it would have betrayed his principles. When an African-American blues-friendly European label came to Chicago and went looking around town for someone to record, Eddie Taylor's name came up. But since Eddie had some whites in his band at the time, the label backed off and Eddie refused to back down. "This is my band," he'd say, "take it or leave it."

Eddie was perhaps the victim of a skewed sense of karma, a man hampered by more than his share of bad breaks. "The thing about Eddie that always kind of got me was, I always kind of compared him to Lowell Fulson, though Lowell did it at a slightly higher level," Shurman notes. "But they both—right up to the end—had been playing gigs they had all along. Eddie was playing in these little dives on the West Side and he would be working sawdust joints and with second- and third-string-type artists. He would tour once in a while, but he was basically just a ghetto-club and local kind of person in terms of his steady career.

He would not be playing the North Side. He might be hired once in a while, and when he was, he was thrilled. Eddie was on another planet as far as guitarists are concerned. Besides the intricate fingerpicking style, Eddie had a rock-solid rhythm foundation, too. I remember Sam Lay and Carey Bell having a discussion about who the greatest guitar player was. Immediately, one of them answered the rhetorical question: 'Eddie Taylor.' The other quickly agreed."

Eddie used his talents, whether always appreciated to the fullest or not, to provide for his family. "He was 100 percent man—a straight-up man," says Eddie's son Timothy, a drummer by trade. "He laid his laws down. He was that type of person. He was an entertainer onstage but he was a father and husband at home. We lived west a lot—Ashland, Lexington, Sacramento, Roosevelt, 13th and Albany, Dublin. We moved around a lot, I guess, because back in the day there were problems with rats and roaches. My daddy was the type of person to do what was best for his children. My sister, she got bit by a rat and we moved out of one apartment and into another apartment. But rats came and we moved again. My father didn't want his children in no danger at all."

By the early '70s, Eddie would be married to his longtime partner, Lee Vera Hill, when his stepson, Larry, was only two years old. "My mother, Vera Hill, was still at home with my grandmom and she moved out and got this apartment at 1131 South Mozart," says Larry. "[Eddie] got an apartment at 1131 Mozart, at the rear of the building. Then eventually they stayed together for years and years and moved from place to place on the West Side—various projects and housings. My biological father deceased in 1969. He was murdered; I think it was mob connected. Then in the early '70s my dad and mom got married, and they lived on the South Side."iv

Eddie and Jimmy both had natural musical ability and both had a family to support, but to oversimplify, perhaps, Eddie was the strong, reliable one; Jimmy the tardy, "let the chips fall where they may" kind of guy. The division line between them, though, is obscure because of their history—particularly their undocumented history. The question is not so much whether Eddie could survive without Jimmy, but whether Jimmy could truly survive without his musical partner.[v]

Without Eddie, Jimmy was off to a shaky start. By the end of 1969, Reed was in hot water with the Chicago American Federation of Musicians. It wouldn't be the first time and it wouldn't be the last time. Jimmy was just not good at following rules. Not in his professional music career, or in his personal life.

Then what Eddie Taylor had been warning Jimmy about became frightening reality. Between the tough touring schedule, his epilepsy, and his drinking, Reed's hard life finally caught up with him. His epileptic seizures got worse and worse; he was having seizures in bunches. For reasons unclear and details not fully known, Reed suffered a kind of collapse and soon checked himself into a nearby V.A. hospital for observation. Reed would later describe the incident to *Living Blues* as his being "shook up," and he blamed his alcohol as one of the reasons why his health was so poor.

Once he was checked into the hospital, his doctor convinced him to lay low for a while, to get out of the music business and stop thinking about the road. Maybe it was out of loyalty to his family, maybe it was the doctor's influential words, or maybe he was just scared to death, but (uncharacteristically) Reed listened and cooled his jets. No one knew how and when he would be "cured," least of all Jimmy. He would be in the V.A. hospital for the indefinite future.

At times, Jimmy would begin to rethink his life, and half believe all the rumors of his death.

Chapter 6
Help Yourself

Jimmy had been at a Great Lakes V.A. hospital system for months. The days were starting to slide into one another, but he was finally getting some rest and relaxation—a world apart from the world outside, the world that had asked so much of him. It was literally what the doctor'd ordered, and he was finally on the road to recovery. Jimmy would later thank God for sparing his life and granting him time to recoup, and for not letting his racked nerves run him into a heart attack.

"That stay was the longest," remembers daughter Loretta Reed. "It was some months. Not quite a year, but it was some months. I know we went to see him there. At that time he was being observed for a lot of things: his seizures, to see if his brain was damaged at all, if the alcohol was bothering, and what-all was happening to him. The doctors were looking at everything."

Though Jimmy may have been far from the music industry, nothing could put a wedge between him and his music. In the hospital's community center, he and others would get together and play. Though Reed never wrote music while he was in the hospital, he kept his mind occupied on creative endeavors. His easier living convinced the doctors to take a bold step: grant him a leave to go home.

After Jimmy left the hospital, Al Smith was eager to get him back in the studio. Jimmy recorded at CBS Recording Studio in Chicago for what ultimately would make up the LP *As Jimmy Is,* a Torrid production for the Roker label. You'd need a scorecard to keep track of all the records Jimmy released in the early '70s. Smith was trying to outsmart the industry. With a trick Vee-Jay had used, these songs were released on different labels for distribution purposes. It was a good business plan: if a DJ didn't like a Reed single released on one label, he or she might like the other.

Canyon, RRG (Wally Roker music, licensed by Al Smith), and Smith's creation, Blues on Blues—it was all done under Smith's supervision or for his very own Torrid Productions. Because both Roker and Canyon issue singles of these songs before the LP was released, the singles were competing for shelf space—what space record stores were affording Reed in the early '70s, that is.

Despite its title, As Jimmy Is was a musical departure for Reed.

And Reed was duplicitous. You never knew what you were getting. On one single he sounded like he was still in that Vee-Jay state of mind. On another, you could sense nothing more than a faint stab at being a bluesy version of James Brown, plying his slow down-home boogie with a hint of funk. Many of the tracks Jimmy did in the early '70s were remarkable only in the sense that they were so instantly forgettable.

In a three-hour recording session on May 26, 1970, at CBS (with engineer Ed Stryzak), Reed, along with William "Lefty" Bates, William Warren, Nick Charles, and Williams McDonald recorded four songs for Al Smith, which would wind up on the Roker/RRG LP entitled *As Jimmy Is*: "Big Legged Woman," an instrumental titled simply "Instrumental" that would later be titled "Jumpin' Jimmy," "Can't Stand to Leave," and "Cry Before I Go," written by daughter Malinda Reed.[i] (Decades later, CDs with such titles as *Cry Before I Go* and *Big Legged Woman* would be released containing the tracks from *As Jimmy Is*.)

Overall, the tracks are trapped somewhere between cheesy and hip, and faintly resemble a theme song from an early '70s sitcom based smack-dab in the middle of South Central. The collision of the slick, urban, black male and the old-world country-blues singer is apparent, sometimes painfully so. But, the songs have their moments and can even be seen as guilty pleasures, mainly because there's something genuine going on that transcends any dated sonic exercises perpetrated by the musicians and producer. Perhaps the large-type liner notes said it all: "If you've heard Jimmy Reed—there's nothing we can add. If you haven't, all we can say is—Jimmy Reed is 'SUM'PM' else."

"Big Legged Woman" was paired with "Funky Funky Soul" when it was eventually released on the Roker/RRG label, and that was, in retrospect, the best choice of the bunch for a single. That old Reed personality shines on "Big Legged Woman," right through the murky funk. The odd mixture of country-fried blues, urban soul, and, in some cases, James Brown–like funk works better than it would seem, or perhaps should. This style—or amalgamated style—is a true departure for Reed (something Al Smith had wanted to capture for Jimmy's ABC material but perhaps never truly did), and even his signature harp squeals are more subdued, dirty, and soulful.

A promo single of "Crying Blind," with "Christmas Present Blues" on the flip side.

"Big Legged Woman" might be another "Crazy 'bout Oklahoma," at least on the surface, or just another song dedicated to a woman—one of the countless women who have inspired blues singers to lust in verse and chorus. Nobody does ramblin' like Reed. He half sings, half talks, the lines: "You really sound good…really sound good to me [laughs]….It got to sound good when I pay the price for supper twice…if this woman just take me back again…." The interplay is actually quite jumpin.' It's controlled chaos, but Jimmy works the harp, from low to high tones. And his lyrics, which can only be seen as heartfelt, speak about a cold-hearted woman who needs to take him back. Reed hits the lower registers here, contributing, the overall laziness of the music's progress. Reed may have been clean, but he sounds knocked out here. And in this case, this was not such a bad thing.

The band roster is unclear on "Funky Funky Soul," but it's apparent that there are at least four guitars on the song, including bass. That, and the fact that Jimmy is manipulating the harp in ways that might be impractical with a "harness," implies that Jimmy is actually only singing and playing harp, without being saddled with playing lead guitar. It would seem Bobby King is on guitar for some of the recording. Jimmy calls out, "I hear ya, Bob" four times. (Shades of his glory days with Eddie Taylor.) It's King on wah-wah-inflected guitar heard in "Funky Funky Soul," "Christmas Present Blues," "Hard Walking Hannah," and "Good Is Catching Up with Me."

"Over the Hump" is a dead ringer for Sly Stone; one can very nearly swap the lyrics to "Thank You (Fallettinme Be Mice Elf Agin)" for Jimmy's lyrics. Jimmy's words are as endearing as they are world-weary. Once again, he plays the wounded-bird card, and it is effective. Just hearing Jimmy's voice, you feel sorry for the guy: the country-hearted bluesman who can (or will) only play his harp, hoping to convert the uninitiated with his style—entertaining the only way he can, with his harp. And he even talks to himself in "Christmas Present Blues," saying, "I hear ya, Jimmy" before he goes into his harp outro.

While Jimmy's personality certainly peeks through, these tracks and the subsequent LP were as adventurous and contemporary as Reed had ever been. More "ghetto" than even his earliest work (when he was a laborer living on the South Side), Reed was speaking as much to the soul of a black crowd as he was to his loyal white following. That's all fine and good, but the problem was that Jimmy was being overexposed. "Hannah," which was slated as the LP's leadoff track, was released (as parts 1 and 2) on a 45 single issued by the Canyon label. "Crying Blind" with B-side "Christmas Present Blues" was released through the Blues on Blues–affiliated RRG label. (Additionally, "Hard Walking Hannah" appeared on the Jewel label with John Lee Hooker's "Dazie Mae.") Where the idea of flooding the market with Jimmy Reed might have worked ten, even five, years earlier, in the early '70s it seemed like someone's desperate attempt to make money: throwing anything the man was doing against the wall, on as many *seemingly* independent labels as possible, to see what stuck.

Al Smith wouldn't be the first in the industry to be guilty of this (and he wasn't or won't be the last), and Jimmy was being pushed through so many labels it was hard to keep track of what was happening and who was in control of his output. For all intents and purposes, Jimmy didn't truly know himself—or care. It seemed his thoughts were being occupied by elements outside the music business universe. And anyway, the man had conquered that frontier, having sold hundreds of thousands of records, climbed up the pop charts, and crossed over into a mainstream white world where few blacks had gone before him.

Having been snakebit by Vee-Jay—and Al Smith—and not very well taken care of at ABC, Reed wasn't really impressed or fazed by much about the business; he had been to the puppet show and seen the strings. He resolved to say that all he wanted to do was "play these blues." And that's it. There isn't anything deeply profound or even very artful in these tracks, but they are fun underscoring Jimmy's reason to play.

Although Jimmy was back in the swing of recording, 1970 was not a great year for him. He'd soon check into Downey V.A. hospital for treatment, spending months under observation for his nerves, epilepsy, and alcoholism. But before this came to light, big plans were in the works. If Jimmy behaved himself, and took care, Al was set to take him on a European tour (as part of the American Folk Blues Festival) in 1972. The idea behind taking Jimmy on the AFBF would be the same as it was in 1968: let the Euros have a crack at him. They love 'im. Of course, looking at the various trips Reed had made over to that continent in the 1960s reveals a mixed bag of musical performances. Many Europeans remember a drunken Reed (onstage and off) as much as they do his performances. The AFBF was no different. Could Smith convince a jaded or savvy European concertgoer to pony up for a ticket to see a sloshed and unfocused Jimmy again? *Yes,* Smith thought, defying logic. "He and I plan to do at least 30 countries," Smith explained in the liner notes for *Let the Bossman Speak!*

The difference, of course, between the planned 1972 tour and the one in 1968 was that this would be a new and sober, yet fragile, Reed. The years were getting up on him. He was only in his late forties but he looked much older. He simply couldn't stand a grueling schedule.

Despite Smith's assertion that Jimmy was "feeling fine these days," he still had to be watched, and no one, not even Smith (the best of the bunch, save Mama Reed) could control Jimmy, his bad attitude toward his handlers, or his alcohol intake. (Thirty countries would, indeed, be too much for Jimmy, and he embarked on a 13-country in 1972 as part of the Blues on Blues package tour.)

One saving grace was that Boonie had just returned from a tour of duty in Vietnam and was available for Daddy if he ever needed him in the studio or on the road. "I was in the Marine Corps in Vietnam, and I saw action," says Jimmy Reed, Jr., of his tour of duty. "I joined the Marine Corps on June 7, 1967, and from that point up until November 10, 1967, I was in training. I flew over to Okinawa, Japan, on November 10 and went through a staging area and then they sent me over to Vietnam.

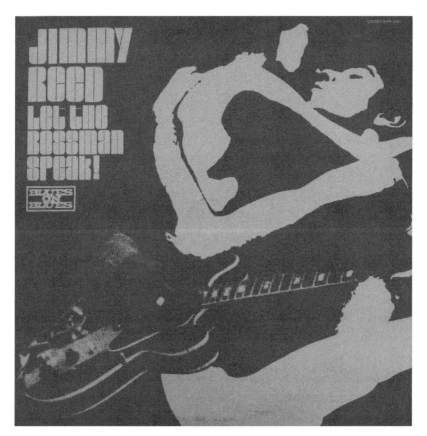

Reed recorded something familiar and something new for "Let the Bossman Speak," one of the first releases to appear on Al Smith's Blues on Blues label.

"After my tour was up, I extended my duty over there for six months to play with the First Marine Air Wing Band," he continues. "I was playing bass drum for the marching band and bass guitar for the jazz band."

The time out of mind from the war and music in general had torn him apart from his dad. Not only had he gone months without seeing his family, but he knew that when he returned from his tour of duty he'd put down his father's blues and start off on a new musical path.

The thought of his son not wanting to follow in his footsteps as a bluesman perplexed, even saddened, Reed. His son was someone who was a near prodigy when he was waltzed onto the stage as a child, to the amazement of those in attendance. At age nine, Boonie was playing with Reed, flooring people. Mama Reed told of how one night Memphis Slim and Brook Benton had been in attendance at the Persian Ballroom and the crowd said, "We want to hear Junior. We don't want to hear you [Jimmy] no more."

Junior's tour of Vietnam sparked an interest in a more sophisticated, guitar-driven, jazz-influenced blues—the kind people like B.B. King had pioneered and were making immensely popular. "Dad didn't like that jazz stuff," Reed, Jr., says. "He didn't like it at all. He would always tell me, 'Don't play all these other people's stuff. Get your own stuff and play it....' "

Despite his yearning to play what he deemed to be more challenging music, Jimmy Reed, Jr., entered the studio with his dad to play rhythm guitar for another round of boogie blues Reed, Sr., style. Jimmy still had a thing or two he could teach Junior. Jimmy knew that all that "junk" Boonie was throwing down was clouding his musical judgment, timing, and feel.

Though Junior would be the first to admit that he didn't want to follow in his father's footsteps and yearned to be seen as anything but "Jimmy Reed's son" (in the musical sense), his dad failed to see Boonie's versatility working for him in the long run. Reed's hopes had been that his son would pick up a thing or two from him, let his dad in just enough to influence his decision to help him find his unique voice—his own sound—on the instrument. If Reed brought anything to the table as a musician, it was his ability to make his music instantly recognizable. What did his son learn?

Regardless of his personal ambitions, Junior decided to stay with his dad. There had always been a support system in place for Jimmy, Sr. In this case, in addition to Junior, it was Malinda Reed, his 18-year-old daughter, who also picked up the bass. (Malinda would soon join Reed's nephews Allen and Darnell James and a host of others in the jazz-pop-rock-blues concoction called One Step Beyond.)

"She's doing rehearsals just as Mama Reed has done for years, and also doing a little writing," Al Smith wrote in the liner notes for *Let the Bossman Speak!* Smith made it sound like Malinda was a newcomer to the music business. She wasn't. She was writing songs at age five and had been accompanying her father in the studio since the late '60s. Malinda also played shows with Jimmy, and the two would duet on the song "Goin' by the River" onstage. She certainly proved to be a lot of things to a lot of people.

Reed's poor health also affected Malinda and her musical ambitions. Once Reed wound up in the hospital in 1969, she found herself out of a father—and a gig. She had been contributing songs to the Reed music cause, as it were, and she, along with some of the family members (including Mama) and Al Smith, were counting on Reed to stay healthy.

Smith knew Jimmy was still unstable, still getting back on his feet. In an interesting move, he decided to record the Big Boss Man again. Jimmy cut two quick sessions for Smith for his new Blues on Blues label. The LP, *Let the Bossman Speak!* (also later released as *Cold Chills* on the Antilles label, distributed by Island), was one of the first releases to be stamped with the Blues on Blues label, after both Reed and Smith broke away from BluesWay (though BluesWay would unearth unreleased and previously released Jimmy Reed material in the early 1970s). Though Smith would release a few blues records nearly simultaneously through Blues on Blues (the others by Homesick James, Big Joe Williams, and Earl Hooker), none had the potential for a crossover hit like Reed's.

The marketing schtick for the record was very much like the first ABC-BluesWay album, *The New Jimmy Reed.* Smith was trying to portray his music as something new—Jimmy having a new "bag" to jump out of. No one knew that Jimmy's health was heading south. It appeared as though he was doing O.K., and Smith himself reported on Reed's progress in the liner notes to *Let the Bossman Speak!*: "Jimmy Reed is feeling fine these days," wrote Smith. "He had a pretty hard spell of sickness for about eight or nine months, but now his voice is strong; he is drinking less; and he is looking good. He's not working the string of one-nighters he used to work during the time he was with the Al Smith Band for so many years on the road. He is doing some college dates and specials like that."

Roy Hytower, having changed his name to Doktu Rhute Muuzic, was one of five guitarists (including Jimmy Reed, Boonie, Lefty Bates, and bassist Nick Charles) who were present at the second tracking session for the LP. (The first session had Jimmy with bassist Dave Myers, guitarist Louis Myers, and Fred Below on drums. Jimmy later would dispute these lineup credits, but it appears as though they were correct on the album's notes.)

Hytower had met Reed in the late '50s in Mobile, Alabama, at the King Club. He was a fan through his brother, who bought all of Reed's music and introduced him to the wonders of it. Muuzic learned quite a bit from watching and listening to Reed, and got his lazy, laconic harmonica style down.

Muuzic had the opportunity to open up for artists like Ray Charles and Fats Domino in Mobile at the Harlem Dukes Social Club, and when he came to Chicago the first band he played in was Otis Rush's smoking outfit, replacing Mighty Joe Young. Eventually he ran into Lefty Bates, and Lefty was impressed with then-Hytower's playing. He was the perfect support player: he was familiar with the tunes he was playing, he wasn't interested in stealing the spotlight, and he was young. Suddenly, Hytower was on Al Smith's radar.

"Later on I came to Chicago and I learned to play the harmonica and guitar the same way he [Reed] did," Muuzic explains. "So, when I came to Chicago I wanted to meet him again, except he was in the hospital at the time. His manager, Al Smith, knew that I played very similar to Jimmy and he wanted me to do some dates that Jimmy had planned, but I had talked with some other musicians and friends of mine who said that it was probably not a good idea to cover for Jimmy because people are actually looking for Jimmy.... I never did do it, but that was how I met Al Smith and that led me to do some studio work with Jimmy.

"What they were trying to do was point him in a different direction," Muuzic continues. "They were looking for a new approach. Jimmy wasn't having any of that. They was trying to introduce him to a new beat, something that was a little more contemporary than what he had been doing. So, finally he just said, 'I'm Jimmy. This is what Jimmy do. Let's just do what I do.' He'd always refer to himself in the third person, you know? I can't quite remember the rhythm of all the songs, but I think a few of them were in a little bit of a different direction. But mainly, the only thing Jimmy would stick to was what he was doing and he would call you on things if the rhythm wasn't right. Then he'd just say, 'Hey, that ain't right. I got to play my rhythm the way I know it.' He would complain if the music was going too far off his path. He said, 'No, no, no. That ain't me. I can't feel that.' He couldn't tell you what he was playing, but you could figure it out. That was different from John Lee Hooker, who would change whenever he was ready. You just had to be on your Ps and Qs. When he change, you change. When he goes around, you go around. No rhyme or reason. Jimmy was pretty much the same, but he had a little more structure. He would play a 12-bar blues and John Lee Hooker would play a 13-and-a-half-bar blues or something."

Even though some of the same elements of *As Jimmy Is* were present for the *Let the Bossman Speak!* tracking sessions, the latter LP is more coherent and consistent, perhaps despite itself. *Blues Unlimited* would call it a "dire" attempt from Reed to claw his way back to the top, but the record boasts some funny, funky, poignant soul-blues moments. Some moments, while musically enthralling, are also downright bizarre. In "Jimmy's Hotpants" (credited to Al Smith), for instance, Reed says, "I love your mini-skirt, but these hotpants outta sight."

In some instances, such as "I Had a Dream" (another song credited to Al Smith), Reed is on lead guitar and harp, and he speaks simply but deeply. He sings, "I had a dream, but the dream never come true…I dream I walked through a river by you, 'cause you was on the other side…I do the same ole thing again if I could keep our love alive." And just like 1963's "Shame, Shame, Shame," in which Reed envisioned Mary Lee leaving him, he is once again singing about being without his bedrock—his lover, partner, and adviser—and wondering what went wrong. However, unlike "Shame, Shame, Shame," the words of "I Had a Dream" reflect the advanced stages of his embattled psyche. Reed was no longer as young or confident (or indignant, for that matter) a man, and "I Had a Dream" clearly shows him in a position of relative frailty; he is someone who accepts failure as a sad and harsh aspect of life. There's no laughing at the blues here, and perhaps for the first time, the man who made everyone get up and dance and laugh and drink nearly brings a tear to your eye. There were other solid efforts on the record ("You Just a Womper Stomper" and Malinda's "Help Me at Dinner-time"), perhaps making this LP one of the only truly shining aspects of Reed's professional life at the time.

No matter where he went, though, temptations abounded. They dogged him. "I know when [Reed] got out [of the hospital], that is when we went into the studio. I can't remember exactly who came into the studio, but they had a bottle of alcohol and Al Smith had a fit," Muuzic says. "At that point, Jimmy Reed hadn't been drinking. Since he had been in the hospital he hadn't been drinking and they was keeping a close eye on him. But this guy came in and it created this big uproar. They got him out of there quickly. You know, 'Don't come in here with that.' I don't know if this guy was trying to slip Jimmy a drink to get him loose, or what."

Al had to look after Jimmy physically, emotionally, and financially. But Smith, it appeared to some, couldn't help but take advantage at times. "For my concept he might have took [Jimmy] a little bit," says Muuzic. "A lot of times managers have tendencies, though I didn't have access to any paperwork or books. But we all kind of figured that he was holding out some of the money because Jimmy was under the influence of alcohol and really didn't keep up with his money as he should have. So, it seems as though Al was probably holding up quite a bit on him. Al was also a sheriff and he carried a big .45 all the time."

But to see only that side of Smith is to ignore all of the other aspects of the Reed–Smith symbiotic relationship. Al Smith never raised his voice to Jimmy, but he would to everyone else. And if anyone else pandered to Jimmy's alcohol problems, he was a pariah. Al seemed to have some sort of power over Jimmy, as if Jimmy couldn't escape if he even wanted.

"You can't deny his role in making Jimmy Reed a star and keeping him out for a while," says Dick Shurman, Chicago blues maven, writer, and producer who's worked with Jody Williams, Johnny Winter, Roy Buchanan, and Albert Collins, among others. "There is no doubt that he put Jimmy on a higher plane than he would have been without him. Plus, I'm sure he had to put up with a lot from Jimmy Reed; he had to literally and figuratively prop Jimmy up a lot of the time. He certainly did a lot for him but he doesn't seem to be a guy who was particularly into Santa Claus, either. And Jimmy was probably incredibly poorly equipped to call him on it. Somebody needs someone who knows business to do business. We [Smith and Shurman] had a couple of conversations where it would veer into business things. With his reputation and evasiveness, I really didn't want to take it very far. I knew him enough not to trust him. You have to feel ambivalent about him, because on the one hand he certainly caused a lot of good things to happen [for Jimmy], and on the other hand he certainly took his opportunity. I think Al is always going to be the Svengali figure of the Jimmy Reed story—maybe the Colonel Tom of the Jimmy Reed story."

Despite all of the planning, self-preservation instincts, and good intentions Smith had, Jimmy's downward slide continued. Smith was simply ill-equipped to handle the enormity of Jimmy's disease, and soon Reed found himself back in Downey hospital for observation.[ii] He checked himself in; it was time to really get clean. No fooling around.

There he met Dave Riley, a Vietnam vet who had seen some serious action. Riley had come home without much of a hero's welcome. He came back to the same rundown projects that he had found himself in before he was shipped out to fight for his country. As he was adjusting to life after the war zones of the Vietnamese jungles, Riley was involved in a scuffle at a party one night.

"I grew up in the projects, O.K.? And I was a different person back then," Riley says. "I was drinking and some guy got on my nerves and I wound up throwing him out a window. Cops came and they took me away. But they found out I was a veteran, see? So they didn't put me in jail, but took me to one of the V.A. hospitals, Downey, for psychiatric observation. That is where I met Jimmy. We'd just talk sometimes. He didn't really know that I was interested in music, and as I said, I didn't really know who he was. We'd just hang around sometimes. Jimmy was into swimming a lot. I lost touch with him after that. I was in the hospital for about a month, and Jimmy was there before I got there—he left long after I did. Seemed to me he had his problems but he was also hiding out from the music industry, you know what I mean? He just wanted to get away."

As Riley admits, he didn't really know who Jimmy was at first, but he would soon discover it once he got out of Downey. "I guess I thought the guy was so unassuming it didn't cross my mind. Jimmy didn't really know how important he was. In all honesty, my father had to explain it to me when I finally got home just who this gentleman was. It was Jimmy Reed."

In the early '70s when John Denver was churning out gold records, he had intimated that Jimmy Reed was a heavy influence on him. While some of us might be hard-pressed to find common musical threads between Denver and Reed, perhaps what Denver learned from Reed was his ability to put across songs that were instantly recognizable. A military brat, Deutschendorf (aka Denver) was, in his own words, a "global citizen"—a true "folk" singer in its purist definition, as Reed had become. Similarly, a sonic cousin to John Denver, James Taylor, seemed to allow a Jimmy Reed–style blues to seep into his plaintive music. Listen to his "Steamroller" (on *Sweet Baby James*) and you'll hear an approximated classic Reed "lump." Taylor has always maintained that the song was written as a tongue-in-cheek commentary on white artists' rediscovery of the blues. He didn't want to be left out, and "Steamroller" was the result.

But aside from these references and other subtle, unlikely coincidences in the mainstream popular culture, Jimmy Reed was slowly being forgotten. Some had even suspected that he died. Those in the know had to soldier on and hope for the best. Meanwhile, on the outside, it was business as usual for Al Smith. He was securing more diverse music contracts through his Torrid Productions. Cary Baker remembers visiting Smith's buzzing-with-activity office at 1321 S. Michigan Avenue in the early '70s. "Gene Chandler also had an office in that building for his labels Mr. Chand and Bamboo," Baker says, who was a teen at the time. "Smith had the indie Torrid Records and seemed to be the Chicago go-to for L.A.-based Canyon Records and Boo Frazier's Perception Records. He was promoting Dizzy Gillespie's soul-jazz single 'Soul Kiss' alongside Jimmy Reed and a single called 'In Over My Head' by the revived doo wop group the Eldorados."

Though blues was certainly Al's first love, he was beginning to branch out. Reverend Stanley Keeble was a Chicago gospel singer who recorded "The Gospel Truth" for Al Smith's Torrid label in the early '70s. Keeble describes his relationship with Smith, which was far from what Reed had experienced. "It was a real pleasant relationship with Al," Keeble says. "I was introduced to Al by a good buddy of mine, Tyrone Kenner, who was the deputy director of the Chicago Committee on Urban Opportunity at the time. I sang at an affair that Mr. Kenner had presented at one of the churches and he had asked Al to come and hear me. I am hoping it was my ability rather than the friendship with Mr. Kenner that convinced him. It seemed to be a great night that night. [laughs] Al was a professional and insisted that things be like they really should have been.... He had a label called Torrid. I think he was at the point that he was getting into gospel with his Torrid label."

In the 1960s and early '70s, artists like Edwin Hawkins and Reverend James Cleveland were either crossing over and/or scoring megahits in the gospel genre. Al Smith sniffed a bit of commercialism in spirituals. "He was a smart guy," notes guitarist Lonnie Brooks. "He was *very* smart. That cat could talk his way into heaven, man."

"You don't go in business *not* trying to make business profitable for you," Keeble says. "I understand and don't have any problem with it. People who have a talent ought to be paid. Now, I am not sure what Al's feeling was in the beginning. Like I said, we were introduced because of my friend Mr. Kenner, who went on to become an alderman in Chicago. I guess Tyrone felt that nobody on the planet could sing but me. I am sure that he prompted Al, because he wanted to see something positive happen with his friend. Al even contacted Albertina Walker, the Queen of Gospel, and his interest had deepened at that point.... I think he foresaw that gospel music would make this great surge.

"I was still young at the time when I was dealing with Al," Keeble continues, "but I had been trained and coached by people who were a lot older than I was. But basically Al was a great guy. He loved the industry and he did what he thought would make the industry a better product for people."

It was a good thing Al Smith was branching out, because his long-time client was about to go south, literally and figuratively. Jimmy got the news that his mother had died while he was in the hospital. His mother had been living alone in Mississippi and Reed was desperate to get down there for the funeral. Rumors have circulated as to how Reed was actually given the news and what was said. Booking agent Bill Tyson of Inner City Trade Productions, who would soon manage Reed, explained to *Living Blues* the way he saw it: "Al booked an engagement down in Mississippi and told [Reed] he could only go to his mother's funeral if he played that engagement. Jimmy played that engagement and got to the funeral too late. They were burying her when he got there."

We have to look upon this story with some skepticism. Tyson was positioning himself to be Reed's manager, firstly. Secondly, Al Smith had a reputation and it is easy to see how someone could embellish some details to make him look bad. Thirdly, Reed had power over himself—sort of. If this account is indeed true, we can only speculate that Jimmy was some sort of victim to Svengali Al Smith.

With that one supposed act, Al Smith and Jimmy Reed parted company. Tyson said that Reed later told him, "God will take care of Al Smith."

Jimmy had been given a 14-day leave from the hospital, and when he returned, the doctor turned him loose. For the final time, Reed got his hospital walking papers—if he would promise not to push himself. Jimmy could work if he wanted to, but he had to avoid alcohol and stress associated with the music business. Reed agreed and was back on the streets of Chicago.

Jimmy was welcomed into the arms of family friend and fellow musician Johnnie Mae Dunson. Effectively, Johnnie Mae had, more or less, become Reed's manager and confidante by default. Dunson brought Jimmy into her house after he was discharged from the V.A. hospital. "Jimmy was at the V.A. because he was a veteran," Dunson says. "I remember when my husband took him in there and put him in there. I can tell you one thing, my son, when he was 13 years old, gave him some special care. My son was 12, 13, when Jimmy Reed taught my son to play. He took care of him like he was his own father. I know that. When I wasn't around and my husband was at work, he helped."

The Reed family, thinking it might be best to give Jimmy some distance, green-lighted Reed's move to Johnnie Mae's place on North Elizabeth in Chicago (though it turned out to be a big and bold move).

Johnnie Mae got to know Jimmy very well when he was living with her. "I lost my mother the day Jimmy Reed came back from the doctor," Dunson remembers. "He was crazy about my mom, and she was crazy about him. They used to sit down and drink coffee together and he told me when he came and wanted to see me, I just told him, 'Mother died.' He went down. He started crying. I tell you that already had took something out of me—my mother leaving me."

Keeping her own family together, keeping an eye on Jimmy, and getting him motivated to stay focused and positive was not easy for Johnnie Mae. "But I did it," she says. "That's right. People saw it and didn't believe it was Jimmy Reed. They thought it was Jimmy Reed, Jr., but I said, 'Ain't no Jimmy Reed, Jr,. here.'"

Johnnie Mae did help rehabilitate Jimmy, get him back on his feet. But Jimmy not only needed someone to keep an eye on his drinking and potential seizures, he needed a shot to his ego: he needed to record.

Meanwhile, in June 1972, Frank Scott, a Brit with a taste for American blues, had decided to record Eddie Taylor's first full-fledged solo LP, *I Feel So Bad,* for the Advent label. "I really wanted to capture him at his best," Scott says. "Eddie, though he primarily played with Jimmy Reed, he just played with everyone. When I was in Chicago in 1969 he was playing with Muddy Waters because Sammy Lawhorn got into an accident. Jimmy had decided to hang it up not long before, and Eddie kept plugging away even though there was not a whole lot for him. Most of the money he got was from hustling from gig to gig."

Scott first met Taylor in 1966 and had gotten to know the guitarist then. They rekindled the friendship in 1969. "When I decided to start a record label and put out a blues record...I really was thinking what else to do," Scott says. "I was thinking that nobody has done an LP with Eddie Taylor. I remember from Chicago what an enormous talent he was."

i feel so bad

the
blues
of
EDDIE
TAYLOR

Eddie Taylor's first full-fledged solo LP didn't break sales records, but it represented a personal milestone for the Chicago-based guitarist.

Eddie was about to team up with former Vee-Jay label head Jimmy Bracken to record new material, but Bracken died in 1972, nixing for years any chance Eddie had of having a recording home. "Pertaining to music, Eddie was hard to beat," says Bruce Bromberg, who offered assistance throughout the entire recording process. "Most of those guys were scuffling. How much money could someone make from an occasional record session? Sidemen probably got $30 or $50. Eddie played the clubs and did what those people do to raise his family."

It was Frank Scott who brought Eddie to California, and the solo LP was recorded in Eldorado Studios in Hollywood and Advent Studios in Glendale. "Basically, I was the one who got Frank the band," Bromberg explains. "Now, Eddie came out [to California] and stayed in Frank's house in Glendale, which in those days was not a black-friendly town. Frank had this place in the hills—he was renting in those days—and was married to his first wife then. Eddie was pretty much stuck there during the day; there was no place for him to go. Frank had a day job. I remember one day I thought I'd be nice to Eddie and take him out to a soul-food restaurant in L.A. I remember he wasn't unpleasant, but he wasn't a particularly forthcoming guy. It was a long time ago and I'm sure I tried to get information out of him, but he wasn't particularly talkative. I took him to this restaurant and thought I was doing him a favor and he gets in there and sits down. The first thing he does when he sits down is inspect the silverware. If he had a microscope, I'm sure he would have used it. I didn't even think he wanted to eat there. We *did* eat there and he seemed somewhat happy after that."

As usual, Eddie's taste was impeccable. His musical ability and depth provided the bulk of what was recorded for *I Feel So Bad*. "Eddie really had an amazing repertoire," Scott says. "Just about everything on that album was stuff *he* wanted to do. The only thing I had suggested was Charlie Patton's 'Jersey Bull Blues.' We had been talking about Charlie Patton and I think he may have seen Patton once or twice. Immediately, he launched into the song—he knew it. He also did 'Stop Breaking Down,' which is basically the Robert Johnson song 'Stop Breakin' Down Blues.' I think musicians around Chicago, some of them, were doing Johnson songs. If you look at the song 'I Feel So Bad,' it is really based on 'Terraplane Blues.'"

Eddie also recorded a jumpin' version of "Goin' Upside Your Head"—a favorite from the Reed days—and "12 Year Old Boy," a song Eddie had recorded with Elmore James as part of the latter's contract with the Chief label. That song and others would later be released by Vee-Jay. On the 1972 version, Eddie plays electrified acoustic guitar.

Second guitarist Phillip Walker and Eddie would mess around with the songs before actually recording the tunes, just to get their feet wet. The final lineup of the LP included Taylor, Walker, David Ii on saxophone and percussion, George "Harmonica" Smith, Jimmy Sones on piano, drummer Johnny Tucker, Charles Sones on bass, and Little H. Williams on percussion. They combined to record a total of 12 songs in two days on an 8-track recorder.

"One funny story: Eddie brought this amp on the plane with him that was bigger than Houston," Bromberg says. "It was a big amplifier that had more bells and whistles on it than a Cadillac. He plugged the amp in, played two notes, and it blew up. He was a grouchy little fucker, but I'll tell you what, boy, if there were mistakes made on any cuts, it was never by Eddie."

"I think one of the only things that we regret to some extent was that Eddie's amplifier went out and we had to run it through the board, which didn't give it as punchy a sound as it might have been if we were able to record his amplifier," Scott explains. "It probably sounds strange in a way, but in those days money was tight, we were young, we were in the session, and we had to make do with what we had."

"We had Eddie play through Phillip's amp," Bromberg says. "It was cut on an 8-track. Phil used to play a Tele in those days. People think of him with that red Gibson that he played, that Pete Welding gave him. If you took those direct, you didn't get much zip out of it. If you listen to Phillip's sound it really doesn't sound like he does on his own records. Those were two things I remember about it. I remember it turned out pretty good."

Eddie would go on to record *Ready for Eddie* in England in the winter and early spring of 1974 under the moniker Eddie "Playboy" Taylor for Jim Simpson's Big Bear label. Eddie's band consisted of guitarist Roger Hill, bassists Graham Gallery and Bob Brunning, Bob Hall on piano, and drummer Peter York. They mesh well together to produce such driving and rockin' numbers as "I'm a Country Boy," "Playboy Boogie" (with a nod to Magic Sam's "I Feel So Good—I Wanna Boogie"), "Gamblin' Man," and a cover of "Cross Cut Saw" (written by R.G. Ford, recorded by Tommy McClennan in 1941, and cut most notably by Albert King with Booker T. & the MGs and the Memphis Horns for the Stax label in 1966).

As Eddie did for the Advent label, he gave a nice sprinkling of his raw talent and influences. Fittingly, producer Simpson seemed to have a similar experience with Taylor as Frank Scott did in the recording process. "Eddie always seemed to have a chip on his shoulder," says Simpson. "He always seemed to resent that he wasn't as famous as Buddy Guy or somebody. He always felt that Jimmy [Reed] was a bit of a passenger. This is only Eddie talking—I don't know how true it is. His musical expertise was way above average, in my opinion. I think he was one of the best blues players who ever lived. I think he thought the world owed him a little more respect for what he was doing. Ate too much chicken, too often. Besides that, he was a very difficult person, and a lot of people were worried about him.

"He was resentful, I think," Simpson continues. "I think he always had a chip on his shoulder that he wasn't more well known. He recorded for me, he toured with me, we did broadcasts together, we did TV, and he was 100 percent professional, but a real miserable sod."

"Like Jimmy Rogers, Eddie didn't have the kind of personality that could hold a band together," Scott admits. "If you have someone like Muddy, he was the master of all he surveyed and he kept his band in line. He could always rely on getting the best musicians in town, whereas Eddie and Rogers couldn't. When we were together recording, I was a young, enthusiastic blues fanatic and was excited by the prospect of recording someone who I thought was an exceptional talent, and someone who could capture the sound I liked in the blues.

"Later on," Scott explains, "things got a little tense between us, I think because he felt he wasn't receiving sufficient royalty payments. About two or three years after we did the first album together, I wanted to do another one with him. I had spoken with him and he was up for it. And I made the arrangements and bought him a ticket and waited at the L.A. airport and he never showed up. I called him up and asked if everything was O.K. and where he was and he said he didn't think things were fair and he'd seen the musicians around town driving around in expensive cars. A few years after, he came out to play the San Francisco Blues Festival and we got together and had dinner. I spoke to him and was a little more direct. I said, 'I've got all the figures, you got paid what we agreed on. We didn't really make any money. My only goal was to put out the album and still have enough money to put out another album by someone else. But I'm not in the business to make a fortune.'"[iii]

"Frank Scott called me because he wanted Eddie to do a second album for him," recalls Dick Shurman. "I talked to Eddie and once I gave him a few hundred bucks advance money. I met him at Else where. I remember he had just gotten his hair processed and was getting ready to get the money, but he had blown off two or three plane tickets that Frank had bought for him. Even after taking that advance money, he told Frank that he wasn't going to do the album. He didn't like the deal or whatever. I don't remember it being anything to justify keeping the advance money. That was unfortunate. That was probably the one time I had saw him give his word on something and then gradually back out of it. Not that another album for Eddie would have put him on Johnny Carson or anything. He might not have been the type of guy who was as successful surmounting obstacles as much as the type of person who created them. Having said that, he was a steady enough guy—he was always playing."

In fairness to Eddie and Frank Scott, Eddie was not the only blues musician Scott had business dealings with who felt, quite unjustifiably, that he was being burned by a deal. "I had the good fortune of getting the rights to put out an Otis Rush album." Scott continues, "I helped set up a tour on the West Coast with him, and I helped put together a band that was familiar with the material. One of the things to help publicize the tour was to manufacture some T-shirts for the record, *Right Place, Wrong Time*. When he got back to Chicago he was threatening to sue me over the proceeds from the sales of the shirts, even though we made no money; the T-shirts were merely for promotion. In other words, *we made no money.* A lot of musicians, black blues musicians, have a real paranoia. They automatically think they are being taken advantage of."

Under the watchful eye of Johnnie Mae, Jimmy was touring again, though lightly. He was doing places like Mother Earth in Austin, Texas, Nutcracker Lounge in New Orleans, and Pepper's, North Park Hotel, and Duke's in Chicago. A memorable visit to Liberty Hall in Houston, with Texan firebrand guitarist Johnny Winter on the bill, is at the heart of a small Reed controversy. Two bootlegs of Jimmy Reed's performances at Liberty Hall have been circulating for years, and in recent years, two CD releases of the performance have been issued: *Liberty Hall Sessions Featuring Jimmy Reed* (Magnum Music Group)

and *Live at Liberty Hall, Houston, TX, 1972* (Fan Club Records/ New Rose).

Winter and Reed are heard doing "Big Boss Man," "Signals of Love," "You Don't Have to Go," and "Bright Lights, Big City." The problem with low-budget releases is the accuracy of the liner notes, spelling of names, and sound quality, not to mention that the artists are cheated of their royalties. According to Andre Fanelli's liner notes (which are in French) for the New Rose release, the "summit meeting" took place in June 1972. Magnum insists the concert was recorded in the mid-to-late '60s. While the former date might be closer to the truth, there is very little verification, and everyone—from Eddie Taylor to Jimmy Reed, Jr., to Johnnie Mae Dunson—has been bandied about as having appeared with Reed on these recordings.

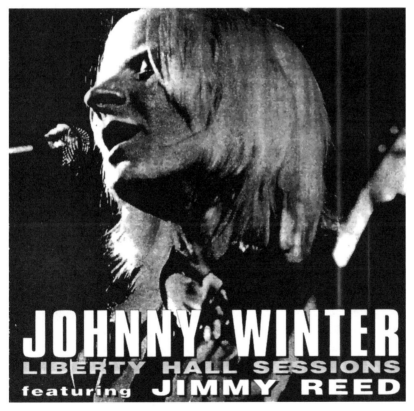

Some claim a Johnny Winter/Jimmy Reed musical summit never occurred, but this seems unlikely.

A quick search on Amazon.com reveals customer doubts about the authenticity of these CDs. While some scoff at the sound quality, others argue that it is not even Winter playing guitar with Reed on the four tracks. This assertion may not necessarily hold water, however. Anyone who has listened to Winter's first two Columbia releases (self-titled and *Second Winter*) can't deny that the person on those four tracks is, at the very least, a very good Winter imitation. And Winter's unmistakable, gruff blues voice asks the crowd at Liberty Hall to put their hands together as the record fades out.

Consistency and accuracy are lacking, but these CDs are interesting historic documents, a snapshot freezing Reed and Winter in time forever: the Big Boss Man and the new guitar whiz kid on the block, who had been the subject of one of the most massive record-company bidding wars in rock music history. If these CDs are good for one thing (and they are just that), it is to hear Reed speaking to the crowd. His heartfelt rambling, both comical and endearing, shows a man grateful to be onstage and happy to be performing for an enthusiastic crowd again. "We want to have you to know…we hopin' each and every last one o' you out in the audience are enjoying yourselves, because we really are enjoying ourselves tryin' to perform fo' ya…. I want to thank God for lettin' me sitting [sic] up here before you tonight…."

Reed's subdued, even consciously restrained harp playing and comatose vocal delivery are more often than not in cooperation—not competition—with Winter's blazing guitar work. Despite Reed's warning that "some of these things may not be just direct on the head," there is nary a mistake to be heard with Winter and the second guitarist (perhaps Jimmy Reed, Jr.?), especially when they lock in for the classic Reed turnarounds.

One wonders what would have become of these two artists had they recorded together in the studio. The closest Winter would come would be to officially commit to a cover of "Baby What You Want Me to Do" (11 minutes' worth) with brother Edgar for their 1975 record *Johnny and Edgar Winter Together*. While the song is perhaps the best example of misapplication of Jimmy Reed minimalism (the band maximizes, not minimalizes, in effect), the down-home blues pokes through Winter's near-psychedelic playing. "Winter's whiplash lead guitar in this extended 'live' jam is challenged by Edgar's bootin' sax in fine fraternal duel," wrote Mark Humphrey for the liner notes of *Johnny Winter: A Rock 'n' Roll Collection.*

Guy Schwartz, whom some have called the godfather of the Houston local music scene, played a few times with Jimmy Reed at Liberty Hall in the early and mid-'70s. "The blues revival thing that happened in the late '60s and early '70s—I was here in Houston when that was going on," Schwartz says. "Liberty Hall was a great fuckin' hall with a Bill Graham booking policy—in and out of the mainstream. Discovering new artists, you know. People like Springsteen played Liberty Hall and called it one of their best gigs when they first started. There are a lot of artists like that because they would take a chance on an unknown artist just because they liked the tape. Even before they had a record deal. Often they often got visits back when the people got popular enough. They could have shunned the room because of its size. They had 300, 400 downstairs and another 100 people upstairs. It was a hippie room.

"I was living a block away from the Hall and so when they would get one of the bluesmen who were playing one of the festivals, not too far away, they would get 'em to play at our Hall," Schwartz continues. "At the same time they would play the Vulcan. So these guys were usually traveling by themselves and needed a pickup band. I've always been one of the guys to call to play on bass. No rehearsal; last minute. I was called with that kind of gig for Jimmy the first time; the other times I was called because I was the guy who had already done it. And Johnny [Winter] used to sit in all the time at Liberty Hall.... Then there was Billy Gibbons, who was always there but never sat in."

Jimi Shutte was playing with Luther Allison at the time when he got the call to back up Reed at a Liberty Hall show in the same time frame. "Jimmy was using Luther's band, and I remember that because I had just joined Luther's band," explains Shutte. "I know we were playing there three nights. I remember we did 'Big Boss Man' and I was doing a kind of Chicago shufle behind it. Jimmy turned to me and smiled, and said, 'Don't be playing all that jazz, now.'"

Though Shutte is unclear on whether he is actually on the low-grade tracks that are now circulating, his memory is not fuzzy when recalling other aspects of Reed's appearance at Liberty Hall. "I remember I was sitting upstairs with Larry [Byrne] and I don't know what we were drinking," Shutte says. "The dressing room was upstairs and they had a dumbwaiter. So, we sent up for drinks.

"I knew he had this reputation as a drinking mutherfucker, but I just didn't see it," Shutte continues. "It could be because at that point I was not too fucking self-destructive. Or maybe he was drinking so quietly I didn't know it. But I don't think so. The show had more of the vibe that Jimmy Reed was back on the road again. You know, 'Jimmy Reed has been sick and hasn't been on the road, but he is better and kicking ass,' or something like that. And, indeed, they were good sets, played to packed houses. You know, musicians might take it lightly that Reed's music seemed like it was the same three chords, and it was in *E* and it was the same pattern, but lyrically and melodically Reed's songs were different songs."

With the coming of spring came a new season of hope and newfound vigor. "The best way to get off [liquor] is you have to be a man [about it]," Reed told Norman Davis. "And you know what I call a man? The average person that can give somebody they word, and back up his own word that he give to that person."

Jimmy was being good: he didn't want to drink (for the time being), but music—his main means of support—just couldn't be avoided. It was Johnnie Mae's idea to get Jimmy in the studio again. She and Jimmy were out in California, relaxing and doing a few shows and living in Sherman Oaks for a while. Johnnie Mae placed a phone call to Bill Tyson (who once claimed that Jimmy Reed was a passenger in his taxicab and that was the first time they met), convinced that if Jimmy had a real manager he could make it big again. He was a star, a tarnished one but a star nonetheless, and his name could carry the session. And if the song or songs they recorded were good, well, so much the better.

Johnnie Mae and Jimmy flew back to Chicago—without telling Jimmy's family—and Tyson put the session together. Tyson tapped, among others, bassist Nolan Struck and Johnnie Mae herself on drums to back Reed. And that would be it—no pre-production prep. Just turn the tape on and go. Just the way Jimmy would want it. The proof, as they say, is in the pudding.

Released on Tyson's own Magic label, two singles, "Same Old Thing" (with B-side "Milking the Cow") and "I Got the World in a Jug" (with "We Got to Stick Together"), were among the best material Reed had done in the last six or seven years of his recording career. Johnnie Mae must have kicked some life into Reed; the two play off each other well, and Johnnie Mae even takes the lead on "Milking the Cow." For Reed, it would be the closest he'd come to reviving the "old stuff."

That was not how the family saw it, however. It was just another part of the music business that they didn't like or understand, and it drove their father away from them. "[At that time] he was being grabbed by so many people," explains Loretta Reed. "She [Johnnie Mae] was one of the people who was grabbing him. We hear some things that are out there that we don't know anything about. So, they grabbed Daddy somewhere, got him in the studio, and cut some stuff. That's how mercenary some of these people were."

"I used to think that she and my mother were very good friends— they were," Jimmy Reed, Jr,. says. "To think she would do something like she did is kind of, it kind of raises a few flags, you know?"

Reed at the 1973 Ann Arbor Jazz and Blues Festival.

Though Tyson himself would later cast aspersions on these performances, at the time Johnnie Mae had convinced Scott and Inner City Trade Productions to begin representing Jimmy and to stick with him, get him much-needed gigs. The only way Jimmy was going to survive was to get back on the road, and to do that people had to know that he was still out there, still alive.

Ann Arbor, 1973.

It wasn't an easy sell to booking agents and club owners. The first calls Tyson and Scott made were met with cackling laughter: *What you mean? The Jimmy Reed? You have the Jimmy Reed? C'mon. What'cha tryin' to pull? Jimmy Reed's dead.* Others were just as blunt and no more courteous: *You have* Jimmy Reed? *O.K. Now, how are we supposed to book a ghost?*

But Inner City Trade broke through miraculously with a few gigs, two of which were Ethel's in Detroit and the 1973 Ann Arbor Jazz and Blues Festival, a two-day, two-night festival. The show was star-studded and the organizers, Rainbow Multi Media, were keen on having Jimmy Reed. "Jimmy Reed, man, when I was a kid in the '50s, Jimmy Reed was our favorite blues artist," says John Sinclair, the former artistic director of the Ann Arbor festival. "White teenagers were crazy about him. He was a genius lyricist. One of the reasons that he got over with teenage kids was because he had a teenage outlook...."

Reed, playing a low-end Ariel guitar, earned $750 for his Ann Arbor appearance.

Reed at the mike with backup guitarist Lacy Gibson onstage at Ann Arbor.

Like giddy teenagers themselves, the organizers handed out money liberally for the festival's talent. In August of 1973, when the expenses were being forecast, Luther Allison was scheduled to rake in a respectable $1,125; Count Basie $1,250; Charles Mingus $1,750; Freddie King $1,750; Ornette Coleman $2,500; Ray Charles $2,500; John Lee Hooker $875. Jimmy Reed? $750. By September, Peggy Taube, Rainbow's central accountant, had allotted $6,660 for Ray Charles and Ornette Coleman was bumped up another grand. Jimmy Reed? $750.[iv]

Reed was outfitted for the Ann Arbor show with an Ariel guitar—a cheap, unauthorized Japanese Les Paul Custom knockoff. Though the Ariel was undoubtedly a low-end, low-performance guitar, it was ironically one of the best, most reliable "boxes" Reed ever used. The question was, what could he still do with the thing?

By the time Reed was supposed to perform on Saturday night (September 8), there was a problem. Reed hadn't showed. Sinclair recalls: "Jimmy almost didn't play because he didn't make it to the show on time. He was on the big Saturday night show with Ray Charles and the Raelets, and the Charles Mingus Jazz Workshop. Big Walter Horton was the opening act, I believe. Jimmy had about 20 minutes and had a terrible band—some kids. [According to festival documentation, Reed had Jimmy Prior on bass, Lacy Gibson on guitar, Jimmy Mayes on drums, and Jimmy Smith, Johnnie Mae's son, on third guitar.] These guys were not selected for their prowess, it seemed. It could have been an issue [that Smith was Johnnie Mae's son]. How are you going to make Jimmy Reed sound bad? You have to go a ways—that is something to accomplish for a musician. Not that they made him sound bad, but, you know what I mean, to hear him with Eddie Taylor on the other guitar and the solid drummer…it was not the same. It gets sterile [without them]. These guys were driving all that way for little money. But they were late."

Sinclair was keeping his fingers crossed that Reed's temperament didn't get the best of him, like the first time he saw him. Sinclair remembers catching Reed in Detroit years before and he was stunned at Reed's reaction to the audience. "I think he was too drunk to sing," Sinclair says. "He came out to start the show and sat there and slumped down. People were howling, 'Play, Jimmy, play.' Then he said, 'I don't want to play.' I will never forget that. I was about 19 and it was the east side of Detroit, some little place that had blues for about a month."

Sinclair got his wish, though barely. Reed, with not nearly enough time to get himself together, went on stage and performed for 15 minutes. *Living Blues* described Reed's performance: "Jimmy Reed came running breathlessly on stage and puffed through a few numbers, but he seemed to be healthy and reasonably together, and the world's been waiting for that for a long time." (An MP3 file of "Big Boss Man" supplied by

Sinclair underscores the claim that Reed was indeed healthy enough to deliver crowd-pleasing renditions of his songs.)

"I don't remember that he played very much with the band that night," says Shurman, who was in attendance. "But it was certainly nice to see him. I remember Lacy Gibson—I knew him pretty well, did a CD with him—said that besides the big crowd, that there was a bunch of people in the trees listening to him. Jimmy came up briefly and on and off at the end."

"He looked happy," adds George Thorogood, also in attendance. "He also looked slender and healthy."

Jimmy was on the comeback trail and getting well. Although he was not completely cured of what ailed him, he was turning heads. In fact, he was very much alive and able to tell people so. "They had it out there: 'Jimmy Reed drank hisself to death. That cat died,'" Reed told interviewer Bill Scott. "I met many cats…that when they see me they just, like, they been had a heart attack. 'No, man this can't be you.' 'Yeah,' I say. 'This is what's leff of me.'…'Man, you been dead so long, I'm thinkin' I'm looking at a spirit.'"

To officially welcome Reed back to the "land of the living," Inner City Trade booking agent Howard Scott (no relation to Frank Scott) and Bill Tyson threw a "welcome home" party for Reed at the South Side club the High Chaparral on October 1. Scheduled to perform at the gala event were Nolan Struck, Eddie C. Campbell, Johnnie Mae's son Jimmy Smith, and others. For just $4 a ticket, a capacity crowd of 1,200 was treated to a show with Master of Ceremonies Manuel Arrington.

Arrington had listened to Reed on the jukebox at the Hi Hat club in Hattiesburg, Mississippi, in the 1950s. He had come to Chicago in the late '60s and had gotten to know Reed, and even shared bills with him at places like Pepper's and clubs along 69th Street. "The High Chaparral show was excellent, and the crowd turnout was very good, because the club seated about 1,200 people," Arrington recalls. "It was practically full. And Jimmy Reed had done sobered up—what I mean by that was he had stopped his drinking. He had on a red suit and he said, 'Tonight I am goin' play real weird guitar.' He put on a performance unlike any I had ever seen. Meaning: he wasn't as intoxicated as he normally would be. And his personality was Cousin Peaches, though. Everybody loved him."

A handbill advertising Jimmy Reed's "comeback" performance at the High Chaparral.

What could have—and should have—been a fine night was dampened by personal issues. Always those damned personal problems dogging Reed and everyone connected to him. Although Jimmy had left the hospital and moved in with Johnnie Mae to recuperate (with his family's blessing), their creative/business relationship had since evolved into something more. He brought Johnnie Mae instead of Mama Reed to the High Chaparral show—his "welcome home" party—and that was unacceptable. It revealed yet another step Jimmy had taken away from his family. He had cracked open a wide rift that would not be bridged easily. And Johnnie Mae rebuffed Mary Lee—her longtime friend—at the show, saying nary a word to her.

"Jimmy was one of many in this big revue of people and…he came there with Johnnie Mae [Dunson]," explains *Living Blues* co-founder Jim O'Neal. "I didn't know any of them at the time. Some of Jimmy Reed's family was there and they got into it. One of Jimmy Reed's daughters was in tears and said, running up to Johnnie Mae, 'Don't you remember me, Johnnie Mae? I was the flower girl at your wedding.'"

Johnnie Mae feels her instincts to nurture Jimmy have been grossly misunderstood and misrepresented. "I know the whole family," she says. "I know every one of them. A bunch of lies were told there too, but that is O.K. I know God knows. As long as I know that I am in peace with God, I'm O.K. I sure as hell been deceived and not believed. Anybody who knows me, knows that I ain't gonna be coatin' nothin' with no sugar."

If the family seemed to have abandoned Jimmy while he was in the hospital, it was only to motivate the Boss Man to stay dry once and for all. But Johnnie Mae thought it cruel. She had no qualms, then, about picking him up from the depths he had sunk into and working towards a better day.

Despite, or perhaps because of, his state of repair, Reed got to know Johnnie Mae's family like never before. "God knows that Jimmy [Reed] is my son's godfather," Johnnie Mae says. "And Mary Lee is his god-mother because those are the first two people who helped me when I came out the hospital. Ain't nobody helped him [Jimmy] when he needed help. Who do you think brought Jimmy Reed back to the world? Everybody else was grabbing for money. I couldn't even find a notebook to write in. I couldn't understand why the family didn't care, myself. They didn't want nothing to do with him because he was a drunkard and he was an alcoholic, and this and that."

Slowly Reed was making the scene. A show here, a show there. By the fall of 1973, things were improving for the Big Boss Man. On the strength of gigs like those at Ethel's in Detroit and the Ann Arbor festival, Scott and Tyson were starting to make their pitches heard by believers. Regardless of the level of talent exuded at these shows, and how much Jimmy still had left to flash to audiences, people were just happy to know he was still alive. Trips across the border into Canada to places like Le Coq D'or in Toronto were planned, as was a three-night stand in December at King Pleasure in Ann Arbor, which booked artists like Sun Ra and organist Jimmy Smith (not to be confused with Johnnie Mae's son).

Mark Brumbach, a veteran Chicago piano player, played Toronto with Jimmy Reed when Reed was beginning to mount a comeback. The band, surprisingly, included Eddie Taylor. "It was at the Colonial and we did two weeks on Yonge Street," Brumbach remembers.[v] "It was fun, but it was kind of a mess. The usual road story. But it was a great band. It was three guitars, Jimmy Reed, Eddie Taylor, and Eddie C. Campbell. I was on piano, and a guy named Cornelius Reed, who they called 'Mule,' was on bass. The drummer was Robert Plunkett. Like Muddy, Reed would carry two guitars plus himself, all the time. It was something like a New Orleans jazz band; each guitar had its role and if it was working well, it would stick to its role. One guitar would run the bass, the other would play the chords, and the third would do arpeggios. I have to tell you, when we rehearsed in Chicago, it was really, really nice. It was as good a band as I had played with at that time."

Brumbach recalls the experience as something close to being in the army: not always pleasant, but something he will never forget. "Eddie C. Campbell, man," Brumbach notes, "Eddie was then—as much as he is today—a pain, to be honest. He's a character. I was driving and he kept telling me, 'Turn here...' 'Turn there...' I had just gotten through playing a couple years in Toronto and I knew where I was going, right? It was kind of like a personality clash, which wasn't a big deal, but it was just enough for it to be a pain."

Campbell being a backseat driver wasn't the worst of it. It was as if Murphy's Law was acting on the Chicago blues crew, and the group was destined not to make it across the border. "We almost didn't," Brumbach says. "It was not great logistics. Jimmy and Johnnie Mae had rented a van that was a piece of garbage. If you or I were going to rent a van to

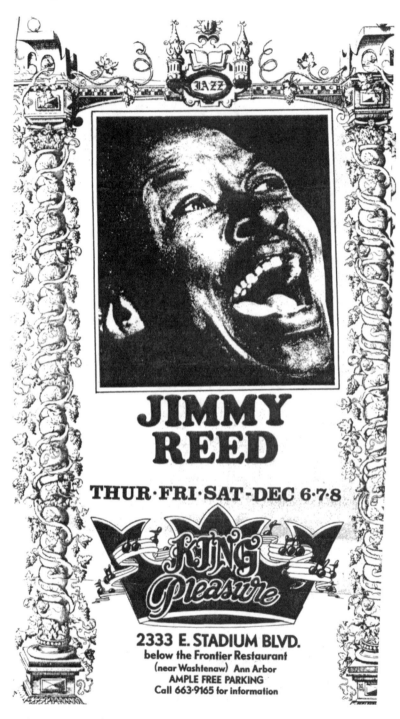

A three-night performance at King Pleasure cemented Reed's reputation as a changed man, and one who was very much alive.

go to Toronto we would either rent a good one or have a van already. It didn't speak of the organizational skills of Jimmy Reed or Johnnie Mae. So, what happened? The van broke down…right before we reached the border, in Michigan somewhere. We were stranded, stuck in this coffee shop, for eight or ten hours while the van was being fixed. It was a comedy of errors, and all I can remember really about it is sitting in this coffee shop and telling this waitress, pointing: 'See that guy over there? He's the guy who wrote "Bright Lights, Big City." ' I didn't think she knew the name Jimmy Reed, but she knew the song, and she was impressed. I remember telling her, 'That is the great Jimmy Reed.' But the whole time it was a pain in the ass."

With Campbell dogging him and an unfortunate road travesty, Brumbach didn't really get motivated to talk to many of his traveling companions. He didn't really start a conversation with Jimmy, and Eddie Taylor appeared unapproachable, at first. "Eddie was a sweetheart," Brumbach says. "Eddie obviously had been on the road before, but I didn't really engage him in conversation. Eddie was quiet if he didn't know you. But he was a very nice guy and very gregarious and funny when he was comfortable with you. He did a lot of imitations and would imitate Jimmy Reed and he would do his voice. He would do kind of exaggerations of him. Jimmy was kind of a comic character because of his voice, which was a real high-pitched voice. And Jimmy would get into farcical situations."

Brumbach had played with Eddie before, when he was a member of Sam Lay's and Johnny Littlejohn's band. Eddie liked the way Brumbach played and recommended him for the Reed gig. "I know Eddie wasn't playing with Jimmy a lot around that time, but he was definitely there," Brumbach says. "In fact, if it wasn't for Eddie, I wouldn't have had the gig myself. Eddie liked my playing and looked out for me. Eddie would call up and ask me what I had for dinner, and he'd tell me stories of raccoon hunting in Mississippi, which I am sure were the real thing. He was definitely from the country. Just like Sunnyland Slim was someone who had actually picked cotton and had a lot of experience with mules and so forth…. It was still kind of a feudal society down there."

Once the van was fixed, Reed and company had to get across the border. While security was not then what it is now in our post-9/11 world, there was some US/Canadian border crackdown. "We came through Canadian customs, and they gave us a hard time," Brumbach says. "The band was kind of a ragtag, funky, Chicago West Side, almost bum-looking bunch of guys. The band was superb, but the authorities wouldn't let anyone but me and Eddie Taylor play, maybe because we had our birth certificates with us. I think it had to do with ID and stuff. These guys may not have even brought driver's licenses.... I had been going back and forth [from the US to Canada], doing that trip for a good year or two before then. So, I kind of knew what to expect."

Some of the others didn't, however. When it came time to do the first show, as Brumbach remembers, they went on stage with the bare-bones minimum. "I think, although I could be wrong, me and Eddie Taylor wound up playing the gig with Jimmy," he says. "It was just the three of us. It was a nice audience, jazz club–like audience, and the room was similar to New York's Lone Star Roadhouse, now defunct. It was not a chitlin circuit thing, which I had played with many artists before. The three-piece was very, very nice, but I really regretted that those guys were nailed at the border. After that we hired some Canadian guys who were O.K., but not as good."

Perhaps of more importance than the quality of music was Reed's quality of life at that time. What stands out about these shows is that Jimmy was taking his promise to live a clean life as seriously as he could. "He seemed fairly healthy," Brumbach says. "I don't remember him smoking cigarettes or drinking, and I didn't see any evidence of his epilepsy. By the way, he was sober—I can't stress that enough—I never saw him take a drink. Over the next few years, I saw signs around Chicago hanging in the window of clubs reading: 'Jimmy Reed: Live on our stage drinking Pepsi only!' I guess it meant that people didn't have to worry about him falling down in the first set. I do remember he was not eating very well, however, on that trip. He ate a diet of Kentucky Fried Chicken—your usual ghetto diet.... But then again, even Eddie Taylor smoked on that trip. He didn't drink, but it was obvious that his wasn't the healthiest life. He smoked and he played in nightclubs.

"Did I tell you that his [Jimmy's] girlfriend at the time was Johnnie Mae Dunson?" Brumbach continues. "Apparently, from the impression

I was given, Jimmy Reed always needed a strong woman in his life to tell him what to do and keep him out of trouble. And she did just that. She was sharing a bed with him. Not that it was any big thing. She had a son, nice kid, Jimmy Smith. He was hanging around [but] didn't do the gig. And she could cook, let me tell you. She cooked pork chops in the hotel on a hot plate. And they were good, and she is a really good cook. I remember her pork chops, and the fact that she cooked them on a hot plate, in a hotel, was very Mississippi."

"Johnnie Mae has built her career, whatever she has, on the story that she was Jimmy Reed's—not wife, now—associate, but much more," Loretta notes.

Johnnie Mae has denied that she was Jimmy's girlfriend on different occasions, and she denied it in one of the conversations I had with her for this book. But some have always been suspicious of Reed's relationship with Dunson, as if she were either a money-hungry manager who snatched a world-weary, dazed, and sickly-to-recovering Reed right out of the hospital, or perhaps something else altogether. She calls claims that she was more than Jimmy's business associate ridiculous. Johnnie Mae argues that she was good for Jimmy's recuperation, and that was all. "A lie will go over this world and the truth will die," Johnnie Mae says. "A lie will go over the world. They keep on tellin' lies on me—they tell lies on Jesus—and yet they saw the change [in Jimmy]. They can't tell me they didn't. People are damned fools, and I am going to go on letting them be fools, as far as that's concerned."

Bluesman Homesick James—who is about as stubborn as they come in offering information—says, "I knew his wife and I knew [Reed], too. He used to come over my house all the time. I prefer to stay out of some things that are just really bad. I know they were bad so I would rather not say anything about them."

For what it's worth, the proof was in the pudding. Jimmy appeared to be getting healthier and he was making the scene, more so than he had for the previous three years of his life. Producer Dick Shurman, who had first met Jimmy Reed in September 1969 as he was taping Earl Hooker at Theresa's Lounge, agrees with this assessment of Jimmy's condition. "He seemed to have gotten himself somewhat back together and was more on the scene than he had been," Shurman says.

Reed and Boonie had sat in with Hooker that night at Theresa's and performed workmanlike versions of "You Don't Have to Go" and "Honest I Do." Not Reed's finest hour by any stretch, but Shurman began to see him more and more around town, appearing more coherent and lively than he had in previous years.

"He spent quite a bit of time hanging around Louisa's South Park Lounge," Shurman notes, "and I would see him there and talk to him at times. I have a tape or two of him sitting in, I think…. There's a question of long-term damage he had done to himself over the years, but he was in a good place. He wasn't drinking and he was performing and he was a very friendly and warm person. But his appearances in Chicago were sporadic and his personal life seemed kind of tangled. He had left his family to go off with Johnnie Mae Dunson, and got involved business-wise with her. It was Bill Tyson who recorded that stuff with Johnnie Mae."

Shurman had recorded Jimmy at Louisa's (more than once, he believes), and remembers one night when Marcelle Morgantini of MCM Records was in the house. "Morgantini was scouting to see who to record and he came to Louisa's and he brought a horde of people who wouldn't have been there otherwise," Shurman recalls. "A bunch of West Siders—Jimmy Dawkins, Mighty Joe Young—really outdid themselves that night, as if it were some sort of audition. The reason I bring it up is because Bobby King was singing right to Jimmy Reed. I was with Jimmy at the front booth by the bandstand and Bobby did a version of "It's a Man Down There" and had grabbed someone's beer glass off the table, dumped it out, and began using it as a slide."

Wherever Jimmy went, his reputation as a songwriter preceded him. Where ten or so years earlier his rep for drinking would precede him, now it seemed he was gaining a newfound respect. "Jimmy had surmounted some of his problems and it seemed as though his head was back on his shoulders and that he was trying to make a fresh start," Shurman explains, "and he wanted to get more serious about it. He would occasionally go to town. I would occasionally see him at Louisa's where he would be singing and getting up to do a song every once in a while. Of course the people loved him and other musicians would talk to him and play songs for him…they are up there and a lot of them called him 'Cousin Peaches.' He was an approachable and modest type of guy, though he had been beaten, somewhat, by life by that point. If you didn't know he was a star, you wouldn't have singled him out. A person who looked like him—he wasn't a derelict, but he wasn't looking real sharp either. He was very approachable and friendly. I had a friend who is into assault poetry, who lives out in California, and he'd come and visit me and go to the blues clubs. One night Jimmy was sitting at our table in one of the clubs. I introduced my friend to Jimmy Reed and my friend saw how open and warm Jimmy was. So, my friend started reciting his poetry to him…I can't imagine what Jimmy thought of it—this outrageous, stoned, free-verse kind of poetry. I remember Jimmy just nodding, 'Yeah, that is real nice.' "

By February 1974, Al Smith, who had become a gun-toting deputy sheriff for the Illinois State Attorney's office, had suffered from diabetes for years and succumbed to a massive coronary in Chicago. Smith was a plugger, a go-getter, but he couldn't outrun his poor health.

According to the Cook County–issued death certificate, Smith was just two and a half months shy of his 51st birthday. Chicago Mayor Richard Daley, Lefty Bates, and Jewel Records' founder Stan Lewis were some of the pallbearers at Al's funeral. Reed and Boonie were also pallbearers. It seems despite his love-hate relationship with Al, Reed showed his respects to a man to whom he owed much. As Ed Winfield, a Reed tour manager and Smith partner, told *Living Blues:* "I think that in a way Al Smith was the greatest thing that ever happened to [Jimmy], because [without Al] I don't think Jimmy's career would have lasted nearly as long…. The outside world don't even know about the house rent, the car notes, and how many times Al had to go to bat for Jimmy just to get his mere keep. Al was very dutiful about sending Jimmy's family money, and this is what Al and Jimmy fought about constantly."

In Smith's funeral program saxophonist Marcus Johnson wrote, "Al organized many benefits for underprivileged children in Chicago and held many prison performances with top artists."

Reed had not required Smith's management skills in the latter years of Smith's life, and their run at BluesWay had been about to end.

ABC/Dunhill planned to release 25 records on BluesWay produced by Al Smith, but by the time of his death only 20 of them had made the cut. One completed Jimmy Reed record went unreleased. Producer Ed Michel remembers: "I wrote a memo on July 8, 1970, about projects in the can that mentions Jimmy Reed BLS-6041, *If You Want It Done Right,* which notes, 'already done with cover.' A follow-up memo two days later talks about the same, noting, '…all paid for; cover in mechanical stage….' This July 10 memo also talks about '…a possible Jimmy Reed album in addition [to 6041] that Al Smith is supposed to deliver—the last one under his contract." (A later Michel memo from September 1972 notes that BluesWay 6041 was indeed finished but had been referenced as "unreleased.") "Obviously, I couldn't convince the powers that be to let me release things in the can," Michel says. "Some of those memos went on for several pages, and detail lots of recordings that never saw the light of day." (After years of thorough searches of the MCA vaults, which were once the ABC vaults, Michel is convinced that the tapes are no longer where they should be—in the MCA vaults!)

A general lack of interest in the music from those working at the BluesWay label combined with a vinyl shortage due to the 1973–1974 oil and energy crisis caused manufacturing of LPs to become quite difficult. ABC was going to pull the plug on BluesWay records one way or another, regardless of the oil embargo. While there had been talks that Smith was going to take Reed to a major label at some point, that never materialized—a point that exacerbated the strained relationship.

Larry Cohn, a former Sony executive, says he was approached by Al Smith about recording Jimmy Reed and releasing his old material in the early '70s. "Smith was the frontman for the Vee-Jay company, and before I got together with [Vee-Jay reps], Al had gotten in touch with me," Cohn says. "He was the major-domo, the producer, and he was taking care of other things that needed to be taken care of for the sessions. We never closed the deal; the rights were so cloudy."

It is intriguing to think what would have come of Reed's material if it had landed on a major label like Columbia, but it was not to be. Indeed, it is a sad swan song to the Smith–Reed relationship to know that Reed's final studio BluesWay record, 1973's LP *I Ain't from*

Chicago, limped out of the gate with hardly a notice.[vi] The record does sport a few gems, but a horrid title and even more horrid cover seem to make this a record a collector's item for completists, and perhaps for good reason. (On the cover, someone, it appears to be Reed, is sitting on a chair along a main drag in Chicago. The camera catches him from the side, and Reed—if it is indeed him—looks old, older than his actual years. The point is enhanced by the fact that the image is a photographic negative.). The LP was compiled from tracks that had been recorded prior to 1973, and surprisingly the atmosphere of some of the recordings is reminiscent of classic Vee-Jay. "Turn Me On" is a jaunty little number, for instance. Johnnie Mae is credited with writing two of the tracks, "If You Want It Done Right" (perhaps a track that might found its way onto BLS-6041) and "Life Won't Last Me Long," the latter seemingly a reflection on Reed's time in the hospital. A few others were written by Reed and co-written with Al Smith or Mama Reed.

There was something cheesy about the entire proceedings for *I Ain't from Chicago.* "This guy Al Smith, I'm sure, was just sitting on tracks—a catalog of these sessions—that he cranked out and BluesWay was just a convenient way to get them out," explains former ABC promo man John Dixon. "I'm sure he got the lion's share of the money."

By this point, Smith had become so businesslike, so outwardly disinterested in his work with Jimmy Reed, that the BluesWay cats hardly paid attention when he'd hand in tracks. "I didn't even know that Al was coming in to turn over Jimmy Reed tapes—he just appeared," says Michel. "Obviously, one of the corporate suits told him to give them to me. He did. I listened to them, cleaned up what needed cleaning up—beginnings, endings, clarifying the sound where it wanted it. I didn't do any major work—no overdubbing, re-editing, or major remixing. What I got were two-track tapes. If I wanted to do fixes, it would involve principally re-equalizing or riding overall levels. Al was a good producer, and I was neither inclined nor had I time to remake work he did.... Al didn't call for anything—he was just turning over recordings to a record company, and was in a hurry to be somewhere else. Al would just show up at The Village Recorder, hand me tape boxes, and say, 'Here they are.' I just said, 'Thanks.' Then, he split. We were both busy guys with projects that had to get done."

BLUE LABOR & KENT COOPER
PRESENT
A NIGHT OF THE BLUES
THE FIRST TIME IN NEW YORK IN
TEN YEARS! THE RETURN OF
THE BIG BOSS MAN

JIMMY REED
AND
LIGHTNIN' HOPKINS

Plus: **BLACK NIGHT ROAD**

SATURDAY, MARCH 30 - 8 & 11 PM
HUNTER COLLEGE
69th STREET, BETW. LEX. & PARK

ALL SEATS RESERVED. TICKETS 4.50, 5.00, 5.50   AVAILABLE AT TICKETRON OUTLETS
FOR INFORMATION CALL   644-4400

The show that never was.

Jimmy had an epiphany, as if Al's death had caused something to snap in his head. Perhaps it was just that Al's grip, whether real or imagined, had loosened, but now Reed wanted to make his own decisions. Maybe he thought he had had enough of listening to other people, even those who were committed to helping him. Jimmy needed freedom, and he didn't want anyone to tell him to be anywhere, at any time, for any reason.

He was free, yes; but his freedom, it seemed, came at a cost.

Kent Cooper of Cooper Productions had spent thousands of dollars on promotion hyping a Jimmy Reed show at Hunter College. Ads were placed in the *Village Voice,* the New York *Amsterdam News,* and on WWRL-AM and WNEW-FM. On March 30, 1974, Jimmy Reed for the first time in ten years (Cooper alleged) was making an appearance in New York City. It was being billed as "Night of the Blues" with the co-headliner Lightnin' Hopkins. Reed and Hopkins would perform two shows, one at 8:00 P.M. and another at 11:00 P.M. Hunter College's Assembly Hall was licensed to Cooper and room #142 plus two dressing rooms were being reserved specially for Reed. He was going to be treated like a king.

A Village Voice *invoice showing the amounts Kent Cooper was billed for ads promoting a Jimmy Reed/Lightnin' Hopkins show at Hunter College.*

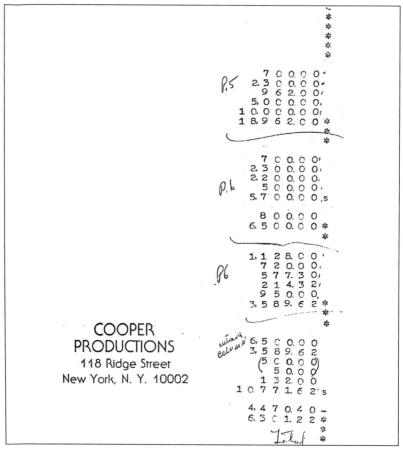

Proof that at least one check was deposited and/or cashed by Inner City Trade Productions.

COOPER
PRODUCTIONS
118 Ridge Street
New York, N. Y. 10002

Cooper's tally of losses.

Problems with "Night of the Blues" emerged weeks before, however. Booking agent Howard Scott was having trouble locating Jimmy and securing his appearance in New York. Cooper explains: "I had a long conversation with this Bill Tyson, by the way, to make sure that everything was on the cool and so forth. Tyson maintained that [Reed] was coming, but as the time grew closer he became more evasive. I do recall when I talked with Tyson, he was calling up almost bawling that he had talked to [Reed] and that [Reed] wasn't going to appear. That was right before Tyson went out of sight. He wasn't saying, 'I gave Reed the money,' but he was saying that Jimmy wasn't going to go, and that he couldn't get Jimmy to go. The son of Dixie Hummingbirds' Ira Tucker called me and said that he, or someone he knew, had been talking with Jimmy Reed, and that [Reed] was not coming to New York. So, when I found out about Jimmy, I got on the phone trying to reach this Bill Tyson."

Cooper could not get ahold of Tyson, who, in Cooper's words, "fell off the edge of the earth." On the night of the show, Reed was nowhere to be found. "There were a lot of people there, but about half of them walked out when they heard Reed wasn't there," Cooper says. "There were a lot of people who were there [to see him].

"You have to understand that by the night of the show, I had talked to Ira Tucker's son and he said that Jimmy Reed never saw the money and he wasn't going to move until he saw the money," Cooper notes. "So, by then Tyson had disappeared and I lined up the Dixie Hummingbirds through Ira Tucker's son, to replace Jimmy Reed. You also have to understand that we were never sure of anything. Jimmy might just show up. Anyway, when he didn't, Tom Pomposello, who was the Master of Ceremonies that night, announced that Jimmy Reed was not going to be there and perform. A lot of people walked out. Still, the first concert at 8:00 P.M. went well.

"But the second one was another story," Cooper continues. "Lightnin', who I knew very well, had gotten real drunk…the Dixie Hummingbirds were waiting to come on and he couldn't finish the songs. It was ridiculous. But then the Dixie Hummingbirds were great. Anyway, after it was over, I tried to track down this Tyson and even tried to look for him in Chicago once when I was out there. [I was] just pissed about his leaving me hanging there. He had completely disappeared."

-28-

Hunter College
OF THE CITY UNIVERSITY OF NEW YORK | 695 PARK AVENUE, NEW YORK, N.Y. 10021 | CONCERT BUREAU

Telephone
(212) 535-5350

April 5, 1974

Mr. Kent Cooper
Kent Cooper Productions
118 Ridge Street
NYC, NY 10002

Dear Mr. Cooper:

Because of the cancellation by Jimmy Reed on the Night of the Blues
concert March 30, 1974, your income was reduced by approximately
50% (of anticipated income).

Cancellations for the 8:00 p.m. show totalled $600.00. This does not
include loss of income incurred when patrons refused to buy tickets on
hearing that Reed would not appear. Also, and this cannot be measured
accurately, the loss of additional income when patrons were informed
by telephone of Reed's cancellation. Our box office phones were ringing
incessantly, with everyone asking for Jimmy Reed, and expressing disappointment at his cancellation.

Refunds for the late show (11:00 p.m.) totalled $362.00.

I have estimated at least 1,000 people, roughly 500 people per show,
walked away when they heard about the cancellation.

I must express my concern for the reputation of Hunter Arts Concert
Bureau. Since we are the only ones visible, we have to bear the brunt
of all reactions, -- abusive and otherwise -- and cancellations of this
type tend to endanger our good reputation for excellent programming.

Yours sincerely,

Ken Ernest
Assistant to Director

KE/nm

EXHIBIT "J"

In this letter, Hunter College's Ken Ernest blasts a hapless Cooper for Jimmy Reed's no-show.

Cooper didn't take it sitting down. A letter dated, ironically, April 1, 1974, was sent from Cooper's office to the Chicago musicians union, claiming that Cooper held up his end of the bargain. "I would like to complain heatedly about Jimmy Reed/James Reed, a singer/guitarist with whom I had a contract written out and signed by him on your sta-tionery," wrote Cooper. "It was sent to me on January 1, 1974. I com-plied with all the terms at every point. On the evening before the show, which was to be on Saturday evening, March 30 at Hunter College, I received a call from some woman who was with Jimmy Reed and she wanted a thousand more dollars...." (The original contract was, indeed, signed and sent to Cooper on January 1, 1974.)

Cooper tallied the costs of the show (which included the cost of a damaged reputation, he explained) for the union. He maintained that he was out not only the amount for the artist retainer, advertising costs for radio spots and print ads, sound engineering services, and other costs, but over $20,000 in addition—damages due to Reed's alleged breach of contract and disappearing act. Neither booking agents Howard Scott and Bill Tyson nor Reed himself had given any satisfactory reason for the no-show, and Hunter College was starting to breathe down Cooper's neck about ticket-sale losses. He was taken to task for not only the financial hit, but for helping to facilitate what the college saw as a public humiliation. A Hunter representative expressed concern over the college's reputation for excellent programming. Hunter estimated that 1,000 people walked away after learning Reed was not performing, and an immeasurable number of others either stayed away or refused to buy tickets at the venue when they learned of Reed's "cancellation." At an average ticket price of $5, it amounted to some fairly big bucks back in 1974.

A hapless victim of either a devious plot or genuine absentmindedness, Cooper had an answer for none of it and was being held responsible for the actions of a third party. And Reed's name was once again deleted from the membership roster of the Chicago musicians union.

The "musical services" contract for the Hunter College show clearly states: "Please make all checks or money orders payable to: Inner City Trade Productions." Of course, Howard Scott and Bill Tyson must surely have understood how easily Jimmy could lose his money, spend it frivolously, or simply piss it away. They could have been protecting Reed from himself. However, the check being made payable to Inner City Trade Productions is curious. Managers do invariably take their cut (the good ones advise that checks be made payable to the *artist*), but can we assume that only a percentage of the money was earmarked for Inner City, with the bulk intended to go to Reed?

Whether any of this has sinister implications we'll never fully know. One thing is certain: no one could motivate Reed to do anything, not even his friend and sometime handler/manager Johnnie Mae Dunson. It also shines a light on the lack of meaningful communication Reed had with his booking agents, promoters, and managers.

Some, who were entrenched in a tussle for control over Reed, have their theories of what happened with the Hunter College show—and what was happening with Reed at the time. "That whole thing was a lie," says Johnnie Mae. "That was Bill Tyson and Howard Scott bullshit they had going. I am gonna tell you the truth. Bill Tyson has been dead and gone. Howard Scott is still trying to tell people his story. They thought they were going to have Jimmy—this, that, and the other."

It is hard to distinguish whether anyone was generally and genuinely looking out for Reed or there was something far more contrived unfolding. Did Reed know of the Hunter College show but have someone else sign the contract? Did he sign the contract but not care enough to come to New York? Was Reed aware of the show at all? To be fair, Reed's case does have extenuating circumstances. He had spent the last few years in a fog, recovering from alcoholism and grappling with epileptic seizures. He needed someone to care for him and look out for his career and business interests. Since Al Smith's departure as his manager (and death just a month before), no one could offer the Big Boss Man sufficient support to gain his trust. We must also consider that at the time Reed was separated from Mama and living with Johnnie Mae.

Dunson thinks the negative energy and competitiveness surrounding Jimmy—which seemed to always follow him—finally got the best of whatever professional situation she had with him. "Somebody is always lying and making up stories and excuses—because of jealousy. They didn't do a damn thing for him. When he needed somebody they didn't do nothing for him. I couldn't understand it myself. Jimmy Reed sat down and talked to me about many, many things. The man was all right, but he was sick, sicker than anybody knew. Yes, yes, yes… I can't even tell you what me, my son, and my husband went through. It makes me angry to even think about—how people were like vultures. They didn't want nothing to do with [Reed] because he was a drunkard and he was an alcoholic, and this and that. As soon as he straightened up, my god! And they still lie because they don't know what they are talking about and I ain't trying to straighten them out. I don't care what they say, I know and God know. Jimmy ain't here to speak for himself. Wished he was.

"I could tell you some stuff that you wouldn't believe it, yourself. That's right," Johnnie Mae continues. "Jimmy Reed had some God in him, too. A lot of people didn't know that. I know a lot of things about him…I know things about him from when he was a little boy on up—everything, including the service record. He would sit down and talk to me many times. I can tell you that when he left me, he was not drinking nothing but Pepsi-Cola, milk and water, and coffee. He was looking so good, yes he was. But I had a family. I couldn't…I had a son to raise and during that time when boys get that age they need more attention than when they were little bitty boys, 'cause you want to know where they at and what they done. You want to try to keep them from being in the streets…. Nobody slighted [Reed]. He was included. People don't know, see? Nobody wanted to be bothered until he got on his feet. When he got on his feet, everybody wanted him then. Yes, Lord!"

But the local musicians union had unceremoniously dropped Reed from their roster because of the Cooper/Hunter College misadventure. In a letter dated June 6, 1975, Reed—or more probably attorney William Yale Matheson—wrote to the secretary-treasurer of the Chicago chapter of the American Federation of Musicians, J. Martin Emerson: "For the past several years I have been seriously ill and confined to hospitals most of the time. I have never signed any agreements with the Cooper Productions, and any signature he has is definitely a forgery."

The letter bore a Jimmy Reed signature, but it is doubtful his hand touched the pen that wrote it. The handwriting is not consistent with other chicken-scratched, half-scripted, half-printed Jimmy Reed signatures I have seen on other documents. (While it is safe to say that Reed was aware of the letter being sent to the union, we have to be cautious in applying similar logic to the contract for the Hunter College show.)

The Reed/Matheson letter explained: "I had the occasion to go to Local 10-208 and was surprised to learn that my name had been removed from the membership roster for failure to pay a $2,500 claim due Kent Cooper, d/b/a Cooper Productions, New York City…. In view of the fact that I have never received any of the correspondence on this case, I respectfully request the case be REOPENED [Reed's caps] and the entire brief mailed to me, so that the matter can be handled by my attorney."

Kent Cooper remembers that legal action ensued involving the Hunter College show, though not much came of it. "There was a lawsuit and we won it," he says. "But, of course, there was no collection. I don't really remember how it was resolved. I know we won, but I don't remember how much. I know [the award] never was collected. Some time afterward, it may have been in 1975 in Atlanta down at the Great Southeast Music Hall, I am down there with Louisiana Red and we were hanging around with a friend of mine and Muddy Waters. Some guy, I forget who he was—one of the hangers-on or one of the musicians who played with Muddy—he said, 'Yeah, yeah, you know Jimmy Reed was supposed to play for this dude in New York and he never showed up.' I said, 'I'm the dude you are talking about.' This guy looked surprised and everything. And, Jimmy Reed was there with us—he was not in that room and I hadn't seen him, but I was unaware that he was on the show, though I was not sure. Anyway, I am at the bar a couple hours later and this guy brings Jimmy Reed in to me. And, we had a drink and talked and he apologized. He said he never got the money and that he didn't trust this guy and, well, what the hell. We had a few drinks together. And that was what happened.

"Jimmy seemed like a real decent guy when I met him," Cooper continues. "He was sober when I [first] met him. His reputation had him to be [otherwise]. He sang just as good drunk, anyway. I always liked his singing, which is why I had him come to New York, for my own enjoyment [laughs]. But obviously there were a lot of people there who wanted to hear him. [His not showing up] was a real blow and we had to give a lot of money back. It was a big loss, the whole thing."

From my talks with people who knew Reed—and those who spoke with him on occasion—Jimmy loved his life, mistakes and all. He loved making music, and the missteps, or what an outsider might view as missteps, really didn't compute. His was a humanistic view of the world, so humanistic that he accepted his actions for what they were; he didn't read into them or assign them more meaning or weight than they were due. That's a very existential philosophy: whatever happens is natural, and perhaps what happens is meant to happen.

However, Reed never had the same kind of guiding force that he'd had in Smith, ever again. Whatever some might say about Al Smith, he was far more stable than Reed ever was; he needed to be in order to manage the blues star. The fictional character Svengali has been bandied about in reference to Smith, and perhaps in one sense, he was a bit of a hypnotist/manager, one whose reach was felt even beyond the grave.

In some sense, the *lack* of Smith's presence perhaps made Reed's life more chaotic than it had to be. Whatever Reed did from here on in would be his own doing. For some that might be a frightening prospect, but Reed eased into this position, as he did so many other things in his life. What helped with the transition was Jimmy's attitude: no illusions about who he was or what he was supposed to do. As a title of one of his records explained, he was *just Jimmy Reed*. "What you sees is what you gets," Reed was fond of saying.

Without anyone he could truly call "manager," Jimmy would emerge solitary, but stronger. "It was not about being [Jimmy's] manager," Johnnie Mae says. "Jimmy was his *own* manager. You didn't manage Jimmy. It was about trust, because [Jimmy] had had it [with people] and he didn't trust nobody."

Despite the Hunter College debacle, Reed's reputation was starting to snowball. He had just played the University of Chicago in December 1974 and a club called Else Where (with old Gary, Indiana, pal John Brim)—two major turning points in his career. Then *Living Blues* did a monster feature on him, covering his entire career. Reed's comeback was nearly complete.

A few months later, a chance meeting at a Chicago nightclub between Howard Scott and Jimmy rekindled a business interest for both Inner City Trade Productions and Reed. "Howard said he'd talked to [Reed] and he was a changed man," Bill Tyson told *Living Blues*. "I just saw all the headaches of getting involved again, but he was not the same Jimmy Reed."

Eventually, Jimmy learned to trust Scott and Tyson, so much so that Tyson was planning on recording new Reed material for an LP. "We want this album to be Jimmy Reed as the world knows him," Tyson said in *Living Blues.* "I think he is a tremendous talent and believe he's a tremendous man. But he needs guidance, too. I think Jimmy is on his way."

It was indeed a new Jimmy Reed. Cleaner than he had been in decades, the Big Boss Man was looking forward to new gigs and a new-found freedom. He had no true manager and he wasn't back with his family, though the deep freeze was beginning to thaw with Johnnie Mae more or less out of the picture. Having lived with Johnnie Mae for months, he was separated from Mama and was under the care of Levi Reed, his cousin. It was Levi who would see to it that Reed's messages were answered and that he would perform when booked. Boonie, who was so diligent in providing support for his father, had all but given up the blues business and left Chicago. As Jimmy Sr. put it in a *Living Blues* interview, Junior moved out to California and got "a job and gone to work."

It truly was time to start anew. "I'm Not Going to Let You Down" (also filed under the title "Keep the Faith"), one of Jimmy's songs from the period, said it best: "Just keep the faith, baby/Honey, I'll be home one day/And when I do come, baby, you can bet your life I've come to stay."

Chapter 7
Can't Stand to See You Go

By the summer of 1975, the US—and the world—was a strange amalgam of turmoil, deep division, and mild contentment. The nation had just been redeemed and relieved from prolonged military action in Vietnam, even as images of military and civilian personnel being rescued from the roof of the US embassy in Saigon flooded TV screens worldwide. Having resigned in disgrace in 1974 rather than face certain impeachment, President Nixon was succeeded by Gerald Ford, who did his best to hold the country together amidst political scandal and social upheaval. Americans were terrorized by a fictional shark called Jaws at the movies while the all-too-real horror of mass extermination was perpetrated by Pol Pot's Khmer Rouge guerrillas on the other side of the world in Cambodia.

It was a time of shifting ideals and social introspection, and more than at any time, people were dropping out, copping out, and tripping out. This freewheeling attitude had always pervaded rock music, but the mid-'70s were in many ways rock's most heady days. No longer were bands doing gigs; they had achieved almost god-like stature, playing to huge crowds in arenas. The bigger the show, the crazier the trip, the better the music. Or so some thought.

In the face of all this, it seemed almost insignificant that Jimmy Reed, who became a pop star while most of the soon-to-be young rock stars who idolized him were in grade school, was mounting a comeback with his relatively simple style of blues music. It was a bit of a miracle that Jimmy Reed was even alive to tell the tale of his exploits, his regrets, and, perhaps, his non-regrets. Clifford Antone, a young blues fan, had opened a blues club in Austin, Texas, in June and had just hired Sunnyland Slim to perform at his venue. Having been treated right by Antone, both personally and professionally, Sunnyland went back to his friends in Chicago and spread the word about 'this kid down in Austin.' "

"Antone's was a life-saver in Austin," says Warner Brothers executive and onetime Austin writer Bill Bentley. "It was an old furniture store, and Sixth Street downtown at the time was mostly little Chicano bars, transvestite hangouts, and other sundry places. But immediately, Antone's started bringing in all the great Chicago blues artists, and nurtured local talent like the Vaughan brothers. With Antone's opening, it was like Austin's musical rainbow was finally complete. There was a ton of music in that town, but not any Chicago blues, which had no place to call home in Austin aside from the sporadic booking at the Armadillo World Headquarters. Clifford Antone created a clubhouse, and for all of us blues lovers, it was like going home to Mama."

Word got around fast, and Antone was using his newfound capital to lure his blues heroes to Texas. "The first person to call was Eddie Taylor," Antone told me. "In those days, Eddie didn't have much work, even in Chicago. He calls me and I was shocked that it was Eddie Taylor on the line because he was a hero of ours. Here's Eddie trying to get work and hoping someone would book him. And we were like, 'Oh, my god. If he would only come here.' Eddie Taylor, to me, is the king of all music. Eddie Taylor is the most, he and Hubert [Sumlin] are the two most influential musicians there are. So, it was a really funny thing. You have to remember the times—this was 1975. I would say the blues was at its lowest point. Eddie said he wanted to come."

As they talked further, the "world's greatest guitar player" asked Antone if there was anyone he could bring with him to make a better show. "Immediately I said, 'Jimmy Reed!' He said, 'O.K., no big deal.' So, he calls Jimmy Reed, Jimmy says yeah, he'll do it. Now, I am 24 or 25 years old. I am talking to Eddie about a date. I said, 'We will let you come on out and play your set and then you and Jimmy can play a set.' Eddie said, 'No, no, no. I don't play with Jimmy Reed no more. He gave me ulcers and I love him, and he is my favorite harmonica player, but I don't play with him anymore.' "

Taylor proceeded to tell Antone about Jimmy's exploits and how it tore him up to play with the Boss Man. Antone backed off, but in the back of his mind thought something *had* to be done to get these two together again. But he let it go.

An hour later Taylor called back, Antone recalled. " 'Mr. Antone, my wife talked to you and she said you sound like a good guy, so I am going to do it.' That was his answer—Vera told him to do it. So, he did."

Eddie agreed to not only play at Antone's, but to play with Jimmy Reed. "I didn't know how long they had gone without playing together, but that was it," Antone said. "In those days we booked our shows from Tuesday through Saturday. Five nights."

Eddie and Jimmy arrived separately (Jimmy with cousin Levi), and the immediate concern was, is Jimmy going to behave himself? "Jimmy Reed was the worst-behaved drunk in the business," Antone admitted. "But, when he was with me, he had already quit [drinking]. I saw him in Austin in the earlier days when he was drunk and it was not too good. But just to be in his presence…. You knew you were around greatness. People say that Bobby Bland doesn't sing like he used to. Maybe not, but just being in his presence, it is a great thing to me. And, as far as I was concerned, Jimmy was putting it down. He was still young and still strong."

Blues vocalist Angela Strehli, Antone's onetime love interest whom he has often said was the real driving force behind the success of his venue, remembers Jimmy coming to Austin. "I just think it was monumental that Clifford tried to get Jimmy back together with Eddie Taylor to re-create Jimmy's real sound," says Strehli. "Eddie was so much a part of that sound. The truth of it was that almost nobody ever covered Jimmy Reed and pulled it off. I have never seen anybody do the Jimmy Reed stuff. You'd hear them and just laugh. I think the reason was that everything had to be perfectly the way it was on record. I think that is really hard, especially for white people. Muddy Waters would say, he'd tell us when he was in town, 'Tell those drummers to play behind the beat.' It was hard for people to really do that. But that is where the groove is."

When I visited with Antone in 2005 in his swanky Austin apartment, he told me that the first thing he ever learned on guitar was the Jimmy Reed boogie beat—what he called "the Eddie Taylor sound." His love for Reed's music and Eddie Taylor is still apparent, and he demonstrated the classic boogie beat on his acoustic guitar. At one point he was so focused on playing that he seemed not to care whether I was asking him questions or not.

"The first thing you learn is that Jimmy Reed backbeat," Antone explained. "The first key is E, of course. A 'Jimmy Reed' played in E.... The key is those turnarounds and that is where I saw Eddie Taylor teach Jimmie Vaughan and Derek [O'Brien] and all those guys. When Eddie gets hold of it, he turns it into a symphony. He'd take the most simplistic thing in the world and turn it into a symphony."

Because of Reed's visit, and Eddie Taylor's professionalism opening the door, Antone and Reed were becoming close. At night the boys would stay up and talk about life and Jimmy's music. "One particular time he wanted to learn the words to his own songs," Antone said. "So, we would sit up at night, at the Steven F. Austin Hotel at Seventh and Congress and actually play. I would teach him the words to all of his songs, you know? We would just go over the songs, and, of course, he had forgotten the words and he, of course, couldn't read. Still, he was in great shape. He was sober and a gentleman. He was just doing so well at that time. You would have never dreamed that could have happened, you know?"

During the day, they'd troll the streets like giddy hooligans in search of new experiences and, of all things, clothes. "The first thing we would do in those days back on Congress was to hit the clothing stores. They had a lot of soul clothing stores down there," Antone remembered. "They had a shoe store. We would shop for shoes—that would be the first thing we'd do, you know? I'd buy him whatever he wanted. But he found some black-and-white checkered shoes, man. He just loved them and we bought them right away. We'd walk up Sixth Street, we'd walk up Congress, and spend the day talking. It was a unique perspective. He had told me about 'Big Boss Man'—that he had gotten into a fight. Did you ever hear that story? He told me on the plantation he wanted a drink of water. Just like in the song: wanted a drink of water but you won't let Jimmy stop. The boss man wouldn't let him. They got into a fight and they were rolling in the ditches and all of that. That was it for him and that was when he left. That is why he wrote 'Big Boss Man.'[i] He would tell me different stories like that and he would tell me about his wife catching him in the back of a Mercury with a girl after some gig, and there was a big fight."

Reed had found a friend. And for Antone, it was like he had reunited with an old high school buddy. Antone had been listening to Reed for the better part of his life, so when he met the man—and became his friend—it was as if it was meant to happen. "There were places you could hear the Wolf or Muddy, but not generally speaking even on black radio in Port Arthur, KJET, which I used to listen to," Antone said. "My father had a liquor store and our warehouses and offices were in black neighborhoods—Louisiana black people—and that was who raised me, thank god. But on those radio stations, you weren't hearing Wolf or Muddy—you were hearing R&B type of music. You were hearing Jimmy Reed. But Jimmy Reed also crossed over. The skating rink, which was the big activity for young people, you could hear Jimmy Reed as you skated. And that *At Carnegie Hall* LP—every young person had that record. And you played it until it wore out, just like that Bobby Bland record *Two Steps from the Blues* or James Brown's *Live at the Apollo.*"

The two became so close that Antone even threw a party to celebrate Reed's 50th birthday. "All the young girls who worked here, you know, you know how girls are—they like to celebrate birthdays—and they want to make a party out of it," Antone said. "We had him a big ole birthday party. Somebody got him a cowboy hat, just all of these nice presents. The coolest thing was he had a Super Reverb, which is open in the back. By chance the birthday cake wasn't a regular rectangle cake. He takes this cake—about this long and about this wide—and it fit in the back of his Super Reverb. He said, 'Do you mind if we don't eat this? I am gonna take this cake back to Chicago and show them that I had a birthday party.' Now, I can't swear to this but Jimmy told me that he had never had a birthday party before. He told me, 'This is the first birthday party I ever had.' Maybe he just never had one like that one, I don't know. I *can* swear to *that*.

"He called me *Antwine*. He said, 'Antwine, it's a *stoooone* pleasure to be here whitcha.' He said, 'Whenever you need me, just call me. But please, don't talk about no money. Just pay me what you can.' You know, those words haunt me to this day. You know how much greed there is in the music business, and ego. So many of the musicians are on a trip; they act like prima donnas and stuff. Here's Jimmy Reed—one of the greatest recording stars in the world, if not the greatest—he was so humble and loved us so much to say, 'Please don't talk about no money.'

"The music business, man," Antone continued. "You have managers and booking agents who don't care about any relationships. Here's a guy like Jimmy Reed saying that. All through my life it just gets more heavy and important that he told me that. On the same line, Clifton Chenier, the King of All Music who I put on the level of Ray Charles—Clifton Chenier was the first band I ever brought—we would pay $1,500 for the week. It was something like that. But when he was out of the hospital, he'd get in a van and drive all the way to New York and back. All these kids with their damn tour buses and won't go here and there without this rider and such. But when Clifton Chenier was all sick, he turned to me and said, 'Antwon'—he called me 'Antwon.' He said, 'Antwon, you know I am not as good as I used to be, so you should just pay me less.' I said, 'No, Cliff. It ain't like that.' Can you imagine one of those rock stars doing that? That is so heavy, that kind of stuff. It haunts you all your life that you even had to hear it, you know? It is like, how does this fit?"

Reed may have left behind some of his truest friends when he left Austin. And coming home to Chicago offered little in the way of comfort or luxury. For a man who was supposedly on the rise, you'd never have known it.

Drummer/Chicago blues producer "Twist" Turner met Reed in Chicago for the first time in 1975, when Reed was living just above the poverty line. "Basically, at the time I was living not far from Billy Branch and he was over here every day and somehow Billy and I were hanging out a lot with John Brim, Jr.," Turner says. "Then we were at John Brim,

Sr.'s house every day. So, John Sr. was doing some stuff with Floyd Jones and Jimmy [Reed]. Somehow I wound up doing this gig with Jimmy, John Brim, Jr., Floyd Jones, and John Brim on the West Side, a place called the Sac-A-Delic Shack on 59th Street. Jimmy was kind of like…he did about half a dozen songs—he came up to do what he was doing and went away. I had seen him once or twice before that. I was sharing an apartment with guys who were DJs at the University of Chicago and they had put on some show that Jimmy Reed was on. They kept saying, 'Let's go to Jimmy Reed's house.' We did, and when we got there, I realized that Jimmy didn't have any money at that time. He was living in a basement apartment on Peoria Street. It was very stark linoleum on the floor with stark, white walls. Heating pipes were exposed. I remember going over there and a lady was there and a couple of other neighbors were drinking [in the basement]…Jimmy wasn't drinking. I think Bill Tyson was managing him at that point and was trying to keep him halfway together. Eventually, we actually set up a tape recorder and they let loose. They were just fiddling around—the music was pretty bad. Not that good at all. It was informal—Jimmy was on the bed playing and there were people wandering in and out and stuff.

"I was surprised that when I went over to Jimmy's house how much Jimmy played guitar," Twist continues. "I always thought it was Eddie Taylor who was doing all of those fills, but it was Jimmy, because he was playing them. Turns out Eddie was doing the bottom."

Twist has one odd memory of Jimmy. The images are still whimsically puzzling to him, even as he recalls them. "One night we decided to take Jimmy out to the Michigan Avenue Restaurant and Café Society, which was owned by this black guy named Sweet Pea," Turner says. "It was actually a place that Big Bill Hill broadcast from—there was this little room that overlooked the big room and he used to sit up there and broadcast from there. Before we left, we were preparing to go, the first thing [Jimmy] does is look in the mirror—he has one of those Afro pick things. He is, like, fiddling with it. Then, he starts spraying Right Guard in his hair—and that shit smells *bad*. I am just thinking that this is weird, you know? He had this polyester shirt, a shiny shirt. All of a sudden he starts to raise his arms and starts spraying on the underarms of the shirt. Not on his person, but on the shirt. I am thinking, 'That is even weirder.' Then he had these black-and-white platform shoes. Those platform shoes—checkerboard patent leather shoes. He starts spraying the Right Guard in those. Then we took him out to the club and George Beasley, who worked with Magic Sam quite a bit, was yelling at Jimmy, 'Come on, Jimmy, and blow some.' Jimmy was sitting there with us saying, 'Well, I have a baaaad tooth.' He couldn't blow with a bad tooth, I guess. We took him around the corner and the Scott brothers were doing the top hits of the day. It was really weird to see him in that setting. They were doing 'Float On' by the Floaters."

The luxury and eventual irony of being a bluesman from Mississippi is that you can influence so many people, remain relatively anonymous, and walk among the crowds relatively unharmed—and unnoticed—and those who have been influenced by you often achieve wider success. Still, Jimmy never gave any outward indication of being resentful toward younger players, or white people in general who liked his music. And by the mid-'70s, even the most talked-about bands in rock music were covering Reed's material or paying homage to him in their live shows.

Bands like the Who had made "Big Boss Man" a concert staple, and the Texans ZZ Top, shunned by the critics early in their career (a career, by the way, that by 1975 had garnered the band two gold records), loved Reed's records and were as much a band of as for the people. Dusty Hill, Billy Gibbons, and Frank Beard were Jimmy Reed fans, and indeed Beard and Hill had even backed up Jimmy and Lightnin' Hopkins on occasion.

But while rock bands were touring the world to sold-out audiences, Reed had hit a bump in the road. He was scheduled to perform at the Chicago Amphitheater in November 1975 as part of DJ Pervis Spann's multi-act, two-city blues tour. (Everybody who was anybody would have the chance to perform a show in Chicago and then another in Memphis, Tennessee, the following day.) Dick Shurman's article in *Living Blues* explained that Reed was advertised as a performer on the tour, but he never showed. (Some speculate that Jimmy's handlers at that time could not convince him to make the public appearance. For reasons that remain unclear, he simply was a no-show.) Harp player and club owner Bob Corritore, who had come down to the Amphitheater specifically to see Reed, was disappointed but couldn't argue with the lineup.

"That particular show's placard boasted Bobby 'Blue' Bland, B.B. King, Albert King, Little Milton, Otis Clay, and Jimmy Reed," Corritore says. "The one I was most excited to see was Jimmy Reed because I had never seen him. It was a great, historic show, but he didn't show up. Luther Allison was added to that, but he was part of this huge array of talent. I tend to think it was a funky chitlin circuit thing. You couldn't argue that you got your money's worth. Reed just wasn't playing around Chicago very much at that time and I was 18 years old with an ID that read 19 and I would hear after the fact that Jimmy Reed made an appearance."

Reed's reputation as a man recovered took a hit as people left the theater scratching their heads. Reed made sure he didn't totally disappear, however. In fact, the camera seemed to love Jimmy Reed at the end of 1975. Film was rolling for a Reed performance at Eddie Shaw's 1815 Club on Roosevelt Road in South Chicago. And on December 4, Reed perches his ass down on a chair, flashes a gap-toothed grin, and performs a slightly slowed version (as compared to the original) of his first true breakthrough hit, "You Don't Have to Go," for KPRC-TV-2 in Houston, Texas.

Reed is outfitted with a harp in his rack, a white thumbpick, a blue blazer, red pants, and dark shades for this broadcast, taped in what appears to be a poorly lit television studio. If nothing else, the performance does reveal that Reed's edge (and with Reed, "edge" is a relative term) had been restored, as well as his sometimes overlooked ability to perform two (three, if you count singing) musical functions at once. Due to some nice camera work, we get a view of Reed's fingers moving quite confidently over the strings as his mouth slides from side to side across the holes of the harmonica to achieve that classic melodic wavering harp solo. It is also interesting to note that Jimmy is using more than two strings to achieve his sound. He clearly knows his way around the fretboard, but it was the exact opposite that had become popular belief. (The "accepted" view of Jimmy's guitar skill is that he had none; anyone who demonstrates how to do "a Jimmy Reed" inevitably plays on two strings over three frets. Not so on this television performance.)

The great Roy Buchanan once remarked concerning Jimmy's guitar playing: "Everybody talks about the simplicity of Jimmy Reed's songs, but the guy didn't take any shortcuts. He was using all six strings and playing his chords just right to fill the sound out."

Guitarist James Solberg and pianist Larry "Third Degree" Byrne were members of Luther Allison's burning band and they remember the no-show in Chicago (which happened to be the final public appearance of Howlin' Wolf) and also a December 1975 performance in Houston at Liberty Hall that boasted both Reed and Allison. I sat down with Byrne and Solberg before a gig they were playing at a blues club on the Connecticut–Rhode Island border.

"The gig at Liberty Hall was Lightnin' Hopkins, Luther Allison, and Jimmy Reed," Solberg says. "I think we were in Jimmy's dressing room or something, backstage, and Jimmy said, 'Get me this bottle of booze and I'll give you this guitar I got here.' It was an old National and I know he had a couple of those. It had the stupid six knobs on top. Mine was the ornate one with the ivory back."

"Luther Allison and his extremely drunk band…" Byrne chimes in. "He had an extremely drunk band…."

"Who was also expected to be Jimmy Reed's band," Solberg interjects. "Jimmy had brought Levi [Reed] with him. Neither one of them could tune a guitar and Levi was supposed to be there to tune Jimmy's guitar. So I ended up tuning Jimmy's guitar and we played a bit together before the show. We'd play with Jimmy every once in a while, and a Jimmy Reed gig was like doing a folk gig, doing colleges. Not a blues show."

"It was like a dream come true," Byrne admits. "I had been playing with Luther for about half a year. Everything that I had hoped might happen in my life was happening. I was playing with a group in which I was learning something every night and the band was getting better every stinkin' night…. We were not making any money and no one was complaining I think because there was always something to look forward to. So, the fact that we were playing with Jimmy Reed, and we were in Houston? I knew right away I would be kissing his ass from the moment I saw him.

"We get down there and I started talking to him: 'Hey, Jimmy. Nice to meet ya,'" Byrne continues. "He autographed a picture for me that I still have—'To My Boss Man, Larry.' He was really nice, but not very talkative. I would start naming off all of my favorite Jimmy Reed songs.

He'd just smile and say, 'I don't remember that one.' I said, 'How about 'Going to New York'? He didn't remember the words. Oh, man! He didn't remember anything. I am thinking, 'Alcohol did a lot worse to his brain than I had thought possible.' But, still, he and Levi were swell. So the last thought I had was, 'If Jimmy didn't do "Going to New York," what did he do?' Then he took the stage and what does he do? 'Going to New York.' And he kept on trying to start, singing, '. . . goin' to New York.' I remember Jimmy going out and doing 'Boss Man' and I think he did 'Bright Lights.' But every once in a while he'd stop and just start singing, 'I'm goin' to New York....' He might tear off a couple of licks and then start smiling."

Solberg seems to remember that Lightnin' was up first and that Luther had more or less ordered the band to go out and play with this solo acoustic act, notorious for his skill in writing music that seemed to lack any set structure. "Yeah, Luther said, 'C'mon, we're going on stage and playing with him,' which I kind of thought was a bad idea," Byrne agrees. "But, it was like, 'Yes, sir.' [We] jumped into the trenches and we got through that. I don't remember if we went on next with Luther or Jimmy came on." "Luther would do this thing where he would sit on the roadie's shoulder—roadie's name was Hannibal—with this 300-foot guitar cord and this big buzz would come out of his amp," Solberg says. "So here's Jimmy playing his set and there is Luther, being a hot dog, sitting on the roadie's shoulder, walking all over the club, during Jimmy's set. Dropping Luther-isms on guitar." "Luther was doing all of this stuff," Byrne explains. "And then we got to the end of the show, just about, and Jimmy was still singing, 'Well, I'm goin' to New York.' You could tell that this was a wonderful, big human being, and that he must have had some horrible fears inside him. That is the only way I can figure it."

In January of 1976 Howlin' Wolf died, and, just a month before that, Chicago mainstay Hound Dog Taylor. It seemed Jimmy Reed may be approaching the same fate. By the late spring and early summer of 1976, Reed was suffering massive tonic-clonic seizures, no doubt a by-product of his quitting alcohol so abruptly. It was about this time that an enterprising young promoter in the Oakland, California, area who went by the name of "Robert Johnson" and other aliases such as Andrew Lee Ashford, Ashford Ashford, Lee Sensation, and Lee Ashford began shopping Jimmy around.[ii] And Eddie Taylor had once again rejoined the Big Boss Man after their pleasant experience in Austin. Perhaps seeing how much Reed's music meant to a younger generation, Eddie had a change of heart. He *wanted* to play with Jimmy. "If Jimmy needs me, I'll play anytime, anywhere," he said.

With Eddie by his side, Jimmy was ping-ponging about the country. He had played the Great Southeast Music Hall in Atlanta and was making a West Coast swing through California clubs like the West Dakota Club in Berkeley, the Bodega in San Jose, and the Savoy Tivoli in San Francisco's blues club haven, North Beach.

Guitarist/keyboardist Ron Thompson, San Francisco Bay Area blues vet, was backing John Lee Hooker when he got the call to play with Jimmy from a "promoter with a lot of aliases," Thompson says. (Probably "Robert Johnson.") Thompson sat in with Jimmy and Eddie at the Bodega. He never thought he'd see the day. "My older sister had an LP of his *Found Love*. It was almost like underground music in a sense. I grew up southeast of Oakland, where there were a lot of Mexican-Americans. They used to have record players in the car—this was before the Beatles, basically. They would have these record players playing Jimmy Reed records. That is how I got into it, man. Then I bought a harp. I really patterned myself on Jimmy Reed. I saw him play when I was really young in Hayward, California, and they had a Battle of the Blues at a place called Frenchy's. I couldn't get into the club, but that night it was John Lee Hooker vs. Jimmy Reed, you know? I had to go see that. I was just hanging out in the front door listening and it was great.

"I was playing with John Lee Hooker and through John Lee, I met Eddie Taylor," recalls Thompson. "One time we were playing in Chicago, and this was supposed to be a blues club, and it is starting to snow. Eddie Taylor was out there but no one would let him in. I told John Lee Hooker about it and Eddie was let in. Eddie Taylor always remembered me from that. So, I wound up playing with Jimmy maybe five or six times at the Keystone in Palo Alto and a place known as the Bodega in San

Jose. When I played with Jimmy he had a million people shouting out different songs they wanted to hear. He got real soulful with stuff, and when I was onstage with him it felt like I was in the audience watching him. It was a trip, you know? I heard other stories about him drinking, but he was in top form when I was with him."

Stephen Gordon, who runs the Savoy label and books the Waterfront Blues Festival in Portland, Oregon, ran the Savoy Tivoli nightclub in San Francisco and booked Jimmy Reed twice in 1976. "I started the Savoy on Christmas Eve of 1975," Gordon says. "I have mostly been into blues and roots music and rock 'n' roll. Jimmy, of course, is one of my heroes. What happened is that I had all of my heroes come play for me: Hooker and Waters and all those people. I had John Lee play for me, right? I am 25 years old when I opened this club. He was one of the first guys I had and at that time I was still starstruck. I was 25 years old and this is John fuckin' Lee Hooker, right? John Lee comes in early in the evening and he's sitting up at the bar and I walk up to him and say, 'Mr. Hooker, I own the club. I'm Stephen Gordon. I can't tell you what an honor it is to have you here.' The usual—blah, blah, blah. He kind of looks at me, with those dead eyes: 'That is fine, son. Just make sure you pay me at the end of the night.' It was like a bucket of cold water in my face.

"What people don't realize when they come to see a band," Gordon explains, "is that to the musicians it is just another night. When you see Jimmy Reed, maybe you haven't seen him in 20 years. To these guys, it is just another night of work. After a while, when you are in the music business, it all turns into one long night. I had Muddy there once and I asked him if he wanted to do a sound check before the show. Muddy looks at me and says, 'Son, I got my sound together 40 years ago.' So, I asked, 'So, you don't want a sound check?' He said, 'Sound check? Do I get paid for that, too?'"

Jimmy had played twice for Gordon, who clearly remembers Robert Johnson and even still reflects on his exchange (of sorts) with him: "The first time [Jimmy] was repped by this black guy by the name of Robert Johnson—obviously that was not his real name—he came out and asked if I would be interested in doing a show with Jimmy. And I said, 'Yeah.' I used to do four-night stands with the right act, right? So, I had

Jimmy in there the first time and he sold out every goddamn night—all four nights. And people like Boz Scaggs and all the rock guys from San Francisco were coming to see him. That was in the spring of 1976.

"Anyway, this guy Robert Johnson just burdened the shit out of Jimmy," Gordon remembers. "Seemed to me this guy Robert Johnson was ripping him off. At the end of the first run, the band members would be put together—local guys from San Francisco. So I walked up to him, the place was empty, just me and my crew and my wife. The musicians are all over in the corner bitching about not getting paid. I walked up to him and said, 'You oughta pay these fuckin' guys. What is this bullshit? I gave you money. Pay them.' He turns around and bull-cocks me. Knocked me flat on my back and then jumps on top of me. I remember thinking, 'What the fuck are taking my guys so long to drag him off me?' My wife was the first person to get to him and she proceeded to kick the crap out of the guy. She hit him with a chair, a table. She went nuts. So, anyway, that was the end of Robert Johnson and Jimmy."

Norman Davis with Jimmy Reed, 1976.

"The story I heard from Eddie [Taylor] was that he had been burned by [Robert Johnson] the first time he came out with Jimmy and he never came back," Bay Area blues harp man Mark Hummel says. "He also tried to book him on a Big Walter Horton tour but he never showed for that. This guy was backstage saying, 'You got Big Walter Horton, what do you care about Eddie Taylor?' Well, Eddie's name was on the damn bill. People are paying the cover and are not being able to get a refund. Sure, I was happy to see Big Walter Horton, but it would have been phenomenal to see them both. The promoter was named Robert Johnson—not the King of the Delta Blues, but King of the Rip-offs. I had a really negative experience with him some years after this. By 1982, I think, I did a gig with Percy Mayfield that this guy completely ripped us off on. He left Percy standing in front of the club with no way back to his motel. This guy used to call me up and threaten me and stuff. He'd say, 'I know where you live and I'm coming to get ya.' I used to go, 'Fuck you,' and hang up. This was the same promoter who had brought in Jimmy Reed."

"I think I met [Robert Johnson] at Big Walter's hotel room once," says Bay Area blues vet Mike Henderson, who had played with Sunnyland Slim, Albert Collins, and Mike Bloomfield, among others. "I remember that there was talk about the business of booking, which was making Walter nervous and I didn't understand any of it. I never did work for the guy, but I could read the brother, you know what I mean? It is body language—it was everything." Norman Davis, a DJ at San Francisco's KSAN radio, was in the production room when he got a phone call from his DJ friend Bill Scott—"Wild Bill"—who worked at KTIM in San Rafael. Wild Bill explained that Jimmy Reed was coming to the Bay Area, and Davis had to ask to make sure Reed was still alive. Scott assured him Reed was, and Davis scheduled an interview with Reed. "The production room was already booked when Jimmy showed up at the station," Davis recalls, "so I took him down to the basement where we talked for about an hour, surrounded by racks of old records and radio equipment. Jimmy's deep Delta dialect had me leaning forward in my chair most of the time to hear every word. Jimmy talked about growing up in Mississippi, how he went to work in the cotton fields as soon as he was big enough to handle a hoe, how he snuck up to the house at lunchtime to hear the King Biscuit Show with Sonny Boy Williamson on the radio, and how he built his first guitar.… He discussed his problems with alcohol…and his success in quitting…and getting back to his music again. I was thrilled to hear him tell it in person. That night I went to see Jimmy play [at the Savoy]. I stayed through both sets and Jimmy sounded great."

"He was in marvelous form," remembers Lee Hildebrand, a Bay Area drummer and blues writer. "It was sort of a comeback San Francisco gig. I remember Geno Skaggs was the bassist that night. It was good to see him in good form.[iii] I saw him at Winterland, around 1966 or 1967, and he shared a bill with John Lee Hooker. They were both backed by organ player Stu Gardner, although Stu Gardner's band wasn't the most stylistically appropriate to back Jimmy. But he did a thoroughly professional job. But the first time was the Berkeley concert. And that was, well.…"

Having opened for Reed, Mike Henderson offers a unique perspective of Jimmy's first shows at the Savoy: "I had a guitar amp—I was playing acoustic—and Eddie Taylor asked if he could borrow my amp. He said, 'O.K., I'll pay you for it.' I said, 'Give me fifteen dollars for the four nights you are using it.' So, anyway, I'm carrying it to the show and when we got to the last night he gave me five dollars. I said, 'No, man, you owe me ten dollars.' I admired him—and if it had been Jimmy it might have been free, right? I carried it, too. I had a lot of respect for Eddie Taylor, but business is business. I felt I was showing him respect by carrying it and bringing it every night, and so forth. Anyway Jimmy takes me to the side and tells me this great story: He said, 'Man, this Texas millionaire takes me into his house one time and the guy said, "Jimmy, take anything you want—money, car, clothes, jewels. Anything." Jimmy told the guy, 'I don't want anything.' The guy didn't understand. There was something about that story that made me realize that money wasn't everything. That was maybe the first conversation I ever had with him one-on-one. By the way, Eddie Taylor gave me the ten bucks. He was sort of staring at me with a cigarette in his mouth the whole time."

Not long after his swing through the Bay Area, Reed was heading south again, to Austin, Texas, and Antone's nightclub. Although he had Eddie Taylor with him and his shows seemed to be going better than in the recent past, Bill Bentley saw a different side of Reed. "I met Reed in the upstairs dressing room at Antone's in July of 1976," Bentley says. "He was very quiet and reserved, but smiled and shook my hand. I asked him how he was doing and he said he'd forgotten most of the lyrics of his songs, but with Eddie Taylor's help during the show, he hoped he could do some of his songs. Then I asked him if he was performing much, and he said, 'Once in a while I'll wake up and someone has put a contract under the front door of my apartment, so I gotta go do the show.' He seemed very resigned to the fact that things weren't going well for him. As I was leaving, he said, 'I guess I just drank too much wine.' But he smiled when I said goodbye."

Ironically, Reed's performance at Antone's was nothing short of joyous. "He had Eddie Taylor playing guitar with him, and the rhythm section, I believe, was from the Fabulous Thunderbirds' first line—Otis Lewis on drums, and possibly Keith Ferguson on bass," Bentley recalls. "Reed came out with a big smile, kicked into 'I'm Mr. Luck,' and proceeded to tear the house down. He played about 15 songs, and many were off-the-wall originals like 'I'll Change My Style' and ones you wouldn't expect. Maybe those were the ones he could remember the words to, or possibly personal favorites of his or Taylor's. The house was full and I think everyone there knew they were seeing the man who had brought the blues to the masses in the '50s with his hit songs on AM radio. In Texas, his first singles got a lot of radio airplay, right next to Elvis Presley, Chuck Berry, and anyone else who was on the charts."

Harp player and vocalist Kim Wilson of the Fabulous Thunderbirds was a fixture at Antone's in the 1970s and 1980s. He knows full well the impact of Reed on Austin, and the world. The blues, and Jimmy Reed's music, was designed to bring people together, sometimes close together. "There ain't nothing technical about Jimmy Reed, yet he is one of the heaviest mutherfuckers in blues history," Wilson says. "That is about as lowdown as you can get. He had a great band: Earl Phillips, Eddie Taylor. That is all you need if you are Jimmy Reed."

But Jimmy wanted to go back to the West Coast, and they wanted him back. "I forget who called me, but maybe it was Jimmy or his wife," the Savoy Tivoli's Stephen Gordon remembers. "He knew that I paid [Robert Johnson] and he wanted to know if he could come back. I said, 'Sure.' He was going to play from Thursday through Sunday."

In a rush, Jimmy grabbed clothes for only two or three days and dashed off—without Levi or any other escort, and without packing his epilepsy medication. It was late August 1976.

When Mike Henderson had heard that Jimmy was playing again at the Savoy Tivoli, he asked Gordon if he could open for him again. "This time the owner says that, 'No, Jimmy is out here without Eddie Taylor.' That meant that maybe I could get a chance to actually play with him," Henderson says.

Because of his experience with Robert Johnson and the Savoy months earlier, Eddie turned down the chance to play again in San Francisco with Jimmy. "Eddie had been burned once, he wasn't going to be burned twice," Mark Hummel says. "So, the story was, this guy put together another tour. The first one was so successful he wanted to bring Eddie back but the bottom line was that Eddie wasn't going to go. I think [Gordon] had Geno Skaggs on bass, Doug Kennedy, and I think he had Mike Henderson, who lived in the Bay Area."

Henderson opened the show, and in fact spoke with Jimmy very often during that last week of August. Henderson recounts a story about Jimmy faking out one of his handlers and caretakers, most probably Al Smith: "One story Jimmy told me was, 'This man come to my house and spent the night with me and then he cleans all the liquor out of my room and he stayed with me 24 hours. We go to the plane and we get on the plane…then we get off the plane and he is right there next to me. We go to the bathroom and he is there. He took me to the club, put me in the dressing room, and went out there and introduced me. He don't know it, but by the time I get to the stage, I was tore up! That man don't know I got tore up between the dressing room and the stage—and he don't know it.' It was always these little anecdotes like that that he would come up with about something. He was like a…I don't know, he wasn't like a grandfather, he was like being around a sage or somebody like that."

"The first night it was just me, Jimmy, Doug Kennedy the drummer, and bassist Geno Skaggs," Henderson continues. "Geno had the sound and he knew how to play. He grew up in Chicago and he knew how to play. The drummer was kind of happy and he would be screaming at him, 'Jimmy, do "Big Boss Man."' I kept saying, 'No, man, let Jimmy call the show himself.' It was crazy—the crowd was screaming at him, too, to play stuff. Jimmy kept saying, 'Nah, nah, nah, nah, let me do this, let me do this....'"

Henderson thought Kennedy's overenthusiastic show of emotion was not proper etiquette for a musician to have on the bandstand. "I'd played with Sunnyland and Albert Collins and with those guys, the first thing you learn is discipline when you are onstage with them," Henderson notes. "It may look free and easy, but, damn, there is an etiquette there. I knew Jimmy was used to doing his show. He talked to the audience and he would go into one song or another with a story about his life."

David Leishman, who was working on a story for *Rolling Stone* about Jimmy Reed's so-called comeback, remembers the New York punk rockers the Ramones opening for Reed Thursday night at the Savoy. "They came out and did the Ramones thing: 27 minutes and 27 songs," Leishman says. "Very loud and very fast. Jimmy came on after they did.... I think it was on a whim—I don't think it was part of any planned tour. He came alone for this trip, but the first time around, Eddie Taylor was onboard. I think this second time, he went directly from Chicago and snuck out of town, maybe Levi wasn't watching. Not to put any burden on him. Literally he hadn't told anyone he was going and he had just caught a plane and headed west. Whether he loved San Francisco, or whether he loved the name of the town, I can't even begin to imagine. There was no retinue, there was no anybody. He was walking around carrying his guitar."

The following day Gordon took Henderson aside and explained to him that he needed to step aside. At first, Henderson thought it was politics. Henderson recounts: "Steve [Gordon] said, 'Jimmy isn't really happy.' I said, 'Is it because of the arguing?' Steve said, 'No, I think it is about the music.' I said, 'Well, number one: nobody can sound like Eddie Taylor.' I dropped it and then later asked Jimmy: 'Jimmy, is there something I am doing wrong?' He said, 'No, no. It is just not Eddie Taylor.' Eddie Taylor kept him taking his medicine. That was when I first realized that they were both one at that point—they were both that sound. Jimmy Reed was Eddie Taylor and Eddie Taylor was Jimmy Reed."

Henderson knew that the connection between Reed and Taylor went beyond music. It was something he could not compete with—nor should he have—as a guitarist or human being. "I said, 'Don't know what to do,'" Henderson recalls. "I said, 'Maybe I can find you another guitar player.' Jimmy just repeated, 'No, man. Eddie Taylor.' I couldn't get *Eddie Taylor.* I found another guitar player and I opened the show instead. And then there was another guitar player who was heavy into the English rock—heavy sustain, you know. That was a Friday night."

The following night, between sets, Henderson had an epiphany. "I will never forget that night. I was walking through that park. It was like going to play with Jimmy Reed, going back to my studio to work on the painting. I was working on something that I thought resembled a Chagall painting—you know how weird they are, with the cows and horses falling from the sky. It was surreal and abstract. I can remember just thinking how surreal my life was at that point. It was a real honor to be able to talk with him. I remember the name of the painting I was working on: 'The Speed of Light.' And, it was this period working in black and red—very striking colors. It all had to do with energy. Life coming together at the speed of light. Every solid is made up of molecules and it's just vibrating so fast that when you look at it with the naked eye, it looks solid."

When Henderson returned to the club, who did he find, much to his surprise, but Mama Reed and Jimmy Reed, Jr. They had come up from L.A., where they were staying while Jimmy was touring in the northern part of the state. (It was also reported that one of the Reed daughters, perhaps Malinda, made the trip to San Francisco as well.) Mama and Boonie sat in with Jimmy on that Saturday night. Dressed in white, Mama was like an angel of mercy: Jimmy's blues angel.

"I was living in California, in L.A., at the time, and Mom had flown from Chicago to L.A. to visit me," says Jimmy Reed, Jr. "Mom was there with me when Dad flew from Chicago to San Francisco.... Loretta called me and had spilled the beans on Daddy."

"The reason I called," explains Loretta, "was because Daddy had gotten Jimmy's number before he left. He said that when he got to

Frisco—that is what he called it—he said, 'I will call him.' I said, 'Yeah, you should because Mama is there.' He said, 'O.K. They'll be surprised.' He talked to me again the next night, after he had gotten there and he told me that he had tried to call [Junior] but he wasn't getting through. So, that is why I called [Junior] and said, 'Daddy is in San Francisco and he is trying to get in touch with you.'"

"Me and Mom drove up [to San Francisco]," Junior says. "I got there in time to play the gig with him that night. Mama sang and I played rhythm guitar."

"I remember the show. Me and my sister-in-law attended it," explained Sharon Helgerson, blues and Jimmy Reed fan who had seen Jimmy the previous night at the Savoy. "I had been listening to Jimmy Reed forever and when we found out that he was playing the Savoy, we were like, 'He is playing *here?* We have to go.' The Savoy was this place that had an odd assortment of tables and chairs and a cloth that covered the door. It was a funky little place. We meandered in and out of the place and we were able to sit right by the stage. We couldn't believe how close we were. And the thing I remember most about the show was Jimmy's checkerboard shoes, Jimmy Reed, Jr., playing guitar, and Mama Reed standing onstage with Jimmy. She was wearing this white dress and was with Jimmy all night that night, talking with him, probably telling him the words to the songs."

"The show was just incredible and I remember this high harmony that Mama sang," Henderson says. "Jimmy and his son, Jimmy Reed, Jr., was going to play guitar and that was as close as you were going to get to Eddie Taylor that night. It was a real high moment. And I knew Geno just kept it in the pocket and the drummer kept his mouth closed and just played the snare.... Jimmy, when he was playing and telling these stories, he would say how much he drank. 'I was so drunk...I'd get into the studio and Mama Reed, she be telling me the words...I couldn't remember the words and Mama Reed, she would be telling me the words. Sometimes I would remember the song, sometimes I didn't.' And he would start laughing. Their encore set was longer than the original set. People just wouldn't let him go. Jimmy closed the doors and people just stood. I was looking forward to seeing him for the last night—Sunday."

Jimmy Reed's last performance, August 28, 1976, at the Savoy in San Francisco.

Call it an omen, call it supernatural, call it meaningless. But something happened that Saturday night, August 28, 1976, that still haunts Stephen Gordon. "My club was like an 'L'-shaped thing, and at the long end of the 'L' was my bar and next to the bar was the doors that went out to the bathroom," Gordon says. "I am going to the can and I am not the kind of guy who is into psychic phenomena or any of that kind of shit, but I started walking down the stairs, the music is blasting, and I hit the second step and all of a sudden I couldn't hear a damn thing. It was like dead silence. I went, 'What the hell?' I ran to the door and—boom!—there was the music again. But the music was usually so loud you could hear it through the door normally. I never had that kind of thing happen to me before or since."

Jimmy is ready to leave the Savoy Tivoli and hitch a ride back to the place he was staying for the duration of the San Francisco tour: a friend's rooming house in Oakland on Monte Cresta Avenue. Before the party breaks up for the night, Mama and Boonie say good-bye to Jimmy and they warn Gordon about looking after him.

"When Mama Reed was there, she said to me, 'You take care of Jimmy, now,'" Gordon recounts. "I said, 'I will, I will.' They leave and Jimmy walks up to me, puts his arms around me, and asks if he can tell me a story. He goes, 'Steve, I'm worried about you, man.' I said, 'What do you mean, Jimmy?' He goes, 'Man, I have been watching you running around, chasin' all of those women, snortin' that weird powder.' I said, 'Jimmy, don't worry about me. I'm fine.' He says, 'Let me tell you a story.' I said, 'O.K.' He goes, 'Let me tell you how I quit drinkin'.' He told me he went on a real bender in 1963, and he said, 'When I woke up in the hospital, it was after about a two-week run. When I started drinking, John Kennedy was president. When I woke up Lyndon Johnson was president.' I told him I liked the story and I would be fine. He said he was going to the house in Oakland and 'I'll see you tomorrow evening.' I said, 'Fine.'"

Henderson: "On Sunday, I get to the Savoy and L.C. Robinson was there, I think Sonny Rhodes, and a few of the Oakland cats who showed up at the show. Anyway, I go into the club where everybody is and say, 'Where is Jimmy?' And nobody answered. They shrugged their shoulders. I thought it was par—he was stuck in traffic somewhere, or getting ready. So, then it got to be where the people were showing up and asking where Jimmy was."

Gordon: "The next night I come in, I used to come in around 4:00 or 5:00 P.M. I used to clean the place myself; I did a better job and it was cheaper. I am sweeping the floor and I knew that Jimmy always got there around 6:00 or 6:30 P.M. and had dinner. We'd shoot the shit. So, 7:00 P.M. comes, 7:30 comes, and he is due on stage at 9:00 P.M. and he is not there, right?"

Henderson: "The guy—it seemed something was wrong. I asked and pressed the issue, 'Where is he? Who has the number? Who is going to look for him?'"

It is unclear at this point what happened next, or when.

Gordon: "I didn't know where he was staying, but I got a ride over to Oakland and went there with a friend of mine. I wanted to see what the hell was going on. We get there, they let us in, and he is lying in bed. He wasn't moving. I knew that Reed had just had an epileptic attack about the week before he came in. Looks like he is asleep, right? But I knew he is dead.

"So, I call the Oakland cops. I don't know if you know anything about the Oakland cops, but this was right in the aftermath of the whole Black Panther thing, and Oakland cops, Philly and L.A. cops, are badass mutherfuckers. So, the cops come—one's a white guy, another's a black guy—and the first thing they say to me is, 'What the fuck are you doing here?' I said, 'Well, I own a nightclub in San Francisco. This is Jimmy Reed, the blues guy. He has apparently died in his sleep, and I know he has a few thousand dollars and all his guitars. So, I want to make sure everything is done correctly. I am responsible for him.' Then the black cop sticks his finger in my chest, pushes me up against the wall, and says, 'You *were* responsible, boy. He's dead. Now, get the hell out of here.' I refused to leave and, you know, I wanted a receipt for his money and his guitars. They were worth money. It was not like Jimmy's family was rolling in dough or anything. So, we went back and forth. It seemed like hours to me, but it was only minutes, I would say. It finally came down to where they were either going to have to whack me or give me the receipt because I wasn't going anywhere. They ended up giving me the receipt. I made sure Mama Reed got the guitars and the money. When they came in, they may have thought I killed him. They were pretty surprised to see two white guys sitting there waiting for him. I didn't want to leave because I had paid him, and four or five grand and all his guitars were in the room. I wanted to get a receipt for everything."

Henderson's account differs:

"On Sunday night, [Gordon] said, 'I saw him this morning and he wasn't moving.' I said, 'What do you mean, you think he's dead? Didn't you check?' He said, 'Mike, I was afraid.' I said, 'Goddamn.' I panic and run out the club and think about who to call. I knew Mike Bloomfield was playing two blocks down. I knew Mike and I knew he knew everybody—he had connections. So,

I went down there and he was actually coming up the street and he said, 'Hey, Mike, how is it going?' I said, 'Hey. Can I talk to you for a second?' I said, 'I am playing with Jimmy Reed up the street.' He said, 'I know, it is going to be like Chicago tonight.' I said, 'Yeah. Mike, I think this guy said Jimmy Reed is dead.' Mike said, 'Oh, god. Call Norman Dayron. Norman knows where Mama Reed is.' I said, 'Mama Reed was here playing with him last night and then went back to L.A.' I get on the phone and call Dayron and I tell him and he gets in touch with the family and they came up and took him away. That was that Sunday night."

"We did that gig that night and then I had to leave to get back to Los Angeles 'cause I had to go to work," Jimmy Reed, Jr., says. "After the gig was over, we parted and got on the road and when we came back to L.A. we got a call, I think, from Geno [Skaggs] who said Daddy had passed. We had to turn around and go right back."

According to the death certificate, the immediate cause of death was "postictal respiratory failure" on Sunday, August 29, "due to or as a consequence of grand mal seizure disorder." The investigation was sealed by Stewart Gross MD/local registrar on September 24, 1976. As laidback as he was in life and in his music, Mathis James Reed left this world in a violent burst, just a week shy of his 51st birthday.

"[Jimmy] said he was taking clothes for only two or three days, as if he had a feeling or something was going to happen, "Lubirda Williams, Jimmy's aunt, told *Rolling Stone* magazine in Reed's obit." He left without saying good-bye to hardly anyone, just a few of us."

Jimmy Reed was buried in Lincoln Cemetery on Saturday, September 4, 1976, two days before his birthday. His body was viewed at Unity Funeral Parlors on South Michigan in Chicago. The list of honorary pallbearers reads like a who's who in entertainment and sports: Muhammad Ali, Bobby "Blue" Bland, Eddie Taylor, James Cotton, Ewart Abner, Muddy Waters, Bill Tyson, B.B. King, John Lee Hooker, Memphis Slim, the Spaniels, and others. John Brim, Michael Reed, Lefty Bates, and Levi Reed were a few of the active pallbearers.

Jimmy Reed, Jr., contributed a touching eulogy to the funeral program:

As a man and father, Mr. Reed was as loving a person as anyone could be. He taught his family to learn restraint, and to be tolerant in situations of anxiety and depression. Being the man he was, not only as a father but as a dynamic

Blues singer, somehow he'd always bring joy to people around him. Mr. Jimmy Reed, Blues singer, was practically the first Blues singer to turn the younger generation's head towards the "gutsy" sound of the Blues. There can never be another Jimmy Reed, but his music will live forever in our hearts and lives.... Mr. Reed projected a feeling that made his many fans feel better and have a healthy attitude towards life. He was and always will be "The Boss Man of the Blues" and the "Pied Piper of Our Lives."

The aftershocks of Reed's death were felt by the entire San Francisco Bay Area blues community, and the rumblings traveled to all corners of the country—and the world. Immediately, questions were asked: How did this happen? Why? Wasn't someone with him? Who was looking after him? None of them were helpful in starting the healing process.

"It took a long time for me to forgive those guys," Henderson says. "I would just see them on the street and walk past. If someone had asked me about those guys, I would tell them: 'There goes the man who killed Jimmy Reed.' I was thoughtless of my criticism of them. When I thought about that I apologized to Geno about that because I knew it hurt him. I'm glad I told him that before he died. I knew it was not that way at all. I knew the guys were scared. If they were scared, they were scared. I was blaming [Gordon] for bringing out Jimmy Reed without Eddie Taylor—all because of money. I got on top of it—everybody. I ripped everybody. None of that brought him back."

When I spoke with Gordon he seemed reflective, but he also apparently has learned to let go and move on. He even recognized that he had been a young man in the 1970s in San Francisco; it was a heady time. "Whatever you do with your book, Jimmy was a good man and a God-fearing man," Gordon says. "I can tell you that."

If people were looking for guilty parties, Eddie Taylor probably thought his name could rightly be at the top of the list. "Eddie, I think, always felt guilt about that," says harp man Mark Hummel, who would go on to play with Eddie in the 1980s. "I mean, Eddie would look after Jimmy and saw all of the seizures and all of his alcoholism.... When he found out that Jimmy died, I don't think he ever got over it. The story I got from Eddie was that if he would have been there, Jimmy probably wouldn't have died. I guess Eddie had had a whole lot of experience [with Jimmy's epilepsy] because they would room together and he would watch out for him. Eddie seemed to have some guilt about not being there. He also seemed to think that Jimmy didn't take his medicine with him."

Born: September 6, 1925

At Rest: August 29, 1976

In Memoriam

James Mathis Reed

FRIDAY, SEPTEMBER 3, 1976

Visitation: 7:00 P.M.   Funeral: 8:00 P.M.

UNITY FUNERAL PARLORS, INC.
4114 South Michigan Avenue
Chicago, Illinois

"A lot of times Jimmy would sneak off and do shows and he wouldn't take Eddie Sr., wouldn't know nothing about it," says Larry Hill, Eddie's stepson. "The only thing he knew was when he went and came back. If Eddie had gone with him when Jimmy went out to California, Jimmy would have been alive today."

There is something to be said for the power of free will. Jimmy had slipped away and traveled without Levi, or Jimmy Reed, Jr., or even the companionship of Eddie Taylor. He seemed destined to be his own man and go out the way he lived his life: by doing it *his* way.

"You could tell he loved his life," Henderson says, reflecting on all the stories Jimmy told him. "If there was a mistake he made, he enjoyed doing it. He was just incredible. I can see him right now, thin as a rail but loving life and enjoying it. He really loved that he had that musical gift and was a natural. I remember him standing on the stage. I had the same feeling when I saw Muddy and Otis Spann and heard this sound that these guys were making. It didn't exist before these guys. It would be the same as meeting Picasso and Van Gogh. An artist. 'They want a song, I just make up a song fo' 'em, you know what I mean?' I was around him just about every second I could. I knew what a treat it was."

"I will never forget him," says Zakiya Hooker, John Lee's daughter. "I'll never forget what he looked like. What he wore. He was more flamboyant than all of 'em…. As a matter of fact, when my dad moved to California and lived in Oakland, Jimmy came into town because he was performing over in San Francisco somewhere. Jimmy came by for a visit and they spent some time together, reminiscing. The very next day, that is when Jimmy died.…"

Tom Mazzolini, who hosts the radio show "Blues by the Bay," interviewed Jimmy for his midnight–3:00 A.M. program on KPFA. Mazzolini is generally seen as one of the last—if not *the* last—person to interview Jimmy Reed. "He came by right after one of his shows," remembers Mazzolini. "It was this late-night interview. Not long after that he died. I remember he had stopped drinking. The irony of the whole thing was that he had finally given up drinking…there were so many stories about his performances and people substituting for him. The irony was that he had given up drinking and he was reinvigorating his career.

"The thing about it was, sometimes if a person has a life of drinking they convey a sense of that period that is still with them. An aura of alcoholism, of being intoxicated. It was synonymous with Jimmy Reed. His whole persona and history was surrounded in drink. The thing I remembered was that he was not drunk and he had not been drinking. Yet, there was this overwhelming feeling that his years of drinking had lingering effects on him. I've noticed it in other musicians who have been drunks and it is hard to shake that perception. It is intangible."

Jimmy had been scheduled to perform several nights at the 1815 Club in Chicago when he returned from his San Francisco trip, and Clifford Antone had big plans for Jimmy's next trip to Austin. "He was supposed to come down here and I was going to record him," Antone said. "I had never really lost any of the big blues players yet. You know, I didn't know how to take it. I was crying for hours and hours and hours.... When you are young you don't know how to deal with grief like that. You've never dealt with grief."

"I think Clifford had finally convinced someone that the meeting of Eddie Taylor and Jimmy Reed should be recorded, but before it could happen, Jimmy Reed died," adds Angela Strehli.

"Jimmy Reed was spectacular for me, and I wished he would have lived so I could have been old enough to really delve into who he was," admits guitarist D.C. Bellamy. "His music was phenomenal."

It seems unfair, as if our flawed hero (but a hero nonetheless) had the desire to change his life, had made those changes, and then disappeared at the moment of his virtual redemption. At the time of his death, Reed seemed happy and whole, perhaps for the first time in his life.

Just before those final Savoy Tivoli shows, Reed sat for an interview with DJ Wild Bill Scott at KTIM in San Rafael. "I feel fine," he told Scott. "And, fact of business, you can believe, all I got I'm gonna try to put it in, whatever it take to satisfy the people and try to make everybody feel fine...."

And that he did. To his dying day.

Reed's unfortunate demise was echoed in the lives of many, but perhaps none with greater resonance than that of William Clarke, the late Californian harmonica player of incredible potential and talent. When Clarke collapsed onstage in Indianapolis in March 1996, he was diagnosed with congestive heart failure and vowed to take himself out of temptation's way and get clean. By November 1996, Clarke had lost weight and even returned to his usual heavy touring schedule. But he collapsed onstage again and died the next day. "It is the same sad story of someone making efforts to get themselves together and then they just don't survive the transition," says Dick Shurman. "William Clarke was a severe alcoholic and he finally faced up to it. He was just starting to get on his own two feet in terms of sobriety and then his body takes him out of here."

The debate goes on as to what would have happened if Jimmy had lived longer. Unlike when he first started in the music business, there would have been a bidding war between labels. It had been reported that Reed was in negotiations with the record label The Roots, which had issued *Jimmy Reed Is Back* (a compilation of earlier tracks Reed recorded) in 1976 before his death. Whichever label Jimmy might have gone with, he would have had a number of options as far as what music he recorded and when. Also, if he had lived just a few years longer, he would have made the festival circuit. In that case, Jimmy could have easily done a dozen or even half a dozen shows a year to make a comfortable living. Things would have gotten easier for him.

"If he was still around like Hooker was," says drummer and former Fabulous Thunderbirds member Richard Innes, "then there would have been Jimmy Reed with Carlos Santana and Eric Clapton—and they would be playing on *his* records. I think that would have happened, no question, but he didn't make it."

Around Chicago, at least, Jimmy wasn't forgotten. Many nights Muddy Waters, the Hoochie Coochie Man himself, played Reed's songs onstage. "I never heard [Muddy] mention Reed, but I know he loved his style and his songs because he played them a lot," says John Primer, who played with Muddy as a guitarist and opening act during the late '70s and right up to Muddy's death in 1983. " 'You Don't Have to Go'— Muddy loved that one." ("You Don't Have to Go" appears on Muddy's early '20s "Live at Mr. Kelly's LP.)

Recounting an epitaph of sorts to Reed's life, Dan Duehren, co-owner of a vintage guitar and amp shop in Sherman Oaks, California, remembers heading to the Rock Bottom in Simi Valley, California, one night in the late '70s. "We used to play [there] a lot and one night they had a big sign out in front that said Jimmy Reed was coming in two weeks," Duehren says. "The only problem was that this was about three years after Jimmy died. Juke [John "Juke" Logan] and I had to check it out, so we went out there and there was George Smith sitting in the corner by himself. I knew George Smith because I had backed him up quite a bit. [Juke and I] said, 'Hey, how are ya, George?' He shh-ed us down and said that he *was* Jimmy Reed and that we should be quiet and not call him George. He didn't play guitar—he played harp and stood out in front and played Jimmy Reed tunes. He put on a great show. He was a great harmonica player and great singer and he did all of Jimmy's hits. He was Jimmy for the night, put on a great show singing Jimmy Reed songs, and everybody left happy thinking they had seen the real thing."

Did Jimmy really get what he deserved while he was alive? All the royalties, the respect, the admiration? Was it enough? Was it fair? Former Vee-Jay labelmate Jerry Butler puts things in perspective: "Well, you know…if you look at it from that point of view, at least he died a natural death. Compare that to Martin Luther King. As Les McCann would have thought to say, 'Compared to what?' I think it was Sinatra who said it best when he said—paraphrasing here—'It was more than I expected but not enough as I deserve.' Whatever Jimmy Reed got was more than he expected but probably not as much as he deserved. He was very creative and he played the harmonica and guitar and he was the foundation garment of Vee-Jay Records."

Jimmy Reed's popularity has waned in the last couple of decades among the general population, while the stature of other bluesmen such as Howlin' Wolf and Muddy Waters has risen (despite the fact that from 1955 to 1962 Reed had more record on Billboard's Hot 100 chart than any other blues artist). Nonetheless, many musicians haven't forgotten Jimmy and throughout the years have tipped their hats to the Big Boss Man and his music. Singers have even been known to risk physical harm in order to approximate Reed's mush-mouthed vocal style, by fastening a paper clip or two to their tongue. Others have taken Jimmy with them to their dying days—literally.

"I'll tell you something that was sweet. Luther's [Allison] last couple days of consciousness, I thought what I could do to cheer him up,

I would bring Jimmy's [Reed] guitar around," explains James Solberg. "Luther was barely able to get out of bed. We were naïve about the disease he had [lung cancer and brain tumors]. We thought we couldn't tour as much, but we could still write and I was still bringing guitars down and jamming on the couch. One day I brought Jimmy's guitar down and Luther was just like a little kid on Christmas morning when he saw that. As sick as he was his eyes bugged out, and remember the big smile he had? You know, 'Where the hell did you get that?' He had recognized it right away. He said, 'Let me see that....' He took it and I remember he had these big-ass feet, too. Just like Jimmy Reed. He started playing that guitar and that big foot started tapping. He had a cabin down by my house in Wisconsin. Now that…I wish I would have had that on tape. Luther broke into about a half-hour of the perfect Jimmy Reed imitations for Rocky [Carolyn Brown, life partner] and me. It was probably the last ounces of energy he had.

In 1986, Steve Miller, who had sold nearly 22 million records in the US alone (at the time of this writing), devoted the entire second side of his *Living in the 20th Century* LP to Jimmy Reed and other blues songs. Miller's professional misfire in 1984 known as *Italian X-Rays* was a far cry from his successful 1982 LP *Abracadabra*. He needed a hit to claim redemption and instead of selling out to the pop world, he seemed to thumb his nose at the record company by returning to the music he had grown up with: the mid-'60s Chicago blues scene. "As soon as I formed my first band, we played Jimmy Reed stuff," Miller told the *Chicago Tribune*. "So it wasn't like I was a white kid who was learning the blues from B.B. King records."

Reed sufficiently embedded himself in Neil Young's musical identity and psyche. Young and Crazy Horse's 2003 concept record, *Greendale,* about a fictional California town, is pure Reed. And the eight-plus-minute "Baby What You Want Me to Do" on 1995's *Broken Arrow* showed Neil hadn't roamed far from his roots. "Jimmy Reed proved that it doesn't matter what you play—it's the feeling," Young told biographer Jimmy McDonough, " 'cause you played the same thing almost every fuckin' song—the changes were a little different, but always that riff—that turnaround riff, 'Dededededuhduhduh.' "

Governor Howard Dean and Michael "Hawkeye" Herman performed "Baby, What You Want Me to Do" at a political event in Des Moines, Iowa, during Dean's 2003 run for the presidency of the United States. Jimmy Reed was long gone, but his music "of the people, by the people, and for the people" was infused into a campaign for the most powerful office on the face of the planet. Hawkeye explains how this came to pass:

> "Basically, I had a meeting with Howard Dean before we were supposed to do this to find out what he could do on the guitar and harmonica, right? Because he doesn't want to get up there and make a fool of himself. His campaign manager for the region had set this up and he agreed to do it. So, what I had to do was, in a nice way, find out what he is capable of so that he doesn't make a fool of himself. I said, 'Well, Mr. Dean, pick up the guitar and let me see what you can do.' He fingerpicked a Dylan tune and then he played a Dave Van Ronk blues tune. Right then and there I knew where he stood as a musician. His abilities. I said, 'Here's what we are going to do. We are going to play this Jimmy Reed tune. The reason why we are going to do it is because everybody knows and likes it and everyone in this room will be press corps—jammed with international press. What we are going to do is what appeals to everybody and what appeals to everybody is Jimmy Reed.' So I played the tune for him and he jammed along. I was carrying it and I would nod to him for a solo, etc. The only advice I gave him was, 'Smile—all the time. A good time is contagious and so is a bad time. No matter what happens, just keep smiling.' "

Delbert McClinton's 2005 record *Cost of Living* features Reed's "I'll Change My Style," also known as "I'll Change That, Too." "I just think it's the most different song I've ever heard him do, in a way," the Texan told the *Cleveland Plain Dealer* in 2005. (Quite fittingly, McClinton replaces the classic Reed harp solo with a sax interlude.)

Harp player Paul deLay often gets requests for "Big Boss Man." "Yeah, but they always request it " 'Big Boss Man by the Grateful Dead,' " De Lay says. "People may not know that the song is a Jimmy Reed song, but one thing is for *damn* sure: the way they react. The crowd, more or less, goes crazy every time."

The young, Austin-born Gary Clark shoved a harp in a rack, strapped on an electric guitar, and took the stage at Antone's nightclub for a killer version of "High and Lonesome." Clifford Antone leaned in to me and asked what I thought of his "young gun." It was indeed refreshing as well as odd to find someone so young, so talented, so well versed in the blues, pulling out "High and Lonesome" and doing it justice. Later that evening, on the same stage, veterans Hubert Sumlin, Willie "Big Eyes" Smith, Calvin Jones, and longtime Antone's house guitarist Derek O'Brien spoke the international language of the blues: "Big Boss Man."

Reed's laidback feel has even been the backdrop of many Hollywood movies over the last 30 years or so. And I've argued that some bluesmen have gained in popularity—even in death—and Reed has not perhaps because his soulful, down-home blues has so seeped into the landscape of American popular music and culture that it's sometimes taken for granted. A well-received 2002 Reese Witherspoon flick, *Sweet Home Alabama,* brings this idea full circle:

> A crowd in an Alabama honky tonk gets juiced by the house band as they play "Bright Lights, Big City" and "Shame, Shame, Shame" in two separate scenes. Considering the setting—a solid white audience down South—the songs and scenes are quite fitting, and the music fades into the very fabric of the story.

Obviously the movie's music editors knew what they were doing; I wonder if the film audience was aware.

Epilogue

After Reed's death, Eddie Taylor was haunted by guilt. "It just seemed to me that Eddie Taylor had this dark cloud about his head," says harp player Mark Hummel. "Things would be going fine and then something would happen that would make you wonder what was wrong with him. One time we were playing and he was using an amp from the previous band. The amp was working fine. All of sudden, Eddie takes the stage, starts to play, and the amp doesn't work. All of these little unexplainable things would happen to him. Like I said, he had this dark cloud above his head."

Nonetheless, Eddie Taylor would perform and record for nearly ten years after Reed's death, usually in Chicago bars with his sons but also the occasional big-ticket venue, covering the occasional Jimmy Reed tune. Eddie cut records that would appear on such labels as Germany's L+R, Antone's (*Still Not Ready for Eddie*), Blind Pig (a live performance recorded in Japan in 1977), and others. Fittingly, on the Blind Pig release, *Long Way from Home,* the song "You're Gonna Look for Me (and I'll Be Hard to Find)" appeared. In many ways, Eddie *was* hard to find, and hard to fathom. He was a quiet man and a top-flight guitarist with a solid sense of professionalism and an unfortunate (though perhaps unavoidable) simmering anger about his lack of wider recognition outside the Jimmy Reed universe.

On Christmas Day, 1985, Eddie Taylor, 62, passed on. Though the mainstream public hardly blinked, the world had lost a gifted musician and a vital link between Delta and Chicago blues. "I shaved him, bathed him, and took him to the hospital when he wasn't feeling well," explained son Timothy Taylor. "By the time I took him to the ER room he went into cardiac arrest—he didn't die. They got him breathing again. The doctor told me to go home, he'd be O.K. That morning about 5:45 we got a call that say it was urgent to come down to the hospital. We had that kind of connection where it was more like two brothers than father and son. We was real close."

"We believe he had cancer because Antone down in Austin was sending him to special doctors down there and believe he had lung cancer from smoking too much," says Larry Hill, Eddie's stepson. "I asked [Eddie] if he wanted me to take him to the hospital. He said he would be all right. Then later my sister and them took him to the hospital right across from where they stayed. They were staying at 2635 12th Place and took him to Mt. Sinai Medical Center hospital on the West Side and he went in and he died. He didn't come back out. He knew he was going to die. He knew it. He didn't want to die around us. He was sick and he got up and groomed himself as a gentleman....I knew he was going to go because he had this one brown suit that he had bought and he would never wear it. He had it in the closet. So, I figured out that was what he wanted to be buried in."

Eddie was laid out in A.R. Leake Funeral Home on Sacramento Boulevard, where Chicago stalwarts Howlin' Wolf and Magic Sam were viewed. Eddie's legacy was his contribution to the blues and his ability to get the job done with proficiency and taste. Unlike Reed's, Taylor's musicians union file was spotless when death benefits were handed to Eddie's wife, Lee Vera, in 1986.

"A lot of standard 12-bar blues that people play today comes from that pattern Eddie Taylor developed in the early '50s," blues historian Jim O'Neal told the *Chicago Sun-Times* upon Eddie's death. "He brought it up from the Delta and kind of standardized it. Musicians always credited Eddie Taylor with being the backbone of that style, which you still hear in every club in Chicago."

In December 1988, Mama Reed and the eight Reed children (Jimmy Reed, Jr., Marlene Reed Butler, Loretta Reed, Malinda Reed, Roslyn Reed Pulley, Rose Mary Reed Sullivan, Michael Reed, and Avery Reed) filed suit in the United States District Court, Southern District, New York, against Arc Music Corp., Gene Goodman, Phil CHess and others, for the sum total of $18 million for damages arising from the defendants' fraud, unlawful appropriation, unjust enrichment, and "conversion" of plaintiffs' property rights. The lawsuit also alleged that the Reeds were not knowledgeable enough of their legal rights or the legalese used in the December 1965 and November 1967 letters of agreement to comprehend their substance, and that, in fact, Jimmy's and Mary Lee's signatures were forgeries. (The latter assertion seems unlikely, as a notary had signed both documents.)

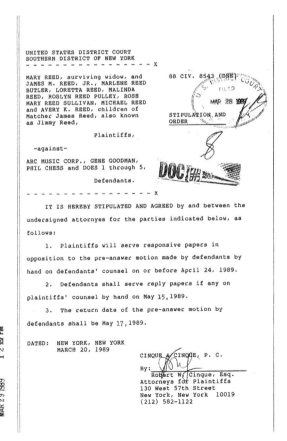

With this letter (see next page also), the Reed family commenced legal action against Arc Music, Gene Goodman, Phil Chess, and others.

```
                    GOLD, FARRELL & MARKS

                    By: _____
                         Of the Firm
                        Attorneys for Defendants
                        41 Madison Avenue
                        New York, New York  10010
                        (212) 481-1700

  SO ORDERED: 3/27/89  3/28/89

  _____
       U. S. D. J.
```

```
                                2
```

The 1965 and 1967 documents seemingly gave Arc Music Corp. the rights to all of Reed's compositions, relieved them from paying writer's royalties, and protected them from any future actions Reed or anyone in his camp might take. But the Reed family's 1988 lawsuit stated: "Goodman, Chess, and their confederates had thrust at the Reeds a document by which they would forfeit valuable rights in exchange for nothing other than a fraction of the money already due them."

The two sides reached a settlement for an undisclosed amount in the fall of 1991, and it was rumored that Mama and family had done very well. Jimmy Reed, Jr., told me the family receives royalties from their dad's music. Maybe there was justice for Jimmy Reed after all.

Endnotes

Chapter 1

iMaxwell House coffee brand was marketed in the late nineteenth century.

iiNot everyone saw eye-to-eye with the station's marketing plan. In 1942, as the story goes, John Lee Williamson took a little trip down to Arkansas to see Rice Miller about using the Sonny Boy Williamson name, but as Lockwood told Chicago blues producer/maven Dick Shurman: "[Miller] chased Little Sonny Boy away from there. He couldn't play with Rice. Rice Miller could play Sonny Boy's stuff better than he could play it!" Though no legal action was taken by John Lee Williamson, as fate would have it, Rice Miller would soon be the only Sonny Boy left to hear in Chicago and would be dubbed "King of the Harmonica."

iiiThe Social Security program, spearheaded by President Franklin Delano Roosevelt, was signed into law in 1935. Regular payments were first doled out just three years before Reed applied for membership.

ivAccording to military records that I obtained, a Mathis Reed was drafted into the United States Navy on August 20, 1943.

vAccording to military records I received, Mathis Reed was given an honorary discharge from the Navy in February 1946.

Chapter 2

iFloyd Jones, a vital link in the development of the blues from acoustic to electric Chicago, was born in 1917 in Marianna, Arkansas. Like Eddie Taylor, Jones was exposed to some of the greatest country-blues artists in history: Charlie Patton, Robert Johnson, and others. (Jones' father, who uprooted Floyd as a child and brought him to Mississippi, worked with Patton.) Jones came to Chicago in 1945 and worked for tips on Maxwell Street with his cousin Moody Jones, Baby Face Leroy, and James "Snooky" Pryor.

iiHorton was asked by Muddy to appear on a couple of his sides, though Little Walter would be the harp player of note in Muddy's band. Horton, however, would go on to record the harp tour de force "Hard-Hearted Woman.")

iiiBut the interstate highway system, trucking companies, and mechanization changed the industry forever and the stockyards were eventually closed in the early '70s, some 20 years after Reed had worked there.

ⁱᵛIt's Merriweather's tinkling and pounding you hear on "Strange Man" and "Mean Man Blues," recorded with the John Brim Combo in Detroit in 1950—Maceo's last recordings.

ᵛThe Appalachian/bluegrass sound came to the US with European immigrants in the nineteenth and twentieth centuries. With the confluence of elements from African, ragtime, classical, basic European waltz, Celtic, and Euro-folk music, the "high lonesome" sound was born. While I am not suggesting that Reed's music is bluegrass, the bumping and bobbing rhythms of bluegrass (and of later interpreters such as Elvis Presley, for example) certainly share a common ground with Reed's boogie.

ᵛⁱBill Monroe is perhaps best known for his high tenor harmonies, which became a trademark of bluegrass music. In 1954 Elvis recorded Monroe's 1946 waltz "Blue Moon of Kentucky" and captured glimmers of the high falsetto that helped define the "high lonesome" sound.

ᵛⁱⁱEddie was strangely missing from Reed's first recorded sides. Vivian Carter, upon hearing Jimmy play with Eddie—who, ironically, was the frontman—had suggested that Eddie take a backseat and let Jimmy come up front. This would be a point of contention between the two men for their close yet sometimes competitive relationship. Eddie always felt he was the real backbone of the "Jimmy Reed sound."

ᵛⁱⁱⁱKing didn't need these Vee-Jay sides. Chess Records resident songwriting maven Willie Dixon had ushered him to Al Benson's Parrot label, where King had recorded three songs—as a singer/guitarist. And King wanted to leave the Chicago/Gary area. He didn't know it then, but this session would be his last hurrah for a while. He'd emerge years later with his Gibson Flying V—a guitar slinger for Stax Records, wowing white kids on both sides of the Atlantic with his passionate combo of soul and blues.

Chapter 3

ⁱHarp technique on "Honest I Do" explained to me by Glenn Weiser, a harp player, recording artist, and educator. The trademark high squeal is a technique harp players frequently use in first position. Reed is using an *A* harp.

ⁱⁱBrayton Fogerty, the executor of Vee-Jay Ltd. Partnership (at the time of this writing), does continue to mail royalties to all their artists. He explained, "Little Richard called me and said, 'Hello, Vee-Jay....' He wanted to tell me his new address so he could get his checks."

ⁱⁱⁱSome believed then—and some believe now—that epileptic seizures are the basis for artistic, even religious, visions. One of the most famous stories involving such occurrences, some historians believe, happened to the apostle Paul. On the road to Damascus, Saul (later Paul), who at first was weary of the new sect of Jews, heard a voice and was brought to his knees by a blinding light (which left him without sight for three days, according to *Acts* in the Bible). That voice, Saul believed, was God.

Once in Damascus, Saul was baptized, regained his sight, and converted to a new sect of Judaism—what was to be Christianity. Some modern-day medical experts and Biblical scholars have interpreted this episode as an atonic epileptic seizure. For years, "seeing the light" or having a *eureka* moment was believed to be a "by-product" of epilepsy. Vincent Van Gogh called it "the storm within." Did epilepsy give Reed extra creative power and vision?

[iv]We now know one shouldn't thrust a finger or any other object into the mouth of a seizure victim. The person should instead be turned on his or her side to ensure the windpipe is clear. According to the Epilepsy Foundation of America, it is impossible to swallow one's tongue during a seizure; the term "swallow" refers to the ability of the tongue to block the airway.

[v]Lester was dubbed "Lazy" by Louisiana recording maven Jay Miller because, as Lester puts it, "I was never in a hurry. [Miller] gave all the artists stage names. He came up with all those stage names: Slim Harpo, Lonesome Sundown, Lightnin' Slim—I don't know where he got that Lightnin' Slim from. He gave me the name Lazy Lester—you know, never in a hurry. I'm a fisherman, and a fisherman is not lazy. More crazy than lazy."

[vi]Charles Singleton wrote for R&B artists and should not be confused with the Charles Singleton who wrote hits for Pat Boone and collaborated with Burt Kaempfert on "Strangers in the Night," among others. "Take Out Some Insurance" would later be covered by Frank Ifield with the Beatles, appearing on Vee-Jay.

Chapter 4

[i]Some compilations, including a Vee-Jay box set, identify the recording date as August 1959. Dee Clark's "Raindrops" was recorded in March 1961 and its single number was 383. "Big Boss Man" is Vee-Jay 380. If Reed recorded "Big Boss Man" in 1959, that would mean the single was shelved and didn't reach the charts for nearly two years.

[ii]During the height of Reed's popularity in the 1960s, more effective epilepsy medication had not been developed. After 1974, new and better forms were marketed, but Reed was never able to truly take advantage of them.

[iii]Dave Tough, a swing drummer, also suffered from both alcoholism and epilepsy. In Burt Korall's book *Drummin' Men,* bandleader Woody Herman said: "[Tough] was a gentleman, a hell of a player, and a bright man. I found out just before he was wheeled out of the band that he was a victim of epilepsy. People never understood. He was worrying he'd get an attack. [The epilepsy] would work on him and build the pressure to the breaking point. And that was when he had his first drink."

[iv]It is still unclear exactly why Earl left the Vee-Jay inner circle—and Jimmy Reed's successful sound in particular—but some stories have circulated for years. One story has Earl playing live with Howlin' Wolf when things went awry. Wolf was driving the band, but Earl, uncharacteristically, was dragging ass. The tempo kept getting slower

and slower until Wolf turned around to see why: Earl was falling off the stool and trying to play on the way down. Wolf demanded sober musicians on the bandstand at all times, so that was all she wrote for Earl. Perhaps to get cleaned up, perhaps to find a safer outlet for his expression, Earl forsook the blues and the heavy drinking atmosphere surrounding it. (He did, in fact, turn up in gospel circles later and retreat into his religion.)

[v]*More of the Best* is noteworthy because it was pressed in stereo. (*The Best of Jimmy Reed, At Carnegie Hall,* and 1964's *At Soul City* were all stereophonic, while LPs like *Rockin' with Reed* were originally released in mono.) If nothing else, this showed how much Vee-Jay catered to its audience's new thirst for hi-fi, which enhanced the listening "experience." The stereo medium was becoming more and more desirable; it re-created and reflected the recording session experience more accurately than mono. Pressing *More of the Best* in stereo also showed how much Vee-Jay valued Reed's material. (His singles, after all, were selling hundreds of thousands of units.)

[vi]What is remarkable about the 1962 sessions is the absence of Mama Reed's vocal coaching on most of these songs. The lack of her voice proves, if nothing else, how creative Jimmy was; he *did* have the ability to make songs up on the spur of the moment.

[vii]Vee-Jay's subsidiary, Tollie, had taken orders of roughly 500,000 for the Beatles' single "Twist and Shout." But this also signaled the beginning of big changes and even bigger troubles for Vee-Jay: the Beatles would be at the heart of a bitter legal battle between Vee-Jay and Capitol.

[viii]By the time Carter was in his mid-twenties, the civil rights movement was well underway in Birmingham. Dr. King was organizing demonstrations for desegregation of the downtown area and, ironically, one of them was against the wishes of entrepreneur A.G. Gaston. Luckily, Reed and Carter were never affected by the violence in Birmingham or on other travels together.

[ix]Bramhall himself got caught up in a world of alcohol and drugs. "In the 1960s and into the 1970s it seemed as though it was almost acceptable and even encouraged…I was really dying and I was starting to get into heroin…I was walking around and in a lot of pain." Bramhall sobered up in January 1986 and teamed with blues-rocker Stevie Ray Vaughan to write about substance abuse and recovery. "At an early age we listened to the same music…we partied together, and we helped get recovered together. We did a few songs like that—'Live by the Drop,' 'Wall of Denial'—about recovery…we would write and back off and just go, 'Wait a minute. There is an easier way to say this,' which would bring us right back to people like Jimmy Reed. Jimmy Reed was just so powerful. I can't think of another artist that I can listen to every day and say, 'I have to change this.' "

Chapter 5

[i]Documentation does corroborate this. Case in point: an August 1970 session for *Blues on Blues* that left trumpeter/bandleader Burgess Gardner and pianist Floyd Morris unpaid and pissed off—to the tune of over $1,500. Checks Smith wrote for additional fees in connection with the session bounced. The matter was not resolved in full for four years. Similarly, blues guitarist Lee Jackson and his band—including none other than Sunnyland Slim, Carey Bell, Willie Williams, and William Carter—did a session with Smith in August 1973 at Universal and they, too, had to sweat for their money. Some checks Smith and Torrid Productions issued to these musicians bounced as well.

[ii]Another point, which holds true for most blues artists of the era, was that Reed was releasing singles first and foremost; albums would come just a bit later. This meant no one was thinking of how a Jimmy Reed LP side's worth of material would impact the listener. There is no evidence to suggest that Reed or anyone at Vee-Jay, including Al Smith, was concerned about repeating or wearing out a certain feel. The curatorial angle simply was not a concern.

[iii]It was rumored for years that Elvis had actually played with Reed. Mississippi native Manuel Arrington told me that Elvis—Jimmy Reed fan that he was—drove his motorcycle from Memphis to Hattiesburg in southern Mississippi to see Reed perform at the Hi Hat Club. There he supposedly joined Reed onstage for two songs. What those songs were, no one knows. Indeed, I tried to confirm the story with local authorities, Hattiesburg residents, and one person in particular, Willie Stokes, who had worked at the nightclub for years. Neither Stokes nor anyone else could confirm that Elvis was ever at the Hi Hat Club, but the people of Hattiesburg keep the myth alive.

[iv]Eddie and Vera would raise eight children: four sons and four daughters. Says Larry: "My mother had 14 kids. Six died. She was the mother of 14, and I was the firstborn."

[v]A close comparison to Eddie is guitarist Hubert Sumlin, who lurked in the shadow of the blues monstrosity known as Howlin' Wolf. I have often argued that Sumlin's musical contributions should be more widely recognized—and they should—but we also have to realize that Wolf would be the enduring blues icon he is today regardless of who played in his band. Can the same be said for Jimmy Reed?

Chapter 6

[i]A promotional 45 rpm disc of a song called "Crying Blind," released through the Wally Roker/RRG label in 1971, was credited to Jimmy Reed and "Doc Oliver" (Marion Oliver, aka Mr. Soul Popcorn, who also wrote music for Dee Clark, among others)—not Malinda Reed, as is generally thought. The BMI-cleared disc credits Al Smith and Renee Marks with writing the flip side, "Christmas Present Blues."

Incidentally, I searched www.bmi.com for Marion Oliver, Oliver Marion, and Doc Oliver, but none are listed as a writer for "Crying Blind."

[ii]In all fairness to Smith, medical health professionals and recovered/recovering alcoholics I spoke with attested to the fact that Reed may have had a biological predisposition toward alcohol. Researchers have attempted to identify the DNA strain that "causes" alcoholism, succeeding in identifying the genes that predispose someone to being "at risk" for alcoholism. For Reed, alcohol flowed freely in studios and venues, and being exposed to these "environmental triggers" was undoubtedly one reason drinking became such a big part of his life. We also can't overlook the concept that Reed's roots in the South may have helped foster a life dependent on liquor. As one recovering alcoholic told me, "I can attest to how much drinking was a part of the social fabric [of the South]."

[iii]Scott claims to have talked with Eddie about Simpson's Big Bear record. Scott told me: "I asked Eddie Taylor: 'By the way, have you ever gotten any royalties from Big Bear?' Eddie said, 'No.' I told him, 'So I am the only person who has paid you royalties....' The good thing is that I think we actually reached an understanding. I think he knew I wasn't one of the cutthroats in the industry." Simpson has nothing but good things to say about Eddie and their dealings. "Business-wise he was O.K. to work with," Simpson says. "He never challenged any payments, and he was always happy to work for acceptable fees."

[iv]Ironically, Eddie Taylor was scheduled to play (for $150), but not with Reed. Despite his talents, Eddie was never a major draw and was asked by Al Smith to take part in the festival if only he didn't play with Reed. "Al Smith played a part for us that year," says Sinclair. "He put together a Chicago Revue for us with Mighty Joe Young, Homesick James, Carey Bell, Eddie Taylor, Otis Rush, and Lucille Spann."

[v]Brumbach is a bit uncertain if the venue was indeed the Colonial Ravern. It may have been Le Coq D'or, also in Toronto.

[vi]BluesWay would later release a greatest-hits record, *The Ultimate Jimmy Reed,* which culled some of Jimmy's top hits from earlier in his career.

Chapter 7

[i]Despite the seemingly personal nature of "Big Boss Man," Jimmy Reed is not credited with writing the song; it is credited to Al Smith and Luther Dixon, as explained in chapter four.

[ii]Many of my sources vaguely (though some quite vividly) remember a promoter using the name "Robert Johnson." Few knew where he went or what he is doing now. Word has it he is producing hip-hop artists.

[iii]Hildebrand does not remember the venue, but it was most likely North Beach's Savoy Tivoli, in early 1976.

Selected Jimmy Reed Discography

LPs

I'm Jimmy Reed (Vee-Jay, 1004), 1958.

Rockin' with Reed (Vee-Jay, 1008), 1959.

Found Love (Vee-Jay, 1022), 1959.

Now Appearing (Vee-Jay, 1025), 1960.

At Carnegie Hall (Vee-Jay, 1035), 1961.

Just Jimmy Reed (Vee-Jay, 1050), 1962.

T'aint No Big Thing...But He Is (Vee-Jay, 1067), 1963.

Sings the Best of the Blues (Vee-Jay, 1072), 1963.

Plays 12 String Guitar Blues (Vee-Jay, 1073), 1963.

At Soul City (Vee-Jay, 1095), 1964.

The Legend—The Man (Vee-Jay, 8501), 1965.

The New Jimmy Reed Album (ABC-BluesWay, BLS-6004), 1967.

Soulin' (ABC-BluesWay, BLS-6009), 1967.

Big Boss Man (ABC-BluesWay, BLS-6015), 1968.

Jimmy Reed's Soul Greats (Up Front, UPF-101), 1968.

Down in Virginia (ABC-BluesWay, BLS-6024), 1969.

The Very Best of Jimmy Reed (Buddah, BDS-4003), 1969.

If You Want It Done Right (ABC-BluesWay, BLS-6041), 1970 (unissued).

As Jimmy Is (Roker Records, 4001), 1970.

Let the Bossman Speak! (Blues on Blues, BOB 10001), 1971.

I Ain't from Chicago (ABC-BluesWay, BLS-6054), 1973.

The Ultimate Jimmy Reed (ABC-BluesWay, BLS-6067), 1973.

At Carnegie Hall (BluesWay, BLS-6073), 1973.

Cold Chills (Antilles, AN-7007), 1975.

Jimmy Reed: Archive of Folk and Jazz (Everest, 234), 1975.

Jimmy Reed Is Back (The Roots, 1001), 1976.

Blues Is My Business (Vee-Jay, 7303), 1976.

Cry Before I Go (Drive Entertainment, DE2-41072), 1995.

Big Legged Woman (Collectibles, COL-5721), 1996.

Selected Singles

"High and Lonesome"/"Roll and Rhumba" (Chance, CH-1142) (released under Jimmy Reed and His Trio), 1953.

"I Found My Baby"/"Jimmie's Boogie" (Vee-Jay, VJ-105) (issued on red vinyl as Jimmy Reed and His Trio), 1953.

"You Don't Have to Go"/"Boogie in the Dark" (Vee-Jay, VJ-119) (issued on red vinyl under Jimmy Reed and His Trio), 1953.

"I'm Gonna Ruin You"/"Pretty Thing" (Vee-Jay, VJ-132), 1955.

"I Don't Go for That"/"She Don't Want Me No More" (Vee-Jay, VJ-153), 1955.

"Ain't That Lovin' You Baby"/"Baby Don't Say that No More" (Vee-Jay, VJ-168), 1956.

"Can't Stand to See You Go"/"Rockin' with Reed" (Vee-Jay, VJ-186), 1956.

"I Love You Baby"/"My First Plea" (Vee-Jay, VJ-203), 1956.

"You've Got Me Dizzy"/"Don't Let Me Go" (Vee-Jay, VJ-226), 1956.

"Little Rain"/"Honey, Where You Going?" (Vee-Jay, VJ-237), 1957.

"The Sun Is Shining"/"Baby, What's on Your Mind" (Vee-Jay, VJ-248), 1957.

"Honest I Do"/"Signals of Love" (Vee-Jay, VJ-253), 1957.

"Down in Virginia"/"I Know It's a Sin" (Vee-Jay, VJ-287), 1958.

"I'm Gonna Get My Baby"/"Odds and Ends" (Vee-Jay, VJ-298), 1958.

"Take Out Some Insurance"/"You Know I Love You" (Vee-Jay, VJ-314), 1959.

"Baby What You Want Me to Do"/"Caress Me Baby" (Vee-Jay, VJ-333), 1959.

"Found Love"/"Where Can You Be" (Vee-Jay, VJ-347), 1960.

"Big Boss Man"/"I'm A Love You" (VJ-380), 1960.

"Close Together"/"Laughing at the Blues" (Vee-Jay, VJ-373), 1961.

"Bright Lights Big City"/"I'm Mr. Luck" (Vee-Jay, VJ-398), 1961.

"Good Lover"/"Tell Me You Love Me" (Vee-Jay, VJ-449), 1962.

"I'll Change My Style"/"Too Much" (Vee-Jay, VJ-459), 1962.

"Shame, Shame, Shame"/"There'll Be a Day" (Vee-Jay, VJ-509), 1963.

"Oh, John"/"Let's Get Together" (Vee-Jay, VJ-473), 1962.

"Heading for a Fall"/"Help Yourself" (Vee-Jay, VJ-593), 1964.

"I'm Going Upside Your Head"/"The Devil's Shoestring Part II" (Vee-Jay, VJ-622), 1964.

"I'm the Man Down There"/"Left Handed Woman" (Vee-Jay, VJ-702), 1965.

"Dedication to Sonny (Boy Williamson)"/"Knockin' at Your Door" (Exodus, EX-2005), 1966.

"Crazy 'bout Oklahoma"/"Cousin Peaches"/ (Exodus, EX-2008), 1966.

"I Wanna Know"/"Two Heads Are Better than One" (BluesWay, 61003), 1967.

"Don't Press Your Luck Woman"/"Feel Like I Want to Ramble" (BluesWay, 61006), 1967.

"Buy Me a Hound Dog"/"Crazy 'bout Oklahoma" (BluesWay, 61013), 1968.

"Peepin' and Hidin' "/"My Baby Told Me" (BluesWay, 61020), 1968.

"Don't Light My Fire"/"The Judge Should Know" (BluesWay, 61025), 1969.

"Hard Walking Hannah Part 1"/"Hard Walking Hannah Part 2" (Canyon, 38), 1970.

"Big Legged Woman"/"Funky Funky Soul" (RRG, 44003), 1970.

"Crying Blind"/"Christmas Present Blues" (RRG, promotional-44001), 1970.

"Cold Chills"/"You Just a Womper Stomper" (Blues on Blues, BOB-2000), 1971.

"Same Old Thing"/"Milking the Cow" (with Johnnie Mae Dunson) (Magic, 81172-1, 81172-2), 1973.

"I Got The World in a Jug"/"We Got to Stick Together" (with Johnnie Mae Dunson) (Magic, 81172-3, 81172-4), 1973.

Compilations

With More of the Best (Vee-Jay, VJLP 1080), 1964.

Various Artists: *14 Golden Recordings from the Historic Vaults of Vee-Jay Records* (ABC, ABCX-785), 1973.

Various Artists: *A Taste of BluesWay* (BluesWay, BLS-1973), 1973.

Various Artists: *Vee-Jay: Celebrating 40 Years of Classic Hits 1953-1993* (Vee-Jay, NVS2-3-400), 1993.

Speak the Lyrics to Me, Mama Reed (Vee-Jay, NVD2-705), 1993.

The Vee-Jay Years (Charly, LC 8477), 1994.

The Vee-Jay Box: The Complete Singles and Other Rarities (P-Vine, PCD 5454-5459), 1998.

The Very Best of Jimmy Reed (Rhino, R2 79802), 2000.

The Essential Boss Man: The Very Best of the Vee-Jay Years, 1953-1966 (Charly, SNAJ 728 CD), 2004.

With Individual Artists

John Brim and His Stompers: "Tough Times"/"Gary Stomp" (Parrot, 799), 1953.

John Lee Hooker: "Mambo Chillen'"/"Time Is Marching" (Vee-Jay, VJ 164), 1955.

Elmore James: *Street Talkin'* (with Jimmy Reed and Eddie Taylor) (Muse Records, MCD 5087), 1975.

John Lee Hooker: *The Folklore of John Lee Hooker* (Vee-Jay, VJD 81033), 1991.

Jimmy Reed and Johnny Winter: *Live at Liberty Hall, Houston, TX, 1972* (Fan Club/New Rose, 422286), 1992.

John Lee Hooker: *On Vee-Jay 1955-1958* (Vee-Jay, NVD2-713), 1993.

Johnny Winter, featuring Jimmy Reed: *Liberty Hall Sessions* (Magnum Music, CDTB 175), 1996.

John Brim: *The Chronological John Brim 1950-1953* (Classics, 5086), 2004.

Selected Eddie Taylor Discography

Still Not Ready for Eddie (Antone's, ANT-0005), 1988.

I Feel So Bad (Hightone, HCD 8027) (originally released as Advent, 2802, 1972), 1991.

My Heart Is Bleeding (Evidence, 26054), 1994.

Floyd Jones and Eddie Taylor: *Masters of Modern Blues* (with Otis Spann, Big Walter Horton, and Fred Below) (Hightone, TCD 5001) (originally released as Testament, T-2214, 1969), 1994.

Long Way from Home (Blind Pig, BPCD 5025), 1995.

Big Town Playboy (P-Vine, PCD-5259), 1997.

Ready for Eddie (Castle, B000084TRQ) (reissued as *Ready for Eddie…Plus*) (originally released on Big Bear Records, 1973), 2003.

Live in Japan 1977 (P-Vine, PCD-25005), 2003.

Selected Bibliography

Books

Aykroyd, Dan, and Ben Manilla. *Elwood's Blues: Interviews with the Blues Legends & Stars*. San Francisco: Backbeat Books, 2004.

Blakey, G. Robert, and Richard N. Billings. *Fatal Hour: The Assassination of President Kennedy by Organized Crime*. New York: Berkley Books, 1992.

Broven, John. *South to Louisiana: The Music of the Cajun Bayous*. Gretna, LA: Pelican Publishing Company, 1992.

Butler, Jerry, with Earl Smith. *Only the Strong Survive: Memoirs of a Soul Survivor*. Bloomington: Indiana University Press, 2000.

Docks, Les. *American Premium Record Guide 1900–1965*. 6th ed. Iola, WI: Krause Publications, 2001.

Du Maurier, George. *Trilby*. Oxford: Oxford University Press, 1995.

Harris, Sheldon. *Blues Who's Who: A Biographical Dictionary of Blues Singers*. New Rochelle,NY: Arlington House Publishers, 1979.

Hoffmann, Frank, and George Albert, with Lee Ann Hoffmann. *The Cash Box Album Charts, 1955–1974*. Metuchen, NJ, and London: The Scarecrow Press, Inc., 1988.

Hoffmann, Frank, with Lee Ann Hoffmann. *The Cash Box Singles Charts, 1950–1981*. Metuchen, NJ, and London: The Scarecrow Press, Inc., 1983.

Jung, C.G. (R.F.C. Hull, trans.). *Synchronicity: An Acausal Connecting Principle*. Princeton: Bollingen Series/Princeton University Press, 1973.

Korall, Burt. *Drummin' Men: The Heartbeat of Jazz: The Swing Years*. Oxford: Oxford University Press, 2002.

Kornblum, William. *Blue Collar Community.* Chicago: University of Chicago Press, 1974.

Leadbitter, Mike, ed. *Nothing but the Blues: Compendium of Blues Unlimited Articles.* London: Hanover Books, 1971.

Leadbitter, Mike, and Neil Slaven. *Blues Records 1943–1966: An Encyclopedic Discography to More than Two Decades of Recorded Blues.* New York/London: Oak Publications/Hanover Books, Ltd., 1968.

McDonough, Jimmy. *Shakey: Neil Young's Biography.* New York: Anchor Books, 2003.

Murray, Charles Shaar. *Boogie Man: The Adventures of John Lee Hooker (in the American Twentieth Century).* New York: St. Martin's Press, 2000.

Oliver, Paul. *The Story of the Blues.* Philadelphia: Chilton Book Company, 1969.

O'Neal, Jim, and Amy Van Singel. *The Voice of the Blues: Classic Interviews from Living Blues Magazine.* New York: Routledge, 2002.

Palmer, Robert. *Deep Blues: A Musical and Cultural History, from the Mississippi Delta to Chicago's South Side to the World.* New York: Penguin Books, 1982.

Pruter, Robert. *Chicago Soul.* Urbana and Chicago: University of Illinois Press, 1991.

Rowe, Mike. *Chicago Blues: The City & the Music.* New York: Da Capo Press, 1975.

Sadie, Stanley, ed. *The New Grove Dictionary of Music and Musicians.* 2nd ed. New York/London: Grove's Dictionaries, Inc./Macmillan Publishers Limited, 2001.

Schuller, Gunther. *Early Jazz: Its Roots and Musical Development.* New York: Oxford University Press, 1968.

Sillers, Florence Warfield, and Members of Mississippi Delta Chapter, Daughters of the American Revolution, and the County History Committee. *The History of Bolivar County.* Bolivar County, MS: (no publisher), 1986.

Sinclair, Upton. *The Jungle.* New York: Signet Classics, 1990.

Spizer, Bruce. *Songs, Pictures, and Stories of the Fabulous Beatles Records on Vee-Jay.* New Orleans: 498 Productions, 1998.

Toffler, Alvin. *Future Shock.* New York: Bantam Books, 1971.

Turk, Dorothy. *Leland, Mississippi: From Hellhole to Beauty Spot.* Leland, MS: Leland Historic Foundation, 1986.

Whitburn, Joel. *The Billboard Books of Top 40 Hits: Complete Chart Information about the Artists and Their Songs, 1955 to 2000.* 7th ed. New York: Billboard Books, 2000.

Liner Notes

Callahan, Mike, and Billy Vera. *Celebrating 40 Years of Classic Hits* by various artists. "The Vee-Jay Story 1953-1993." Box set. Vee-Jay, 1993.

Dahl, Bill. *Sings the Best of the Blues* by Jimmy Reed. Vee-Jay/Collectables/Rhino, 2000.

Escott, Colin. *Memories: The '68 Comeback Special* by Elvis Presley. RCA/BMG, 1998.

Fanelli, Andre. *Live at Liberty Hall, Houston, TX, 1972* by Jimmy Reed and Johnny Winter. Fan Club Records/Red Rose, 1992.

Harris, Sheldon. *Soulin'* by Jimmy Reed. ABC-BluesWay, 1967.

Harris, Sheldon. *The New Jimmy Reed Album.* ABC-BluesWay, 1967.

Koide, Hitoshi. *Jimmy Reed: The Vee-Jay Box.* P-Vine Records, 1998.

Oliver, Paul. *Story of the Blues* by various artists. Columbia/Legacy Recordings, 2003.

Robins, Wayne. *Best of the Vanguard Years* by John Hammond. Vanguard Records, 2000.

Magazines

Ackerman, Paul. "Rhythm & Blues Notes." *Billboard,* March 5, 1955.

Ackerman, Paul. "Rhythm & Blues Notes." *Billboard,* September 24, 1955, 16.

Baker, Cary. "Jim Bracken 1909–1972." *Living Blues,* no. 8, Spring 1972.

Baker, Cary. "Records." *Living Blues,* Winter 1971–1972, 34.

[no author]. "Best Sellers in Stores." *Billboard,* November 11, 1957.

[no author]. *Billboard,* March 5, 1955, 36.

[no author]. *Billboard,* March 12, 1955, 46.

[no author]. *Billboard,* March 26, 1955, 138, 142.

[no author]. *Billboard,* April 2, 1955, 40.

[no author]. *Billboard,* April 30, 1955, 47.

[no author]. *Billboard,* May 7, 1955, 49.

[no author]. *Billboard,* May 14, 1955, 48.

[no author]. "Blacks, Whites and Blues: The Story of Chess Records." *Living Blues,* November/December 1989.

[no author]. "Bribe Case Turns Touchy & Go." *Billboard,* March 4, 1967.

[no author]. "Britain's Beatles' Sales Top 300,000." *Variety,* November 13, 1963.

Broven, John. "Low and Lonesome." *Blues Unlimited,* August/September 1974.

Cogan, Jim. "Analog Dialog: Bill Putnam, Sr." Pts. 1 and 2. *uaudio.com,* May 2005 and June 2005, http://www.uaudio.com/webzine/2005/may/content/content8.html, http://www.uaudio.com/webzine/2005/june/content/content8.html.

[no author]. "Combine Bids for VJ—With Condition." *Billboard,* May 14, 1966.

[no author]. "Crown Prince Is Dead." *Rolling Stone,* January 20, 1968.

[no author]. "45's." *Living Blues,* no. 13, Summer 1973.

[no author]. "5,000 Vee-Jay Masters on Auction Block on February 24." *Billboard,* February 11, 1967.

[no author]. "Hot 100." *Billboard,* February 29, 1960.

[no author]. "Hot R&B Sides." *Billboard,* June 5, 1961.

[no author]. "Houston's Company Takes Vee-Jay Spin." *Hollywood Reporter,* January 25, 2000.

[no author]. "Jimmy Reed, 'Big Boss Man,' Dead at 50." *Rolling Stone,* October 7, 1976.

Jones, Max. "A Legend Comes To Life." *Melody Maker,* November 1964.

Kozinn, Allan. "Ewart Abner, Jr., 74, President of Motown Label." *New York Times,* January 12, 1998.

[no author]. "Lasker to Vee-Jay; Move to Coast Hint?" *Billboard,* October 5, 1963.

[no author]. "Malinda Reed." *Living Blues,* no. 22, July/August 1975.

Mazzolini, Tom. "Blues News: San Francisco." *Living Blues,* no. 29, September/October 1976.

Morris, Chris. "Reed's Widow Sues Pub: $18 Mil. Action Alleges Fraud." *Billboard,* December 24, 1988.

[no author]. "Music: Beatlemania." *Newsweek,* November 18, 1963.

[no author]. "New Vee-Jay Regime Broadens Horizons." *Billboard,* September 7, 1963.

O'Neal, Jim. "Jimmy Reed 1925–1976." *Living Blues,* no. 29, September/October 1976.

O'Neal, Jim. "Living Blues Interview: Jimmy Reed." *Living Blues,* no. 21, May/June 1975.

O'Neal, Jim. "Al Smith." *Living Blues,* no. 16, Spring 1974.

Patoski, Joe Nick. "Jimmy Reed, Emancipator of the South: An Oral History." *Blues Access,* Summer 2000.

[no author]. "Potpourri." *Down Beat,* April 1989, 12.

[no author]. "R&B Best Sellers in Stores." *Billboard,* November 4, 1957.

[no author]. "R&B Best Sellers in Stores." *Billboard,* December 2, 1957.

[no author]. "R&B Best Sellers in Stores." *Billboard,* December 16, 1957.

[no author]. "Review: 'Masters of Modern Blues: Vols. 1, 2, and 3.' " *Rolling Stone,* January 21, 1969.

[no author]. "Review Spotlight on…" *Billboard,* September 26, 1957.

[no author]. "Reviews of New R&B Records." *Billboard,* September 17, 1955, 57.

[no author]. "Settlement Reached on Jimmy Reed Royalties." *Living Blues,* November/December 1991, 5.

Shurman, Dick. "Chicago…". *Living Blues,* November/December 1975.

[no author]. "Top 100 Sides." *Billboard,* October 14, 1957.

[no author]. "Top 100 Sides." *Billboard,* November 4, 1957.

[no author]. "Vee-Jay Randy Wood Assumes Presidency." *Billboard,* August 31, 1963.

[no author]. "Vee-Jay Records Unveil New Tollie Label." *Billboard,* March 7, 1964.

[no author]. "VJ Calls in European Rep." *Billboard,* June 19, 1965.

[no author]. "VJ Hopes to Open Negro Gospel Door." *Billboard,* February 27, 1965.

[no author]. "ZZ Top: Power to the People." *Rolling Stone,* August 26, 1976.

Newspapers

Chicago Defender. "Gary Has Always Had Nightlife, Bright Lights, Vendor Hops, Jives," June 9, 1956.

Chicago Defender. "Steel, the Life of Gary, Nation's Barbecue: Gary Works, Men Who Run Them Put Imprint on Town," June 9, 1956.

Chicago Defender. "Where There's Steel, There's Steel Workers: Organizing Efforts Span 20 Years, Aid 30,000," June 9, 1956.

Chicago Sun-Times. "Eddie Taylor, Leading Blues Guitarist Here," December 31, 1985.

Chicago Tribune. "Gary Leads 34 Suburbs in New Home Building," January 22, 1956.

Chicago Tribune. "Jimmy Reed, Musician, Dies," September 1, 1976.

Johnson, Billy. "The Forgotten Blues Highway." *The Leland Progress,* May 29, 2003.

Kostanczuk, Bob. "Vivian Carter Built Vee-Jay into Top R&B Label." *Post-Tribune,* November 2, 1992.

Kostanczuk, Bob. "Label Matriarch Turned to God After Collapse." *Post-Tribune,* November 17, 1991, lifestyle section.

Leibovich, Mark. "Candidate with the Blues: In Iowa, Howard Dean Sets His Campaign to Music." *Washington Post,* August 15, 2003.

Los Angeles Times. "Blues Singer Jimmy Reed Dies," September 2, 1976.

Masters, Jim. "Blues Pioneer Dies in Gary." Northwest Indiana News.com, October 3, 2003.

Matre, Lynn Van. "A Return to Roots: Steve Miller's New LP Has a Very Blues Hue." *Chicago Tribune,* December 14, 1986.

O'Neal, Jim. "Review: Jimmy Reed Is Back." *Chicago Reader,* December 10, 1976.

Reich, Howard. "Mother of the Blues." *Chicago Tribune,* June 10, 2005.

Saunders, Barry. " 'Livin' with Vivian's Just the Beginning.'" *Post-Tribune,* May 14, 1989.

Smith, Sid. "Musical Biography of Blues Star Offers the Same Old Song." *Chicago Tribune,* February 27, 1991.

Selected Original Interviews and Personal Correspondences

Charles "C.C." Adcock

Linsey Alexander

Johnnie Allan

Murray Allen

Clifford Antone

Manuel Arrington

Cary Baker

Don Otha Baker

Richard Banks

Chuck Barksdale

Robert Barry

D.C. Bellamy

Marc Benno

Tab Benoit

Bill Bentley

Steve Binder

Doyle Bramhall, Sr.

Bruce Bromberg

Lonnie Brooks (Lee Baker)

John Broven

Mark Brumbach

Gary Burbank

David Burns

Jerry Butler

Larry "Third Degree" Byrne

Al Cabaj

Clarence Carter

Walter Carter

Franco Chiappetti

Randy Chortkoff

Mike Clark

David Clayton-Thomas

Larry Cohn

Hampton "Hamp" Collier

Kent Cooper

Bob Corritore

Steve Cushing

Kenny Daniels

Patrick Day

Dick DeGuerin

Paul delay

John Dixon

Dan Duehren

"Little" Arthur Duncan

Johnnie Mae Dunson

Steve F'dor

Billy Flynn

James Fraher

Herstine Franklin

Earl Lavon "Von" Freeman

Grady Gaines

Ernie Gammage

Tom Hambridge

John Hammond

Jerry Haussler

Sharon Helgerson

Mike Henderson

Michael "Hawkeye" Herman

Lee Hildebrand

Larry Hill

William "Bill" Hill

James "Red" Holloway

Milton Hopkins

Thornton James "Pookie" Hudson

Mark Hummel

Don Hyde

Richard Innes

Tom Jacobson

"Homesick" James
   (William Henderson)

Earl Jones

Marvin Junior (the Dells)

Delbert Kauffman

Rev. Stanley Keeble

Eddie Kirkland

Bill Kornblum

Jimmy D. Lane

David Leishman

Lazy Lester (Leslie
   Johnson)

Billy Magee

Janiva Magness

Portia Maultsby

Pete Mayes

Tom Mazzolini

Mickey McGill

Tony McPhee

Ed Michel

Doktu Rhute Muuzic
   (Roy Hytower)

Jon Paris

Paul Petraitis

Rod Piazza

Michael Powers

Walter "The Thunderbird"
   Price

Jimmy Reed, Jr.

Li'l Jimmy Reed (Leon
   Atkins)

Loretta Reed

Rose Reed

Fred Reif

Dave Riley

Bobby Rush

Guy Schwartz

Frank Scott

Frank "Little Sonny"
   Scott, Jr.

Rod Sellers

Dick Shurman

Jimi Shutte

John Sinclair

Byther Smith

James Solberg

Bruce Spizer

Mavis Staples

Jim Stevens

Chris Strachwitz

Angela Strehli

Hubert Sumlin

Eddie Taylor, Jr.

Timothy Taylor

Jimmy Thackery

Ron Thompson

George Thorogood

Dorothy Turk

Twist Turner

Phil Upchurch

Sal Valentino

Billy Vera

Donnie Walsh

Dick Waterman

Brad Webb

Bill Weilenman

Mark Weinstein

Mark Wenner

Charles White

Dave Williams

Kim Wilson

Wally Wilson

Johnnie Wood

Richard Young

Web Sites

http://ajp.psychiatryonline.org/cgi/content/full/159/4/519 (American Journal of
   Psychiatry online)

www.archives.gov

http://www.bbc.co.uk/religion/religions/christianity/features/stpaul/st_paul_
   script.html (BBC's religion and ethics homepage)

www.bmi.com

www.chigmm.org (Chicago Gospel Museum)

www.cin.org/saints/roaddama.html (Catholic Information Network)

www.epilepsy.com (The Epilepsy Project)

www.epilepsyfoundation.org (Epilepsy Foundation of America)

www.epilepsymuseum.de (German Epilepsy Museum, Kork)

www.frankscottjr.com

www.georgethorogood.com

www.jazzinchicago.org

www.sfsa.org (Steel Founders Society of America)

www.veejay.mu

Other Sources

The Bible. King James Version. Great Britain: CollinsBible, a division of Harper-Collins Publishers.

City Directory, 1952, Gary, Indiana.

"In Memoriam: James Mathis Reed." Funeral Program/Obit. Chicago: Unity Funeral Parlors, Inc., September 3, 1976.

Jimmy Reed TV appearance, KPRC-TV-2. Houston, December 4, 1975.

Jimmy Reed radio interview, KTIM. Conducted by Bill Scott. San Rafael, CA, 1976.

Jimmy Reed radio interview, KSAN. Conducted by Norman Davis. San Francisco, Spring 1976.

Jones, Earl, Ph.D., and Jihad Muhammad, MS, CED, William Hill, and John Gunn. "Midtown: The Central District Tour Guide Map: Historic Black Community, Gary, Indiana." Gary: Historic Preservation and Revitalization, 2005.

Knighten, Stacey. "Powder Puffs and Sponges." In *Steel Shavings: Cruisin' the Region in the Fifties.* Gary: Indiana University Northwest, 1978.

Legal Case No: 88 Civ. 8543. Mary Reed, etc. Plaintiffs against Arc Music Corp., Gene Goodman, Phil Chess and Does 1 through 5 Defendants. Filed: United States District Court, Southern District New York, 1990.

McIntyre, James R. "The History of Wisconsin Steel Works of the International Harvester Company." Courtesy of Wisconsin Historic Society, circa 1951.

Musicians Union File: Jimmy Reed, Eddie Taylor, Albert Smith.

Report of the President's Commission on the Assassination of President Kennedy, "Appendix 16: A Biography of Jack Ruby." The National Archives.

Sinclair Papers. Bentley Historic Library, University of Michigan, Ann Arbor.

Village Voice ad, March 14, 1974, 50.

Acknowledgments

This manuscript was truly one of the toughest assignments I ever had to complete. I did the best I could sifting through a lot of info, and somehow saw this endeavor through to the end.

There are a number of people I want to thank for getting me to the finish line. Here goes:

Thanks to Richard Johnston at Backbeat Books for allowing me the opportunity to write about the blues. Thanks to everyone on the Backbeat team, including Julie Herrod-Lumsden (for her superior editing), Gail Saari, Nina Lesowitz, Kevin Becketti, and Steven Moore.

Thanks also to Jimmy Reed's family: Junior, Loretta, Rose, and granddaughter Chava Flesche.

As for those who helped in the research process, special thanks must go to Norman Davis for his professionalism and, of course, his own research. He and "Wild Bill" Scott unselfishly opened their vaults and allowed me to peek inside. Props go to blues maven and author Scott Dirks, who allowed me access to some incredible video footage. Thanks to Vee-Jay's Brayton Fogerty, who helped kick this mutha off, Eddie Sadlowski, Al Cabaj, Ezra Kotzin, musician/historian Paul Petraitis, Rod Sellers of the South Chicago Historical Society, Franco Chiappetti, Carolyn Meek at the Houston Blues Society, Pathway Records, and Marguerite Moran (at the Wisconsin Historical Society).

A virtual standing ovation goes to Bob Corritore and Glenn Weiser for their technical insight. Thanks to Walter Carter at Gruhn Guitars and Mike Robinson of Eastwood Guitars. Thanks to pianist and LP collector extraordinaire Steve F'dor (for your expertise and patience in personally trying times; as you said, "It's for the blues!"), Lee Hildebrand (for racking your brains concerning "Robert Johnson"), Shane K. Bernard, Ph.D., Stephen McShane, Ronald Cohen, Ph.D., Professor of History and Co-director of the Calumet Regional Archives at Indiana University Northwest (thanks for the e-mails and access to the Calumet archives), Greg Johnson, blues curator and assistant professor of the blues archive at the University of Mississippi's Department of Archives and Special Collections, Christopher Popa of the Harold Washington Public Library in Chicago, Rob Hudson, assistant archivist at Carnegie Hall in New York City, archivist Karen Jania and reference assistant Christie Peterson at the Bentley Historic Library at the University of Michigan in Ann Arbor, Mississippi's Bolivar County Library and Leland Public Library, Dorothy

Turk, Portia Maultsby, Ph.D., Professor of Folklore and Director of the Archives of African-American Music and Culture at the Indiana University at Bloomington, the kind people of Leland, Mississippi, and the surrounding areas, the resources in the New York Public Library, Dennis V. Hickey, Professor of Political Science at Missouri State University, the National Epilepsy Foundation, the National Institute on Alcohol Abuse and Alcoholism for the extensive research material provided, and Dr. Earl Jones, John Gunn, and longtime jazz musician Bill Hill for their efforts to preserve African-American history.

Thanks to Jerry Butler, the Dells, Mavis Staples, and Grady Gaines (all of whom recognized the importance of writing about Jimmy Reed). Thanks to Ed Michel (for the much-needed info), Don Hyde, Von Freeman, Red Holloway, Johnnie Allan, Larry Byrne, James Solberg, Mitch Diamond, Janiva Magness, Barbara Logan, Doyle Bramhall, Sr., Rod Piazza, Ron Thompson, Larry Cohn, James Fraher, Dwayne Gilley, Twist Turner, Fred Reif, Lazy Lester (for making me feel at ease talking to a living harmonica legend), Jimi Shutte, Steve Cushing, Anthony Summers (for attempting to pinpoint some meaningful data for me), Detroit Junior (rest in peace), Hedy Langdon and Eddie Kirkland, Eugene Skuratowicz, Linda Knipe (Jazz at Chardonnay), Zakiya Hooker, John Lee Hooker, Jr., for adding another dimension to Jimmy Reed's personality, Kenny Daniels of Kenny and the Kasuals, Roger "Hurricane" Wilson, Gary Burbank (for mixing laughs with serious vignettes), Wally Wilson, Homer Henderson, Sharon Helgerson, Cary Baker, Tom Mazzolini (for your vital work), Reverend Stanley Keeble, Sal Valentino of the Beau Brummels, Billy Flynn (re: Eddie Taylor), Justin Time Records and David Clayton-Thomas, Lisa Becker and John Primer,

Betsie Brown at Crows Feet Productions, Phil and Ernie Gammage, Murray Allen, Marc Benno, Michael "Hawkeye" Herman, Frank "Little Sonny" Scott, Jr., Little Arthur Duncan, Herstene Franklin and the Pilgrim Rest Baptist Church, the McMurchy family, Mayor Charles Harvey of Shaw, Mississippi, Mayor Gene Alday of Walls, Mississippi, Paul deLay, Bill Bentley at Warner Brothers, Steve Binder, Richard Marcelli, Lonnie Brooks, Clarence Carter, Hampton "Hamp" Collier, Bill Weilenmann, Willie Stokes, Patrick Day, Dick DeGuerin (a high-profile lawyer's work is never done, but you found time to talk about the blues), John Dixon, Marvin Barnes, Johnnie Mae Dunson, Milton Hopkins, Richard Innes, and Houston guitar ace Pete Mayes.

Thanks to Clifford Antone (who always freely offered his time when the blues was the topic of discussion; may you rest in peasce, Cliffor), D.C. Bellamy, Mike Henderson, Stephen Gordon, Dick Shurman (thanks for contributing), Jerry Haussler, Robert Carvounas, John Sinclair, and Susan Criner at Gulf Coast Entertainment. I'd also like to thank Groundhog Tony McPhee (thanks for the tour info), Dave Williams for the vote of confidence, and John Broven—first for his knowledge, intelligence, and work in this field, and secondly for his invaluable input.

Thanks to Christopher Phillips, new friends Richard Young, Rick Vito (for your enthusiasm and guitar work), Dan Duehren of California Vintage Guitar & Amp, harp man Mark Hummel, author and Long Beach neighbor Bill Kornblum (keep sailing and watch those golf balls), Peter Bochan (thanks for your support), Jerry Schaefer of Graveyard Blues Radio, *Blues Revue,* Gil Anthony, Tanya Junior, *Goldmine's* Wayne Youngblood and Catherine Bernardy, George Thorogood—a famous name and guitar player—who heard about this manuscript and responded to my request in the affirmative, and John Hammond.

To my brother Mike, for introducing me to the world of musical instruments, to Murphy and Judy Bailey for bringing their lovely daughter, my wife, into this world. And to my wife, Sharon: you've put up with my shit, late-night work sessions, ignorance, utter stupidity, pigheadedness, chauvinism, pride, and obliviousness. You deserve a solid-gold medal. Now I just have to figure out how to get one! My undying love and appreciation, babe.

Lastly, to God. Sometimes I am not sure how to define that slippery term, but I want to believe. I want to believe in something greater, and hope…. Hey, J.C., if you're out there (up there?), thanks for listening when I needed you the most. In your infinite wisdom you realized, why let a little thing like a coma come between us? See ya later. *I hope….*

About the Author

Will Romano is the author of *Incurable Blues: The Troubles & Triumph of Blues Legend Hubert Sumlin* (Backbeat Books, 2005). His writing appears in *Writer's Digest Handbook of Magazine Article Writing (All-New Second Edition)* and *The Drummer: 100 Years of Rhythmic Power and Invention* (Modern Drummer Publications). He has written for such diverse publications as the *New York Post, New York Daily News, Guitar Player, Bass Player, EQ, Goldmine, Modern Drummer, Military History, FOH (Front of House), Popular Electronics,* VH-1.com, and others. He lives with his wife, Sharon, and Molly, their Labrador retriever, in Long Beach, New York.

Photo Credits

Index